Mighty Lewd Books

Mighty Lewd Books

The Development of Pornography in Eighteenth-Century England

Julie Peakman

First published in 2003
First published in paperback 2012 by
PALGRAVE MACMILLAN

Palgrave Macmillan in the UK is an imprint of Macmillan Publishers Limited,
registered in England, company number 785998, of Houndmills, Basingstoke,
Hampshire RG21 6XS.

Palgrave Macmillan in the US is a division of St Martin's Press LLC,
175 Fifth Avenue, New York, NY 10010.

Palgrave Macmillan is the global academic imprint of the above companies
and has companies and representatives throughout the world.

Palgrave® and Macmillan® are registered trademarks in the United States,
the United Kingdom, Europe and other countries

ISBN 978–1–403–91500–9   hardback
ISBN 978–1–137–03396–3   paperback

This book is printed on paper suitable for recycling and made from fully
managed and sustained forest sources. Logging, pulping and manufacturing
processes are expected to conform to the environmental regulations of the
country of origin.

A catalogue record for this book is available from the British Library.

A catalog record for this book is available from the Library of Congress.

10   9   8   7   6   5   4   3   2   1
21   20   19   18   17   16   15   14   13   12

Printed and bound in Great Britain by
CPI Antony Rowe, Chippenham and Eastbourne

For Jad

Contents

List of Illustrations

List of Abbreviations

Ashbee, Vol. I	Fraxi, Pisanus [Henry Spencer Ashbee], *Index Librorum Prohibitorum*
Ashbee, Vol. II	Fraxi, Pisanus [Henry Spencer Ashbee], *Centuria Librorum Absconditorum*
Ashbee, Vol. III	Fraxi, Pisanus [Henry Spencer Ashbee], *Catena Librorum Tacendorum* (London, privately printed, 1877)

All reprinted as *Bibliography of Forbidden Books* (New York, Jack Brussel, 1962).

BL	British Library
DNB	Dictionary of National Biography
KB	King's Bench Records
MS	Manuscripts
PRO	Public Records Office
SP	Session Papers

Acknowledgements

My thanks are extended to the various librarians who have helped me, at the British Library, London; The Wellcome Library, London; The Huntingdon Library, San Marino; Sylvia Merian at the Pierpoint Morgan Library, New York; Dr. Norman H. Reid at the University of St. Andrew's University Library; and to Jilly Boid at the Artefact Museum of St. Andrew's University, for their assistance in providing me with the manuscripts and artefacts for viewing. Many thanks to the Isobel Thornley Bequest Fund for their kind financial assistance.

Thanks to my friends and colleagues at the Wellcome Institute who have made me feel 'at home', Sally Bragg, Alan Shiel, Kristina Alverez, Natsu Hattori and Lesley Hall who have shown much kind attention and encouragement, as have visiting colleagues Helen King and Marie Mulvey Roberts.

I particularly want to thank seven women with whom I banded together on the Women's History MA and still meet for regular mutual support and discussions on our various theses/work/life: Sara Bailey, Meg Irving, Linda Massie, Diana Pechsier, Deirdre Palk, Stephanie Spencer and Cally Ward. Also, thanks to Jess Mookherjee for her encouragement and enthusiasm, and again, for reading my work; thanks too to Jean Kysow for kindly proof-reading it.

I would like to thank my family: Paul Peakman has, in the past, helped financially with my studies in earlier days; both he and his wife, Karen Peakman, have been a great source of emotional support. Thanks to my parents, Leslie and Maureen Peakman, both now dead, who inspired and encouraged me in everything I wanted to do.

My greatest gratitude is reserved for two people: The ebullient Roy Porter saw me through the ups and downs of writing this book, ever-supportive and inspiring me with his confidence. His premature death was a personal tragedy as well as a great loss for scholarship. He supplied me with countless references, jolly japes and hours of thoughtful discussion. His tireless efforts in reading countless rewrites were sterling. Any scrap of professionalism I owe to him. Without his continual unflagging support and many helpful suggestions, this would have been a much lesser work. And finally, to the indomitable Jad Adams, without whom I probably would not have undertaken the task at all. He has remained a constant companion in times of difficulty and provided many transports and joys. He talked with me through many a sexual topic from anal sex to auto-asphyxiation and helped me find the wonderful world of Henry Spencer Ashbee and eighteenth-century erotica.

Preface to the Paperback

When Palgrave contacted me to talk about bringing *Mighty Lewd Books* out in paperback, I was pleased it was to be made more accessible. We discussed adding or altering it, but the work still stands within discussions of pornography today.

Since this book was first published there has been an explosion of pornography on the internet with access for an unprecedented number of people. Our understanding and perceptions of sexual acts have shifted unalterably in terms of both accessibility, the type of acts available for viewing and the type of people who can view them. For all the censorship laws and the anti-pornography campaigners, I am pleased to say that pornography is still thriving.

However, the current claims for its apparent ability to corrupt have challenged credulity – it has been blamed for all sorts of problems from sex addiction and adultery to murder and rape (which incidentally leaves the perpetrators dangerously less culpable). It has been used as a hook on which to hang all societal ills.

The use of pornography as a scapegoat is reminiscent of the scares of the eighteenth century in which similar claims were made about its detrimental effects. It was supposedly responsible for causing everything from personal 'disorders' such as masturbation and nymphomania to blasphemy and the degeneration of nations. Most of the claims still come from religious fanatics, politicians or journalists basing their 'facts' on inadequate (or even fabricated) examples. As for its ability 'to deprave and corrupt' – an accusation going back at least to the eighteenth century – it would seem that some things have not changed at all. It would be good to see the government asking experts in pornography (those who write about it, those who read it and those involved in its production) for their opinions before making laws – instead of accepting the opinions of anti-porn campaigners who provide very little in the way of firm statistics and have their own political and moral agendas.

Meanwhile, the history of pornography has taken off in its own way and has helped to put pornography in its proper context. Pornography often can (and does) convey unexpected insights about a society – it reflects and helps implement new developments in technology; it undermines authorities such as the Church, State and medicine; it shows the fantasies of its audience, it can satirize the hypocritical, and transgress the class system; it portrays rich and poor, young and old, and different races, reducing everyone to the same level.

When I first set out to examine eighteenth-century pornography, it was a fairly new territory. In general, over the last decade there has been a surge in interest in both the history of pornography and the history of sexuality with more students and academics investigating the topic, as well as the general public, keen to understand the workings of the mind and body. Since then, others have expanded the subject backwards into the seventeenth-century and forward into the nineteenth-century. Investigation into the history of the book and explorations of print culture have also added to the understanding of how people obtained pornography in the past, what they thought of it, who wrote it, read it and sold it. What interests us, is what pornography tells us about our culture, past and present.

After the initial publication of *Mighty Lewd Books*, I expanded my research to incorporate the history of sexuality in the eighteenth century in *Lascivious Bodies*, and edited eight volumes of *Whore Biographies 1700–1825* in which I identified, categorized and assessed this genre. More and more publishers are now bringing out complete volumes of the history of sexuality to cover all countries, classes, types of sexualities and nationalities – my recent edition of *A Cultural History of Sexuality* in six volumes being one example. Since then, I have moved into exploring alternative sexualities (so-called 'sexual perversion') and have investigated global perspectives of sexuality in world history.

Currently, other areas of research on pornography have concentrated on the expansion of porn on the internet and its effects (amateur porn being particularly healthy in undermining mainstream producers of porn providing it free for all). A healthy sex life is a happy one – and for many this includes pornography. So do please continue reading...

Introduction

This is a book about the development of pornographic literature and an exploration of a great diversity of other sexually-oriented printed matter, which circulated in eighteenth-century Britain. Some erotica revelled in innuendoes and allusive terminology as a means of continuing a discourse on and around sex, particularly in the public arena. Other, more explicit material was directed at the private consumer; this would be the beginnings of what we would now recognise as 'pornography'. I have looked at both ends of the spectrum and have concentrated on its progress, its major elements, and how both this amatory material and 'mighty lewde' works fitted into a broader scheme of the world. I have also looked more specifically at the themes that would be taken up in this material and the sources of these themes.

Ribald poems, salacious prints, sensational trial reports, medical advice manuals, religious attacks, scandal sheets, racy memoirs and obscene fictional tales were printed and dispersed through booksellers and hawkers throughout the main towns and cities. This material ranged from light-hearted lascivious humour to hard-core graphic descriptions of sexual activities, but, more importantly, it carried contemporary attitudes to certain subjects, such as science and religion.

The eighteenth-century world was one of rapid change. Ancient views were being questioned and new ideas taking their place. Science was developing in leaps and bounds. Advances in natural philosophy, medical experiments and exploration of foreign continents all led to an expansion of the world-view, the scientific revolution having a profound effect on how people saw themselves and life around them. Certain new findings were pivotal in their influence on bawdy material, which took up new scientific terminology and satirised recent experiments. However, within erotica, a process of assimilation and elimination of particular issues was evident. Ideas were either incorporated or rejected within the context of erotic material against a backdrop of contemporary beliefs and practices, as seen in oral traditions, folklore and everyday activities. Rather than accept new promulgations often perceived as far-fetched, frequently erotica retained ancient beliefs.

The external world had an impact on the sexual language, rhetoric, activities and didactics within lascivious material, many of the ideas and beliefs springing

1

from occurrences and attitudes in general culture. Political, social and ideological forces all had an obvious influence. Thus, erotica did not merely deal with sex but was highly influenced by popular contemporary topics circulating in the public domain, frequently acting as a conduit for debate on various subjects, ranging from generation and the workings of bodies, to botany, electricity and anti-Catholicism. Moreover, erotica often ratified contemporary notions about socio-sexual relations between the sexes, depicting men and women in 'normal' sexual hierarchical roles, highlighting the extreme characters of the passive female on the one hand, and the uncontrolled lascivious female on the other, both images prevalent in the real world.

The examination of the erotic book trade (chapter 2) is an attempt to understand how and why the erotic book developed when and where it did. Since little evidence has so far been unearthed on the circulation of the erotic book and its various formats, publication details of the books under survey have been scrutinised to see what they reveal regarding not only when and where the material was produced, but also class and gender issues. Were both men and women involved in erotic book production? How much did the material cost? In other words, did erotica reach across the class divide? Were only men reading erotica? Was it only élite men? Or did women and labourers have access to the material? My findings have been placed within the context of other evidence on the history of more general printed material in an attempt to provide an overall probable pattern of production and circulation of erotica, and of its readers and writers. In the section on censorship, the trial accounts of prosecutions have been examined to see which books were considered obscene and why. This sheds light on the changing attitudes towards certain material and, in some cases, a continued confusion as to the definition of obscenity.

Procreation, disease and degeneration are all topical subjects reiterated in erotica, highlighting the very real fear of poverty and ill health, which permeated eighteenth-century society. Yet descriptions of the erotic body and its fluids (chapter 3), while often subversive, nevertheless retained surprisingly conventional views. Although historians have highlighted the radical nature of pornographic material,[1] the conservative element in erotica is an issue which has not previously been examined. This analysis therefore raises unasked questions about the nature of taboo in pornography. Is pornography always radical or subversive? If not, when not? Which traditional components are maintained and why? Images in erotica, although radical in some respects, continued to retain dominant contemporary attitudes towards men's and women's bodies, particularly in respect to genitalia and bodily fluids. This affected the way in which bodies were depicted, the display of fluids within any particular body depending on their sex. Essentially, this exhibition of bodily fluids unleashed the 'uncivilised' erotic body.

New scientific developments arose specifically around discussions about botany, reproduction and electricity (chapter 4). Terminology from the new sciences was used to discuss sexual organs, scandals and sexual activities within the boundaries of metaphor, whilst simultaneously ridiculing new scientific proposals. Travel, explorations and discoveries of new lands (chapter 5) would also affect erotic writing and its interpretations of the world and the body.

But it was religion, or more specifically anti-Catholicism, which would serve to provide the overriding themes in the emergence of a more graphic sexual material (chapter 6), most notably its harnessing of flagellation as a sexual theme. Anti-religious erotica and identifiable themes in early pornography related tales of debauched monks and nuns, seducing priests and their corrupted penitents. The culmination of these ideas can be seen in the emergence of a new pornographic world of flagellatory fiction (chapter 7).

This book came out of many ideas which the material itself proffered. Because of its great wealth as a source, this work can look at only some of the aspects which were presented by the material. I have attempted to pull together prominent themes in erotica, current in culture, science and religion. I am particularly concerned with the emergence of pornographic strands which emerged amidst a plethora of other erotica. I also attempt to draw out the main contemporary notions of female and male sexuality and identify the multifaceted images which were prominent.

I have chosen to concentrate on heterosexual sex, since much of the fictional pornography was aimed at heterosexual readers. Although I mention homosexuality and tribadism, it is only in so far as it is mentioned within the material examined. Unless other material is uncovered, as far as we can tell with current available sources, fictionalised pornography directed at homosexual readers did not emerge until the nineteenth century. However, certain erotica was in evidence which reported homosexual activities, usually in factual or semi-factual reports of trials. But this appears to be related merely for newsworthy titillation rather than having any immediate and profound effect on the development of pornographic fiction at the end of the eighteenth century. The case is the same for British anti-aristocratic erotica and pornographic political attacks, which were produced more for entertainment value and as scandalous gossip than to help formulate themes in new forms of pornographic fiction (although this was not necessarily true in France).[2] All these subjects warrant fuller arguments of their own, but this book is not the place. The subject of erotica as a literary genre, although touched on, will not be examined in detail as this, again, is another book.

Two historians, Roy Porter and Robert Darnton, have particularly influenced my work on eighteenth-century erotic material. Roy Porter has been instrumental in devising ways of investigating sex and society. In his section in *The Facts of Life*,[3] he explores the 'creation of sexual knowledge in Britain' during the seventeenth and eighteenth centuries through an examination of sexual advice literature. In this investigation, he has shown how certain literature can be used as a way of understanding sexual knowledge in eighteenth-century society.[4] In his book *The Great Cat Massacre*, Robert Darnton attempts to understand what he calls 'l'histoire des mentalités', which incorporates cultural history and the history of ideas. He aptly points out that cultural history has previously been directed at 'high' or 'intellectual' culture with the exploration of 'low' culture as still unmapped territory. Where Darnton succeeded with story tales and fables in unravelling complex threads of cultural history, this book will attempt to do the same in relation to sex in cultural history.

Erotica was very much part of eighteenth-century culture, ideas within it being influenced by external events and attitudes. When reading this erotica, it became evident that it was not part of a separate fantasy world devoid of any stimulus from reality, but played a major role in the construction of gender identity. Hierarchical patterns emerged in erotica which commented on the dominant ideology. Erotica sometimes accepted the 'norm' and followed the path of accepted gender ideals elsewhere, but it would just as easily invert or reject them altogether.

1
Erotica or Pornography?

One person's smut is another person's sensuality. Similarly, distinguishing between erotica and pornography has been a topic of great debate among historians of sexuality. Problems with defining the material, to a large extent, result from attempts to fit the material into a cultural and sociological pigeonhole which did not exist when it was written. Erotica has been seen to be written as 'a matter of intent in that the authors and publishers had in mind to provide the reader of their wares with sexual stimulations of one sort or another'. Pornography has been described as that which is prohibited, 'the written or visual representation in a realistic form of any general or sexual behaviour with a deliberate violation of existing and widely accepted moral and social taboos'; 'the explicit depiction of sexual organs and sexual practices with the aim of arousing sexual feeling'. The terms for erotica and pornography have even been used interchangeably, which denies the differentiation between graphic descriptions of sexual acts and suggestive innuendo or sexual parodies. This corpus of work has also been described as 'sexual fiction'.[1] Yet not all pornographic descriptions can be described as fiction, as we can see by trial reports.

Definitions of erotica and pornography within this body of writing have proved problematic, and many of the arguments are not always helpful. They confuse the issues which are important by continually querying characterisation. Certainly, the eighteenth-century reader did not use the same categorising faculty that we use today. No boundary was made between pornographic, erotic, libertine, gallant or licentious images, or differentiation from other forms, such as philosophical, political or moral genres.[2] Writings of a sexual nature have been labelled somewhat indiscriminately as pornography, erotica, smut, obscenity, clandestine or forbidden texts, sexual fiction and libertine literature – different terms often applied to the same works. To add to the confusion, many of the arguments have been applied within the conceptual framework of the twentieth century, which blurs the real issues that were important in the erotic writings of the eighteenth century. Furthermore, French and English erotic writings have frequently been lumped together, ignoring the important distinctions which need to be made between the two sets of material. An artificial delineation between mainstream literature and erotica has been made in today's world which simply did not exist at the time it was published and first being read. This 'low-life literature' therefore needs to be fitted into a broader, wider cultural context.[3] Our notion of pornography existing as a separate entity is fairly specific to the last 150 years.

If the word 'pornography' did not exist, should we use it to describe material in the eighteenth century? Assertions have been made that 'pornography' cannot be used on the grounds that it would be anachronistic, the term being first mentioned in the *Oxford English Dictionary* only in 1857. It has also been argued that the use of *érotique* in the context of 'sexual' rather than 'amorous' emerged in France only in 1825,[4] so, if we reject 'pornography' as a term, we would be obliged to reject 'erotica' for the same reasons. Furthermore, similar terminology was circulating in ancient Greece, so it would be erroneous to dismiss the terms on the basis of anachronism. Plato's *The Symposium* refers to 'erotic' in the sense of both love and sex. Eighteenth-century writers frequently alluded to Greek and Roman references and often used the same connotations, writing about love and sex as synonymous, and they frequently equate sex, lust and love with being 'amorous'. In *Deipnosophistae*, Athenaeus mentions πορνηγράφος (pornography), referring to one who writes about harlots.[5] Therefore, since Grub Street writers also wrote about prostitutes, why not call their work pornography? But the term 'pornography' no longer alludes only to writings of or about harlots. More recently it has been imbued with political meaning, certainly not the intention in this book.[6] We do need, however, some sort of definition of the material to assist the modern reader.

A set of works called 'pornography' can be traced as a specific chronological and geographical development from sixteenth-century Italy and seventeenth-century France.[7] Certainly, we can trace a definite development of English material in the eighteenth century which includes graphic descriptions of sexual activities – what we could call 'pornography' in the modern sense of the word. For clarity, my definition of 'pornography' is material that contains graphic description of sexual organs and/or action (for example, detailed descriptions of masturbation, or anal, oral and penetrative sex) written with the prime intention of sexually exciting the reader. Pornography is not merely a series of repetitive scenarios, but a particular way of writing to fulfil a particular function, to create the desired effect of physical pleasure.[8] But it was specifically seventeenth-century France which first developed a more graphic style, English 'pornographic' work becoming 'an aim in itself'[9] (for the main purpose of sexual excitement) only from the middle of the eighteenth century. There was a traceable crucial period in the development of more pornographic English-grown material (as opposed to translations of foreign work) which would take off from the 1770s onwards (with the notable exception of *Memoirs of a Woman of Pleasure*, 1749). Stylistically improved in order to render a sexual reaction from its readership, the fictional scenarios became more imaginative. New narratives emerged combining the techniques of the novel with explicit sexual scenarios to form an authentic pornographic voice. Although elements of this were evident in earlier works, they would fuse only in the late eighteenth century.

For the purposes of this book, I place pornography as one genre within a superfluity of other types of erotica, erotica being used as an overarching description for all books on sex. On a general level, bibliographers of erotica include the same books, and I adhere to their precedent.[10] All the material I have included comes from one bibliography of erotica or another and shall therefore be referred to as 'erotica' as an all-encompassing term to depict material pertaining to the bawdy, amorous or sexual, including pornography.[11] A distinction needs to be made here between the noun 'erotica' (the bulk of the material) and the adjectives 'erotic' and 'pornographic' when describing it. A consensus exists that 'erotic' material pertains to sexual matters, either overtly or in a 'hidden' form; for example, through metaphor, innuendo or implication. Eroticism is usually recognised by implication of the sexual rather than its explicitness, through the use of euphemism or innuendo. Erotic (rather than erotica) material can therefore be defined as that which is descriptive of amatory or sexual desire made through insinuation. This is generally written to amuse rather than sexually stimulate, unlike pornographic material which is more explicit and carries that intention. Certain types of specifically English erotic material were circulating during the early eighteenth century (and would continue through the nineteenth century), running parallel to the development of pornographic works. In his study of pornographic, obscene and bawdy works of the seventeenth century, Roger Thompson uses the definition 'bawdy' as meaning to provoke amusement; and the definition 'obscene' (as a general rather than legal term) as 'intended to shock or disgust'. Both terms fit aptly for other texts dealing with sex or desire.[12]

The only hard-and-fast definition which can be easily identified is the legal term 'obscenity', as applied to books in cases which saw successful prosecutions against the publishers of certain types of material.[13] Those British pioneers who have traced the publication and censorship of books generally regard the writers and publishers of such material as a vanguard of resistance to authority. Erotica identified as obscene can be defined as writings about sex which officials or dominant groups have suppressed on the grounds that they are morally corrupting or degrading.[14] It therefore follows that if writing about sex is a revolt against authority, that authority is likely to react, usually through censorship of the material.[15] Obscene books, in this context, play the role of opposition, a balancing force within society, and cannot be seen as separate from it, but merely a resistant force within it.

Developments in pornography

Both the emergence of the novel and the growth of the urban world had a major impact on the development of pornography. English erotic writing saw stylistic developments in the language. Earlier themes of 'gallantry' or 'amatory' were maximised into full-blown sexual avarice or lust, although systematic cursing and abusive terminology was not to develop until the nineteenth century.[16] Furthermore, substitution of the metaphor with sexually explicit Anglo-Saxon terminology allowed for the replacement of the suggestive for the graphic description of sexual organs or activities, although euphemistic material would continue to be popular.

A further development can be seen in the relocation of the settings in the pornographic scenarios; these will become evident in this book. Throughout the eighteenth century, in the creation of the British pornographic world, the setting became increasingly 'hidden' or 'secret', often introducing a more claustrophobic atmosphere than encountered in earlier erotica, although this was a gradual and uneven process. The draped, voluptuous boudoir and the airy open pastoral scenarios of erotica gave way to secluded, middle-class, family parlours and the enclosed convent cells of pornographic works.

All forms of sexual activities abound. Straight, missionary position sex was still evident, but there was an increase in other forms of carnal activities, and this development is significant. Some pornography shows female demands for increased foreplay and less penetrative sex.[17] Surprisingly, flagellation pornography did not always mention penetration, and in some erotic books men do not figure at all. Penetration was therefore not always the ultimate aim in pornography. Although there was an increased concern about masturbation during the eighteenth century, to a large extent, this was connected with the medical assertions that excess loss of sperm affected a man's health.[18]

The increase of the portrayal of sexual activity of any kind is a result, if anything, of new developments in printing and mass production. Sex was increasingly being written about, therefore sexual intercourse was more 'on show' in textual form, pornography increasingly willing to pander to different tastes. A growing interest can be identified not just with vaginas and penises, but with forearms, thighs, breasts and buttocks. This would indicate that there was not merely a concentration on genitalia as desirable sexual parts of the body, but an exploration of other potentially erogenous zones, at least in print.

In erotica, prostitution was seen as necessary, despite the serious concerns about venereal disease. Men are shown as being in constant fear of cuckoldry, this connected to anxieties about female sexual desire. Often women were seen as powerful and sexually threatening. Yet women were also sometimes portrayed as victims. Positive attitudes towards romance did not grow only towards the end of the century, as Lawrence Stone argues (see below), but were present in early erotica. Also, we can see through pornographic material that, from the mid-seventeenth century, imagery of sex between women was prevalent, at least in the mentality of the reading public. However, this was a positive image and, as yet, still connected to women who also liked sex with men.

This exploration, though, is not without its difficulties. Erotic and pornographic works can add to our understanding of people's sexual knowledge and beliefs and, in a psychosexual dimension, disclose personal desires. But erotica does not necessary tell us about people's actual sexual experiences. Some of the more explicit material is fantastical; how far these fantasies were indulged in reality is difficult to determine. What we can see from some of the sources is that some fantasies *were* played out in reality – flagellation, for example. Furthermore, sexual meaning and debates were frequently buried under layers of obfuscatory language, sometimes culminating in complicated forms of metalepsis, layer upon layer of figurative terms (particularly metaphors) distancing the real subject (sex) under discussion. Decoding disguised messages, which would have been easily accessible to the eighteenth-century reader, reveals both the continuity and changes in notions about sexual behaviour. It also reveals the multiplicity of images and understandings of men's and women's bodies which were current, many of them conflicting, some of them constant. Close scrutiny of the sexual texts uncovers a real concern with social and intellectual authority, with many of the writings questioning dominant scientific or cultural viewpoints.

Finally, whims or desires were replaced by fetishes, degeneration or 'unnatural' sexual acts. Again, this was a gradual and sporadic process in English porno- graphic fiction, and most recognisable from the last quarter of the eighteenth century. Why there was such hiatus between this fictional work and those that followed is an interesting, if probably unanswerable, question.[19] It might simply mean that the material is no longer extant, although popular pieces would see many editions, which made survival more probable.

Although I have pointed to the differences between certain alleged sexual prac- tices and their reflection in erotica, care must be taken in using erotica to demon- strate actual sexual behaviour. Various other sources exist, such as court and police records, hospital records, newspapers and journals, letters, diaries and memoirs, which, while containing particular biases, can help to verify sexual practice. Some of the behaviour described in erotica, if not necessarily widely practised, was certainly widely written and read about in other printed matter. For example, popular magazines printed letters on flagellation, and significant quantities of pamphlets were based on real trials of debauched clergymen, sodomites and criminal conversation. Other pieces of erotica would appear to be directed at a select few, with debaucheries crossing the line of 'normal' behav- iour, or even inverting it, thereby representing not a popular trend but a devia- tion from the acceptable (for example, the work of de Sade). Some lascivious scenarios went out of their way *not* to represent the normal.

Most importantly, both satire and writings of graphic sexual fantasies fre- quently invert and subvert dominant ideology. Some satire has been misinter- preted and a straightforward reading of the material has completely reversed comprehension of its true intent. For example, the humour of Juvenalian satire can sometimes be overlooked because of its self-consciously and seriously moral tone. Furthermore, because pornography transgresses taboos, it crosses cultural boundaries, taking the reader into the world of the 'hidden' and forbidden. This leads to potential pitfalls of inverted realities, subversion of 'truths' from a gov- erning external discourse, or submerged meanings within a text. Conversely, it has been argued that when sexual repression occurs in a society, sex becomes the primary focus of discussion. Michel Foucault has stated:

> Rather than the uniform concern to hide sex, rather than a general prudish- ness of language, what distinguishes these last three centuries is the variety, the wide dispersion of devices that were invented for speaking about it, for

having it be spoken about, for inducing it to speak for itself, for listening, recording, transcribing, and redistributing what is said about it: around sex, a whole network of varying, specific, and coercive transpositions into discourse.[20]

The history of sexuality

The history of erotica and the development of pornography are essentially part of a wider history of sexuality and gender. The history of sexuality involves differentiating between sexual *mentalities* (thought, knowledge and opinions) and sexual *realities* (experience, actions and what actually happened), the history of erotica being substantially about the former, a history of ideas. Meanwhile, the history of gender has provoked questions about oppression, submission, passivity, assertion and, most importantly, discussions around public versus private spheres which need to be incorporated into the study of erotica.

Within the history of sexuality, there has been a trend towards depicting broad shifts in sexual behaviour. In *The Family, Sex and Marriage in England 1500–1800*, Stone asserts that a new mentality arose during the eighteenth century whereby shows of affection were more commonplace, as was an increased desire for sexual pleasure and privacy. This was accompanied by the weakening of the extended family network and support systems, and the isolation of the nuclear family.[21] Problems with such sweeping teleologies became evident with the publication of essay collections which have had a major impact in questioning entrenched historical views about the eighteenth century. These books have assisted us by adding more cultural layers to previous all-encompassing paradigms on repression and libertarianism and have demonstrated how the eighteenth century was a highly diverse society.[22]

Since the 1970s, women's history has provided new theories, which have helped to expand our understanding of women's roles and status in society while shedding new light on the history of sexuality.[23] Yet debates have raged between feminist historians in the race to construct new sexual paradigms.[24] First, gender was described as a social construction, a useful category of historical analysis, whereby both men and women can be studied.[25] This, in turn, was criticised in that gender as a category is an illusion; it does not exist as a distinct and separate classification and cannot be divorced from other historical variables such as region, economics, ethnicity and class.[26] A reassessment has been deemed necessary whereby relationships between men and women should be seen not as one overriding, entrenched stance, but as mutable, effecting both long- and short-term transformations.[27]

However, women's history has been guilty of applying its own restrictive frameworks, as shown in the 'separate spheres' framework which divides society into private and public spaces.[28] In this depiction, men dominated the public arena, whereas women were relegated to the private sphere. Enslaved in a life of domesticity, the woman became a prisoner in her own home, an 'angel in the house'. The 'ideal' woman was chaste, or at least sexually passive. Furthermore, this history, in which feminist historians have pinpointed increasing restrictions on women's behaviour, does not necessarily mesh with the impressions of other historians, who point to an openness of sexuality during the eighteenth century. While much work has been undertaken on middle-class women, the straightforward utilisation of public/private divisions simply does not work when applied to other classes, as can be seen in the case of rural plebeians[29] and the gentry.[30] Recent work suggests that women's public role in the eighteenth century was not as restricted as first thought, and women continued to play a prominent social role in the public domain.

None of the feminist frameworks works when attempting to place women in one of two opposing roles; either as victims, or as active agents of their own history. A multiplicity of images can be found exemplifying both, but these polarities are too melodramatic. Both representations can be found, but so can a plethora of other images ranging between the two extremes. Straight rendering of dichotomies has to give way to investigations of multi-layered facets allowing for more complex visions.[31] What is needed is an analysis of cultural influences and social incorporation in a more pluralistic approach.

The argument around men, women and sexual licence, and submissiveness or assertiveness, has seethed with suggestions of revolutions and crises with every new study. There have been suggestions of a 'sexual revolution' for women, in which they actively pursued sexual pleasure;[32] a prevalence of sexual unconventionality among wealthy female plebeians which brought with it vulnerability, culminating in a sexual 'crisis' around 1780–1820;[33] a sexual revolution where a heterosexual phallocentric sexual culture reigned;[34] and another occurring in London around 1700 wherein sexual relationships were redefined as a result of the emergence of a third gender, this being the adult effeminate sodomite or homosexual.[35] All these studies have attempted to shed light on the shifting sexual cultures of the eighteenth century. However, 'revolution' is too strong a word to use in defining new emerging patterns in erotica. What can be seen is a definite development in erotica which led to the major new English pornography. This is most evident in the depiction of the up-and-coming middle-class domestic household in flagellation material, a striking example of English writers of erotica creating a new private sphere as a setting for sex.

2

The Erotic Book Trade

> A naked male figure at a bookseller's shop is one way of telling the public what *kind of books* the proprietor had to dispose of: – but, however the ingenuity may answer a private purpose, it is certainly a disgrace to public modesty, and ought to be taken down by the magistrates if this hint for its removal had not the desired effect.
>
> *The Times*, 20 August 1788

By the end of the eighteenth century, London was awash with all sorts of printed matter, which could be bought from a wide variety of outlets. Part of this cache of reading material was highly erotic, including licentious novels, adventurous travelogues, rude prints, ribald songs and racy poems, and some pornographic. The most explicit material was subject to prosecution and therefore was purposely kept 'hidden'. It had to be more carefully sold and was aimed at a specific audience.[1]

False dates of publication, aliases or omission of writers' names and disguised place of publication all make for difficulties in establishing the exact date of publication. Some erotic religious and political tracts can more easily be identified since internal evidence relates to real events reported elsewhere. Reference to current scandals can also help to date a piece. However, some older scandals held their titillation value long after the event; for example, Lord Audley's trial for sodomy, which took place in the seventeenth century, continued to attract readers well into the eighteenth.[2] Typographical evidence of printing styles, types of fonts, layout and particular bindings sometimes helps link erotic books to publishers of semi-erotic or 'official' books, the latter containing names and addresses where the material could be purchased or where it had been published. Occasionally, old popular prints were used to accompany new works, but also new prints were bound together with texts from an earlier period. Artists' depictions of erotic books within their pictures provide us with proof that the book had been published at that time, and was no doubt easily recognisable by a common audience. One such example can be seen in Hogarth's 'Before' picture, in *Before and After*, where a book of *Rochester's Poems* is displayed (Figure 1). Gillray's print, *A Sale of English Beauties, in the East Indies*, 1786 (Figure 2) depicts a box of erotica telling us what was available in his day, including *Fanny Hill, Female Flagellants, Crazy Tales* and *The Sopha*. This is particularly helpful, for example, in the case of *Exhibition of Female Flagellants* since the dating of this book has so far been conflicting.[3]

References to erotica, both popular and élite, were given in other printed material; for example, there was a series of advertisements for *School of Venus* carried in newspapers, including the *Daily Advertiser* for 25 August 1744, in the *General*

Invented Engraved & Published Decr y.^e 15.th 1736 by Wm Hogarth Pursuant to an Act of Parliament.

Figure 1   William Hogarth, *Before and After*, 1736. Note the woman is reading novels and Rochester's poems – an indication of her lascivious nature. *The Practice of Piety* is a satirical joke on Hogarth's part.

Figure 2 James Gillray, *A Sale of English Beauties in the East Indies*, 1786. Bottom left, note the crates 'For the Amusement of Military Gentlemen'. The imprint of the birches on the crates indicates the flagellatory nature of some of the books contained: *Female Flagellants*, *Fanny Hill*, *Sopha* and *Madame Birchini's Dance*. All these books were available before 1786, the date of Gillray's print.

Advertiser (20 August), *Daily Post* (21 August) and the *Daily Advertiser* (22 August).[4] Publishers of erotica frequently published pseudo-medical or 'gallant' works, which advertised to the readership other types of raunchy ware which were available. Risqué memoirs advertised books on sex manuals, giving details of where they could be bought, connecting the book back to the publisher.

Publishers responded to public demand for more suggestive and explicit sexual material and increased production to incorporate a wide range of tastes and to suit all pockets. They expanded the market by circulating more widely, and changed the format to reduce costs for the readers in order to reach a larger audience. The price of the material varied from penny sheets and sixpenny chapbooks to expensive, leather-bound books costing up to six guineas, the majority of them falling somewhere between one shilling and three shillings. Similar stories and poems could be found in chapbooks, magazines, newspapers and pamphlets. This provides compelling evidence on how accessible erotica had become to different economic groups. From the number of reprints and editions a book or pamphlet went through, we can ascertain a book's popularity.

Cultural, social and literary changes encouraged the development of English erotic and pornographic styles with an increasing array of images of sexually active men and women. However, these developments were not independent from external influences. It was earlier Italian and French works which would help to shape English erotica.

Foreign influences

Italy took the lead in the publication of erotic works during the sixteenth and early seventeenth centuries, followed by France in the later seventeenth and early eighteenth centuries. Sexually explicit printed material found in eighteenth-century England was often imported and erotica emanating from Europe proved popular. Both pornographic engravings and texts would find a market in eighteenth-century Britain, encouraging reprints, translations and emulations. Some of the original editions are extant in the British Library,[5] numerous copies testifying to the interest and demand of the British public.[6]

The earliest erotic Italian works to have an impact were by Pietro Aretino (1492–1556). He wrote *Sonetti lussuriosi* (1534) to accompany erotic illustrations undertaken by Giuilio Romano and engraved by Marcantonio Raimondi. This led to a genre of engravings known in eighteenth-century England as *Aretino's Postures* (Figure 3). His second publication, *Ragionamenti* (1536), was first seen in London in 1584.[7] English writers were inspired to produce their own versions, such as *The Crafty Whore* (1658), a free rendering of the third dialogue of the first part of *Ragionamenti*, which deals with the life of whores.[8] Further renditions of whores' stories include *La Puttana Errante* (1660),[9] translated as *The Accomplished Whore*; and Ferrante Pallavicino's *La Retorica delle Puttane* (1642), translated as *The Whore's Rhetorick* (1683).[10] The latter incorporated common elements of pornography using the story of a whore's life to satirise the Jesuits and the hypocrisy of religion. Pallavicino was beheaded in Avignon at the age of 28 for his anti-clerical writings.

Italian influences have been traced back to the works of Aretino, Rocco and Franco, yet evidence of direct influences on English material still needs to be explored. Some of the themes assumed to be English can be traced back to earlier Italian work. One example is the theme of the eel, which was to become so popular in eighteenth-century English erotic satires;[11] this had already been mentioned in Marini's *Adone*. In this tale, a fisherman describes a domestic eel with two hangers which he is saving for Lilla, and which raises its head if anyone touches it.[12] Another theme can be found in Niccolò Forteguerri's burlesque poem *Ricciardetto* (1738), which relates the tale of a priest who resorts to Boccaccian stratagems in order to enjoy the favours of a young bride. This theme was developed in French and English anti-Catholic material. Furthermore, versions of Italian books, although not nearly so prevalent as French erotica, do appear in English-language versions in the eighteenth century; for example, *Libro del Perchè*[13] (Book of Wherefore) came out in England as *The Why and the Wherefore* (1765).

Italy's culture was to have an influence on other European erotic and pornographic writings. The infamous Marquis de Sade believed Italy to be inhabited by

Figure 3   Agostino Carraci, *L'Arétin de A. Carracci (à la nouvelle Cythère*, 1798).

the most decadent race, and this influenced his choice of setting for Juliette's sexual adventures. The French novelist Stendhal was also moved to include themes evident in the sexual lives of Italians in his *Chroniques Italiennes*, which he based on historical facts of a sodomising bishop and a report of incest.[14] Italian material also influenced the use of the Arcadian, the pastoral or mythological setting, which were to become prevalent in later eighteenth-century French and English erotic material. However, erotica shifted in its perceptions and representations of sex with a move from *volupté* (in which sex was seen as essentially good and ruled by sensual pleasure) to *debauché* (in which sex was seen as bad and directed by corruption). In the sixteenth century, Italian 'rococo eroticism' had presented sex as problem-free. But by the time the libertine novel emerged, France was depicting sex as the source of all problems. This evolution was not quite so clear-cut in English material, where both *mentalités* are evident.

Although Italy was the forerunner of pornography during the sixteenth century, its production of obscene literature had all but died out by the eighteenth. Nor did it experience the rise of realistic sexual fiction as seventeenth-century France and eighteenth-century England did. The evolution of English erotica was to be more heavily influenced by French material, which was at the forefront of the development of earlier more sexually graphic types of work.

An eager audience for French pornography already existed in England in the seventeenth century, erotic French classics such as *L'Escole des Filles* (1655), *L'Académie des Dames* (1680) and *Venus dans le Cloître* (1683) proving popular. All three books carried themes of sexual initiation, defloration and interest in body parts and bodily fluids, which were to become essential elements in English pornography.[15] The French original of *L'Escole des Filles* (Figure 4) was first published anonymously in 1655 and was available in London by 1668. Samuel Pepys read it, as shown by his much-quoted diary entry for 9 February 1668 in which he describes it as 'a mighty lewd book, but yet not amiss for a sober man once to read over to inform himself in the villainy of the world'. Twenty years on, an English translation, *The School of Venus*,[16] was the focus of Curll's prosecution in London, and again in 1745. Both Millot and L'Ange, publishers of the first edition, had shares in the book and, on his arrest, the latter admitted that although the manuscript was in his handwriting, Millot was the author.[17] The text consists of a dialogue between an experienced woman and a virgin, a technique inherited from Aretino, which would be used in eighteenth-century erotica.

The dialogue style continued in *L'Académie des Dames* (Figure 5). Written by Nicolas Chorier, the earliest edition was published in Latin as *Satyra Sotadica* in 1659 or 1660. The French edition, *L'Académie des Dames*, appeared in 1680 and was translated as *The School of Women* in 1682, and as A *Dialogue Between a Married Lady and a Maid* in 1688 and 1740.[18] *Venus dans le Cloître* (Figure 6) was originally published in France, written by Jean Barrin in 1683, vicar-general of the diocese of Nantes. Again in the form of dialogue, this time between two nuns, the book introduces a religious setting which was to play an important role in creating a separate sub-genre of erotic literature. *Venus in the Cloister* was translated for the English market by Henry Rhodes and published in 1692,[19] and republished by the pornographer Edmund Curll in 1725.

Although the interaction between English and French pornographic novels was considerable, one of the most important features of English translations is that they were frequently 'free translations'; in other words, they were not literal interpretations but liberal ones, often containing interesting additions or omissions. These interspersions highlight 'hidden' English tastes and are significant in pointing to particularly English desires or abhorrences. For example, in the original *Rettorica delle Puttane* (1642), 'Le figure dell'Aretino' was recommended, but

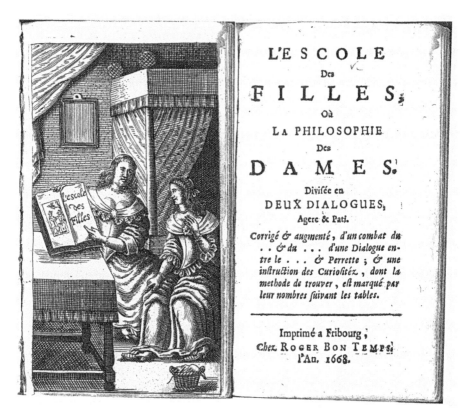

Figure 4 Title-page and frontispiece from Michel Millot, *L'Escole des Filles Où La Philosophe des Dames*, '1668'. False imprint. The pedagogic theme of sexual initiation contained within the text is depicted in the frontispiece showing the older woman introducing her younger friend to pornography.

in George Shell's English version, *The Whore's Rhetorick*, an anti-sodomitical stance is indicated, and the figure rejected for its depictions of what appears to be anal sex. The character of Mother Creswel [*sic*] (a well-known bawd in London) declares: '*Aretin's* figures have no place in my Rhetorick, and I hope will find no room in my Pupils Apartment. They are calculated for a hot Region a little on this side of *Sodom*, and are not necessarily to be seen in any Northern Clime.'[20]

Subtle differences can also be found in the English *School of Venus*, again not a literal translation of *L'Escole des Filles* but adapted for English audiences. It was also shorter and therefore could be sold more cheaply at prices ranging from 1s to 3s 6d, thus reaching a wider audience. Additionally, the philosophising on love in the original disappeared in the English translation and gave way to more explicitly sexual terminology. There are also references to incest, which are not present in the original French version.[21] This points towards an English predilection for incest, which was to evolve further during the second half of the eighteenth century. These developments might well have been a reaction against the increasing importance being placed on family values.[22] As has been mentioned,

Figure 5   L'Academie des Dames, 1680.

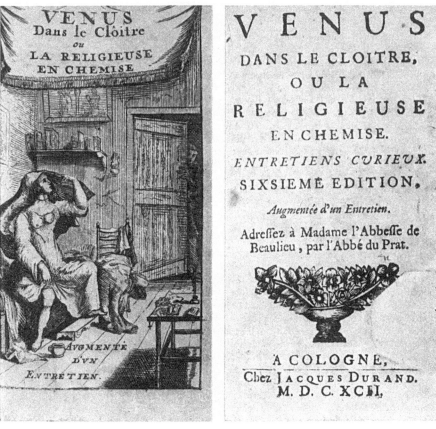

Figure 6 Frontispiece and title-page to an early edition of *Venus Dans Le Cloître*, 1683, a work ascribed to Jean Barrin.

the breaking of taboos was part of pornographic format;[23] in some pornography, the taboo being broken was the unity of the family – in order to create tension, the family was placed under threat.[24]

Differences can be seen in a comparison of the English *Dialogue Between a Married Lady and a Maid* (1740) and its French original, *L'Académie des Dames*. The defloration scenes are less aggressive, the sexual encounters less frequent and Tullia more passive.[25] In the French version, Octavia and Tullia indulge in tribadism.

> *Octav.*: Ah! ah! Tullie, comme tu me presses! ah deux, quelles secousses! tu me mets toute en feu, tu me tues par ces agitations. Etiens au moins les flambeaux, car j'ai honte que la lumière soit témoin de ma patience. Crois-tu, Tullie, que je soufrisse cela d'un autre que de toi.
>
> *Tull*: Ma Chère Octavie, mon amour, embrasse-moi entièrement, et je reçois ... Ah, ah, je n'en puis plus, je décharge, ah, ah, ah, je meurs de plaisir![26]

This was omitted in translation. In fact, most of the third dialogue dealing with lesbian love is excluded from the English version. *Dialogue Between a Married Lady and a Maid* consists of only 47 pages, but the French original was well over double that.

In French pornography, attacks on the priesthood and the cloistered existence of the nunneries were common. These themes were to influence English erotic writing, fitting neatly with the contemporary Protestant British train of thought, which was decidedly anti-Catholic. English satires from the sixteenth century onwards had already seen attacks on the Catholic clergy in the form of bombastic recitations against the Church of Rome and Popery in general. English erotica would refashion itself to include attacks on the Catholic Church common to French literature, creating its own stereotypes of lecherous friars and lascivious nuns. *Venus in the Cloister* became particularly popular in England. Other anti-Catholic erotica followed and included fictional convent tales, revelations of excommunicated Catholic priests and reports of French priests' trials incorporating details of their sexual deviations.

Kearney states that little new erotic writing emerged at the beginning of the eighteenth century until the publication of John Cleland's *Memoirs of a Woman of Pleasure* (1748/49) and in France, *Thérèse Philosophe* (1748) and *Histoire de Dom B...*, *Portiers Des Chartreux* (1741). This is perhaps more true in relation to the lack of pornographic fiction published, since other erotica was produced during this period, most noticeably from Curll's production line.[27] *Memoirs of a Woman of Pleasure* has been recognised as one of the first major pieces of the genre of the pornographic novel. However, the French introduced *Histoire de Dom B...* in 1741/2, which had a huge impact in Britain, the translation being available as early as 1743. The book was attributed to Jacques Charles Gervaise de Latouche and was frequently reprinted under various titles, including *Dom Bougre, Portier des Chartreux, Mémoires de Saturnin* and *Histoire de Gouberdom*.[28]

In England, French material had a reputation for being indecent or obscene. French words were therefore often inserted into the title, in the frontispiece or in adverts of a book to act as an indicator of its sexual nature. Buyers and readers would therefore be able to identify the kind of book it was.[29] English books would also often insert French words into the text and reference them to French originals to make them seem more sensual. Erotic books frequently 'borrowed' from each other, lifting material from one book and inserting it into a newer version. French erotica was often immediately available in England, followed by English translations. Likewise, English exports to France, such as *Memoirs of a Woman of Pleasure*, were available in French translation, in this case within two years of its publication in England.[30] The book was very popular, going through numerous editions, including both French and German versions, though poor Cleland was perhaps the last to benefit. Fortunately, when he was summoned to answer for his work, the Earl of Granville was on the Privy Council and awarded him an annuity of £100 per year.

Although English publishers would go on to advance their own brand of erotica, foreign material would provide some of the essential subject matter which would be explored in English pornography, namely that of defloration, bodily fluids, anti-Catholicism and flagellation. However, English material would adapt these themes to cater for specific English sexual predilections. The English book publishers would respond to the impact of foreign pornography by developing their own domestic market.

Publishers, printers and sellers

The book trade expanded rapidly during the eighteenth century and obscene books could be purchased all over London, including *Rochester's Poems*, *School of Venus*, *Tullia and Octavia* and 'A percel of Cutts'.[31] Nor were sellers of erotica afraid to advertise their wares. One correspondent to *The Times* complained:

> At one of the public academic exhibitions in Somerset-House, within these last four years, some naked figures stood in the sculpture-room, that highly displeased their Majesties. There was not so much as a fig-leaf. The public afterwards complained, and they were removed. It was indecent for a moment – what must be the continuance of a similar figure over a bookseller's shop in the Strand – the whole as large as life? Surely it ought to be taken down?[32]

The extent of the growth of the book trade can, to some extent, be gleaned from Plomer's *Dictionary of Printers*, although not all those involved in the book trade would have been registered; 1,700 firms are listed for the period 1668–1725, double the number that had existed twenty-five years previously. Between 1725 and 1775, 2,500 firms were producing reading material, the market now having expanded to include the provinces. By the 1790s, there were four times the number of printers as there had been at the beginning of the century.[33] A rise in demand for printed material was stimulated by increased educational opportunities, the growth of the middling classes, a growing periodical press, the increase of circulating libraries, reading clubs and private subscription libraries.

Publishing, printing and selling were interlinked and were not always separate lines of work, the same person sometimes being responsible for several parts or all of the operation. For example, Edmund Curll both published and sold erotic material. Trade publishers were in fact wholesalers, acting as agents through which other retailers could obtain copies. The publisher would often hire the printer and binder separately as books were mostly sold in sheets and bound prior to publication. Frequently, the printer remained unnamed unless he was also the publisher or seller; for example, John Nutt (who also published *Swift's Tale of A Tub*) printed and sold *The Account of the Seducing of Ann, the Daughter of Edward Ketelbey* (1700); A. Baldwin printed and sold *Reasons Humbly Offer'd for a Law to Enact the Castration of Popish Ecclesiastics* (1700) in Warwick Lane. Some printers sold material from the address where they were printing; *The Palace Miscellany* (1732) was printed and sold by J. Dormer, at the Printing-Office, the Green Door, in Black and White Court, in the Old Bailey. Although printers had been a key component in publishing, by the eighteenth century 'it was above all the booksellers who specialised in what we call publishing'.[34] The terms bookseller and publisher were, to a large extent, interchangeable.[35]

London was the centre of book production in Britain and played a dominant part in influencing the market, with an ever-increasing output of books, pamphlets, periodicals and newspapers.[36] Much of the erotica emanated from Grub Street, a real location[37] situated in Moorfields. Full of crumbling tenements, the area was the haunt of pimps, prostitutes, booksellers and publishers and a miscellany of writers. An examination of the publishing details on the title-pages of erotic books shows the main areas of production: from the 1690s to the 1730s, publishers of anti-clerical erotica (one of the most popular forms of titillating material during this period) were based in Fleet Street, St Paul's, Warwick Lane and Stationers' Hall. *A Short History of Monastical Orders* (1693) was printed for Rob Clarvell at the Peacock at the west end of St. Paul's; J. Critchley operated from Charing Cross and published pamphlets such as *The Case of Mary Katherine Cadiere* (1731); J. Roberts in Warwick Lane also produced pamphlets on the same scandalous case, *A Defence of F. John Baptist Girard* (1732) and *The Case of Mrs Mary Cadiere* (1732).

During the 1730s, 1740s and 1750s, book production grew, with many of the erotic books published in Covent Garden and Holborn. Mr W. Hinton, who published *The Ladies Miscellany* (1731), was based at the Kings Arms in High Holborn, next to the Three Cups Inn; J. Leake and E. Curll were based at the Pope's Head in Rose Street, Covent Garden, *Merryland Displayed* (1741) issuing from there. *The Secret of Pandora's Box* came from T. Cooper in Paternoster Row. His wife, Mary, later printed and sold *Lucina Sine Concubitu* (1750) from the Globe in Paternoster Row. By the 1770s, Paternoster Row was still a base for Fielding & Walker, who printed *An Elegy on the Lamented Death of the Electric Eel* (1770), an erotic skit on electricity.

Production of material was often shared. Of eighteenth-century novels for which relevant details are known, half were produced by one publisher, the rest were printed either for 'the Author' or by partnerships of two or more publishers. Congers, or associations of copyright-sharing trade members, were formed as a device to share production costs and protect copyright by controlling distribution.[38] Publishers J. Isted at the Golden Ball in Fleet Street, T. Astley in St. Paul's Churchyard, E. Nutt at the Royal Exchange, A. Dodd without Temple Bar and J. Jollifre in St. James Street all shared in the publication of the popular erotic pamphlet *Tryal of Father John-Baptist Girard on an Accusation for Quietism* (1732).

Publishers of erotica were not confined in the material they produced but also printed scientific pamphlets and books. Mary Cooper, mentioned above, along with C. Davis of Gray's Inn, Holborn, printed scientific pamphlets, such as *An Essay Towards the Explication of the Phenomena of Electricity* (1746). Curll published not only erotica and pornography but also books on history, philosophy and science. The Royal Society brought forward discussions on experiments in science through its publication *Philosophical Transactions*. These were reprinted by other publishers in cheap abstracts throughout the eighteenth century and found an avid readership. This new market was recognised by Grub Street writers, who produced inexpensive versions of scientific tracts and pseudo-medical material which could reach lower down the class scale. Boundaries between science, medicine and literature remained blurred,[39] with erotica as much a part of popular entertainment as art, science and literature, including other types of fiction and non-fiction. Quack medical guides, anti-clerical attacks, romantic novellas and even poems were therefore all seen as popular readable information on sex, and as yet no clear-cut demarcations between book genres had been established.

Floods of ballads, cheap chapbooks and titillating sheets of erotic verse and prose were pumped out by printers based around London Bridge and Smithfield, suggesting that street literature continued to flourish throughout the eighteenth century. In the 1720s, Jacobite ballads were pounced on by an 'abundance of scoundrels of both sexes', with young women targeted for sales at fairs as well as on doorsteps.[40] These ballads and poems were sung in the streets, recited in taverns and the theatre, and were passed on through oral tradition. Seventy-year-old Ellen Vickers and her illiterate daughter Sarah Ogilbie were among many who cried seditious ballads on street corners.[41] Coffee-houses and taverns were also focal points for the spread of titillating tales. The alehouse poet acted as a cultural conduit, absorbing news, stories, ballads and songs. Coffee-houses sold books and made broadsheets and periodicals available to their customers; one of the first of Curll's book sales mentioned in the newspapers took place on 28 February 1705–6 at the Temple Coffee-House.[42] *Arbor Vitae*, a piece of metaphorical erotica based on botanical classification, was part of this genre; the prose version was available in 6 × 12" twopenny sheets printed on both sides, and would have circulated in inns and coffee-houses.[43]

Ribald poems were frequently issued in more expensive collections such as *The St. James's Miscellany*, containing *An Epitaph On a Lady of Quality* and *The Ladies Miscellany* (1732),[44] 'Priced Stitch'd Two Shillings', which included such titles as 'The Happy Slave', 'To Cupid', 'A Drinking Song', 'The Minorcan Lovers', 'The Female Phaeton' and 'To Cloe, having a Tooth-Ache'. Songs and poems frequently reflected contemporary topics in sexual satires; *Festival of Ancareon* [*sic*] (1788) contained Captain Morris's songs on both 'the tree of life' and the 'electric eel'; botany and electricity were popular erotic themes.[45] Similarly, the *Ladies Delight* (1732), price sixpence, contained the verse and prose of 'Arbor Vitae', followed by 'Ridotto al'Fresco', a poem describing 'the Growth of this Tree in the Famous *Spring-Gardens* at *Vaux-Hall*, under the Care of that ingenious *Botanist* Doctor H____GG____R'.

Private manuscripts of racy poems[46] were printed up without authorisation by unscrupulous publishers. Curll was frequently criticised for publishing under other people's names, including other publishers such as John Morphew, John Pemberton, James Roberts, R. Burrough, J. Baker, Egbert Sanger and Charles Smith, which makes it difficult to prove who printed which books.[47] He also published under the names of Jonathan Swift and Alexander Pope. One such unauthorised publication led to the now famously reported incident in which Pope, annoyed by the fact that his *Court Poems* had been published without his permission, arranged via a mutual acquaintance to meet Curll over a 'friendly' glass of wine at the Swan Tavern in Fleet Street. Pope achieved his revenge by slipping Curll an emetic. The whole story was then related in *A Full and True Account of a Horrid and Barbarous Revenge of Poison on the Body of Mr. Edmund Curll*. The *Curliad* gave Curll's account referring to the 'emetic potion' served to him by Pope and led to a succession of satirical exchanges between the two. *A New Miscellany of Original Poems* (1720)[48] priced five shillings, contained poems allegedly by the celebrated Matthew Prior, Pope, Mrs. Manley and Lady Mary Wortley Montagu. Mrs. Manley decided to call on Curll after she heard he was to publish her alleged 'memoirs' without her permission under the title of the *History of Her Own Life and Times* (1724). They eventually came to an amicable agreement.[49]

Women also played a role in the book trade. Plomer cites 87 women printing under their own name during the period 1726–75, amounting to 3.5 per cent of the total.[50] However, women's professional involvement is difficult to trace as Stationers' Company Records usually appeared in the husband's name. Women workers in the trade therefore sometimes remain 'hidden'. It is likely that women were more involved than previously assumed. There is plenty of evidence to show the extensive activity of women in the book trade, with daughters, widows or wives working as part of the family business between 1678 and 1730 in Grub Street.[51] There can be no doubt that women were involved in the production of books in the early part of the century, not necessarily as 'helpmeets' to their husbands but as joint operators of their trade. Three trade publishers were particularly active in the first half of the eighteenth century, two of them being women, Abigail Baldwin (d. 1713), James Roberts (c. 1670–1754) and Mary Cooper (d. 1761). They were known for shifting large quantities of topical works, often through street-hawkers.[52] Women frequently took over from their late husbands and passed the business on to kin, as did Mrs. Baldwin to her son-in-law, James Roberts. Women also formed congers, coming together for the joint publication of books, which made it cheaper and easier. In 1735, Elizabeth Nutt, Ruth Charlton, Mary Cooke and Anne Dodd joined up with James Read to enable a publication of *Annotations on the Holy Bible*. However, with increased capitalisation and professionalisation of the print trade, many workers, both male and female, became disempowered. Major structural changes saw a decline in family businesses and, as a result, women were no longer offered the opportunity to learn the business through their families. By the mid-century, women had all but disappeared as major publishers and printers.[53]

Women were also involved in the seedier, less respectable end of the market. Among the women of Grub Street were Elizabeth Nutt and Anne Dodd (both mentioned above), who were thanked for their work running a group of shops at the Royal Exchange, Temple Bar.[54] Few publishers went under their full names, the use of initials making it more difficult to identify them; for example, E. [Elizabeth] Nutt and A. [Anne] Dodd were listed among those who printed and sold erotic verse such as *St James Miscellany*,[55] which included

Natural History of the Tree of Life and *The Ladies Delight*. Elizabeth Nutt's daughters, Alice, Catherine and Sarah, assisted in the business.[56] Mary Cooper was responsible for publishing *Lucina Sine Concubitu*. Sarah Popping was less fortunate. In 1716, she was taken into custody for the 'injudicious publication' of *An Account of the Tryal of the Earl of Winton* which was advertised for sale at only twopence. On explaining how the pamphlet had come to be printed, the witness said Sarah Popping (being too ill to give evidence) was not its 'onlie begetter'. Consequently, Edmund Curll and John Pemberton were taken into custody. Popping wisely presented a petition stating that she had been ill and her sister, 'who was not acquainted with such things', had published it before she knew. Popping and Pemberton were discharged, while the less fortunate Curll was held in custody for three weeks.[57]

As with any good dealers, female booksellers of erotica would check out their wares before purchasing from buyers.[58] Bridget Lynch, wholesaler, 'own'd she had sold several of the School of Venus'.[59] According to one trial report, Mary Torbuck sold copies of a collection of engravings entitled *A Compleat Set of Charts of the Coasts of Merryland wherein are exhibited all the Ports, Harbours, Creeks, Bays, Rocks, Settings, Bearings, Gulphs, Promontories, Limits, Boundaries & Co*, at five shillings a copy to a bricklayer named Edward Scudamore at St. George's, Hanover Square. Catherine Brett added that she also sent her sons to Mrs. Spavan to purchase it at 2s 6d a copy, and had heard 'one Richards (first cousin to the said Sparvan) say that Spavan had boasted of having obtained a guinea a week by the sale of School of Venus in particular'.[60]

Despite the apparent ease with which erotica could be bought in London, it has been suggested that its circulation might be restricted. Boucé has stated: 'What was readily available in mid-eighteenth century London, would probably be much more difficult to get hold of in the provinces.'[61] However, evidence is emerging which proves that local distribution networks in eighteenth-century England were more widespread than originally thought,[62] and were already well established in the seventeenth century.

Itinerant hawkers distributed ballads and chapbooks across large swathes of the country, to obscure districts and to the humblest social levels. An estimated 2,500 hawkers existed, both men and women. This figure includes only those registered in the first year of the 1679 Licensing Act, and many more illicit traders would have been plying their wares. The type of material became increasingly sensational in the form of plays and pamphlets about murder, earthquakes and monstrous births, complete with woodcuts, with 24-page chapbooks becoming standardised around the mid-seventeenth century.[63] The extent of the spread of material became such a concern that after the Licensing Act of 1679 was allowed to lapse, the Stationers' Company led the attack against hawkers and bawlers, foreign booksellers and scandalous pamphlets. They opposed the sellers who 'wander up and down Citty and Cuntry Selling or dispersing Books contrary to Act of Parliament', many of them libellous pamphlets,[64] and proposed a new Charter, passed on 22 May 1685, which attempted to restrict their activities.

Cheap scandal sheets produced in London could be obtained in the provinces, as witnessed by a gentleman's letter related in the *British Magazine*[65] for June 1749. He declared: 'I have read from time to time in small histories, comprized each in a half sheet, and sent me down into the country as they come out, remarkable accounts of murders, rapes, ghosts, blazing stars, and apparitions, which have been an amazement to this great metropolis', which included 'authentic' accounts of the case of Lord Lovat and the rape of the chaste Mrs. P_____ps.[66] According to the letter-writer's disingenuous remarks, the frequenters of George's coffee-house[67] preferred the 'lying histories' of Tom Jones, Laetitia Pilkington and Roderick Random to these 'true accounts'. A shared collusive culture of sexual innuendo operated, which everyone would have been expected to understand, and the scandal of various affairs, including that of Mrs. Teresia Constantia Phillips would have been well recognised. This 'innocent pursuit' of obtaining such tales reportedly cost the reader ten shillings a year.

Although the eighteenth-century provincial book trade has been seen as mainly distributive rather than productive,[68] some local towns were highly active. Provincial printers produced political squibs, 'dying' speeches and a vast body of material, with no thought for its long-term survival. Some of these were single- sided, indicating that they were produced with the intention of being posted up on walls and doors. Single sheets include material on executions, scandal and love as *The Confessions or Declarations of John Price* (c. 1737), *The Maid's Lamentation on the Loss of her Shepherd* (c. 1782), *Beauty's admirer; or, the lover in Cupid's Snare* (c. 1783),[69] or in chapbooks, as in the eight-page *The Prodigal Daughter: or the Disobedient Lady Reclaim'd* (c.1770s). The printers were clearly cultivating a market among the labouring classes in the towns and countryside.[70]

Whereas single sheets of printed material were produced in the provinces, there is no evidence of erotica being routinely produced outside London. Certainly, the majority of the material under examination in this book was produced in London, with the rare indication of an erotic book having been printed in Bath or Dublin. However, since cheap and portable material was being widely distributed, there is every reason to believe that erotica and pornography, including suggestive chapbooks, scandal sheets, erotic prose, pornographic pamphlets and ballads could be obtained elsewhere in the country.

Readers and writers

Historians have suggested that erotica was mainly written for and read by gentlemen as part of the 'flowering of libertinism'[71] although, as yet, there has been little debate about exactly who read erotica. These historians do not directly assert that it is *only* men who were reading such material, but generally imply that men were the main readers of erotica, with little consideration given to the range of erotica or to the issues of gender and class. Although English élite gentlemen were among the audience for French-language pornography, a more divergent readership is evident for some English-language erotic material. It must not merely be assumed that women did not read bawdy material. Margaret Spufford suggests a shared appreciation of rude humour between plebeian men and women in their reading of cheap, popular, ribald material. She provides evidence that 'even the most cultivated early seventeenth-century ladies enjoyed dirty jokes'.[72] There is, therefore, every probability that similar eighteenth-century chapbooks, including the erotic ones, were read by women. Nor were only élite people reading erotic material. Tim Hitchcock suggests that books such as *The New Description of Merryland* and *Merryland Displayed* were aimed at the middling sort, and that the readership included women. References to tea-tables, the use of 'highly florid language and Latinate expressions' and the indulgence in extended euphemisms (in other words, that which made use of sophisticated sexual metaphors) were all part of the 'middling-sort of culture'. He states that although pornography was 'derived from and directed at a narrow libertine audience', it undoubtedly reached to the lower-middling sort.[73]

Robert Darnton believes that French Enlightenment pornography such as *Thérèse Philosophe* was read mainly by a 'champagne-and-oyster' readership of the élite, but has pointed to cheap, widespread pornographic sheets read by the lower classes. Darnton states that it is 'very likely' that sex books were written by males for males everywhere in Europe, although he admits that little is known about the readership.[74] Goulemot's comments that erotica could be found everywhere in France, 'from the apartments of the highest nobility to the little room of a preacher's servant', indicates a readership which stretched from the upper to the lower classes.[75] So who really did read erotica, and which sort? A reappraisal of the arguments is needed to take into account differences in class and gender of the readership when considering various types and formats of erotica.

One particularly fascinating 'set of records', *Records of the most Ancient and Puissant Order of the Beggar's Benison and Merryland, Anstruther*, has been used as evidence of readership.[76] The male libertine members of the Scottish Beggar's Benison of Anstruther allegedly read and masturbated over pornography. The records were published in two parts – the 'historical portion' and the pornographic supplement – a fact which has some significance, as we shall see. The historical portion lists the members and outlines the history of the secret society for men known as 'Beggars Benison and Merryland' based at Anstruther. The supplement[77] supposedly contains minutes of their meetings from the 1730s. It consists of four printed pages, the rest of the book taken up with songs, toasts and essays on reproduction (including detailed descriptions of genitalia) which had been read or performed at the gatherings. Each record is approximately three lines long, indicating how many attended the meeting, with a brief note on what took place and whether it was a successful meeting or not. For example: 1734 Candlemas, the proceedings took place before a meeting of thirteen 'Knights' where a seventeen-year-old girl, 'fat and well-developed', took off all her clothes for the benefit of the members. 'She spread wide upon her Seat, first before and then behind' while the knights examined her 'Secrets of Nature'; '1734 Lammas. 18 assembled, and frigged upon the Test Platter.'[78] The platter was filled with semen from each knight, most not averaging 'quite a horn spoonful'. According to the minutes of St. Andrew's Day, 1737, 'Fanny Hill was read' in manuscript form. Although not published until 1748, it is possible that *Memoirs of a Woman of Pleasure* was circulating in manuscript form by that date.[79]

However, the Beggar's Benison *Supplement* was probably a money-making scam by the nineteenth-century pornographer, Leonard Smithers, the minutes a fabrication of Smithers himself. According to Kearney, the book was printed by Smithers on the disbanding of 'Beggar's Benison', in London in 1892.[80] To take any book published by Smithers as a serious factual account would be stretching credibility. Not only did he operate as a bookseller, selling a variety of salacious material, but he was a notorious publisher of pornography, commissioning both translations and new writings. He translated *Priapeia* with Richard Burton, which he then published. He also consorted with Ernest Dowson's circle of decadent poets, Dowson himself working as a translator of French pornography for Smithers. Indeed, Oscar Wilde called Smithers 'the most learned erotomaniac in Europe'. Furthermore, Smithers was known for making up tales when it suited him. After selling his correspondence with Wilde, Dowson and Aubrey Beardsley, he then forged further letters to maintain his flow of funds.[81] All matters considered, any pornographic book issuing from Smithers' direction would appear dubious in authenticity to say the least.

This said, there can be little doubt that a libertine gentlemen's group called Beggar's Benison existed during the eighteenth century. Various artefacts and manuscripts are held at St. Andrews University Library and Artefacts Museum.[82] Among them is the pewter 'test-platter' into which the minutes claimed the knights had masturbated. Inscribed around its rim is 'Beggar's Benison Anstruther 1732'; inside, at the base, the platter is inscribed with the phrase 'The Way of a Man with a Maid – Test-Platter' along with an engraving of a large penis inserted into a hairy vagina (Figure 7). The penis has a small purse tied round it, indicative of both commerce and a symbol of a scrotum. According to Captain Francis Grose's *Dictionary of the Vulgar Tongue* (1785), the 'Beggar's Benison' (or blessing) was 'May your prick and purse never fail you', a phrase indicative of both the sexual and financial interests of the society. Other artefacts include various seals imprinted with phalluses, a couple of sashes, five medals, a punchbowl, phallic glass drinking vessels and a silver snuff box[83] (allegedly containing the pubic hair of a courtesan of George IV). Although some of the artefacts suggest a later date, probably nineteenth century, some date from the eighteenth century, suggesting that the club was established then. Nonetheless, this leaves the debate open as to whether the actual minutes were in fact true or not (or whether the members of the Beggar's Benison society read 'Fanny Hill').

Amongst the collection of manuscript papers are seven letters to J. Macnaught Campbell Esq. from J. Leslie, acting on behalf of Smithers from the publisher's address at 174 Wardour Street, London. Macnaught Campbell

Figure 7   The Beggar's Benison Test Platter, into which members allegedly ejaculated.

was a descendant of one of the original members of the Beggar's Benison and Collector at Kelvingrove Museum, Glasgow. He had applied to purchase a copy of the History of the Beggar's Benison from Smithers which had been delayed. In a letter dated for 23 July 1892, Leslie wrote:

> Mr Smithers has handed me your note subscribing for a copy of 'The Beggar's Benison'. The book is with the Binder and will be ready for delivery on Monday or Tuesday next. The subscription price is £2.2.0, your cheque for which I shall be glad to receive.[84]

Macnaught Campbell evidently obliged as Leslie acknowledged receipt of the advance excusing himself for the delay: 'Have been away for a holiday and only returned on Saturday. Will forward you vol. tomorrow. I beg to acknowledge receipt of cheque with thanks.' This was followed by a flurry of letters from Leslie to

Macnaught Campbell with promises of delivery, excuses and apologies for delay: 'By next post you will receive your copy of the "BB"'. When the copy was sent, it was incomplete, minus the supplement:

> Herewith is enclosed your copy of the 'Beggar's Benison'. Kindly own receipts and let me know whether you desire your copy of the supplement ... I must apologise for the delay which had taken place. During my absence an awkward accident happened to 2 of the facsimiles and spoilt the copies. plate 3, the Diploma. plate 9, the 7 seals. and I have been compelled to get fresh copies of these plates done. I have delayed therefore forwarding your copy, waiting for these, but as I learn that they will not be ready until Saturday I think it best to forward your copy at once. I shall send on the 2 remaining plates instantly they are delivered to me, which I expect will be first thing on Saturday morning.

And again:

> Herewith are plates 3 & 9 of the 'BB' completing your set. I am sorry that I had to keep you waiting for them.

By 12 November, nearly four months after the initial contact, Leslie finally forwarded the *Supplement*:

> I have pleasure in herewith enclosing you one copy of [the] second part of the 'beggar's benison'. Kindly acknowledge receipt and return the enclosed form filled up and accept my best thanks for your subscription. Assuring you that my services are placed at your disposal in any matter relative to books.

So why the delay? Despite Leslie's excuses, although the first part of the book was ready, it would appear that Smithers might have been awaiting interest and subscriptions before publishing, and perhaps writing himself, the second part of the Beggar's Benison. Smithers was known to fabricate further writings which had earlier proved popular, so once the history on the Beggar's Benison was attracting interest, he would have had no reservations about supplying the readership with a fictitious follow-up which provided lurid details of the society's activities. Macnaught Campbell wrote to T. D. Murray Esq., a solicitor in Anstruther, on 5 December 1911 about the veracity of the *Supplement of the Beggars Benison*:

> The Minutes or books I know nothing of but I believe the Minute Book was destroyed either by Mr Connolly or by Dr. Gordon, but I have a fancy it was the former gentleman who did so. There was a supposed print of some of the proceedings made some twenty years ago [the Smithers edition] but I have strong reason to doubt their genuineness for reasons which I cannot very well

put in writing. I have tried to find out something of the history of the old Association but with very little success.

No original minutes for the Beggar's Benison have yet been found.

More reliable evidence of male libertine readers lies with a similar group of celebrated libertines. Sir Francis Dashwood, John Wilkes and the members of a notorious Hell-fire Club were certainly readers of erotica. The story of the allegedly depraved society of anti-clerical libertines who dressed up as monks and held secret meetings where they debauched local virgins is now well known and often retold.[85] The society, or the 'Knights of Sir Francis' as they called themselves, was probably founded in the 1740s, the original meeting said to have been at George and Vulture Inn in the City. Dashwood and Paul Whitehead, the secretary, had probably met at an earlier club, the Beefsteak. Dashwood bought and refurbished a dilapidated Cistercian Abbey at Medmenham, which carried the motto 'Fay ce que voudras' (Do as you wish) over the entrance and the main fireplace. The building included a library furnished with popular books including *Tale of a Tub, Gulliver's Travels, Castle of Indolence* and Foxe's *Book of Martyrs*.[86] In his memoirs, Walpole relates how he found in Dashwood's library 'scurrilous novels bound as Books of Common Prayer' and recalls how Dashwood was 'notorious for singing profane and lewd catches'.[87] Most of the books from the library which belonged to Wilkes have his own bookplate inside them and contain his handwriting. One erotic book currently held at The British Library, *Cabinet D'Amour*, is inscribed by Wilkes himself, giving the address 'Medmenham Abbey'. Further proof of the Medmenham set reading erotica can be established by a letter in the private papers held at West Wycombe, the home of Sir Francis. In 1761, Sir William Stapleton, on turning out his own library, forwarded what appears to be erotica to furnish the Abbey, drolly referring to them as 'pious books':

> I unfurnished my library at Twickenham last week and sent the pious books to Mr. Deards [the bookseller] with orders to send them to George Street [Wilkes's address]; if the Chapter think them worthy of the Abbey. I shall be extremely glad, hoping they will now and then occasion an extraordinary ejaculation to be sent up heavenward.[88]

Sir Francis had been responsible for forming the Dilettanti Society in 1732/3, where, according to Walpole, 'the normal qualification is having been to Italy and the real one being drunk; the two chiefs are Lord Middlesex and Sir Francis Dashwood, who were seldom sober the whole time they were in Italy'.[89] Portraits were commissioned of the members and, in 1742, Sir Francis had his painted as St. Francis standing before a naked statue of Venus.[90] The Dilettanti also supported the publication of *Antiquities of Athens* (1762) and an expedition in 1766 resulting in the publication of *Ionian Antiquities*, a precursor to Payne Knight and the expedition which was written up in *The Discourse on The Worship of Priapus* (1786–7). The latter was printed in limited numbers for a specifically private male audience; only eighty copies were to be circulated for members of the Dilettanti Society. Among the recipients were Horace Walpole, Gibbon, Boswell, Malone, Wilkes and the Duke of Portland. However, restriction by subscription was probably more to do with the cost than the erotic content.[91] Ribald poems were occasionally written for private consumption within small libertine groups. *An Essay on Woman* (1763) was originally meant to be read only by friends but was to create a furore for Wilkes.[92] Only twelve copies were made, but its scandalous nature gave rise to reprints and other spurious versions. Bishop Warburton spoke of it as a performance which 'consisted of the most horrid insults on religion, virtue, and humanity, and the most shocking blasphemy against the Almighty'.[93] Walpole called it 'the most blasphemous and indecent poem that ever was composed', and 'a performance bawdy and blasphemous to the last degree, being a parody of Pope's "Essay on Man" and of other pieces, adapted to the grossest ideas, or to the most profane'.[94] The *Gentleman's Magazine* of 1763 gave a full account of *Essay on Woman*, describing the work where 'the lewdest thoughts are expressed in terms of the grossest obscenity; the most horrid impunity is minutely represented; the sex is vilified and insulted; and the whole is scurrilous, impudent and impious to an incredible degree'.[95] Wilkes defended himself in 'Letters to the Electors of Aylesbury' in subsequent editions of the same magazine.[96] Another author of racy poems, Thomas Hamilton, Earl of Haddington, who wrote *New Crazy Tales* (1783),[97] followed by *Monstrous Good Things!! Humorous Tales* (1785) for 'the amusement of liezure minutes', originally intended the poems for private readings before a group of friends, visiting at his home, 'Crazy Castle'. However, target audiences for some erotica were wider and included males of the middling sort. Advertisements for *Memoirs of a Woman of Pleasure* were placed in the *Gentleman's Magazine* in February 1749, and clerics such as Swift and Sterne kept libraries of erotica.[98]

Obviously, literacy levels and cost affected readership. By the late seventeenth century universal literacy existed amongst the male middling sort and above. Within the lower orders, the literacy rate was rising (about 75 per cent in London). Urban men and women were more likely to be literate than their rural counterparts, and men more literate than women, with women's literacy growing between 1600 and 1750, from 15–20 per cent to around 40 per cent.[99] About 40 per cent of plebeian society could read, with figures amongst tradesmen being higher.[100] Cressy states:

> The expansion or improvement of education increases literacy, which in turn leads to a greater demand for books. The rising output of printed matter makes it possible for more people to own books, and may itself stimulate the spread of literacy. The greater circulation of books creates more opportunities for people to learn to read them.[101]

However, arguments about the extent of literacy depend on the wide variety of definitions of literacy used by historians. The fact that a person could read is not always taken as a sign of literacy, if that person cannot also write. The fluency of literacy also blurs the boundaries as although some people could sign their name, they could not necessarily read. Also, many people who could not write could manage to read. Generally though, despite the difference in statistics given for early modern literacy, most scholars agree that literacy grew rapidly between 1600 and 1800.[102]

Although the printed material in English provincial towns and cities included a growing number of books and pamphlets aimed at the middling and upper levels of society, the lower echelons of society were also being targeted as an audience. The eighteenth-century specialist trade in ballads and cheap 'popular' prints had already been developed between 1550 and 1640, with many of the publications for 'lay' people rather than learned culture, written for 'everie man from the highest to the lowest: from the richest to the poorest'.[103] Plenty of reading material was therefore available which was inexpensive and suitable for rudimentary readers. Even the illiterate were not cut off from the printed word. Only one reader was necessary to read to an interested party. Public houses would employ news readers. Oral public discourse further expressed itself in traditional tales, proverbs and jokes, conversations in taverns and through market place and street gossip.

Attempts were being made to reduce costs and thus extend the readership. French pornographic material was often translated and reprinted in cheaper editions, chapbooks and pamphlets. One particular flurry of interest was created by the trial of a debauched French priest, reports of which were published in *The Case of Mary Katherine Cadière, Against the Jesuite Father John Baptiste Girard* (1732) and its many variations. Judging from the number of editions, these obscene pamphlets sold well.[104] Some of the smaller pamphlets, which sold for sixpence, would have been within the reach of labourers, and it would appear that the lower ranks were prepared to spend their small income or savings on reading material. During the 1770s, while walking to Richmond at the age of eleven, William Cobbett spent his last threepence on *Tale of a Tub*. He described the event as 'my eye fell upon a little book, in a bookseller's window: "Tale of a Tub"; Price 3d'. Despite having no supper, he purchased the book and sat down to read it immediately. He declared, 'it delighted me beyond description'.[105] By the late eighteenth century in Portsmouth 'the sailors gave sixpence or a shilling as freely for a book, as a half penny is given elsewhere when times are hard'.[106] Pornographic pamphlets and small chapbooks would therefore have been within the reach of sailors and working people with similar incomes.

Readers who could not afford to spend money on a whole book were willing to buy it in inexpensive parts. Books were often sold by the sheet instead of ready bound, allowing customers to pay 6d a week instead of say, four guineas, in a lump sum.[107] Indecent anecdotes and comic sketches could be found in monthly journals. Ned Ward's *The London Spy*, launched in November 1689, was full of scatological references and tales of the activities of flagellation brothels. Sixpenny issues were sold and read in coffee-shops and taverns.[108] Sensational details of the scandalous *An Apology for the Conduct of Mrs. Teresa Constantia Phillips* (1749) and Charlotte Charke's tales of cross-dressers and female friendships[109] were published in cheap newspapers.[110] *The Female Husband*, a tale of female cross-dressing based on a real case of one Mary Hamilton who had fourteen wives, could be bought for a few pence.[111] Some people would have access to erotica without the need to purchase it themselves, either by borrowing or purchasing for someone else. All this testifies to the fact that erotica was available in a wide variety of forms and offered a choice of cheap erotica to the reader.

The argument for female readers of erotic and pornographic material has, in the main, been ignored.[112] Yet women frequently appear to be the target of erotic material, if the prefaces are to be believed. Authors prefaced their work with an 'address to the ladies' indicating that the writers of erotica either directed their material at a female readership or wished to create the illusion of one in order to add another layer of fantasy for male readers. From the accompanying picture, which depicted women sitting at a tea-table, these ladies appear to be from the middling sort. In *Merryland Displayed*, the author noted that women were indeed reading this book:

> I am sorry to say that some of the Fair-Sex, as well as the Men, have freely testified their Approbation of this *pretty* Pamphlet, as they call it, and that over a Tea-table some of them make no more Scruple of mentioning *Merryland*, than any other Part of the creation.[113]

The book itself purported that women were reading it because there was not a bawdy word in it, merely 'smutty Allusion', thereby implying that if discussion about sex was couched in innuendoes, it was acceptable reading material for women.

Certainly the authors of erotica depicted fictional characters as having read pornographic books. Agnès in *Venus in the Cloister* reads *L'Escole des Filles* and *L'Académie des Dames*; Thérèse in *Thérèse Philosophe* reads *L'Académie des Dames* and *Le Portier des Chartreux*; Fanny Hill had access to pornographic novels which were kept at the brothel as an inducement to sex; Fielding's fictional *Shamela* is seen to have considered *Venus in the Cloister* one of the treasures of her library; amongst her few possessions – included with her four caps, five shifts, stockings and a couple of petticoats were 'some few Books: as, *A Full Answer to a plain and true Account*, &c. *The Whole Duty of Man* ...The Third Volume of the *Atlantis*. *Venus in the Cloyster: Or, the Nun in her Smock* ...'[114] Although the creation of a female persona who read about sex was obviously a literary device in order to establish the sexual nature of a character, most importantly, it meant that Fielding's readers would have had to recognise the titles and known of the contents of such a notorious book.

Lower-ranking women, including servants, were also perceived as readers of such erotica. In *The Cabinet of Venus Unlocked and Her Secrets laid open*, the preface to 'amorous' readers states that the book was intended to inform men of the manner of generation, but the author admits: 'Me thinks I already for-see, that the longing Chamber-maide will read this little book ...' His friend accuses him of writing to incite titillation over which presumably he knows the critics will attack:

> I perceive the intent of your wanton page is rather to incite an itching or titil-lation on whereby women may be disposed to conception, than to stir up the conception of learned men's brains. The Chamber-maid is like to receive a great satisfaction in making a scrutiny, whether she enjoys the integrity of her Hymen, and so be resolved, *quid poterit salva virginite rapi*. She will roul over your pages to see whether she hath not forfeited the notes of her virginity, by petulancy, whilst others (I mean the profoundly learned) make strict inquisi-tion into abstruse Philosophical verities.[115]

In fiction, female chambermaids are so frequently involved in the acquisition of pornography that it would appear to be a common supposition. Tonzenie in *A New Atlantis for the Year One Thousand Seven Hundred and Fifty-Eight* men-tions three erotic books which she was reading which were obtained by her maid: 'Having soon after reached her teens, and by the means of her chamber-maid got a translation of Ovid's *Art of Love, Rochester's works* and the *Memoirs of a Woman of Pleasure*, all her doubts about her inward pleasure vanished.'[116] Significantly, she mentions Ovid in the same category as *Memoirs of a Woman of Pleasure*, suggesting that the eighteenth-century reader made no distinction between classical and contemporary erotica. Female servants and the lower classes certainly had access to and read the material, even though they might not have been the intended audience. Records of eighteenth-century book-sellers between 1746 and 1784 reveal print orders and purchases by fifty ser-vants who, over twenty-one years, bought, bound or ordered seventy books or pamphlets. Entertaining works accounted for 20 per cent, including jest books (4 per cent). Some servants, such as Mrs. Philippa Hayes, housekeeper to a bachelor, George Lucy, had the run of the house (and thereby presumably had access to his library) and sometimes borrowed books from booksellers, although she was an exception.[117] One British seller, Mrs. Roach, 'used to open a portfolio to any boy or to any maidservant ... the portfolio contained a multitude of obscene prints ... she encourages them to look at them ... This was common to other shops.'[118]

Women gave and received pornographic books and particularly appreciated fine copies. The courtesan Mrs. Leeson received a 'beautiful edition' of *Woman of Pleasure* from a female friend, and read similar books including *Guide to Joy, Rochester's Poems, the Cabinet of Love,* and *Kitty and Amynter*.[119] Mrs. Errington, made famous through her adultery trial of 1796, was said by a witness to have shown her the book *Memoirs of a Woman of Pleasure* on several occasions. Fanny Murray and other mistresses of the Medmenham set would no doubt have read the same material as their male counterparts, since it was readily available to them. The playwright Edward Ravenscroft (*The London Cuckolds*, 1682) remarked on girls reading obscene material: 'the other day I caught two young wenches, the eldest not above twelve, reading the beastly, bawdy translated book called the *Schoole of Women'*.[120] Obscene prints were even sold in girls' schools.[121] George Cannon, an infamous pornographic bookseller, even employed people to throw pornography over the walls of girls' boarding schools as an inducement to later sales.[122]

Women were reading about sexual intrigues in women's magazines which occasionally carried risqué trial reports, racy poems and sexual satires. Francis Place noted that *The Ladies Magazine: or, The Universal Entertainer* (1749–53) carried all three, including Hill's *Lucina Sine Concubitu*.[123] Revelations of people's affairs frequently came out in thinly disguised stories in popular magazines or found their way into gossip columns. Sarah Lennox read about such reports in *Town & Country* and *Covent Garden Journal*, and would eventually provide material for the gossip columns herself, based on the rumours of her numerous affairs. She also read memoirs that would have been thought unsuitable for young ladies, and when Rousseau's *Confessions* appeared from 1781 she reverently put each volume beside his other works on her library shelves. She liked to read anything she regarded as 'wicked', such as Voltaire's *Candide* or the pornographic *Le Canapé*[124] of which she exclaimed, ''Tis the filthiest most disagreeable book I have ever read.' She ordered her own books from a female bookseller, Mrs. Harriet Dunoyer, in the Haymarket. Caroline, her sister, married to the politician Henry Fox, possessed a library which held many explicit medical books, including Mandeville on diseases and Venette's *Tableau de l'Amour conjugal*, a sex manual full of advice and amorous illustrations.[125] Another sex guide, *Aristotle's Master-Piece*, was thought decent enough to give as a present to engaged couples, despite the fact that young apprentices masturbated over it.[126]

The range of erotica which could be purchased was extensive in terms of both content and price. In terms of class, it is clear that a much wider readership of erotica and pornographic material existed, which included the middling sort, with the cheaper material stretching to include the lower classes. In terms of gender, it is evident that women read and enjoyed obscene literature, and it was not merely the province of libertine men. Working women might well have been more likely to have shared bawdy humour prose with their menfolk, as Spufford suggests.[127]

Establishing the authors of erotic material is frequently problematic since false trails were purposely laid to avoid prosecutions. The names of some of the British men who wrote erotica are known to us, including John Cleland (*Memoirs of a Woman of Pleasure*), the lesser-known Thomas Stretser (*Arbor Vitae*) and Richard Payne Knight (*Worship of Priapus*).[128] Although Stretser has been cited as the author of *A New Description of Merryland*,[129] the name of 'Dr. Armstrong' appears on the title-page of one edition. John Armstrong is indicated by his full name as the author of *Pleasure of Venus*, where he is described as a 'physician and poet', so he might have had a hand in *Merryland*, or he might simply be cited as a tribute to his work, a common occurrence in this type of material. Writers often hid behind anonymity or false identities. Some authors who wrote under pseudonyms can be traced: John Hill, one of the most notorious popular science writers at the time, who published 96 books with 29 different publishing houses,[130] also wrote skits on sexual reproduction under the names 'Abraham Johnson' and 'Richard Roe'. It was never fully established that Wilkes was the sole author of *An Essay on Woman*.[131] Walpole doubted it was written by Wilkes alone, and believed he was assisted by Thomas Potter, who was having an affair with Bishop Warburton's wife at the time. Many of the authors of the material remain anonymous.

Detecting female writers of erotica is even more difficult. Women's contribution to writing so far has been documented as political or romantic fiction.[132] By 1700, women's publications would enter a rapidly expanding domestic market, and women's increasing literacy and their novel-writing would be fundamental to the creation of sensibility.[133] The nature of their writing frequently carried sexual overtones. Women writers often used erotica and sexual language as a veiled means to express political opinion. This declined with the emergence of the cult of domesticity around 1740, which quelled women's expression of both the erotic and the political.[134] Yet in the late eighteenth century there were more female novelists than male. From 1760 to 1800 about 2,000 novels were by women, and women also represented a significant sector of the readership.[135] Despite women being gradually forced out of Grub Street,[136] it is clear that fiction, from about the 1760s, such as that from the Minerva press, was written by women, about women and for women,[137] and plenty of this material contained a highly erotic charge.

Women were known to have written licentious material. Mary de la Rivière Manley was arrested on 29 October 1709 for the libellous publication of *Secret Memoirs and Manners of Several Persons of Quality. From the New Atlantis, an Island in the Mediteranean* [sic] (1709), a pseudo-novel full of gossip and scandal relating to prominent figures of the day in which she sought to expose the vices of Swift, Viscount Bolingbroke and Robert Harley, and in which she accused Lord Torrington of taking his mistresses to sea disguised as boys. The novel was published anonymously, the title-page of the first volume signalling its salacious content, enticingly declaring 'written originally in Italian'. She also wrote political pamphlets during the 1711 elections and articles for *The Examiner*. Eliza Haywood wrote racy novels such as *Love in Excess: or, The Fatal Enquiry* (1724) which was full of erotic prose, with its 'heaving Breasts' and 'snowy Arms' where 'every Pulse confess a Wish to yield'. Eighteenth-century courtesans frequently wrote their memoirs when they retired from the business of whoring. A Dublin brothel-keeper, Peg Plunket, wrote her life story *The Life of Mrs. Margaret Leeson* (1795–98) in three volumes. A London courtesan, Harriette Wilson, followed suit with her *Interesting Memoirs and Amorous Adventures of Harriette Wilson* (1825). Leeson's book caused quite a stir while Wilson's memoirs were initially banned and she narrowly escaped prosecution by absconding to Paris. Leeson's memoirs are particularly valuable since they provide evidence of female writers of erotica. She ascertained that a certain Mrs. H wrote a series of racy poems including *Guide to Joy*. No copy of the poem is known to have survived.[138]

A number of the publishers of erotica had a good working relationship with female writers. In a comparison of the publishers of erotica under survey here with the survey undertaken by Cheryl Turner on publishers of women's fiction, it is evident that they were often the same. For example, publishers of erotica mentioned above, A. Bettesworth, J. Hooke, J. Pemberton and T. Longman, all published fiction by Penelope Aubin (*Life of Madam Beaumont*, 1712; *Life and amorous Adventures of Lucinda, An English Lady*, 1722), usually in partnership. Bettesworth was one of the publishers of the anti-Catholic erotic work *The Frauds of the Romish Monks and Priests* (1725, fifth edition); the pornographer Edmund Curll published Jane Barker's *Love Intrigues* (1713); James Roberts, who published the sexually explicit exposé *The Case of Mrs. Mary Catherine Cadière Against the Father John Baptists Girard* (1732) and *A Defence of F. John Baptist Girard* (1732), published her *Exilins* (1715) and Eliza Haywood's *Love in Excess* (1719–20); and John Morphew published virtually all Manley's fiction. James Roberts published at least 64 works of women's fiction between 1710 and 1736 and, in partnership with Curll, published material by Jane Barker and Mary Hearne. Most of the partnerships of women's fiction consisted of two or three publishers.[139] If women were seen to be good at racy fiction which titillated readers, there is no reason to suspect that, with the advent of pornographic fiction, women were not asked by their publishers to provide for this market anonymously, particularly since they appear to have had a strong relationship with publishers of erotic material.

Censorship

Printing had been introduced in England by William Caxton in 1476 and, until 1695,[140] all books had been required to be licensed before publication. Initially, licensers appeared to be fairly liberal. Despite complaints, works such as Pietro Aretino's *Ragionamenti* (1588) and Jaggard's *Decameron* (1620) were licensed for publication. The book trade was controlled on behalf of the government by the Company of Stationers and, until the last of the Licensing Acts expired, it was illegal to publish anything without a licence. However, distinctions between acceptable and unacceptable material were frequently unclear. Sometimes a book would be banned, only to be passed by or even approved on a later reprint. In 1683, John Wickens was sentenced to pay a fine of forty shillings for publishing *The Whore's Rhetorick*, yet it was officially approved in the following February. The extent to which a particular book was repressed therefore depended on how threatening the authorities perceived it to be at any one time.[141]

In 1688, the printer Joseph Streater and seller Benjamin Crayle were prosecuted for their dealing with *The School of Venus*, a translation of *L'Escole des Filles*, and both bound over at Guildhall sessions on charges of 'selling several obscene and lascivious books'.[142] The lightness of the fines involved – 40 shillings and 20 shillings respectively – showed the lack of regard which the authorities gave this material, which was evidently not considered dangerous or subversive. Streater and Crayle were again prosecuted in 1689 for publishing *Sodom: or The Quintessence of Debauchery*. Crayle was sentenced and committed to prison, but released on condition of good behaviour. The case did not go to King's Bench (as serious cases did), nor was the charge 'obscene libel', but 'librum flagitiosum et impudicum' (a disgraceful immodest book), with additional charges of being scandalous and lascivious. When the libel law was applied, it was clear from a comment made at the time by Judge Powell that it was insufficient to deal with writings which were considered indecent. Prosecuting James Read and Angell Carter in 1708 under a common law indictment for publishing *Fifteen Plagues of a Maiden-head*, the judge declared:

> This is for printing bawdy stuff, that reflects on no person, and a libel must be against some particular person or persons, or against the government. It is stuff not fit to be mentioned publicly. If there is no remedy in the Spiritual court, it does not follow there must be a remedy here ... . It indeed tends to the corruption of manners, but that is not sufficient for us to punish.[143]

However, the libel law was successfully used in the prosecution in 1728 of Edmund Curll for the publication of the *Venus in the Cloister, or The Nun in her Smock* (1725)[144] and *A Treatise of the Use of Flogging*.[145] A memorandum dated 3 April 1725 ordered the prosecution of Curll for 'publishing foul, lewd and obscene books tending to corrupt the morals of his Majesty's subjects'.[146] Curll was undoubtedly surprised to be prosecuted since the same material had appeared nearly thirty years earlier in London without exciting attention. Despite the sentence,[147] he made the best use of his punishment:

> This Edmund Curll stood in the pillory at Charing-Cross, but was not pelted, or used ill; for being an artful, cunning (though wicked) fellow, he had con-trived to have printed papers dispersed all about Charing-Cross, telling the people, he had stood there for vindicating the memory of Queen Anne: which had such an effect on the mob, that it would have been dangerous even to have spoken against him: and when he was taken down out of the pillory, the mob carried him off as it were in triumph, to a neighbouring tavern.[148]

The reaction of the crowd would suggest that the attitude of the public to porno-graphic material did not equate with that of the law.

Distinguishing obscene material from mere anti-Papist onslaughts posed prob-lems for at least one judge; John Fortescue, one of the trial judges in Curll's pros-ecution, did not regard *Venus in the Cloister* an obscene book, 'And indeed I thought it rather to be published on Purpose to expose the *Romish Priests, the Father Confessors, and the Popish religion'*.[149] Generally, attacks on the Catholic Church were deemed acceptable since Papists were seen as both a social and a political threat. Importation of Catholic books was forbidden.[150] Caches of illicit Catholic books were searched for and destroyed by government pursuivants, and the burning of such books was an officially condoned demonstration against their distribution. Anti-religious texts perceived to threaten the established Church of England were also prosecuted.

The same memorandum that had ordered Curll's arrest simultaneously ordered the prosecution of Mr. Woolston for the 'writing, printing and publishing of a blasphemous pamphlet'.[151] Thomas Woolston[152] (1670–1733), Fellow of Sidney

Sussex, Cambridge, was tried for attacking the literal meaning of the Resurrection and the Virgin Birth in his *Moderator Between an Infidel and an Apostate* (1725) but, despite a conviction, before the court could sentence him, the case was dropped on the grounds that the King's Bench did not know enough theology to try it. He was again prosecuted in 1729 for his work on a series of six *Discourses on the Miracles of Our Saviour* (1727–29), which discredited the biblical accounts of Jesus' miracles. In it, he dismissed the transfiguration as being the effect of Jesus standing in strong sunlight, the voice from the cloud as an act of ventrilo-quism. For this he went to prison for a year and was charged £25 each on four counts of blasphemy.

Various quasi-medical texts were also seen as a potential threat. In 1709, the surgeon John Marten had been prosecuted, but acquitted, for his *Gonosologium Novum* (1709), a book derived from Venette's *Tableau de L'Amour Conjugal* (1686).[153]

By 1745, with the renewed drive against obscene literature, a letter dated 19 March was sent to the Attorney General's office on behalf of the Secretary of State, bringing to his attention *Aretinus Redivivus* and *School of Venus*, two 'very obscene and infamous books, which seem calculated for corrupting the youth of the nation'. On the basis of this, a search warrant was issued, including orders to find the authors of *A Compleat Set of Charts of the Coast of Merryland*.[154] During the same year, John Leake[155] printed an edition of *Venus in the Cloister*, but this was suppressed by the authorities before it went on sale. In a letter to James Webster and James Brettwell, two of His Majesty's messengers, Leake's house was ordered to be searched. The letter stated: 'I have received information that certain lewd and Infamous book intitled "Venus in the cloister or the Nun in her Smock in Five Dialogues" adorn'd with curious Copper Plates are now printing off by John Leake at his house in Angell street St. Martins le Grand in order to be speedily published.'[156] A summons was issued for Leake, along with five others involved in the pornographic book trade, Bridget Lynch, Thomas Read, Daniel Lynch, George Spavan and John Stevens, with issues of £100 to be levied on the goods and chattels of Bridget Lynch and of £200 on the rest.[157]

Daniel Lynch, a bookseller, was indicted for publishing *School of Venus or the Ladies Delight* and *Frances, A Marry'd Lady and a Young Maiden* with 24 plates from Aretino's postures;[158] John Stevens, a London pamphlet seller, was indicted for *School of Venus* including curious plates (the same case as above);[159] John Leake was also charged with publishing *The Ladies Academy* 'from the French, with 24 curious copper plates';[160] and George Spavan, a pamphlet seller of the Parish of Saint Clement Danes, was prosecuted for printing and publishing *Aretinus Redivivus or the Ladies Academy*.[161]

The last quarter of the eighteenth century saw a demand for tighter moral controls. In 1787, the foundation of the Proclamation Society by William Wilberforce ('A Proclamation for the Encouragement of Piety and Virtue, and for the preventing and punishing of Vice, Profaness, and Immorality') aimed to sup-press 'all loose and licentious Prints, Books, and Publications, dispersing Poison to the Minds of the Young and Unwary, and to punish the Publishers and

Vendors thereof'.[162] A wave of prosecutions indicated a crackdown on publishers and sellers of obscene books. In 1788, John Morgan of Hanover Square, London, 'being of a wicked and depraved mind and disposition', was sent to prison for a year and pilloried for

> most lawfully wickedly and impiously devising contriving and intending to vitiate and corrupt the morals of all the subjects of our said present Sovereign Lord the King and to debauch poison and infect the minds of all the youths of this kingdom and to bring them into a state of wickedness lewdness debauchery and brutality ... did unlawfully wickedly and impiously publish and cause and procure to be published a certain nasty filthy Bawdy and obscene Libel intitled 'The Battle of Venus' A Descriptive Dissertation on the Various Modes of Enjoyment.[163]

Such convoluted rhetoric had become the standard legal charge. In the same year, Lewis MacDonald, a bookseller in St. Martin-in-the-Fields, was prosecuted under the same charge for publication of the old favourite *The School of Venus*. He was ordered to be set in the pillory at Charing Cross for an hour with £200 bail on the condition of good behaviour.[164] During 1790, James Hodges was prosecuted at the King's Bench, for publishing *Memoirs of a Woman of Pleasure*,

> exhibiting Men and Women not only in the Act of Carnal copulation in various attitudes and position but also with their private parts exposed in various other lewd and indecent attitudes and Postures;

and *A Dialogue between a Married Lady and a Maid*, which did 'scandalize and debase human Nature'.[165]

Even racy magazines such as *Bon Ton* came under fire. On 18 July 1793, William Locke was charged with 'the printing and publishing of false indecent scandalous and malicious and defamatory Libel hereafter mentioned Clara Louisa Middleton now the wife of William Middleton of Stockeld Park in York and John Rose, groom to William Middleton'.[166] Locke was accused of 'unlawfully and maliciously designing and endeavouring to traduce, defame and vilify the Character and Reputation of the said Clara Louisa Middleton', accusing her of adultery with Rose and 'to expose her to ignominy Ridicule Contempt and disgrace'.

The lack of interest in the licentious publications at the beginning of the eighteenth century compared to the successful prosecutions between 1798 and 1809[167] indicates an increasing repression of literature. In 1794, James Roach was prosecuted for selling *Harris's List of Covent-Garden Ladies* and imprisoned for a year with sureties of £200 for his good behaviour for three years thereafter. In 1798, John Cole, a London bookseller, was prosecuted for publishing *Fanny Hill* and *The Delights of Venus*; the latter had been published in 1709 in *The Cabinet of Love* and had never previously been considered worthy of prosecution.[168] Even bawdy rhymes and songs were targeted. Cole was accused of publishing obscene rhymes on 13 August 1798 in which a 'Mans breeches were immediately loosened waist and knee-bands and slipped over his Ancles clean off his shirt collar was unbuttoned too' together with the following ditty which referred to 'part of the private parts', using the first letters of each line:

> A Knight delights in hand Deeds of Arms
> Perhaps a Lady loves sweet Music's Charms
> Rich Men in store of wealth delighted be
> Infants love dandling on the Mother's knee
> Coy maids love something nothing I'll express
> Keep the first Letters of these Lines[169]

He was also prosecuted for publishing Octavia and Tullia's dialogue. In court on 31 January 1799, he was discharged on giving £250 sureties (in other words, he was bound over).

Similarly, in 1799, Thomas Skillern, a dealer in music, was indicted for his lewd songs which were branded as containing 'filthy bawdy and obscene words and sentences and descriptions not fit or proper to be stated or set forth in any Language or in any Nation'. The song was described in court:

> how the Woman all bounc'd and their blood hurr'd up their faces. He made them all itch from their nave to their breech and their Bubbies burst out all their laces. There was such damn'd work to be F—k'd (meaning carnally known) by the Turk that nothing their passions could vary.[170]

In this instance, it would appear that bawdy poems and songs were deemed acceptable since Cole was only bound over and Skillern acquitted, the sheriff deciding that 'the said Indictment and the matters therein contained are not sufficient in Law that the needs nor is he bound be the Law of the Land in any manner.' James Fenturn was also charged and acquitted for the same.[171] These attempts at censorship show just how difficult it was for the prosecutors to decide what was acceptable and what was obscene and illegal, with no clear definition.

Of course, censorship and reaction against the publication of such material did not necessarily reflect the whole of society's view. Censorship might not necessarily have meant that there was a broad consensus against a certain book, but could be seen as a form of repression from a small select group wielding power against a larger section of the community reacting against its authority. Nor does past censorship tell us about the censor's view on sex alone, as some books were banned for their anti-monarchist or anti-Protestant themes. However, there are obvious distinctions between censorship taking place in Europe and that in England. Lynn Hunt's assessment of French pornography indicates that the control of written and printed material in France mainly arose from political restrictions rather than any objection to obscenity *per se*.[172] But in eighteenth-century Britain, prosecutions for obscenity or libel appear to have been based increasingly on protection of sexual morality rather than politics or religion. Significantly, by 1802, with the formation of the Society for the Suppression of Vice, attacks on moral laxity now included the call for a concerted effort to rid the book trade of obscene literature.[173]

Conclusion

During the course of the eighteenth century, England went from being an occasional producer of bawdy humour to a society awash with erotica. During the 1600s, England's main supply came from abroad with the occasional French pornographic book falling into the hands of upper-middle-class male readers such as Pepys with *L'Escole des Filles*. By the end of the eighteenth century, Britain was not only producing large quantities of cheap erotica but had become an exporter. Within England, the distribution of erotica extended from the major cities into the provinces. During the course of this development, in order to broaden the readership and make it more readily available, the format of erotica had expanded from expensive, calf-skin-bound, high quality books to include penny sheet erotic verse and shilling pornographic pamphlets. The audience extended to include women and the lower orders, and women were involved in the publishing, selling and writing of erotica. Aristocratic women were reading French pornography, while servants were viewing graphic sexual illustrations.

The courts were unsure how to react to this widening sphere of obscene books and, despite arrests, prosecutions were often unsuccessful, and some judges were even lenient. However, in the last quarter of the century, a crackdown on pornographic material can be seen; here the evangelical movement and the reformation of manners played a role. Yet bawdy poems would continue to enjoy a particular freedom despite attempts to contain them.

3
Bodily Fluids

> This violent scene of happiness every night repeated, soon cost the poor fellow his life: for his blood was so inflamed with provocative doses Janneton used to administer to him, and his body so harassed and exhausted by Tonzenie's insatiable demands, that he fell sick of a raging fever, and was carried off in a few days to her inexpressible sorrow.
>
> Anon, *A New Atalantis for the Year One Thousand Seven Hundred and Fifty-Eight*[1]

The 'violent scene of happiness' is the result of a repeated indulgence in extreme passion, the dangers of such limitless sexual activity exemplified by the hero's demise. Here, the heroine, Tonzenie, accidentally kills her footman through sexual over-exertion, assisted by Janneton, her maid, who has dosed him with aphrodisiacs by lacing his food.[2] More significantly, Tonzenie has exhausted him, literally, to death. Such erotica not only contained warnings to men not to overdo their sexual exertions, but to beware of women who demanded them. Excess evacuation of sperm is seen not only to weaken a man, but even proves fatal.

Such beliefs derived from ancient medical notions and reflected popular religious beliefs about the body and its fluids. An example of medical assumptions about the unhealthiness of excess of evacuation of sperm and its connection to his weakening state of health, can be seen in Tissot's treatise *Onanism; or a Treatise upon the Disorders produced by Masturbation* (1766). He declared:

> The human seed ... proceeds from all the humors of the body, and is the most essential part of them. This is proved by the weakness, the faintness which accompanies the loss of it in the act of coition, be the quantity ever so small. There are veins and nerves, which, from all the parts of the body, concur to their centre in the parts of generation.[3]

These concerns about men's bodies, together with certain anxieties about women's bodies, were reinforced in erotic writings. These ideas were expressed within the context of the humoral system, the early modern erotic body being essentially a humoral one.[4]

The humoral body

Early modern men and women described bodily events and sensation in humoral terms, a philosophy derived from Hippocratic belief (fifth century BC) and incorporated into Galenic physiology (second century AD). The humoral body was regulated by the four humours – phlegm (phlegmatic), yellow bile (choleric), blood (sanguine) and black bile (melancholy) – based on the natural elements – water, fire, air and earth, which were responsible respectively for the wet, hot, dry and cold balances in the body. Its fluids, blood, semen, milk, sweat and tears, were all mutable. Female bleeding from various orifices was widely accepted as 'diverted menstruation', the 'menses' taking such unusual routes as through ears, skin, gums, fingers, saliva glands and tear ducts.[5] The balance of humours was to be maintained through a variety of evacuations, as seen in the processes of alimentation, excretion, menstruation and lactation; all were understood to be homologous. Within this model, the body had a set of internal procedures characterised by corporeal fluidity, openness and porous boundaries.[6] Containment of these liquids was paramount. If liquids were to be discharged, then it should be in a controlled fashion.

Although Galenic medicine demanded a balance of the humours if a body were to remain healthy,[7] the body sometimes did not contain itself as it should. If liquids broke out in abundance, it was perceived not only as a problem to the individual, but as a threat to civilised society. This uncontrolled body was dangerous because of its lack of restraint. An example of this can be seen in the body of the early modern male drunkard, which was seen as a volcano, constantly on the verge of erupting in a superfluous production of bodily fluids, thereby creating a threat to social order. It was believed that excessive eating and drinking would create surplus semen, which had to find an outlet. The escape came in the form of unrestrained emissions resulting in ejaculation, vomiting, defecation and bloodshed.[8] This display of bodily fluids was a sign of personal weakness since a lack of control over one's own body meant an absence of control over one's emotions. A further example of this can be seen in the works of John Wilmot, Earl of Rochester, who was notorious for his obscene poems and plays, not to mention his behaviour. His poems of the 1670s describe the masculine desire to master the female body. The futility of these attempts caused men to 'dissolve', 'melt' and 'spend at ev'ry pore'.[9] In this state, men could no longer contain themselves, which indicated not only a lack of resolve but also a loss of authority over women. Men who lacked control over their fluids were considered to be of weak moral fibre and also (if they continued to expend fluids unabated) of weak constitution. Generally though, bodies which escaped their own boundaries through secreting fluids have been depicted as female.[10]

Early modern female bodies were seen as embarrassing 'leaky vessels', their bodies seeping liquids; through lack of control over their own bodily fluids, they would inadvertently express tears, milk, blood, urine and sweat.[11] Women were therefore seen as uncivilised and emotional. Within this model, female blood was demonised and seen as shameful.

Norbert Elias has suggested that a 'civilising process' was taking place, which led to a lowering of the threshold of disgust involving the progressive hiding of body parts and functions.[12] In this civilising process, natural instincts were tamed through a bridling of the emotions and subjugation of the undisciplined body. Shame was used as a mechanism in order to try to discipline 'uncivilised', troublesome bodies, seen to be those of wives, whores, rustics and children (in short, those who failed to control their bodily fluids).[13] Conversely, pornographic material, which traditionally rejected the status quo and embraced taboo subjects, would revel in the display of bodily fluids. This can be seen as a reaction against the 'civilising' process in a direct expression of the 'uncivilised' body. These pornographic elaborations showed an unleashing of emotions, the exposing of the body and the emission of fluids, with a concentration on fluid-related themes involving blood, sperm and female ejaculations. All three will be explored below.

Eroticised blood

Defloration, blushing virgins and torn maidenheads were all themes running through eighteenth-century erotica, all connected to a historical obsession with displays of blood. Female blood had long been a focus for a network of phobias in western culture, with attempts to control a woman's bodily fluids through menstrual regulation.[14] Biblical associations with blood partly explain the blood taboo. Menstruating women are conveyed as dirty or 'unclean'. Leviticus 15:24 applies negative concepts to menstruation, proclaiming, 'And if any man lay with her at all, and her flowers be upon him, he shall be unclean for seven days; and all the bed whereon he lieth shall be unclean'. Religion was one of the major influences on ideas about menstruation, such that social roles and relations between men and women rested on a set of beliefs surrounding the female body.[15] Within this framework, women's sexuality was perceived as powerful, yet simultaneously women were relegated to a secondary and inferior position within a gendered hierarchy. Popular theories and practices evolved from religion, which equated female sexuality with uncleanliness. Menstruating women were attributed supernatural powers and seen as a potential danger. As a consequence, they were prevented from undertaking certain domestic tasks, such as pickling pork or salting bacon, since they might spoil the food.[16] Warnings circulated about how women during the menses could sour wine, curdle milk, wither crops and drive dogs mad.

Ancient myths, old folklore beliefs and quack notions about the body were included in medical, pseudo-medical and erotic manifestations of haemo-centric enthusiasms. In his *Anatomy of Melancholy* (1621–51), Robert Burton reinforced wide-held opinions which saw menstrual blood as problematic. In a chapter entitled 'Symptoms of a Maids', Nuns' and Widows' Melancholy', he defined the symptoms of menstrual blood in negative terms:

> those vicious vapours which come from menstruous blood … the whole malady proceeds from that inflammation, putridity, black smoky vapours, etc., from thence comes care, sorrow, and anxiety, obfuscation of the spirits,

agony, desperation and the like, which are intended or remitted *si amatorius accesserit ardor* [if the passion of love is aroused], or any other violent object or perturbation of the mind.[17]

Burton was one of many who saw women as afflicted with medical problems because of their very nature. Their ills were attributed to either the retention, or excessive loss, of blood in the womb. Green sickness[18] (otherwise known as chlorosis) was connected to menstruation, tending particularly to affect young or pubescent girls. Physical symptoms of the 'wasting disease' included pallid skin, loss of appetite and amenorrhoea, and were often accompanied by behavioural changes, such as lethargy or desire for solitude. Prescribed cures included baths, pessaries, fumigation and bleeding. Sexual intercourse was also recommended as a cure for a variety of women's ills, especially for amenorrhoea.[19]

Humoral notions about bodily fluids, including concerns about blood, were conveyed to the readers through a wide range of sexual advice literature. These books fed off and into each other. Parts of Sinibaldus' *Geneanthropeiae* (1642) were translated into English and incorporated into *Rare Verities, The Cabinet of Venus Unlocked and her Secrets Laid Open* (1657). *Geneanthropeiae* was itself a collection of ancient Greek and Roman physicians' and philosophers' sexual texts.[20] It described itself as 'a collection on some things out of Latin … never before in English', such phrases often used to suggest the sexual nature of a book to prospective purchasers. In turn, *Rare Verities* was popularised by Venette in *Tableau de L'Amour Conjugal* (1686), which first appeared in English in 1703[21] as *Mysteries of Conjugal Love Reveal'd*. This and other sexual instruction manuals, such as the pseudo-anonymous *Aristotle's Master-piece* (1684), were rehashed and reprinted throughout the eighteenth century and would continue to prove popular.[22] The intention of the books themselves was frequently ambiguous. Although allegedly originally written with the purpose of sexual instruction, publishers recognised a market for reprinting old medical texts for the purpose of titillation. Readers were intentionally alerted to the sexual nature of the book through disingenuous 'warnings' inserted in the prefaces. *Rare Verities*, for example, expressed insincere concern that the book might slip into the wrong hands – maid-servants were thought to be reading it, with improper consequences.[23]

Within these books, notions about blood, women and processes of the body were presented within the context of humoral medicine. *Rare Verities* identified the cause of many female ailments as connected to the menses. Under the chapter 'Retention of the Courses', the author states:

> Obstructions do so inflame the womb and genitals, that as they cause a prurition, so likewise they are the origin of a thousand dangerous symptoms. The sign of this indisposition of body is too too [sic] visible to every ones eyes; to wit, a universal paleness.[24]

As well as retention, problems associated with voiding great quantities of blood were considered. Women were warned of the potential frightful consequences of bleeding to death after initial intercourse:

This membrane [the hymen] which is thus broken, yields a greater or smaller quantity of bloud, according to the largeness and fulness, or smallness and emptiness of the veines. Some have immediately died by the greatness of the flux of bloud.[25]

Visible evidence of blood after sexual intercourse was taken as a crucial sign of virginity. *Aristotle's Master-piece* (1690) discussed defloration at some length and suggested that 'pain and bleeding' were a necessary consequence. Green sickness in young virgins and barrenness in women were also considered:

The former of these ill conveniences is too apparent in Virgins, especially such as are of a Flegmatick Complexion, evidently shewing itself by discolouring in the Face, in making it look green, pale, or of a dusky yellow, which proceeds from raw undigested humours ...[26]

All aspects of virginity are dealt with – what it is and how it is violated. Doctors are generally in agreement that the hymen is broken after intercourse:

most are of the opinion that the Virginity is altogether annihilated when this Duplication is fractured and dissipated by violence, and that when it is found perfect and intire, no penetration had been made. Also some learned Physicians are of opinion that there is no Hymen or Skin expanded containing blood in it, which divers imagine in the first Copulation, flows from the fractured expanse.[27]

Venette's *The Mysteries of Conjugal Love Reveal'd* (1712) understood blood to be an indication of virginity. Indeed, he advised unchaste brides to use dried lamb's blood inserted into the vagina on their wedding nights to provide the desired effect and thereby fool husbands. However, he was eager to point out that the lack of a hymen, or the absence of bleeding, did not prove a woman was not a virgin.

Such conflicting beliefs expressed in sex manuals were often reflected in erotica. Fictional characters in erotica often disagreed with medical opinion. In opposition to Venette's belief, evidence of a hymen was regarded as necessary to prove a woman's virginity. Women were inspected for the presence of a hymen, and they were expected to bleed on first intercourse as proof of their virginity. In 'The Young Lady's Catechism' in *The Palace Miscellany* (1732), Betty Sly, the chambermaid, asks her mistress, Miss Forward, to describe the signs of a maidenhead. Her mistress replies: 'According to the new Doctrine of our modern Surgeons, there is no Sign to be perceived, but I believe they FIBB; I would willingly ask one of 'em who Marries a young Gentlewoman, whether his Wife was a Maid, and if so, then by what Sign or Token he knew her to be one?'[28] Her answer embodies the contemporary moral code and popular belief – that a woman should be a virgin upon marriage and that evidence of a hymen is an indication of her chastity.[29] She rejects the medical assumption that a hymen is not detectable. This suggests that there was an understanding amongst the writers (and probably their readers) that a virgin could indeed be identified by an intact hymen regardless of what the physicians of the day decreed.

A woman's honour rested on her sexual reputation.[30] Virginal blood on sexual initiation was perceived as proof of a woman's chastity and a sign of her purity of character. This in turn reflected on the honour of her family. A man's honour, however, was dependent on other characteristics, such as strength, courage, honesty and authority. It also related, in part, not to his own virtue, but to his wife's, since a cuckolded man lost his reputation.[31] Controlling female sexuality was therefore essential since ungovernable women were a threat to both men's honour and to society. If a woman was not a maid when she married, the patriarchal lineage came into question. How was a husband to know that a child born to his wife was really his? But establishing a woman's honour before marriage was a difficult, if not impossible task. Physical inspections of a woman's body were normally undertaken by a female midwife, usually only when a woman was pregnant,[32] or if there was a court case and an examination was necessary to establish virginity.[33] A woman would deny charges of illicit sexual activity to save her reputation. In one case, Thomas Turner, a somewhat naïve overseer of the poor for East Hoathly, Sussex was persuaded of the innocence of a maid-servant because of her vehement denials of any sexual misdemeanours. Eventually, a midwife had to be brought in to 'search' her body in order to establish the girl's pregnancy and to extract an admission.[34] Any investigation of a female patient by male physicians remained a fraught area and was viewed with suspicion.[35] Therefore, unless a physical examination took place, a bridegroom had to rely on the word of his betrothed.

The eighteenth-century interest in defloration[36] was reflected in erotic texts. In *Dialogue between a Married Lady and a Maid* (1740), a frank discussion takes place between Tullia and Octavia regarding the relative importance of maidenheads. Tullia relates the tale of her wedding night, when her husband checks for an intact hymen by inserting his fingers inside her. He 'thrust it a little way up, till he met with a stop, and I complained he hurt me: This he did on Purpose, to be satisfied whether I was a Maid or not as afterwards he himself confessed.'[37] Her husband is pleased at the discovery that he has taken a virgin bride. However, the ravishing causes Tullia some discomfort as she cries out to her husband: 'I never can endure it, it will split me in two, you'll kill me, if all this must go into my Body.' Octavia's future husband also inspects her vagina before intercourse to ensure her maidenhead is intact, the sight of blood necessary evidence of her chastity. Her mother, eager to examine the stains, declares: 'Pluck off this Smock, which I will keep for a Relick since it is stained with thy Virgins Blood.'[38] Erotica therefore followed popular belief in that the sign of blood on bedsheets was thought to be proof of a chaste bride.

If proof of virginity was necessary in a bride, it was at least desirable in a mistress. Unchaste women therefore made efforts to fake their virginities.[39] Financially, for the prostitute, it was worth the effort since men were prepared to pay extra for a virgin. Various brothels, or 'nunneries', were recorded as suppliers of 'virgin' whores. According to *Nocturnal Revels, Or, The History Of King's-Palace and Other Modern Nunneries,* a racy book about the various 'nunneries' or brothels of the day, Charlotte Hayes, a celebrated brothel-keeper, undertook such activities. She apparently passed off her young whores as undefiled, preparing Kitty Young and Nancy Feathers as vestal virgins. The book cites Charlotte Hayes's accounts for 18 June 1759, in which she wrote: 'A Maid for Alderman Drybones – Nell Blossom, about nineteen, has not been in company for four days and was prepared for a state of vestal ship last night', for which she received twenty guineas. She also supplied whores for Dashwood and his 'Knights' at Medmenham Abbey. She noted, 'Twelve vestals for the Abbey. Something discreet and Cyprian for the friars.'[40] Lord Sandwich, one of Sir Francis Dashwood's Knights, said of Hayes, 'She keeps the Stock Exchange supplied with real, immaculate maidenheads'.[41] Allegedly George 'S-l--n' (Selwyn)[42] asked Charlotte how a hymen could be preserved. She was obviously no novice: 'As to Maidenheads, it was her opinion, that a Woman might lose her Maidenhead five hundred times, and be as good a Virgin as ever. Dr. O-PATRICK has assured her, that a Maidenhead was as easily made as a pudding.' The need to have hymens surgically restored was of paramount importance to Charlotte's business because of their economic value; for Charlotte, 'though she had lost hers a thousand times, she believed she had as good a one as ever, as she has been under the Doctor's hands that very morning'.[43]

In John Cleland's *Memoirs of a Woman of Pleasure* (1749), Fanny Hill used pig's blood she had hidden in the bedpost, thereby fooling her clients into believing she has just lost her maidenhead:

> In each of the head bed-posts, just above where the bed-steads are inserted into them, there was a small drawer so artfully adapted to the moulding of the timber-work, that it might have escap'd even the most curious search, which drawers were easily open'd or shut, by the touch of a spring, and were fitted each with a shallow glass tumbler, full of a prepar'd fluid blood; in which lay soak'd, for ready use, a spunge; that requires no more than gently reaching a hand, taking it out, and properly squeezing between the thighs, when it yielded a great deal more of the red liquid than would save a girl's honour.[44]

Kitty's Attalantis [sic] *for the Year 1766,* an almanac of current harlots found in London, reports a Miss Ram— who carried on intrigues at her family home for twelve months, 'which she did with the greatest success, having sold her maidenhead, in that space of time, to fifty different people, when 'twas supposed, by her age, that her father's boy, who used to sweep the shop, got her real one, behind the counter'.[45] At the back of the book, a letter from 'Nancy Laycock', dated 8 July 1765, states: 'Received of *John Goodcock,* esq; the sum of five guineas, for my maidenhead, which is more than any of the *Badcocks* in the parish wou'd give, or any other parish within fifteen miles of this place, having tried every market day for these nine months past'.

Part of the reason for seeking a virgin was related to avoidance of venereal disease and, in some cases, virgins were sought in the belief that they cured venereal disease.[46] More persistent than the doctored prostitutes is the image of a man seeking a virgin so he can 'break her in', thereby proving his virility and his manhood. This is seen in the reports in the *Bon Ton*, of March 1793, of the establishment of the Adam and Eve Club 'in which the qualifications are that every member must produce a similar certificate of having deflowered his virgin, or debauched his married woman, and the more of those feats he has achieved, the greater is his station in the assembly'.[47] This control over a woman's initiation into sex through her defloration was part of this dominant code of morality,[48] reflecting a double standard wherein men were perceived to have property in a woman's body, the value of which diminished if she had sexual intercourse with other men.

Blushing was used in fiction as a way of denoting sexual knowledge or sexual vitality. In erotica, torn maidenheads and blushing virgins were part of the same erotic blood imagery. Female blushing, although thought by some to be a sign of embarrassed innocence, could also be seen as flirtatiousness, an acknowledgement of sexual matters or even sexual excitement. According to medical practitioner, John Gregory, in *A Father's Legacy to his Daughters* (1774), a blush denoted modesty, an attribute any good woman should possess:

> When a girl ceases to blush, she has lost the most powerful charm of beauty. That extreme sensibility, which it indicates, may be a weakness and incumbrance in our sex, as I have too often felt; but in yours it is peculiarly engaging.[49]

A blush on an unmarried woman's cheek was proof of her chastity, modesty linked to sexual continence. The ideal woman would therefore blush at the appropriate times. In another register, however, blushing was seen as a green light for sexual advances and a form of flirtation. In examinations of depictions of modesty in fiction, the blush is seen to depict not only modesty but also knowledge of sexual pleasure and the embarrassment caused in revealing it.[50] In Charlotte Lennox's *The Female Quixote*, Arabella's incessant blushing signals her body's assertion of both her modesty and her availability: 'She blushed with a very becoming modesty'; fell to 'blushing at an insolence so uncommon'; 'blushed with anger'; and 'could not help blushing at her uncle's compliment'.[51] Some women, such as Mary Wollstonecraft, regarded blushing as degrading and blamed some women for succumbing to coquettish ways:

> So far from being ashamed of their weakness, they glory in it; their tender muscles make no resistance; they affect to be incapable of lifting the smallest burden, and would blush to be thought robust and strong. To what purpose this? Not merely for the sake of appearing delicate, but through an artful precaution.[52]

Richard Polwhele commented in the notes to his poem *The Unsex'd Females* (1798), 'That Miss Wollstonecraft was a sworn enemy to blushes, I need not remark. But many of our readers, perhaps, will be astonished to hear, that at several of our boarding-schools for young ladies, a blush incurs a penalty.'[53]

The connection between blushing and desire can be seen in erotica in the previous century. In *The Whore's Rhetorick* (1683), Mother Creswel informs her protégé, 'A reasonable blush is much more prevailing than any artificial supply: it is a token of modest [*sic*], and yet an amorous sign.'[54] Blushes were seen as *à la mode*, simultaneously signifying both a woman's modesty and her sexual availability. Mrs. Manley, in *New Atalantis* (1709), recognised the value of a decent aptitude for blushing, 'for, without regard to that much-in-fashion virtue assurance, next to real innate modesty in ladies (which indeed never fails of giving the appearance) I think the outward blush and seemingly habitude of it one of the greatest ornaments they can wear'.[55] Blushing not only denoted availability but also depicted sexual fervour. In a *Dialogue between a Married Lady and a Maid* (1740), Octavia relates how her lover fills her with passion when kissing her vigorously, and 'with violent Transport', she describes feeling 'a certain Warmth run thro' my Veins, a Trembling in all my Limbs, that I was unus'd to; but he saw me blush as red as Fire, which made him hold a little'.[56] In *Memoirs of a Woman of Pleasure*, one young girl, Harriet, grew redder and redder as she was indulging in sex, the vigorous activity appearing to increase her vitality:

> Her countenance, and whole frame, grew more animated; the faint blush on her cheeks gaining ground on the white, deepn'd into a florid vivid vermilion glow: her naturally brilliant eyes now sparkled with tenfold lustre: her langour was vanish'd and she appear'd quick-spirited, and alive all over.[57]

Concurring with medical opinion, in erotica, sex was deemed good for a woman's health. Pseudo-medical literature, such as *The Joys of Hymen, or the Conjugal Directory* (1768),[58] conveyed the blush as connected to robust and enjoyable sex. One particular scene connects the blush and the blood of the ripped hymen. The maiden 'glows with fierce desire, a florid crimson decorates her cheeks', while her hymen 'purple wines and ceres gifts produce' and 'bloods from chyle, and sperm from blood divide'. Racy novelettes aimed at female readers also connected blushing to a sexual passion. *Confessions of the Nun of St. Omer, Rosa Matilda* (1805) features blushes at the point of seduction: 'For the first time our lips met – it thrilled in liquid fire to my heart – I felt the ardent blushes of my cheek, and returned with transport hither unknown, the kiss of Fribourg, – Amazed, delighted, he pressed me closer to his throbbing bosom.'[59]

In summary, we can see that erotica harnessed existing themes of blushing and defloration as techniques in order to expose blood, in both the cheeks and the vulva.[60] Where these methods were employed, blood became a symbol of a woman's honour, proof of female modesty and chasteness. Conversely, in order to transgress moral boundaries of acceptability which deemed blood to be kept hidden, and in order to make it erotic, blood was conspicuously placed on display. The violation of the hymen was closely linked to blood taboos, which prohibited encroachment into the interior of a woman's body. To produce an element of titillation, the erotic therefore had to 'break into' a woman's body to reveal her 'private' blood, particularly that associated with her sexual organs. This exposing of blood found in defloration and was a continuation of an old social code – the preservation of the family – with the proof of a woman's virginity ensuring a legitimate heir-line. In this erotica, power was wielded within the context of the familiar, usually within a loving or affectionate relationship.

Genitals and their fluids

Medical and pseudo-medical books frequently indulged in detailed descriptions of genital fluids, particularly the production and excretion of the precious seminal liquid. *Rare Verities* expressed concerns about the balance of the humours in relation to seminal fluid. Too long a penis was seen as problematic as it prohibited the rapid flow of sperm necessary for successful impregnation; if 'it is so long before the seed comes through it, (and then too much cooled) that the woman hath spent herself a long time before the mans issueth, and so renders that act ineffectual'.[61] Orgasm for both men and women was seen as a necessary process for conception, particularly important in the heating of sexual fluids. Cooling of the sperm would hamper this process[62] and coldness was blamed for impotence.

Concerns about semen were expressed in various conflicting debates. On the one hand, too much expulsion was deemed harmful; on the other, retention of sperm was viewed as unhealthy. Some medical opinions of the day echoed that of Herman Boerhaave, the influential Dutch physician and philosopher, who, in 1708, expressed his concern about excess seminal loss:

> The *Semen* discharged too lavishly, occasions a Weariness, Weakness, Indisposition to Motion, Convulsions, Leanness, Driness [*sic*], Heats and Pains in the Membranes of the Brain, with a Dulness of the Senses; more especially of the Sight, a *Tabes Dorsalis*, Foolishness, and Disorders of the like kind.[63]

Others supported Robert James, who believed that *too little* sex might be harmful to a man's health. In his *Medicinal Dictionary* (1745), he argues: 'too great a retention of the Semen induces Torpor and languid State of the Body, and often lays a Foundation of terrible Disorder'.[64] A balance was therefore necessary for good health. Sperm was also seen as beneficial to women, and sex proposed as a cure for women's ailments: 'Venery both alleviates and removes various Disorders incident to Women: for the male Semen, consisting of a fine elastic Lymph, rarefies and expands not only the eggs, but also, the Blood and Juices in the Vessels of the Uterus.'[65] James apparently put his theories into practice. In a story in his diary, Dr. Campbell related an incident between James ('a very lewd fellow') and his friend, Dr. Johnson:

> James, it seems, in a coach with his whoor, took up Johnson and set him down at a given place – Johnson hearing afterwards what the lady was,

attacked James, when next he met him, for carrying him about in such company – James apologized by saying that he always took a swelling in his stones if he abstained a month &c – Damn the rascal says Johnson, he is past sixty the swelling wd. have gone no further.[66]

Discussions which raised anxiety about excess seminal loss ran concurrently with debates about the moral and medical dangers of masturbation. One essay played a large part in creating a popular fear of masturbation in the early eighteenth century. *Onania; or the Heinous Sin of Self-pollution, and All It's Frightful Consequences in both Sexes Considered with Spiritual and Physical Advice to those who have already injured themselves by this abominable practice and seasonable Admonition to the Youth of the nation of Both sexes* (1716)[67] went through nineteen English editions by 1760[68] and was directed at unmarried youth, which is where the problem of masturbation was thought to lie. Moral panic over masturbation was linked to concerns about the loss of sperm and its consequential effects, and evolved from biblical implications of the sin of Onan. The 'unnatural' practice of allowing sperm to fall on the ground meant wasting seed intended for procreation. The perceived immorality of the act, together with the debilitating effects of the waste of semen, led to the advocating of 'spermatic economy'.[69] But the sin of Onanism spelt out here was not just the sin of spilling seed on the ground, or *coitus interruptus*, as it was described in the Bible. This sin was one of which women could also be found guilty. However, the expulsion of female fluids appears not to have raised concern, indicating that they were perceived as less precious and therefore inferior.

Expositions of the evil consequences of masturbation concentrated on self-pollution and myths surrounding its debilitating effects. Another book to raise concern over masturbation was Tissot's *Onanism: or, a Treatise upon the Disorders Produced by Masturbation* (1760). Tissot (1728–97) was a practitioner with a huge influence throughout Europe, his book enjoying large commercial success through numerous editions, and translations from the Latin into French, English, Dutch and German.[70] He alleged that masturbation caused medical disorders which included epilepsy, convulsions, boils, disorders and death, and could even jeopardise one's soul. Warnings were given about over-ejaculation and the waste of sperm. One case of L. D. described a clockmaker who began the vice at the age of seventeen, continuing to masturbate three times a day: 'The slightest irritation immediately cured an imperfect erection, which was instantly followed by an evacuation of this liquor, which daily augmented his weakness.'[71] This caused him violent pains, leaving him weaker and weaker until eventually he died in June 1757. He believed that all sexual activity was potentially dangerous, the rush of blood to the head posing a potential threat to one's sanity.[72] The debilitating effects of masturbation in women were equally profound. Tissot described them:

Women are more particularly exposed to hysterical fits, or shocking vapours; to incurable jaundices; to violent cramps in the stomach and back; to acute pains in the nose; to the *fluor albus*, the accretion whereof is a continual source of the most smarting pain; to descents and ulcerations of the matrix, and to all the infirmities which these two disorders bring on; to the excretion and darting of the clitoris; to the *furor uterinus*, which at once deprives them of decency and reason, and puts them upon a level with the most lascivious brutes, till a desperate death snatches them from pain and infamy.[73]

Unlike the over-ejaculations of men, the excess spillage of fluids from masturbating women was not an issue of interest for these medics. Rather, women were perceived to be particularly susceptible to masturbation because of their imagination,[74] and there lay the area for concern. Since women had little control of their minds, masturbation could have great effect on them. Consequently, depictions of insane young female onanists as unbridled nymphomaniacs became common. The *Critical Review*, in 1760, wrote that female nymphomania, or 'furor uterinus' as it was called, could be caused by masturbation or 'titillations of their own sex'.[75] The most prominent Scottish professor of medicine, Dr. William Cullen, in his *Synopsis Methodicae* (1769), described 'a condition of nymphomania' (again referred to as *furor uterinus* or 'mania of the uterus') as a common female disorder. A couple of years later, Bienville's book *Nymphomanie, ou Traité de la Fureur Utérine* (1771) was published, the English translation (*Nymphomania, or Treatise on Uterine Fury*) became available in 1775 (Figure 8).[76] Although savaged by the critics at the time, his theories were indicative of both common medical assumptions about women and an example of how long-standing theories would continue to hold sway within new medical ideas. Bienville recounted the terrible plight into which the female onanist could fall, and traced the immodest descent into passionate insanity:

> The real sensation of pleasures, added to the different ideas of which are incessantly filling their imaginations, in a short time renders these wretched sufferers furious, and ungovernable; it is then, that breaking down, without the least remorse, the barriers of modesty, they betray each shocking secret of their lascivious minds by proposals, to the expressions of which even ears not uncommonly chaste cannot listen without horror, and astonishment; and soon the excess of their lusts having exhausted all their powers of contending against it, they throw off the restraining, honourable yoke of delicacy, and, without a blush, openly sollicit in the most criminal, and abandoned language, the first-comers to gratify their insatiable desires.[77]

Notably, the clitoris was swollen and larger 'than in discreet women'.[78] Bienville believed that nymphomania 'begins by a melancholy *delirium*, the cause of which is in the vice *matrix* [uterus]; it then turns to a maniacal *delirium*, the principal of which is the disorder of the brain', but is essentially a mental derangement caused by the female imagination.[79] Significantly, the condition of a woman's mind, or her 'imagination', was being closely connected to her sexuality. Bienville blamed the imagination for these excesses, 'Lascivious novels' fuelling this behaviour.

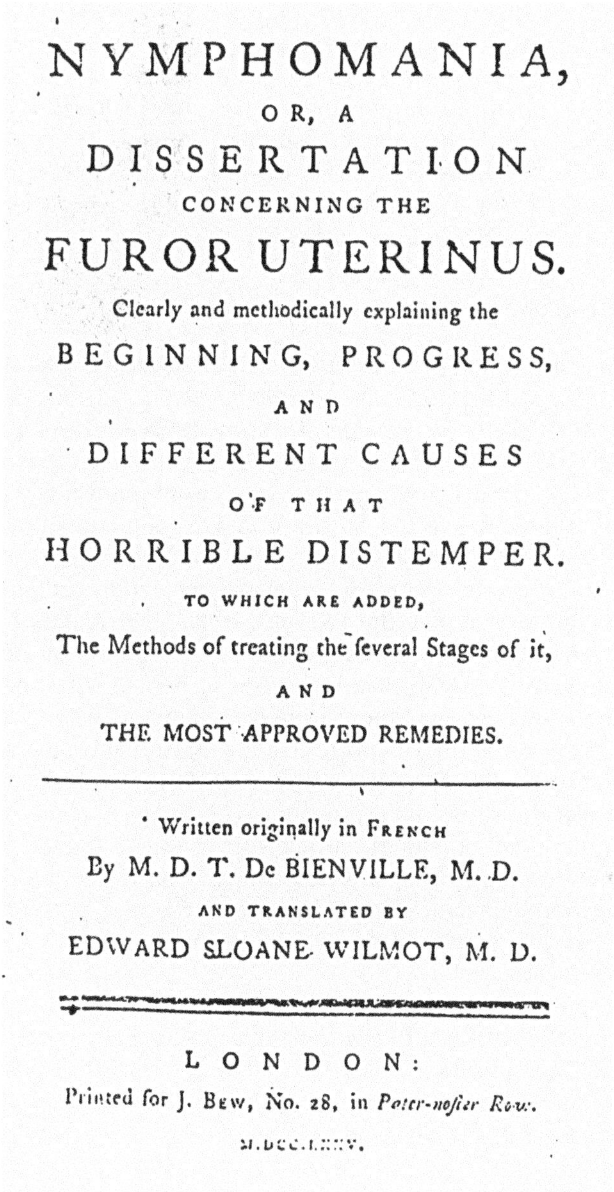

NYMPHOMANIA,

OR, A

DISSERTATION

CONCERNING THE

FUROR UTERINUS.

Clearly and methodically explaining the

BEGINNING, PROGRESS,

AND

DIFFERENT CAUSES

OF THAT

HORRIBLE DISTEMPER.

TO WHICH ARE ADDED,

The Methods of treating the several Stages of it,

AND

THE MOST APPROVED REMEDIES.

Written originally in FRENCH

By M. D. T. De BIENVILLE, M. D.

AND TRANSLATED BY

EDWARD SLOANE WILMOT, M. D.

LONDON:

Printed for J. Bew, No. 28, in *Pater-noster Row*.

M.DCC.LXXV.

Figure 8 Title-page to M. D. T. Bienville, *Nymphomania or a Dissertation Concerning the Furor Uterinus*, 1775.

Although medical concerns raised about masturbation related to both men and women, anxieties were applied differently depending on one's sex. In a man, excessive masturbation was seen mainly to affect his physical well-being, but in a woman, it would affect her mind. As well as becoming physically unhealthy, a man might become slightly melancholic, but a woman would become insane and uncontrollable. Furthermore, concerns about excess spillage of fluids of men and women were not equivalent. Excessive masturbation in a man meant excessive loss of sperm, which was responsible for draining his body of energy: in a woman, masturbation led to deranged imaginings, with loss of vaginal secretions playing no part in this analysis. As such, medical opinions portrayed sexually rapacious women as out of control, deranged and hysterical, whereas men retained control of their reasoning faculties.

Sexual secretions in erotica

Erotic books such as *The Whore's Rhetorick* (1683), *Dialogue between a Married Lady and a Maid* (1740), *The Secret History of Pandora's Box* (1742), *Histoire de Dom B* (1743), *A New Atalantis for the Year One Thousand Seven Hundred and Fifty-Eight* (1758) and *La Souricière Or The Mouse-trap* (1794) all expressed views about medicine in one form or another. Some medical views were shared by erotica, others were ignored or positively rejected. Erotica would expound on all sorts of sexual matters from male and female ejaculation, sexual initiation and tribadism.

Popular medical concerns over the loss of male body fluids, particularly semen, were shared by erotica, as was the *lack* of anxiety over female expulsion of vaginal secretions. Although men's health was portrayed as detrimentally affected by these emissions, women were seen to benefit from their orgasms. Indeed, in erotica, female ejaculations were positively fêted. Furthermore, contrary to scientific postulations, in erotica female masturbation did not pose the threat suggested by medics. Women were portrayed as being able and willing to indulge at their leisure without repercussions. This image of female insatiability in erotic prose therefore sometimes clashed with the medical image of nymphomania. Although women in erotica were frequently portrayed as sexually rapacious, they were rarely melancholic. If anything, they were portrayed as full of *joie de vivre*. If they did become depressed, it was due to a *lack* of sexual activity rather than too much.

Traditional opinions and beliefs on the workings of the sexual organs were carried over from the seventeenth century and continued to pervade eighteenth-century erotica. *Dialogue between a Married Lady and a Maid* (1740) first describes the female genitalia in some anatomical detail, followed by a description of how it works. Tullia describes the labia and vagina:

> This Slit is made with two Lips, which being opened gently, discover another inward as red as a Cherry, with two other Lips, which are called Wings, or Nymphs: and under them, about a Finger's Breadth or more, within, are in Virgins, as their art, four little rising buds, which, joining together, and leaving only a little Hole between, stop up the best Part of the Passage into the Womb.[80]

In *The Compleat Midwife's Companion* (1671; reprinted 1725), its author, Jane Sharp, recognised the clitoris as the font of female pleasure. In direct comparisons between the clitoris and the penis, she declared: 'This Clitoris will stand and fall as the Yard doth, and makes Women lustful and take delight in Copulation; and were it not for this they would have no desire nor delight, nor would they ever conceive.'[81] Similar understandings of the female body are displayed in erotica. The ancient medical notion of female ejaculation is reiterated in a comparison between female and male genitalia. Readers are led to believe that the clitoris is the part responsible for the orgasm, ejaculating a liquid:

> Just before them, towards the upper Part of the C--t, is a Thing they call the *Clitoris*, which is a little like a Man's P---k, for it will swell and stand like his; and being rubbed gently, by his Member, will, with excessive Pleasure, send forth a Liquor, which when it comes away, leaves us in a Trance, as if we were dying, all our Senses being lost, and as it were summed up in that one Place.[82]

Female ejaculation and the loss of vaginal fluid were seen as natural phenomena, with mutual masturbation frequently playing a significant role in sexual initiation. These depictions were inherited from French pornography. In *Histoire de Dom B...portier de Chartreux* (1743),[83] mutual masturbation is introduced by an experienced nun who feigns fear of a thunderstorm in an attempt to seduce her fellow sister:

> I tried to comfort the Sister, who, in the meantime, had put her right thigh between mine, and the left under; while in this position she rubbed herself against my right thigh, thrusting her tongue into my mouth and smacking my buttocks with her hand. After she had done this for some time, I thought I felt my thighs wetted. She gave several deep sighs, which I imagined arose for her fear of the thunder.[84]

Within these scenes, orgasmic women were seen to ejaculate profusely without any harmful effects. Neither excess loss of her fluids nor masturbation made her ill. Books such as *The Uterine Furies of Marie-Antoinette, Wife of Louis XVI* (1791) and *The Private, Libertine, and Scandalous Life of Marie-Antoinette* (1791)[85] (the latter containing an engraving of the queen being masturbated by her lady-in-waiting) would continue to make connections between medical thought, such as those described in Bienville's 'Uterine Furies', and ideas on masturbation and tribadism.

In the 1780s, English directories of London whores depicted women as having copious flows of vaginal mucus. Harris's *List Of Covent Garden Ladies* (1788) describes one Miss L-c-s, of No. 2 York Street, Queen Ann Street East who had such secretions as to drown sperm; 'she is said, like the river Nile, frequently to overflow, but somehow or another her inundations differ from those of that river, as they do not produce foecundity [*sic*], some skilful gardeners are of the opinion that she drowns the *seed,* which is the reason that it does not take root.' Similarly Miss Sophia M-rt-n, No. 11, Stephen Street, Rathbone Place provides an 'impetuous flood' yet 'no one complains, but rather rejoices at the debility she produces, and wishes for repetition which she enjoys with a *gou* peculiar to herself, and is possessed of every *amorous* means to produce it'.[86] Copious vaginal secretions were thereby depicted as an obvious sign of female sexual proclivity, and as such a phenomenon to be enjoyed.

The male genitalia and its ejaculations were equally celebrated in *Dialogue between a Married Lady and a Maid*. The head of a man's penis is portrayed as 'a fine Carnation', and the scrotum as 'a Bag, or Purse' or 'Stones'. Tullia explains to Octavia the amazing and enjoyable power of the male ejaculation 'for it come out with that Force, that it leaps two Foot or more from 'em upon spending'.[87] The strength of an ejaculation is an obvious indication of a man's virility. Octavia describes the seminal fluid in detail:

> I presently felt my Hand and my Belly, as far as my Navel, all wet with a warm Shower which flowed from him: It felt thick and slimy, which made me withdraw my hand, and he immediately giving me a thousand Kisses, seized both, and wiped them with his Handkerchief.[88]

Handkerchiefs and cloths for wiping away seminal fluids add a sense of domestic intimacy. This post-coital ritual is described by Tullia as she relates her wedding night: 'As soon as my Mother had put me to Bed, she gently put a fine handkerchief under my Pillow, and bid me use it when I wanted to wipe myself or my Husband.'[89]

Medical anxieties concerning the loss of semen were echoed in *A New Atalantis For The Year One Thousand Seven Hundred And Fifty-Eight* (1758) where an overindulgence in sex is seen to result in ill health. The two lovers, Clerimont and Essesia, initially blossom after their first sexual encounter, 'their eyes sparkling with such unusual lustre, made all about them prognosticate for their health, since so great and sudden a change had happened in them for the better'. Serious medical assertions about the positive effects of sexual intercourse on the health of both men and women are taken up by erotica in these revelations. Significantly, sexual intercourse is portrayed as more beneficial for women; Essesia's face becomes 'as smooth as polished marble', 'she smiled in every feature' and her lips become ruby red. But while increased frequency of sex for women led only to their better health, for men the positive effects of sex diminished with frequency, too much sex sapping their strength: 'From a frequency of these interviews, Essesia grew better, but Clerimont became quite emaciated. His physicians ordered him to the south of France, which he was glad of being quite tired of the constant drudgery Essesia exacted from him.'[90] Essesia has weakened Clerimont because of her excessive sexual demands. Once Clerimont leaves, Essesia attempts to find a way to recreate her virginity. Hence, she makes the *Economy of Love*[91] her favourite book since it teaches her how to restore her maidenhead and 'from thence had learned the medicaments to close up chasms caused (through an indulgence of passion) by way of a maiden-head restorative'.[92] Essesia needs to reclaim her virginity if she is to attract another man, the value of her person being tied up in her chastity.

The passions of the sexually active woman were seen to run high, and the fulfilment of these desires was perceived as essential in maintaining the equilibrium of one's humours. A woman's libido appeared to lie dormant, but once she had been initiated into sex, her ardour had to be satisfied or she would become ill. Although Essesia gains a husband, he does not live up to her demands and she falls into a depression: 'The sluggish duties of Hymen no way answering the rapidity of her desires, she fell into a melancholy'.[93] Her mentor, the good lady Rocforia, explains the problem: 'Our countrymen, from constitutional gloomy habit, are always for making deep and useless researches. They dwell too long upon a thing, without any intermediate Relievos [sic] which is very disagreeable to their assistants.' However, continental men are regarded as equally disagreeable for other reasons as seen in her tirade against foreigners:

> The volatility of the French, who always play on, or about the surface, by their continual skipping up and down, is highly irritating, but not at all satisfying. I have been frequently obliged to slap them. The Italians are so profoundly respectful and so protestingly tedious, that more of the ceremonial is to be met among them than anything else. So fond are they of overshooting the mark, and keep so awful a distance from what we love to have ever closely approached to, that by most nations they are looked upon as very backwards in love. The Germans or High-Dutch are in the service of Venus; as in that of Mars. To act heroic deeds in either, they must be roused with spirituous liquors. The phlegmatic Low-Dutch are very apt to fall asleep in the trenches. Wherefore, to rouze [sic] and keep them awake, the martinet and finger-spurs are absolutely necessary.[94]

Women are portrayed as sexually demanding, men unable to keep up, and if they do, it is at their own peril. A further tale similarly relates the story of Pertonia and her husband Lord Macer Slender-hams whom she has worn out:

> Lord Macer Slender-hams was the undaunted heroe's [sic] name, whose soul, too active for his body, had almost worn away; but she soon pulled down the former, by entirely exhausting the latter, and reduced him to the figure of a shrivelled skin drawn over a skeleton.[95]

Despite the dangers associated with insatiable females, women and their sexual organs were frequently praised. In *The Secret History of Pandora's Box* (1742), the author pays homage to female genitalia and conveys his admiration: 'What is there in the creation more beautiful than woman! and what is more natural than to pay our veneration to the organ that produces reasonable beings!' Women's sexual organs are awarded a high level of esteem, and praise is lavished accordingly. These parts of women 'preserve the union and harmony of society; they tame the most savage of men'.[96] He denounces the attitudes of men and defends the behaviour of women: 'The fair-sex, who are generally accused of running into the excess of self-love, seem to me entirely justified by the conduct of men towards them. Deification was their undoubted right.'[97] Yet despite the elevation of women, the author acknowledges the power they have over men. Their ability to bring about a man's downfall is obvious from the euphemistic title. A woman's genitalia, once accessed or opened, as with Pandora's Box, allows all the illnesses of man to descend upon the world, the intimation being that women are responsible for spreading sexual diseases. Female genitalia are at the same time 'secret' and mysterious. This mystical power attributed to the female form is however similarly ascribed to the penis in its nickname, 'diving-rod, or magical wand'.[98]

Euphemisms for the male genitalia were extended into full-blown analogies in the racy tale *La Souricière Or The Mouse-trap* (1794).[99] The male 'mouse-trap' is the object which catches the female 'mouse', the latter being an endearment for a woman, sometimes with sexual implications.[100] However, the 'mouse-trap' does not always work as expected. When it fails to respond to the charms of an older woman, the narrator condemns its inertia: 'I wish'd the *Mouse-Trap* at the devil, not "*having all the good gifts of nature*" then at my command'.[101] The book raises the whole question of heat, passion and sexual stimulation culminating in yet another metaphor conveyed in descriptions of the barometer/penis: 'I arose in the morning, and found the *Barometer of health* risen to its *utmost elevation*; and contrary to the *Torricellian Baroscope* when at its highest, *the bottom of the Tube* was greatly overcharged with *Mercury*.' The barometer appears to be the male equivalent of 'the Female Thermometer', the latter a fantastical device which reads women's level of desire. The measuring of female lasciviousness was introduced earlier in the century with a description given in Joseph Addison's *Spectator*, No. 281 (1712) of a thermometer containing liquid taken from a 'coquette's Pericardium'.

Connections between heat and a woman's sexual appetite were made in *An Essay upon Improving and Adding to the Strength of Great Britain and Ireland by Fornication* (1735). Written by a clergyman[102] in the style of a sermon, this encomium on copulation was a pseudo-pious satire which affiliated the heating of fluids to sexual craving: 'Our Blood is heated; the Pulse beats high; we are all a Flame, and can never be cooled, 'till we have dipped into the soft, the sweet, the bubbling Fount of Love.'[103] The author took up the counsel of the Bible from which he quoted, 'Be fruitful, multiply and replenish the Earth',[104] and proceeded to make his own recommendations for the propagation of the nation:

It should therefore, be the greatest Business of our Lives to Plant and Propagate our Kind, To throw the Seed into every fruitful Corner. To get it vigorous into the gaping Bottom of every sweet-natured Vale. We ought therefore to be active and industrious in rearing up great Numbers of young Plants and preparing them for being transported to other more kindly Climates, where they shall all enjoy uninterrupted Sweetness of everlasting Spring.[105]

The book was lauded by a group of libertines who replied in *An Address of Thanks from the Society of Rakes, To the Pious Author of 'An Essay upon Improving and Adding to the Strength of Great Britain and Ireland by Fornication'.*[106] These associations between heat and sexual fervour were expressed in *The Secrets of Women* (1745), a reiteration of a twelfth-century medical text, reprints of which were still popular in the eighteenth century.[107] The book explains how the menstrua heated up the female vulva through an 'abundance of matter' and made a woman desire sex.

The interest in heat and sex continued unabated. The Female Thermometer was again described by the essayist Bonnell Thornton in *The Connoisseur* No. 85 (1754) as an invention for measuring 'the exact temperature of a lady's passions', this time a compound of extract of a lady's love and maidenhead and 'wax of virgin bees' acted upon by 'the circulation of the blood and animal spirits'.[108] Scientific discussions around heat and thermometers are hinted at in one passionate scene in which the narrator describes a fiery young woman as 'ardent in the extreme' but 'had that learned body of philosophers, The *Royal Society*, been present, it might have given rise to a tedious debate, to have investigated, whether *something* more simple in its construction than a *fire-engine*, would not have distinguished the young lady's conflagration.'[109]

Despite bodily fluids being such a focus in erotica, breast milk seems to have been ignored. Meanwhile, both medical and literary sources were redefining the body. The habit of putting children out to nurse declined as the trend for mothers to breast-feed their children became more popular. William Cadogan's *An Essay Upon Nursing* (1748) encouraged mothers to breast-feed their own children.[110] Rousseau's *Emile* (1762) castigated mothers who did not breast-feed their children as selfish and callous. William Buchan in his *Advice to Mothers* (1769) warned: 'Let husbands not be deceived: let them not expect attachment from their wives, who, neglecting to suckle their children, rend asunder the strongest ties in nature.'[111] The breast was also being defined as a symbol of Empire, the mother feeding the sons who fight for King and Country. Yet despite detailed descriptions of genitalia and genital fluids, breast milk played little part in the eighteenth-century erotica under survey, although it had been hinted at in earlier erotica. In *The Whore's Rhetorick* (1683), breast milk is conveyed as the elixir of life and descriptions given of impotent old men who 'fall to dallying and sucking the Pappies as if they expected to extract some sovereign Cordial, that would introduce a new spring into their frozen hearts, and snowy Heads'. The effect of a youthful woman's breast is to rejuvenate the aged man, and therefore 'it is natural for an old Fellow to be fond of the Pappies, if the Proverb be ground on truth, which makes him a Child the second time.'[112] This alludes not so much to the *erotic* nature of the breast but more to its nurturing quality and points to earlier beliefs. Sixteenth- and seventeenth-century imagery of old men sucking at the breasts of nubile women was common and indicated a prevalent belief in the mystical rejuvenating and life-giving qualities of the female breast. This depiction was not to figure in eighteenth-century English erotica.

The reaction of erotica to the contemporary debate on breast-feeding was to claim the breast for sexual purposes alone. During the seventeenth century, small breasts had been deemed preferable since women with small breasts were thought to be more sexually oriented. *Rare Verities* declares: 'Little breasts in women are a greater sign of lust, then [sic] great ones.'[113] But by the eighteenth century, bosoms began to be described in erotica through a variety of exalted adjectives – 'snowy bosom',[114] 'glowing bubbies'[115] and 'angelic orbs'[116] – raising them as a subject of reverence. Big breasts came to be relished, as seen in the description of women frequenting the flagellation brothels, notably, a woman called Grenville, 'with the enormous bubbies'. These breasts were prized as much as a good-sized hip and bottom as to be found on another woman called Bentinc, 'with breadth of hip and splendour of buttock'.[117] Male breasts were not generally cited as erotic. However, in one erotic book, *A New Atalantis for the Year One Thousand Seven Hundred and Fifty-Eight*, a scarce reference is made to the attractiveness of a male bosom, in a surprising reversal of roles, when one heroine grabs her male lover's bosom:

> An immediate blush made him appear more beautiful in her eyes. Then unbuttoning the top of his waistcoat, she thrust her hand into his bosom, which was as fair as man's could be; then put one of his hands on her glowing bubbies, which bounded to, and were electrified at the touch.[118]

This description of the desirability of the male bosom was unusual, if not unique, but it remains unclear why such explorations take place in the story. It might be viewed as 'women on top', a parody in reversal of roles, which depicts control of sexual agency by the woman.

Conclusion

Explicit descriptions of the body were used to enhance erotic value, erotica placing its focus firmly on blood and the exposing of bodily fluids. Not only were bodies exhibited graphically and in detail, but they were placed in a domestic setting, often within a claustrophobic atmosphere, to provide a greater sexual intensity. When exposing fluids, erotica incorporated medical and religious opinions already prevalent elsewhere. Themes present in sex manuals were expanded and developed in realistic pornographic scenarios of sexual activities which discussed anxieties about menstrual blood, fears of seminal loss and unrestrained female fluids/sexuality; these expulsions of fluids were connected to a lack of control over one's own body. However, in erotica, bodily fluids were expressed rather than contained. The more pornographic the descriptions, the more bodily fluids were displayed in a reaction to the advocation of restraint and control in 'civilised' opinion.

A gendered view existed which prescribed one set of values for men and another for women. Men were urged to contain themselves and their fluids, whereas women's fluids were unimportant. Sperm was seen as the vital force of life and, because it was of limited quantity, to be safeguarded. Yet female sexual secretions were seen as copious, unlimited and expendable. Erotica conveyed women as lacking in self-discipline, revelling in their own free-flowing emissions, and therefore irrational and inferior. Moreover, an abundance of vaginal mucus was seen as synonymous with an assertive sexuality, and as such was coveted yet perceived as threatening. A gendered perspective of blood was also apparent in erotica where female blood was frequently displayed yet male blood was rarely exposed, and when it was, it was within a specific context.[119]

Part of the erotic value of the body lay in its interpretation as a humoral body. Although control over bodily fluids was imperative in a civilised body, the very fact that female fluids were portrayed as so free-flowing depicted 'uncivilised' women with 'impolite' or embarrassing bodies. Exposure of blood and bodily fluids signified an underlying concern about female insatiability and ferocious sexual appetites. Women posed a threat in that they were capable of draining men of their fluids (and life force). Men retained control over their fluids or died an honourable, but necessary death, but their bodies were never embarrassing. Implicit in this sub-text was a warning inherited from the common contemporary opinion that men should control their sexual activities or end up as unrestrained (and thereby as inferior) as women. The fact that women were *not* in command of their own bodily fluids contributed to a definition of them as uncontrolled (and uncontrollable) and therefore ungovernable.

The texts and sub-texts of these books raise complex issues and the reading of them is by no means straightforward. Although the radical nature of pornography lay in its deviance from 'civilised' society, in many ways it would continue to uphold traditional views. Themes of male control over female sexuality were depicted in vaginal examinations and defloration scenes, and ancient medical beliefs on bodily fluids continued to be enunciated. The violent scenes of defloration were to some extent a reaction to this undisciplined female sexuality, in that men were in control of women's initiation to sexual intercourse. These scenes depict women being ripped asunder, the action done to them rather than their instigating the action, where men attempted to retain some authority over women through control of their bodies. At the same time, women were very vocal, frequently screaming out, not necessarily accepting their initiation graciously. They were frequently assertive in their demands and rarely depicted as passive in this sub-genre of erotica.

Despite (or more likely, because of) the fact that these women's bodies were embarrassing and uncontrolled, they were nonetheless exciting. But most importantly, at the same time, women's bodies that expressed copious sexual fluids were both happy and healthy bodies (albeit uncivilised) as opposed to the sick bodies of their over-ejaculating male counterparts. These depictions do not always fit with the medical assertions linking female masturbation to derangement. Mutual female masturbation frequently acted merely as an initiation into sex rather than a prelude to madness, as medical opinion suggested. Much of this erotica displayed a certain black humour. Men who over-ejaculated were idealised as a symbol of virility in that they have to copulate until it killed them. In this, there is an inverted boastfulness, in that men have to have sex until they die, the irony being seen in their own wilful self-destruction. The overt theme in the erotica described above was one of celebration of sex, a revelling in bodily fluids, where women and men shared a mutual enjoyment of each other's bodies.

4
Erotica and Science

> *Arbor Vitae, or the Tree of Life,* is a succulent Plant; consisting of one
> straight Stem, on the Top of which is a *Pistillum*, or *Apex* ... . Its *Fruits*,
> contrary to most others, grow near the Root; they are usually no more
> than two in Number.
>
> *Arbor Vitae Or, The Natural History Of The Tree Of Life*[1]

Erotica began to play with reports on findings in botany, reproduction and electricity. Although some of the scientific ideas being reported were based on empirical observation and experimentation, others were spurious and wildly
exaggerated assertions. In reaction to these claims, new forms of erotica sprang
up in the form of scientific satires about the body and sex.

Specific periods can be pinpointed when erotica responded to these leaps made
in science, and incorporated its themes from three topics – botany, reproduction
and electricity. First, the 1730s saw a botanical theme emerging in erotica. This
was as a result of developments in botany, particularly Linnaeus' sexual
classification of plants and new publications by botanists such as Phillip Miller.
Second, by the 1750s, findings about the reproductive process emanating from
the Royal Society were published in *Philosophical Transactions*. This resulted in
erotic parodies by John Hill on experimentation in female self-fertilisation.
Third, in the 1770s, a burst of activity in electrical experiments was quickly followed by erotic satires containing popular gossip of sexual intrigues. These skits
incorporated early theories on 'animal magnetism' and body chemistry. As a
result, particular body images were produced in erotica seen in the Botanical
Body, the Reproductive Body and the Electrical Body.

The themes of botany, reproduction and electricity, once established, would
become part of the erotic tradition and would interact with other expressions
contributing to a general erotic repertoire.[2] Each was a specific reaction to a
certain set of contemporary experiments. All three sorts of erotic material – those
that related to botany, reproduction and electricity – involved attacks on the
Royal Society.

First, an exploration of scientific exploration current in the eighteenth century
will be made in order to understand the world into which these erotic themes

were introduced. This will be followed with a look at the three different groups of erotica – botany, reproduction and electricity.

Scientific developments

Attempts were being made to give structure to a perceived disordered world. As scientists endeavoured to 'tame nature' under the all-encompassing study of 'natural philosophy', they were suggesting new ways of looking at the cosmos and its components. These investigations involved various experiments in reproduction, botany and electricity. From the mid-seventeenth century, William Harvey and his followers, through their investigations into the circulation of blood and reproduction, would identify various processes of the workings of the body; in the early part of the eighteenth century, Carl Linnaeus produced a classification system for plants which would revolutionise the botanical world; and as a result of their experiments with magnetic forces during the 1770s, Benjamin Franklin and Joseph Priestley (along with the lesser known Sir William Watson and Sir John Pringle) would uncover the mysteries of electricity.

Until the development of the mechanical philosophy, nature had been seen as a living organism and traditionally had been seen as feminine. Attitudes to women were closely connected to two opposing views on nature. On the one hand, nature was seen as wild and uncontrollable and could render violence, create storms and wreak havoc; on the other hand, nature was earth, a nurturing mother. This ambivalence was reflected in perceptions about women: the female body was a mystery to be fathomed. This gave rise to certain anxieties expressed in attempts to appropriate the natural world through science.[3] Both Carolyn Merchant and Ludmilla Jordanova have been instrumental in exemplifying science as a penetration of nature. In *The Death of Nature*, Merchant has examined the connections made between woman and nature that developed as the modern scientific and economic world took form during the sixteenth and seventeenth centuries. She states:

> The Renaissance view of nature was based on the organic analogy between the human body, or microcosm, and the larger world, or macrocosm. Within this larger framework, however, a number of variants on the organic theme were possible. The primary view of nature was the idea that a designed hierarchical order existed in the cosmos and society corresponding to the organic integral parts of the body – a projection of the human being onto the cosmos.[4]

In other words, prior to the Enlightenment, a presupposed structure of nature based on the designs of the body had existed. From 1500 to 1700, as the scientific revolution proceeded to rationalise the world, the view of nature as 'nurturing mother' gradually diminished along with the wilder 'female' earth archetype. The earlier organic conception of the cosmos gradually gave way to a mechanistic model.[5] For Jordanova, the developing new science was striving to understand, and thereby take control of, nature by ascribing a structure to a chaotic universe. Efforts were therefore made to organise the world in a way that would make sense. However, the system of categorisation differentiated between male and female in an ideologically biased way. Women were seen as 'natural' and men as 'cultural', gender being used as a cosmic metaphor. The world was thereby divided up, with unequal social relations signalled by language of gendered anatomy and pathology. Within this classification powerful polarities were at work, the male equated with 'active', 'public', 'reason' and 'self', the female equated with negative values of 'passive', 'private', 'desire' and 'other'.[6] The identification of female with nature, materiality, passivity and sentiment was a signifier of lack; for example, lack of reason and rationality. The metaphors of 'the laws of nature' conveyed a presupposition of an ontological hierarchy which ordered mind and matter, theory and practice, normal and aberrant.[7] Scientific investigation into the world of nature, or 'tearing of Nature's veil', was necessary if any understanding of life was to be comprehended. To do this, scientists had to understand the mechanisms of the interior of the body. Attempts were made in new anatomical explorations which reinforced the notion of female inferiority. Within this framework, women were seen as biologically, culturally and intellectually inferior.

Thomas Laqueur adds to the debate, suggesting that the concept of human sexuality changed 'in or about the late eighteenth century' with a shift from a one-sex model of the body to a two-sex model.[8] Prior to this, male and female genitalia had been perceived as coming from the same model, in which women's sexual organs were an inversion of the male. The perception of one sex meant that a single terminology was applied to both male and female parts alike; female genitalia were ultimately referred to by words commonly used for male organs. The uterus was seen as the female scrotum, the ovaries as testicles, the vulva as foreskin, the vagina as the penis. The female genital structure was considered a somewhat inferior model of the human body since it was not properly formed. The genitalia were thought to remain inside the body due to a lack of heat, heat being necessary for its full development. Heat was also believed to be necessary for conception, and the female orgasm seen as a prerequisite for conception. Laqueur states:

> Midwives and doctors seemed to believe that female orgasm was among the conditions for successful generation, and they offered various suggestions on how it might be achieved. Orgasm was considered to be a routine, more or less indispensable part of conception.[9]

However, this belief shifted as new understanding of the working of the body brought with it the knowledge that orgasm was not necessary for conception. Harvey readily dispensed with the notion of the need for female orgasm in conception. He declared that the 'violent shaking and dissolution and spilling of humours' which occurs 'in women in the ecstasy of coitus' is not required for conception.[10] A biological divergence emerged whereby women and men were perceived as two separate sexes, and only one sex, the male, had to ejaculate in order for conception to take place. Thus women's access to sexual pleasure was gradually eroded.[11] Despite the new scientific claims, however, traditional views continued to prevail. As late as 1785, statements were being made about the necessity of female arousal for conception by Samuel Farr. In his legal-medical text *The Elements of Jurisprudence*, he declared: 'without an excitation of lust, or enjoyment in the venereal act, no conception can probably take place.'[12]

The ancient theories of Aristotle and Galen[13] would continue to circulate in the eighteenth century. Menstrual blood and semen were seen to be the most important fluids in the process of reproduction. Aristotle (384–322 BC) believed that the female contributed the matter, while the male contributed the form, or 'vital principle'. Menstrual blood was the matter acted upon by the semen, and was seen as nourishment for the developing foetus. Galen (129–c. 216 ?AD) believed the male and female semen, produced through orgasm, mingled in coition resulting in an offspring resembling one parent or the other. Harvey's thoughts on physiology were strongly influenced by Aristotle, and classical ideas on generation[14] carried through in contemporary speculations about life and propagation.[15] Contradictory theories on generation ran side by side and became increasingly diverse and chaotic. The theory of pre-formation emerged whereby all individuals were created by God and stored in the body, fully developed as a miniature homunculus; spontaneous generation was suggested where life sprang forth autonomously; debates arose around the role of male and female in the process of reproduction. Was the male the provider of the 'vital principle'? If so, what role did women play? Or did both the male and female make an equal contribution? What was the process involved? And what determined the sex of an offspring? The Royal Society of London attempted to address these hotly debated questions, playing a large part in altering people's perceptions of the living world. It provided a forum for discussions of scientific matters and established a means of sharing knowledge and ideas through their publications. The breadth of subject matter in the early volumes of *Philosophical Transactions* of the Royal Society covered everything from plants to monsters, including monstrous births. Initially, the publications reviewed works already undertaken and works in progress, but this gradually changed to incorporate accounts of original investigation.

The heated debates taking place within the Royal Society influenced the emergence of these certain types of erotica. Described as 'a society of gentlemen', the Royal Society was linked to a particular class of gentleman with few financial worries who had time to pursue self-improving hobbies through the study of nature and technology. Its journal, *Philosophical Transactions*, carried the result of experiments and findings of both virtuosi and more serious investigators. Important researchers such as Antoni van Leeuwenhoek and Marcello Malpighi first reported their findings in the society's journal, which was to reach a wide international audience during the seventeenth and eighteenth centuries. Yet discontent was evident amongst members, as seen in disputes between the Newtonians and the natural historians. For example, a natural historian and avid collector, Sir Hans Sloane was characterised as a pompous muddle-headed collector of useless miscellanea. He remained in conflict with the Newtonians, after

Edmond Halley took over, presiding between 1713 and 1721. After Newton died in 1727, Sloane became interim president, retiring in 1741 to be replaced by Martin Folkes who was also president of the Society of Antiquaries, his main interest being archaeology. The Royal Society financed expeditions including Captain James Cook's first trip to the South Seas in 1772. In the 1770s, the journal became the central point for the debate on electricity. Bitter infighting resulted as a result of Franklin and Watson's arguments on the protective power of lightning rods and whether pointed rods or blunt ones were most effective.[16] The reaction to these debates and infighting was an erotica which mocked the ideas emanating from the Royal Society.

The botanical metaphor

> The Tree of which I fain would sing
> If the kind Muse her Aid would bring,
> In *Arbor Vitae;* but in brief,
> By vulgar Men call'd —*Tree of Life*
>
> That is, to take especial Care,
> Not to set *Vulvaria* near;
> Of them two Sorts are frequent found,
> One helps, and t'other spoils the Ground;
>
> *Arbor Vitae, Or The Natural History of*
> *The Tree of Life Verfify'd*[17]

Arbor Vitae (figure 9) was originally published as a poem and frequently emulated. It was regularly reprinted along with prose, and *Natural History of the Frutex Vulvaria*. Both sets of material were probably written by Thomas Stretser, or Stretzer, one of Edmund Curll's hacks, and are in a collection of tracts held in the 'Private Case' material at the British Library. Curll was well known for his publications of erotica and often used false imprints, including false dates to avoid detection.

Botanical metaphors were springing up in all sorts of erotica as a result of contemporary scientific investigations into categorising of plants.[18] Such material circulated in all forms of printed matter and found its way across class divides. Witty poems about the *Arbor Vitae* sold in twopenny sheets were easily accessible to labourers. *Wisdom Revealed, Or the Tree of Life* sold at the pamphlet-shops in London and Westminster for sixpence. Raucous songs would also have been sung in taverns, and were also available in penny song-sheets.[19]

This erotica describes bodies and the sexual behaviour of men and women in terminology favoured by contemporary botanists and was a specific reaction to new developments in science and natural history. New investigations in the plant worlds by botanists such as Richard Bradley, Carl Linnaeus and Phillip Miller[20] attracted the writers of Grub Street, who saw a way to capitalise on the new ideas in nature in smutty prose, poems and songs. Words and expressions were assimilated and used in satirical analogies in bawdy erotica and pamphlets of ribald humour. These botanical metaphors were used as a device to

ARBOR VITÆ:

OR, THE

NATURAL HISTORY

OF THE

T R E E

OF

L I F E.

In Stem moſt ſtreight of lovely Size,
With Head elate this Plant doth riſe;
Firſt bare——when it doth further ſhoot
A Tuft of Moſs keeps warm the Root:
No Lapland Muff has ſuch a Fur,
No Skin ſo ſoft has any Cur;
This touch'd, alone the Heart can move,
Which Ladies more than Lap-Dogs love.

L O N D O N:

PRINTED for E. HILL, in *White-Fryers, Fleet-ſtreet.*
MDCCXLI.

Figure 9   Frontispiece and title-page to *Arbor Vitae, Or the Natural History of the Tree of Life*, 1741

communicate openly about sex and conveyed an image of male and female sexuality, and described a certain set of relationships which operated between men and women in the eighteenth century; in other words, a new erotic world was formulated which allowed for the expression of alternative attitudes on sex differing somewhat from more authoritarian lines of thought on morality. In this 'other world', secret gardens, hidden valleys and cavernous holes contain mysterious erect plant life, furry thickets and bushy knolls, which mirrored the sexual nature of bodies constructed elsewhere. This gendered space was made recognisable for the readership through graphic imagery in the form of trees as penises, caves as vaginas, and so on, in the creation of a 'landscape of desire'.

Assumptions about the mystery of Nature were gleaned from the myths of the ancient Greeks. Fountains and trees, caves and mountains, were considered as seats of the gods, and gifts were offered to certain trees believed to be the seats of gods. Natural caves were connected with religious rites and parts of the body were attributed to natural forms made from the rocks.[21] The authors of botanical erotica would have been familiar with these stories and made frequent references to the classics.

The study of nature included all things on earth and attempts were made to find one unified system which would incorporate and be applicable to all materials living, or innate. The structural organisation of botany and nature reflected the hierarchy of social relations between men and women in the external world. Londa Schiebinger has observed an inherent hierarchy in botany on two levels. First, 'the *implicit* use of gender to structure botanical taxonomy', in other words, using traditional notions about sexual hierarchy and importing them into botanical classification, the male being most important; and second, 'the *explicit* use of human sexual metaphors to introduce notions of plant reproduction into botanical literature', in other words, using sexual language applied to humans to explain the sexual life of plants. Schiebinger highlights the eroticisation of plants in the terminology of the botanist Linnaeus, citing his descriptions of 'nuptuals' of living plants and 'bridal beds' of flower petals. These metaphors, along with Erasmus Darwin's descriptions of 'mild' and 'retiring' plants, expressed conservative attitudes and relegated the female to a secondary role.[22]

Plant sexuality lay at the core of the eighteenth-century revolution in the study of the plant kingdom. Gender was a main principle in attempting to organise revolutionary views on nature and gave rise to the emergence of sexual difference in plant terminology in the late seventeenth and eighteenth centuries.[23] Nature's laws were perceived as a reflection of social and sexual relations between men and women, and within this model, nature was firmly linked with femaleness.

Influential botanists such as Linnaeus (1707–78) were changing the views of the world through the reclassification of nature. Linnaeus was particularly famous for his work as a taxonomist of the animal, vegetable and mineral kingdoms, in particular his sexual classifications of plants in seven volumes.[24] Linnaeus' system of classification had been circulated through papers, seminars and lectures given at the Royal Society. His work was based on the difference between the male and female parts of flowers. He was the first to recognise the sexual reproduction of plants and this system reflected the contemporary gender hierarchy. But Linnaeus was not the first on this route. In 1682, Nehemiah Grew, in *Anatomy of Plants*, had already likened his plant specimens to male genitalia: 'The blade (or stamen) does not inaptly resemble a small penis, with the sheath on it.'[25] John Ray and Joseph Tournefort, two leading botanists working at the end of the seventeenth century, had also made significant inroads into classification of plants based entirely on the structure of their flower and fruit parts.

Critics of the Linnaean system (which conveyed a sexual life for flowers) were quick to take up an attack on the notion as ridiculous. The very sexual nature of the language used by Linnaeus was an obvious target for humorists of erotica, thus allowing sharp-witted satirists a chance to make an easy profit on bawdy parodies. Linnaeus' language was couched in patriarchal terminology; 'marriage beds' of plants echoed language of men and women's relationships, and reflected the same hierarchy of contemporary gender relations. Erotica, however, overturned the natural structure of this sexual hierarchy, challenging patriarchal assumptions and portraying women as sexually powerful, and even dominant.

Castigators of the botanical sexual imagery brought attacks from a variety of sources. One such writer, J. G. Siegesbeck, in his book *Botanosophia verioris brevis Sciagraphicia* (1737), declared: 'What man will ever believe that God Almighty should have introduced such confusion, or rather such shameful whoredom, for the propagation of the reign of plants. Who will instruct young students in such voluptuous system without scandal?' Similarly, Reverend Richard Polwhele, Bishop of Exeter, in his book entitled *Unsex'd Females* (1798), attacked the teaching of the sexual system of botany as it encouraged unauthorised sexual unions, naming Mary Wollstonecraft[26] as the main protagonist in what he called the 'female Quixotes of the new philosophy'.[27]

Phillip Miller, a famous English botanist, also became the butt of many of the Grub Street hacks. Employed at Chelsea Gardens, he had adopted the Linnaean system in *The Gardener's Directory* (1731). His botanical work *Catalogus Plantarum Officinalium* (1730) had an obvious influence on the writing of *Natural History of Arbor Vitae* (1732) as Phillip Miller was given as a pseudonym by the true author, Thomas Stretser,[28] one of Curll's hacks, who was probably also the author of its female counterpart, *Frutex Vulvaria*. This response to botanists draws on an existing tradition in which women were seen in agricultural terms. The metaphors used were not particularly sophisticated and were a satirical reaction created for an audience unwilling to accept highfalutin research theories – the discovery of the sex life of a plant.[29] But the sexual overtones of the allegory are much more than a mere skit on the botanical findings of the time by a public unwilling to accept their conclusions. They reflect a particular attitude to women's bodies and their sexual behaviour in relation to that of men.

The botanical metaphors in erotica are neatly divided into two sets of material, the male and the female, otherwise loosely termed as the trees and the shrubs.

The tree of life

One of the earlier depictions of the male species in erotica can be seen in *Natural History of Arbor Vitae,* a poem first published in 1732, purporting to be a tale of the tree of life, but is in fact a portrait of the male genitalia, and how to deal with its maladies. *Arbor Vitae* was later reprinted in 1741 along with a lengthy description of the tree itself leaving us with no illusions that the penis was the real matter under discussion. An analogy is made between a boy's sexual maturity and the coming of age of the tree and its ejaculations: 'The Tree is of slow Growth, and requires Time to bring it to Perfection, rarely feeding to any purpose before the Fifteenth Year; when the Fruits coming to good Maturity, yield a viscous Juice or balmy *Succus*.' [30]

Conversely, old age is considered, and the use of a support advocated as an aid to ensure an erect tree: 'In the latter Season [winter], they are subject to become weak and flaccid, and want Support, for which Purpose some Gardeners have thought of splintering them up with *Birchen Twigs,* which has seem'd of some Service for the present, tho' the Plants have very soon come to the same, or a more drooping State than before.'[31] As well as the suggestion of the splinting of a withering member, flagellation is implied here as a means to stimulating the flagging male libido. 'Birchen twigs' were frequently referred to in later pornography, flagellation being one of the main themes.

Various infamous quacks are targeted for ridicule throughout these poems, as are their cures. The securing of a ligature around the penis is suggested by one: 'The late ingenius Mr. *Motteux* thought of restoring a fine Plant he had in this condition, by tying it up with a *Tomex*, or Cord made of the Bark of the *Vitex*, or *Hempen Tree*: But whether he made the Ligature too strait, or that Nature of the *Vitex* is really in itself pernicious, he quite kill'd his Plant thereby; which makes this universally condemn'd as a dangerous Experiment.' Removal of the scrotum is also practised: 'Some *Virtuosi*[32] have thought of improving their Trees for some Purposes, by taking off the *Nutmegs.*' Peter Anthony Motteux (1660–1718) had caused a stir amongst the *Bon Ton* of London after he died in a house of ill fame in 1718 in Star Court, Butcher's Row near St. Clement's church.[33] Mr Humphrey Bowen is mentioned, a 'judicious Botanist' who, in his book *la Quintyne*, cautions against the 'poisonous Species of *Vulvaria*' which are 'too often mistaken for the wholesome ones'. He 'has seen a tall thriving Tree, by the Contact only of this venomous Shrub become *porrose scabiose,* and covered with *fungous Excrescence's* not unlike the Fruits of the *Sylvestris*: ... these venomous shrubs have spread the Poison through a whole Plantation'.[34] Similarly, another notorious quack, Dr. Misaubin, a French MD practising in London and specialising in wonderful cures for venereal diseases, is ridiculed because of his foreign accent and eccentric manners.[35]

Other popular botanical poems describe men alternatively as virile trees or sensitive plants playing on *double entendres* as seen in *Wisdom Revealed; OR THE TREE OF LIFE*[36] (1732), *The Manplants: Or, a Scheme for Increasing and Improving the British Breed* (1752)[37] and *Mimosa, or A Sensitive Plant* (1779), the latter declaring 'with ineffable delight have you ascertained that though all the *sensitive plant* is alive to the *touch*, there is one delicate *part* observable in its articulation'.[38] In botany, the 'Sensitive Plant' was given the generic name *Mimosa* (L. *mimus,* mime) as far back as 1619 because the plants 'mimick' the sensitivity of animals. R. J. Camerarius, in *Epistola de sexu plantarum* (1694; translated in Jullian Sachs, *History of Botany, 1530–1860*), ascribes seeds as 'the significance of male organs, since they are the receptacles in which the seed itself, that is the powder that is the most subtle part of the plant, is secreted and collected, to be afterwards supplied from them. It is equally evident, that the ovary with its style represents the female sexual organ in the plant.' The 'sensitive plant' became a well-recognised metaphor; even Fanny Hill made reference to it: 'My fingers too had now got within reach of the true, the genuine sensitive plant, which, instead of shrinking from the touch, joys to meet it, and swells and vegetates under it.'[39]

Flowering shrubs

Celebration of the female body in erotic botanical metaphors saw female sex organs represented as flowering shrubs, caves or valleys. In this material, the female body was synonymous with the natural landscape, but unlike contemporary scientific views on nature, woman/nature was not relegated to an inferior position. Poems sprang up in the same vein as *Arborvitae*, this time parodying the female model. Edward Ward's poem satirised a woman's design as early as 1725 in *The Riddle Or A Paradoxical Character Of An Hairy Monster* (1725).

> When full 'tis round, when empty long,
> Sometimes a Hole, sometimes a Slit,
> Hairy when old, and bald when young,
> Too wide for some, for others fit.
>
> It justly may be stil'd a Well
> At each Spring-Tide it overflows;
> Its Depth no mortal Man can tell;
> That none but he that made it knows.
>
> It Lies obscurely in a Clift,
> That's fenced with Brambles around it.

This was reprinted in 1741 along with *Little Merlin's Cave* (1741), another metaphor for female genitalia. This was an 'in' joke resulting from a feature built by William Kent in 1735 in the royal garden of Queen Caroline entitled 'The Cave of Merlin'.[40]

Just as *Arborvitae* had embraced the metaphor of the penis, *Natural History of the Frutex Vulvaria, or Flowering Shrub* (first published in 1732) would embrace the 'flowering shrub' as a metaphor for the female sex organs. Written under the pseudonym 'Philgynes Clitorides',[41] *Natural History Of The Frutex Vulvaria* was dedicated to 'the two fair Owners of the finest *Vulvaria's* in the three Kingdoms'. The *Frutex Vulvaria* is described as 'a flat low Shrub, which always grows on a moist warm Valley, at the foot of a little Hill, which is constantly water'd by a Spring whose Water is impregnated with very fine Particles, which nevertheless agree wonderfully well with this *Shrub*'.[42] Despite being presented as 'none other than the Female Arbor Vitae', it becomes quite clear that the vulvaria is quite different from the *Arbor Vitae*, with different characteristics, affected by different maladies and requiring different cures.

A small-sized vagina is depicted as a well-prized characteristic of the English woman. Moreover, the English 'shrub' is considered far superior to that of their European counterparts. 'Contrary to the *Arbor Vitae,* which is valued the more the larger it is in Size, the *Vulvaria* that is least is most esteem'd; for which Reason our *English* Shrubs are priz'd vastly more than those grown in *Italy, Spain,* or *Portugal;* and indeed, those that are above five inches in Diameter, are worth little or nothing.'[43] An attack is made on the withering plants of the realm; '*Tho'*

Great Britain *has never been destitute of the finest* Shrubs *in the Universe, yet the* Trees *that have been grafted* upon *them, for these two and twenty Years last past, have so far degenerated, that our* Plants *are held in the utmost Contempt in all foreign Countries, as fit only to be* piss'd upon.' It goes on to tell how plants have deteriorated over the recent years: '*All these Misfortunes the* Naturalists *and* Botanists *ascribe (how truly I know not) to the Degeneracy of our* Trees of Life; *how much then, beauteous Ladies, must the whole Nation be obliged to your* indefatigable Endeavours, *to* restore their Vigour.'

Contemporary medical arguments resulting from experiments in anatomy and physiology were echoed in this erotica. Theories queried ranged from whether or not the vagina produces its own juices, to the necessity of orgasm in sexual reproduction: 'It has long been warmly contested by the great *Botanists,* whether the *Vulvaria* is not a *succulent Plant. Hippocrates* and *Galen,* two eminent *Virtuosi* of former Ages, with abundance of their Followers, very obstinately contended that it was so; and that it has a balmy *Succus,* or *viscous Juice,* which distilled from it, upon being *lanced* ... . But the celebrated *Harvey,* with many other modern *Botanists,* famous for their useful Discoveries and Improvements, absolutely deny this.'[44]

Despite the fact that female enjoyment of sex was increasingly deemed unnecessary for procreation, the erotica recognises women's desire for sexual gratification. Indeed, the traditional theme of uncontrollable female desire is expressed in the concerns about nymphomania: 'Some *Vulvaria* are troubled with a very unaccountable Disorder ... which they shew by the a continual *Opening* of the *Fissura,* or *Chink* above mention'd, and which is not to be remedied but by the Distillation therein of the balmy *Succus* of the *Arbor Vitae.* In this Case, one *Tree* seldom or never discharges a *quantum sufficit* to answer the Intent of Cure'. The depositing of an over-sexed woman in a brothel is seen as one way of curing the nymphomania: 'it has often been found necessary to remove the *Shrubs* to a *Hot-house* where there are several *Trees* provided, in order to compleat the Cure.'[45] 'Several of these *Hot-houses* are to be met with in and about the *hundred of Drury*'; specifically, he mentions those around St James and Westminster, St George's Fields, Vauxhall and Mother Needham's. Mother Needham (1680–1731) was a notorious brothel-keeper given the title 'Female Botanist', presumably because she ran a sideline in abortions.

There is an assumption that women spread diseases and that a woman infected more men than men did women. This held with contemporary views, as did the notion that the pox was more difficult to cure in a woman. We find 'more bad Symptoms in the *Shrub* than in the Tree, but are more difficult to be remedied, and will diffuse their Poison a great deal farther; since, for the one *Shrub* that the *Tree* can hurt, the *Shrub,* when infected, may spoil twenty *Trees*'. The celebrated Dr. Misaubin and his ardent endeavours to cure the pox are also mentioned in this prose.

'Anxiety-making' and trading in fear of the pox were the hallmark of the quack VD doctors; adverts for wonder cures were even carried in such respectable magazines as *The Female Tatler*.[46] The writers of erotica, aware of the proliferation of medical charlatans, were quick to launch an attack on them, warning the reader about the side-effects of alleged medical 'cures'. Uneducated quacks were vilified for their misdiagnoses. Incorrect treatments given to women suffering venereal infections were seen to have detrimental effects. In one instance, in *Frutex Vulvaria,* the preparations given for the pox instead of crab-lice had a harmful effect:

> Some unskilful *Botanists,* who have not been apprised of the Nature of these Insects, have imagin'd that their Shrubs have been infected by the Contact of a poisonous *Arbor Vitae,* and have accordingly applied a Remedy proper only for that Disorder, which instead of doing any Good has quite spoil'd the *Shrub;* whereas had they only applied some *Staphis Agria,* together with a due Quantity of *Axungia Porci,* to the Root of the *Fibrilae,* the *Shrub* would have nerve been the worse.[47]

The risk of pregnancy was ever present and abortion well at the forefront as a means of contraception, with female abortionists available to perform the deed. Such 'tumours' can be removed and 'Female *Botanists'* are available who claim to do this, but the author warns us: 'I would advise no Person, who have a Value for the Wellfare [sic] of their *Vulvaria,* to trust them in extraordinary Cases, but immediately to apply to the *Botanists* above mentioned.'[48] The menstrual cycle is referred to as a disorder 'which makes it believ'd that this *Shrub* is under the Dominion of the moon'. Such old lunar symbolism which connected the moon to bodily rhythms of change and renewal (also with female sexual inconstancy) continued to hold sway in this erotica, while new promulgations were increasingly given short shrift.

Erotica and reproduction

> I began to question, why might not the Foetus be as compleatly hatched in the seminal Vessels of the Woman, as when it passes through the Organs of both Sexes ... whether Animalcula did really float about in the Air, and slide down the Throat as he [Mr. Woolaston][49] described?
>
> 'Dr. Abraham Johnson', *Lucina Sine Concubitu*[50]

Erotica began to explore theories on reproduction in line with natural philosophers and theologians, such as William Harvey and William Wollaston, who were making new considerations about the process of generation during the seventeenth and eighteenth centuries. John Hill (1716–75), the writer of *Lucina Sine Concubitu,* was obviously borrowing from Harvey's assertions on reproduction from his book *On Generation* (1651):

> many animals, especially insects, arise and are propagated from elements and seeds so small as to be invisible (like atoms flying in the air), scattered and dispersed here and there by the winds; yet these animals are supposed to have

arisen spontaneously, or from decomposition because their ova are nowhere to be found.[51]

Hill's sexual satires parodied such serious scientific proposals about the propagation of living creatures in humorous and risqué accounts of experiments in reproduction. His parodies explored two of the most important controversies emanating from these discussions, in both erotica and medical tracts. The first raises the question of which sex was the more significant in the reproductive process, the male or the female; the second asks whether female orgasm was a prerequisite for conception.

Along with *Lucina Sine Concubitu,* two similar tracts on generation were published in 1750, which depicted satirical views on reproduction and female sexual behaviour while simultaneously deriding the contemporary scientific world,[52] all three probably written by 'Sir' John Hill.[53] The first tract, *Lucina Sine Concubitu,* went under the pseudonym of 'Abraham Johnson'; the second was *A Letter To Dr. Abraham Johnson* by 'Richard Roe'; the anonymous third was entitled *A Dissertation on Royal Societies. Occasioned by the late pamphlets of Dr. Abraham Johnson and Dr. Richard Roe.* These tracts raised three main concerns, which emerged as a result of scientific exploration of reproduction. First, was the diminished role of women in reproduction; second, was the problem of unwanted offspring; and third was the entry of both science and the male physician into the female domain of childbirth.[54] Hill's popular satires overturned some of the serious promulgations of physicians on the role of men and women in conception. Hill disregarded Harvey's suggestions that women did not need to achieve orgasm in order to conceive, re-establishing its necessity (and thereby the necessity of female pleasure). Taking the joke further, he completely disposed of the need for men in reproduction. Hill also introduced the figure of the gullible male medical examiner who personified the more ludicrous examples of the professionals in the Royal Society.

Hill was a prolific, unscrupulous man who managed to combine medicine and botany with satirical erotic writings. He appears a pushy and fickle character, keen to turn his hand to anything in his bid for recognition. Rejected by the Royal Society, Hill took refuge in vengeful attacks through his allegorical sexual satires and later made money selling quack remedies. He had started as an apprentice to an apothecary, later setting himself up in a small shop in St. Martin's Lane. In an attempt to increase his profits he studied botany, and was eventually employed by the Duke of Richmond and Lord Peters in the arrangement of their gardens and collection of dried plants. He delved (unsuccessfully) into the world of theatre, as both actor and playwright at the 'little theatre' in the Haymarket and at Covent Garden[55] and even made a slight diversion into the realm of fiction with his *The History of a Woman of Quality* (1751) aimed at a female audience.[56] He also had a column as 'The Inspector' in the *London Daily Advertiser and Literary Gazette* (which Isaac D'Israeli decried as a highly scandalous chronicle). According to G.S. Rousseau, Hill entertained a passion for a courtesan called 'Diamond' for whom he wrote *Letters From the Inspector to a Lady.*[57] However, Hill did not gain the reputation to which he aspired; Rousseau says of him: 'It is sad to report that he emitted but a dim light.'[58]

Hill knew David Garrick, Samuel Richardson, Laurence Sterne, Samuel Johnson, James Boswell, Albrecht von Haller, Carl Linnaeus and the members of the Royal Society. Whether they were friend or foe depended on the day. At various times, he plotted and schemed to ruin the career of various acquaintances, including Tobias Smollett and Henry Fielding. Martin Folkes and Henry Baker introduced Hill to other members of the Royal Society, but he failed to obtain the requisite number of votes to allow him entry. No doubt as a result of this rejection, while editor of *British Magazine* (1746–50), he began to write scurrilous pieces condemning the Royal Society. He went on to attack his former patrons, Folkes and Baker, in a publication entitled *A View of the World of the Royal Society* (1751), ridiculing the Society's *Philosophical Transactions*, to which he had contributed papers only a couple of years earlier. He was, however, recognised for his serious works including a translation of Theophrastus' *History of Stones* (1746), his *General Natural History* (1748–52), a catalogue of animals, vegetables and minerals, *The Vegetable System* (1759) and *Exotic Botany* (1759).[59] He corresponded with the Earl of Bute and with Linnaeus, to whom he dedicated *The Sleep of Plants and Cause of Motion in the Sensitive Plant Explain'd* (1757).[60] Despite portrayals of Hill as a failure and charlatan, he was the first to connect tobacco to cancer in a little-known pamphlet, *Caution against the Immoderate Use of Snuff* (1759).

Lucina Sine Concubitu[61] went on sale for the price of one shilling. Further editions followed and translations were made in French and German, a testimony to their popularity at home and abroad. The author claims that women have no need for men in the reproductive process and aims to prove 'by most Incontestable Evidence, drawn from Reason and Practice, that a Woman may conceive and be brought to Bed without any Commerce with Man'. He attests to a discovery 'entirely new, and which I am sure will equal anything that has been offered to the World since Philosophy has been a Science'.[62] Practised in 'Man-Midwifry', the narrator, a physician, diagnoses pregnancy of a neighbouring gentleman's daughter. Upon being confronted with this suspicion, the 'young lady turned up a Face of inexpressible Innocence and Amazement, and immediately fainted away into her Mother's Arms'. The girl continues to declare her innocence, proclaiming never to have been touched by a man. In an attempt to explain her predicament, the physician refers the reader to a Mr Woolaston's [sic] infamous *Religion of Nature Delineated* (1722). After reading the book, the doctor confesses:

> I was instantly thrown into a *Reverie*, and began to reflect with myself, that if such little Embryos, or *Animalcula* are so dispersed about, and taken in at the Mouth with Air or Aliment ... why might not the Foetus be as compleatly hatched in the seminal Vessels of the Woman, as when it passes through the Organs of both Sexes?[63]

He wondered 'whether Animalcula did really float about in the Air, and slide down the Throat as he [Mr. Woolaston] described?' Here, Hill was satirising the serious work of William Wollaston (1660–1724). His *Religion of Nature Delineated*

(1722) was a popular book selling 10,000 copies 'in a few years' and went through at least six editions by 1738. Wollaston expounded the notion of pneumatic conception.

> If then the semina, out of which animals are produced, are as (as I doubt not) animalcula already formed; which, being dispersed about, especially in some opportune places, are taken in with aliment, or perhaps the very air; being separated in the body of the males by strainers proper to every kind, and then lodged in their seminal vessels, do there receive some kind of addition and influence; and being thence transferred into the wombs of the females, are there nourished more plentifully, and grow, till they become too big to be any longer confined.[64]

With his sarcastic reference to a virgin conception, Hill might also have confused the two philosophers, William Wollaston and Thomas Woolston (1670–1733), a common occurrence amongst contemporaries.[65] Thomas Woolston had been publicly deemed blasphemous as a result of his discussion about the Virgin Birth. He was indicted alongside the pornographer Edmund Curll[66] for his work, *The Moderator Between An Infidel and An Apostate* (1725), which incited antagonism over his disbelief of the Immaculate Conception:

> I do believe the Virginity of the Mother of our Lord, and will by no means be induced to write against it: But it is ridiculous, very ridiculous and absurd to imagine that God should give forth a Prophecy of the Conception of a *Virgin*, which is subject to Counterfeit, and in its Completion liable to unanswerable Exceptions against it. Who can prove the Mother of *Jesus* to have been a *Virgin*, and otherwise than upon her own Word, and the good Opinion her Relations had of her?[67]

Scientific postulations around fertilisation were being ridiculed whilst simultaneously drawing attention to these two popular works. Two contemporary issues were further played out: that of conception without the aid of a man; and that of pneumatic conception, or the notion of animalcula or 'seeds' being propagated by air. William Harvey's (1578–1657) *De Generatione*, a landmark in the scientific revolution, had already established the basic process for formation of life, defining the egg as common to all animals. Yet Harvey had suggested that conception could be through magnetisation, conception of an idea or contagion, and thought the egg was produced *after* fertilisation. He believed that some plants and animals were produced spontaneously and that they might have arisen from seed or eggs so small they could be carried unnoticed in the air. Other scientists helped establish the male's importance in generation. As early as 1677 (not published until 1679),[68] in a letter to the Royal Society, Anton von Leeuwenhoek described his findings of 'spermatic worms' (spermatozoa) and 'animalcule' under the microscope. He also saw the multitudes of animalcules in rainwater as 'seeds' being carried up when rainwater evaporates in the heat of the sun to be returned to earth as rain. Christiaan Huygens confirmed the findings of sperm, along with Nicholaas Hartsoeker, who reported the appearance of little eel-like animals in the semen of the cock. Women's role in reproduction was therefore being relegated to that of mere nourisher.

Significantly, in *Lucina Sine Concubitu*, the narrator questions the need for male involvement in conception in the same fashion that contemporary scientists were questioning the contribution of the female in the reproductive process. Just as the role of the female was being diminished by scientists, the narrator turns their theories on their head, dispensing with the male role altogether. Again, like the scientists, the protagonist ponders alternative methods of fertilisation. Following in the tradition of other writers of erotica, he quotes from Virgil, this time as substantiation that offspring can be born without coition:

> The Mares to Cliffs of rugged Rocks repair,
> And with wide Nostrils snuff the western Air:
> When (wondrous to relate) the Parent Wind,
> Without the Stallion, propagates the Kind.[69]

Aristotle had originally deemed mares to be sexually wanton, for they were said to chase stallions in order to satisfy their sexual urges. If not impregnated by a stallion, the mares would be fertilised by the wind.[70] Taking up this idea, the author suggests that if mares can become pregnant without coition, through sniffing the air, then maybe the same could be done for mankind. He proposes that it is women who are the most fertile and likely carriers of fertility, not men, and to test his theory, builds 'a wonderful cylindrical, catoptrical, rotundo-concavoconvex Machine', which acts as 'a kind of Trap to intercept the floating Animalcula in that prolific Quarter of the Heavens'.[71] He wants to carry out an experiment to impregnate a woman by this method, but his choice is difficult: 'Sometimes I thought of taking a Wife, over whom I could usurp absolute Authority, and lock her up till the Day of her Labour',[72] but he is fearful 'she might grow desperate, when she should find I had only married her to try an Experiment upon her'.[73] He concludes that the wind carries the Animalcula which women then inhale. Impregnation occurs, resulting in the possibility that 'a Woman may be with Child in a single State, consistently with the purest Virtue'.[74]

Women are perceived to be naturally lascivious but because of society's restrictions on behaviour, have become devious from the necessity to conceal their activities. Humorous jibes are directed at women on account of their sexual natures, the narrator suggesting an altered state of affairs regarding female sexual licence. He proposes that, once parthenogenesis is understood, women will be able to indulge themselves sexually without fear of tarnishing their good name, and it 'will be easy for a young Lady to lose her Maidenhead without losing her Character'.[75] Although this was a comic piece rather than a call for sexual liberation, Hill was drawing attention (whether intentional or not) to the problems women faced for their sexual activities.

Unwanted pregnancies and a tarnished reputation were seen as the inevitable results of women's amorous dalliances. By the end of the century, Joseph Banks would castigate the rigidity of the sexual double standard and furthermore blame women themselves for their strict adherence to the rules. In a letter to Mary Ann Radcliffe, he declared: 'the greater part of the Evils to which your sex are liable under our present Customs of Society originate in the decisions of Women'. He blamed women for ostracising their own sex for sexual misdemeanours, stating: 'The Penalty by which women uniformly permit the smallest deviation of a Female character from the Rigid Paths of virtue is more severe than Death and more afflicting than the Tortures of the Dungeons.'[76]

Scientists from Aristotle to Marcello Malpighi had gained much of their empirical knowledge on the progress of generation from the study of eggs and embryonic chicks. René-Antoine Ferchault Réaumur undertook similar experiments, and was another scientist to become a target of Hill's satires. The results had been published in *The Art of Hatching and Bringing Up Domestic Fowls by Means of Artificial Heat* (1750) and described the methods used in Egypt using 'ovens which are very different sizes, but in general capable of containing from forty to forty-score thousand eggs'.[77] Réaumur observed that dung generated heat and so thought it an admirable way to propagate chickens. The pamphlet relates:

> Dung is indeed capable of acquiring a much greater degree of heat, than that which is necessary for the hatching of Eggs: and Mr. De Reaumur has put his eggs into an earthen pot, and lodges them in a layer of dung where they have almost stewed and parboiled.[78]

This was a serious work communicated to the Royal Society. Erotic satires were bound to follow. In a *Letter To Dr. Abraham Johnson, On the Subject of his new Scheme for the Propagation of the Human Species* (1750),[79] a new 'experiment' was created which parodied Réaumur. The experimenter explains:

> I have plann'd out a spacious Area with Walks for the Ladies to take the Air upon, and with Ranges of my *artificial Uteri* disposed on every Side, into which they may at Pleasure drop their Load, whenever they are in a Humour to take the necessary Steps for the procuring of another. In other Words, I have disposed all my intermediate Alleys into hot Beds of Dung; in these I have bury'd Rows of Wine-Casks not to forget a Set of Sugar-Tubs, and other Receptacles of proportion'd Size, for the more corpulent of my Customers; in each of these I have placed a Basket of soft Cotton, and in each I have suspended a Thermometer, to certify me to the utmost Exactness of the Degree of Heat.[80]

A world is proposed in which women could conceive without recourse to sex and leave the incubation of their offspring elsewhere. Furthermore, the doctor in the narration proffers a means of avoiding pregnancy altogether using contraception in the form of an eagle-stone.[81] He states: 'this grave Author at length comes to the Virtues and Uses of this famous Mineral, which I find is no other than that which has been long known among the good old Women of our Country, under the Name of the *Eagle-Stone*'. It could drive away apparitions, cure toothache or, if worn on the arm by a woman with child, prevent her miscarrying. Conversely, if tied to her leg, 'or worn on any Part below the Seat of Impregnation', it would immediately bring on a miscarriage and 'bring forth the little Embryo, of whatever Age, or under whatever Circumstances, it may be fix'd there'.[82] Natural abortifacients were well known in early modern England and used as a means of controlling fertility,[83] and the doctor advocates one particular abortifacient for use as a contraceptive method. The doctor proceeds to buy up all the stocks of eagle-stone he could find to sell to his 'patients'.

> I published among the Neighbours, that every Woman that pleased might now repair to me, and dance without Fear of paying the Piper! that Pleasure was before them; and Virtue, that is to say Reputation, (for that is all the Ladies of the Age means by the Word) was safe; That they might with me have all the Amusement that attended the being made with Child, and that they might be assured of being delivered from all the Effects of their Entertainment, at the End of a Week and three Hours, without the least Pain or Danger.[84]

The implication is that but for the moral regulations controlling women's sexual behaviour and the risk of pregnancy, women would revert to their natural state, embracing sexual practices. Overtly, the satire pokes fun at the more conventional view on women's modesty and ambitions of chasteness. However, there is an underlying tension, which suggests that this alternative world is being shown as a warning to men. Free from their burden of pregnancy, women would be able to indulge their naturally libidinous yearnings undetected. This satire therefore plays on the underlying male fear of cuckoldry, which such unremitting female licentiousness might bring. This world would create a plethora of autonomous women, who could indulge their sexuality at whim, men losing their authority and power. As such, women were portrayed as a potential threat.

In March 1750, a further pamphlet, *A Dissertation on Royal Societies. Occasion'd by the late pamphlets of Dr. Abraham Johnson, and Dr. Richard Roe*,[85] was published which vilified the Royal Society:

> every man is ready to cut the throat of him, who dares to know more than himself: the members of the Royal Society dread to receive a man of real knowledge among them ... Whatever foundation there may be for the scandalous things Dr. *Roe* has charged upon this society, nothing is more certain, that errors are to be found in their works, and too evident proofs of want of science at their meetings ... what must the *French* botanists think of us, when they are informed, that the seeds of a common herb, the bidens, which had fallen into a ditch, were picked out of it, and brought before the Royal Society, under the name of animals: when they see that not one man of that society, knew either what they were, or what was the difference between the seed of a plant, and an animal, but all join'd in the query, as to what would be the form of this creature when perfect, and return'd the thanks of their whole body to the curious and

ingenious gentleman, who had made the blunder they were not able to set right, nor even to comprehend that it was one?[86]

Hill was directing this invective at a mistake made by the Rev. Henry Miles and Henry Baker who had falsely identified objects Miles had found in ditch water. Believing them to be tiny living animals, they related their findings in *Philosophical Transactions* but, embarrassingly for them, the objects turned out to be seeds.[87] In 'A Description of a Meeting of a Royal Society in London and a Coffee-House Conversation', the narrator relates an incident where he hears wildly exaggerated tales as he follows the fellows into a coffee-house. One gentleman tells of a frightful monster 'with Wings and Claws, voided by a Lady, on taking a single Dose of his Worm-Powder; a second, of a living Wolf in one of his patient's Breasts, and a third, of a Toad in a Block of Marble'.[88] These wags collected at 'Wits Corner in the *Bedford* Coffee-House, and behind the sacred Veil at *Rawthmell's*',[89] coffee-houses being a meeting place for the discussion of London's natural philosophers, including members of the Royal Society.[90] Hill, who frequented the Bedford Coffee-House, obviously abhorred the ridiculous claims to which he had been party in discussions at this establishment by Royal Society members. He was not alone in his condemnation of such declarations. *The Gentleman's Magazine* mocked the Royal Society in reports made of a mother who gave birth to a leonine monster 'with nose and eyes like a lyon, no palate to the mouth, hair on the shoulders, claws like a lyon instead of fingers, no breast-bone, something surprising out of the navel as big as an egg, and one foot longer than the other'.[91]

If anyone was left in doubt as to the reason for these pamphlets, Hill made sure that his intentions were well known. The *British Magazine*, in February 1750, published 'A letter from Dr. Abraham Johnson To the Author of the British Magazine' (one and the same – Hill) declaring: 'You are sensible, that the very last thing I was call'd upon to do, was to prove that a natural child might be born without the help of the father.'[92] He was amazed at the consternation the tract caused since he had no other ambition than 'to tickle myself to make myself laugh', although it was obvious to readers that ridicule of the Royal Society and its experiments were at the heart of the matter. The *British Magazine*, in March 1750 under the same title heading 'A Dissertation on Royal Societies. Occasion'd by the late pamphlets of Dr. Abraham Johnson, and Dr. Richard Roe', retold the story of *Lucina Sine Concubitu*, and discussed who was in fact the author of these tracts; could it be 'one author with two names'? Hill further connected himself with the papers by printing the article in the *British Magazine*, entitled 'A *strange* Instance *given by Mr.* REAUMUR, *in his* Treatise *of the hatching of* Eggs'.[93]

Castigations of the more conjectural theorising on reproduction led Hill to attack the speculators and their attempts to understand female fertility. No doubt much of his satire spread from rancour at being refused admission to the Royal Society. Implicit in his writing, however, is an underlying (and common) assumption that women by nature were sexually rapacious. Furthermore, these tracts purposely divorced sexual intercourse from conception. In earlier sex guides (as seen in the sex manuals of Venette and *Aristotle's Master-piece*), sexual activities were closely connected with the desire to conceive, with advice on the best way to perform to become pregnant. Hill's satires did the opposite. In this inversion, he created a grand libertine joke. In his experimental world, sex could take place without pregnancy, and pregnancy without sex, thus disengaging the two. Within this realm, women were made biologically superior to men since the latter were no longer necessary for conception.

The electrical metaphor

> Ye lovely maids, ye amorous dames, attend
> Ye widows, taught by cruel death to feel;
> Here join the griefs of a deploring friend,
> And wail the loss of the *Electric Eel*.
>
> That Eel on earth, in Paradise the first,
> If we Mosaic stories may believe,
> That led weak woman to the tree accurst,
> And damn'd our sex through the all-curious Eve.
>
> That Eel which took the film from Adam's eyes,
> And did electrify his dowdy dame;
> That Eel which made the very dullest rise,
> Is robb'd of vigour and electric flame.

'Lucretia Lovejoy', *An Elegy on the
Lamented Death of the Electrical Eel*[94]

New arguments and theories about electricity, friction and generation emanated from the Royal Society. These were circulated not only among scientists, but were discussed at lectures,[95] in clubs and in coffee-houses,[96] with gentlemen arguing the merits and demerits of various electrical experiments. One such discovery was made by Stephen Hales (1677–1761), who helped promote the notion of electricity as a biological property. In his *Statical Essays* (1733), he suggested that electricity accounted for nerve and muscle function, and 'that a considerable vibrating electrical Virtue can be conveyed and fully act with considerable Energy along the surface of animal Fibres, and therefore on the Nerves'.[97] Another scientist who wrote of electrical bodies was Benjamin Wilson (1721–88),[98] at that time a student of chemistry. His *An Essay Towards An Explication of the Phenomena of Electricity Deduced from the Aether of Sir Isaac Newton* (1746) contained papers he had read before the Royal Society. In one article, 'A Dissertation on Electricity', he discussed his findings:

> It is agreed, that there are some bodies called electrics *per se;* wherein certain matter is excited by friction, by means of which light bodies are attracted and repelled; and that there are other bodies called non-electrics *per se,* to which this matter may be communicated so as to produce the same effects.[99]

He showed his experiments, including his electrical apparatus, to several gentlemen of the Royal Society, including Martin Folkes, Samuel Meade, John Hyde and William Watson, writing further papers including *A Treatise on Electricity* (1750). Further experiments were made by Watson. In a letter addressed to Folkes, President of the Royal Society (1741–52), entitled *Experiments And Observations Tending To Illustrate The Nature And Properties Of Electricity* (1745), Watson explained: 'I take this Opportunity to acquaint you, that on *Friday* Evening last I succeeded, after having been disappointed in many attempts, in setting Spirits on Fire by that Power.' On Monday 15 April, he wrote:

> when about four o'Clock in the Afternoon I got my *Apparatus* ready, and fired the Spirit of Wine four Times from the Finger of a Person electrified standing, upon a Cake of Wax, and once from the Finger of a second Person standing upon Wax, communicating with the first by means of a walking Cane held between their Arms extended … . I placed a Man upon a Cake of Wax, who held in his Hands a Spoon with the warm Spirits, and in the other a Poker with the Thread. I rubbed the Tube amongst the Thread and electrified him as before. I then ordered a Person not electrified to bring his Fingers near the Middle of the Spoon; upon which the Flash from the Spoon and Spirit was violent enough to fire the Spirit.[100]

This is followed by a series of letters by him supporting his finding, concluding in yet another account of his experiments described in *Account of the Experiments made by a Gentleman of the Royal Society in order to discover whether the ELECTRICAL POWER could be sensible at great distances*, 'It has been found, that in proportion as Bodies are susceptible of having Electricity excited in them by Friction, in that Proportion they are less fit to conduct to other Bodies.'[101]

These scientific writings supplied an image too good to miss. Writers of erotica applied the notion of electrical friction to human bodies, providing a connection between electricity, bodies, motion and sex. *Teague-Root*[102] *Display'd Being Some Useful And Important Discoveries Tending To Illustrate The Doctrine Of Electricity In A Letter From Paddy Strong-Cock* (1746) was a direct parody of Watson's experiments. It feigns amazement at the dazzling experiments of the Royal Society:

> you have inform'd the World, that a great Philosopher, with two assistants, by the Help of two Cakes of Wax, a Cane, a Poker, Silk Threads, and a Glass Tube, can set fire to a wholesome Spoonful of warm Spirit of Wine, provided the Air, the Wind, and some other minute Circumstances concur … . The importance of the Discovery transported me so.[103]

The author has borrowed freely from Watson's tracts on the power of electrical shocks in order to create an amusing sexual analogy. Electrical power becomes the means by which the female root stirs the flaccid male into life:

> Amongst the wonderful Properties of the Male *Teague-Root*, this is one, that when the Weather is cold, or where it's not under the Electrical Influence of the Female Root, it shrinks to one Third of its Bulk, and is as limber as a Piece

of Rag: but so soon as it is under the Influence of the Female, that it is, within the Sphere of this Electrical Force, it raises itself to the Height I have mention'd ... and remains so till all the Electrical Fire is spent ...[104]

Similarly, the 'Female Root' amazes 'where it is highly electrical, how it will wriggle itself about, twist, squeeze, and gape, as if it would swallow the Male in its voluptuous Jaws, till the Electrical Fire is spent, in a Discharge of a similar Liquid, which moistens the whole Root'. Women are portrayed as ejaculating and their orgasms are seen to be more prodigious than men's, 'The Flashes are more frequent, and much more discernible than those seen from the highest Electrified Tube. I will not pretend to say that her Finger will set Spirit of Wine on Fire ...'.[105] Despite the introduction of this new electrical terminology, the older bosky metaphors are still in place, as can be seen in this description of the male genitalia:

At the Bottom of the Root issue two round Globes, that are pendulous in a Bag, where they seem to be loose, tho' bound to the Stem of the Root, by small yielding Fibres: The Outside of this Bag is wrinkly, and cover'd with a kind of Down, much resembling Hair, or the Beards of common Leeks.[106]

An equally unattractive picture is painted of the female genitalia:

The Female Root is not a beautiful Root; it's a broad Root with a Hole perforated thro' it, which will contract, or dilate itself on Occasion like the Mouth of a Purse.[107]

Amalgamations of plant and electrical metaphors expressed in *The Man-Plant* (1752) provide an explanation of the process of generation. Although women are recognised as the carriers of the eggs, they are not the vital part needed to ignite life into the cells:

Male-seed, which is itself the Integument, or Wrapper of a Spark or Particle of Fire, essentially quickened with the vivifying electric Touch produced by the Friction of the generative Process, and radiated up the Womb, where that individual Animalcule fostered by a Heat congenial to its ingenuous Essence, grown and develops into the human Form, through the constant Activity of its Fire-Spirit, struggling in vain to get loose from its Entanglement in the ambient, and tenacious corporeal: Matter, or fluid Principles of future Solids.[108]

Man is seen as providing the essential spark needed in the formation of life, but most important is to establish the moment of conception, 'The Points to be settled then were not only how to bring the Woman to lay or extrude this Egg, but to ascertain both the precise Time of her being electrified by the Congress of the Male'.[109] Within this badinage, three contemporary assumptions on generation surface. First, an essential 'spark' is necessary to generate life, and this is provided by the male, in keeping with Aristotle's beliefs that the male principle provides the vital matter in generation. However, mutual passion is necessary to generate this spark through bodily friction ('electricity'). Second, this energy can be spent, usually women sapping the strength of males. And third, women ejaculate juices in a similar way to men, and have better orgasms (more 'flashes').[110]

From the 1750s, scientists were increasingly undertaking physiological experiments with electrical fish. In 1759, Michel Adanson (1727–1806) investigated a fish which could produce electrical effects similar to the Leyden jar,[111] and made a direct comparison between the fish's shock and nerve action; John Hunter (1728–93) published 'Anatomical Observations of the Torpedo' (1774) and 'An Account of the Gymnotus Electricus' (1775) in *Philosophical Transactions of the Royal Society* after undertaking experiments on the electric organ of the ray fish or 'torpedo'. At about the same time, John Pringle discussed his study of electric fish in a lecture delivered at the anniversary meeting of the Royal Society on 30 November 1774, entitled *A Discourse on the Torpedo*.

As a direct result of these new scientific experiments on electrical eel and torpedo fish, a new wave of erotica emerged in the 1770s playing with images of the male genitalia as an eel, and the female as a torpedo (a fish capable of emitting electrical charges). Two erotic pamphlets entitled *The Electrical Eel, or Gymnotus Electricus* (1777) and *The Torpedo* (1774) (Figure 10)[112] again raised issues of foetal formation, and questions about which sex was responsible for generating the life force. The author of *The Electrical Eel* suggests that electricity comes from the eel.

> This Treatise on the natural, secret, powerful, and most effacious Principles of Electricity, Not Derived from the friction of Bodies, but proved and deduced from The Gymnotus Electricus, Is Now offered by an Adept, To Their sagacious considerations That This rare Phenomenon Of Nature, Is the original Serpent Of Sin.

In other words, the male carried all the vital ('electric') material for conception, and mutual orgasm ('the friction of bodies') was no longer deemed necessary.

Part of the intention of the 'electrically' themed poems was not merely to satirise the recent experiments (although this was obviously a main part of the joke) but to gossip openly about notorious libertines and recent scandals. Sarah Lennox was amongst those targeted as a result of her intrigues and sexual misdemeanours.[113] *The Torpedo* was dedicated to Lord Cholmondeley, chamberlain to Queen Caroline, whose affair with Mrs. Elizabeth Armistead was well known.[114] Lady Grosvenor was lampooned as a result of the well-publicised affair with the Duke of Cumberland.[115] Notorious libertines were cited, such as the famous prostitute Charlotte Hayes and politician John Wilkes. Another poem, *An Elegy On The Lamented Death Of The Electrical Eel; Or Gymotus Electricus* (a parody on Grey's famous *Elegy*),[116] mocked Countess H(alifax?), Lord B(ute) (whose 'huge erection'[117] provided a focal point) and Chevalier-Madame d'Eon de Beaumont.[118] *The Old Serpent's Reply to the Electrical Eel* mentions the celebrated actress Peg Woffington; and Mr. David Hartley, Member of Parliament for Hull, an 'ingeneous gentleman' who contrived a tin resistant to fire and undertook experiments to prove it.[119] Popular vulgar songs sprang up to

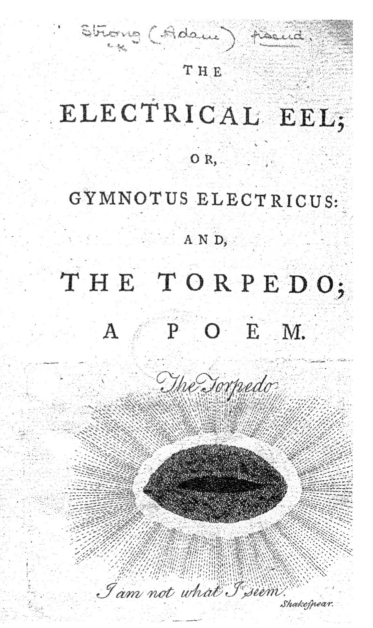

Figure 10   Title-page to 'Adam Strong' (James Perry), *The Electrical Eel, Or Gymnotus Electricus and The Torpedo. A Poem*, 1777

incorporate the lewd metaphors surrounding electricity, such as Jenny's Song in *Captain Morris's Songs* (1788) in which the 'Indian eel' is introduced, which twists in 'strange electric motions'.

Electricity became a powerful new metaphor for sexual attraction. Electricity, animal magnetism and the attraction of bodies were parodies used as an attack on both the scientific assertions frequently seen to be based on spurious knowledge and ill-conceived experiments. These analogies were also means to expound scandalous gossip. Adulterous aristocratic men and women, well-known prostitutes and prominent politicians had their sexually adventurous lives publicly displayed. Within these descriptions, some traditional beliefs on female and male sexuality were upheld, some were overturned. Disease is not mentioned in detail, but reference is made to the diminishing lustre and the dying vigour of the Electric Eel. The facetiae concentrate on conception, on how the 'spark' or vital life force is ignited, the male proffered as the main force in generation.

Conclusion

During the seventeenth and eighteenth centuries, science was attempting to account for the maintenance of living things and for their origination. Theories on botany, generation and electricity affected the erotica and were incorporated into the material. This 'scientific' erotica was a way in which to discuss sexual themes while allowing for criticism of more spurious scientific claims. However, although erotica was highly receptive to new ideas, it often retained scepticism towards new lines of thought.

Botanical works were written in highly erotic terms as seen in Linnaeus' description of plant reproduction. Once sexual reproduction had been deployed successfully as an analogy for reproduction in plants it was explored enthusiastically with respect to human coition. Writing about sex in terms of botany and science thereby allowed for sexual expression without fear of censorship.

Two main points emerge. First, the botanical erotica shows the anxieties men had about women's bodies; fear of catching the pox, fear of making them pregnant and fear of the ensuing medical problems attached to sexually active women. The female 'shrub' comes off worse as depictions are frequently attacking the quality of its fruits and flowers, allusions to the disease therein and its wayward course of reproduction. Men, however, do not escape blame for this deterioration seen in the lack of care or attention on the part of the tree or 'sensitive plant'. Also, it is unsurprising that male writers of erotica concentrate extensively on the possibilities of the spread of 'vermin' or the catching of crabs or the pox, considering the lack of effective cures. Risks of pregnancy, the menstrual cycle, nymphomania and other 'female' disorders are mentioned, but then so are the problems of impotence. Medical cures are suggested for both. Second, despite, or perhaps because of, the apparent discrepancies in science (nature as female and all-encompassing, yet somehow still secondary), satires on erotic terminology were incorporating the genders in a different way, equating woman with nature, yet of primary importance. Despite attacks by science on women's fertility and attempts to see her biological role as inferior, in erotica we see a celebration of female sexuality, a rude efflorescence. More frequently, the female genitalia are praised (as in *Little Merlin's Cave* 'with Spring-Tide it overflows' – a reference to vaginal fluid), adored and revered, and, most importantly, something desperately to be obtained.

The descriptions of male and female genitalia carry equal doses of ribald humour, both elevated to a subject worthy of much discussion and opinion. Both sets of material have intentionally humorous jibes about the failing powers of the genitalia and references to the admirable qualities of the flowers/fruits compare well with the pleasures provided by the proud erect but 'sensitive plant'. Although sometimes there are disparaging remarks about the failings of flowers or the shrivelling shrubs, and the spread of disease amongst the sexually active women of the country, generally, they are given a 'botanical equality' with men. Most importantly, the tree or sensitive plant is only important in its relationship to the vulvaria or shrub. Moreover, the personification of woman embedded in the shrub/fruit/flower is given the key role in botanical erotica: the woman is motivator of all actions and the cause of all woes and delights.

In Hill's fictional world, women are portrayed as biologically superior and men as intellectually superior. The male protagonist assists female 'patients' to fulfil their biological potential, but women have the ultimate power to procreate on their own. As such, the image of the reproductive body is female and perceived as biologically more powerful and therefore threatening. Within this set-up, although a man leads the scientific investigations, men in general are rendered biologically redundant. Despite the implications of Laqueur's findings on changing medical views, in this erotica, women were not considered sexually quiescent but continue to be seen as sexually lascivious, actively pursuing sex rather than passively encountering it.

An alternative is offered in the electrically themed poems, where men are the essential givers of life, providing the 'spark' or essence necessary for conception, women merely the carriers. However, women retain the power to sap men's strength. With regards to insult or veneration, there seems little gender disparity between male and female sexual organs. Both are viewed with disdain (the penis as limp as a rag, a 'wrinkled' scrotum, the female genitalia as an unbeautiful root) and both equally celebrated for their power to generate electricity. Despite the male Electrical Body being procreatively more powerful, the female Electrical Body attains greater orgasms.

Confusion on matters of reproduction continued to express itself through a proliferation of various images in erotica. This was, in some ways, an attempt to make sense of the new sciences and the new roles assigned to men and women in reproduction. Erotica provided a place to express these conflicting views. Botany, generation and electricity would continue to be used as metaphors within erotica through the nineteenth century up to the present day. The significance of such developments in images is crucial to understanding the nature of erotica as reactive to the world in which it was written. These themes arose out of particular disciplines to become part of an erotic tradition.

5
Sexual Utopias in Erotica

> Near the Fort is the Metropolis, called CLTRS [clitoris]; it is a pleasant
> Place, much delighted in by the Queens of MERRYLAND, and is their
> chief Palace, or rather *Pleasure Seat*; it was at first but small, but the
> Pleasure some of the Queens have found in it, has occasion'd their
> extending its Bounds considerably.
>
> Anon, *A New Description of Merryland*[1]

Erotica developed its own sexual utopias in which landscapes were depicted in
the form of a woman's body. Anatomical details were used to depict these 'other
worlds' whilst reflecting both classical and contemporary images of landscapes
and gardens. Within these erotic settings, the body was depicted in various
specifically constructed forms: an agricultural landscape in which the female
body is depicted as the soil/nature; a geographical terrain in which a woman's
body represented a whole country (as seen above); the female body represented
by a ship within a seascape; and a male archaeological body represented within a
neoclassical setting.

These scenes were loaded with agricultural metaphors, pelagic allegories and classical allusions producing the image of the landscaped body as a mini-cosmos. This
use of the human body to describe the workings of the world was an ancient trope,
which had been reiterated through the ages from the Ancients to the Renaissance.[2]
In his *Nature's Work of Art*, Leonard Barkan refers us to the picture of Man as
Cosmos as described by George Herbert (1593–1633), 'For Man is ev'ry thing, / And
more: He is a tree, yet bears more fruit'; he is the cosmos where 'Waters united our
navigation'. The 'combination of total inclusiveness and miniature proportion represents an essential and typical view of man in the Renaissance: man is a little
world'.[3] According to Barkan, when Herbert refers to man as a tree, a house, a
sphere, etc., he is not talking of the human condition, but of the human body. Out
of the desire to simplify man's relation to the cosmos arises the idea that man is a
microcosm, a miniature cosmos. Barkan explains:

> Once a man is viewed in the concrete terms of his fleshly house, he is inevitably
> divided subdivided into a number of parts, for, though the system of his body is

closed and finite, it is clearly composed of a large number of elements. This concrete multiplicity becomes the vehicle for either concrete or abstract multiplicity in the world around him. Thus the human body as a metaphoric vehicle has considerable range, whether in philosophy or literature, since it is capable of subdividing its referent into a great number of parts, while at the same time controlling the total range of the body's essential unity.[4]

The cosmological view of the individual man characterised the study of natural philosophy and lasted until the Copernican Revolution. To study man was to study the cosmos. In a similar way, towards the end of the seventeenth century, popular medical handbooks were using the rustic landscape as a metaphor for the body. Agricultural analogies were used to describe procreation,[5] reflecting an essentially bucolic view of the world, as seen in Jane Sharp's *The Midwives Book*:

> Man in the act of procreation is the agent and tiller and sower of the Ground, Woman is the Patient or Ground to be tilled, who brings Seed also as well as the Man to sow the ground with. I am now to proceed to speak of this ground or Field which is the Woman's womb ... we women have no more cause to be angry, or ashamed of what Nature hath given us than men have, we cannot be without ours no more than they can want theirs ... . At the bottom of the woman's belly is a little bank called a mountain of pleasure near the wellspring ... . Under the hill is the springhead.[6]

Both the Renaissance cosmic view of man and medical analogies of women/nature depicted the body as a metaphor for the cosmos. Erotica would use the same ploy to describe the sexualised body.

The early modern female body in the guise of nature was perceived alternately as passive/submissive and wild/passionate.[7] Yet in the erotica which depicts the broader landscapes, the image of woman is generally both sexually powerful and essentially more lascivious than that of man. Conversely, the erotica which uses the male body to describe the landscape shows it in the form of a stiff, controlled, man-made classical architecture, the antithesis of the image of the wild, feminine, natural landscape. Its beauty lay in its formal construction rather than the image of uncontrolled nature, as seen in the female Landscaped Body. Yet another kind of utopian setting in erotica took on the Arcadian world of the classicists. In this world, the landscape was not depicted as a body but was described as a mini-sexual universe with its own lusty inhabitants. All these utopias had their own laws or methods to ensure the continued enjoyment of sex.

Major cultural influences can be seen in the development of this erotica dependent on man's perception of his surroundings. This world-view was shifting with man's increasing attempts at controlling nature. The altering perception of the visible space was effected through three main changes. First, the rural landscape was changing, brought on by the encroachment of enclosures and a gradual shift towards urbanisation. Second, there was a notable increased interest in botany and gardening, which brought with it the landscaping of parks and estates through the likes of 'Capability' Brown, Nicholas Revett and Humphrey Repton. Finally, the world-view was expanding as a result of expeditions to foreign territories, and this saw a remodelling of perceptions of global space. In turn, these changing spatial perspectives in the eighteenth century would be reflected in erotica in the sexual landscape and the erotic garden. However, within these changes, the classical tradition of the erotic landscape and garden would continue to resurface. Erotic grottoes, caves and gardens, which had long existed in Greek mythology, still featured in the eighteenth-century erotic backdrop. Thus the 'natural' versus 'constructed' landscape in erotica needs to be examined in order to understand how these utopias conveyed a certain set of images about male and female sexuality. But first, it is necessary to explore the background to these changes in spatial perspectives if their influences on erotica are to be recognised.

The eighteenth-century landscape

Erotic themes were influenced by changing attitudes to the English landscape; one of the major transformations which affected this shift was enclosures. By 1700, half the arable land was already enclosed, mainly through private agreement, and from the 1750s onwards increasing numbers of enclosures took place through Acts of Parliament, a revolution that affected about 3,000 English parishes.[8] The transformation was rapid, if erratically dispersed, and visually transformed the open heath and rough pastures to miles of flowering hedgerows and enclosed small fields.[9] On his travels, Tobias Smollett declared: 'I see the country of England smiling with cultivation; the grounds exhibiting all the perfection of agriculture, parcelled out into beautiful enclosures, cornfields, hay and pasture, woodland and common ...'.[10] Space was being cut up, fenced in and more enclosed.

It became the fashion to make one's grounds look more the way nature intended. This was attempted through the augmented irregularity of the gentleman's estate in an attempt to make it look more wild and natural.[11] The leaning towards this more 'natural' look was summed up by Anthony Ashley Cooper, 3rd Earl of Shaftesbury in his *The Moralists* (1709):

> I shall no longer resist the passion in me for things of a *natural* kind; where neither *Art*, nor the *Conceit* or *Caprice* of Man has spoil'd their *genuine Order* by breaking up the *Primitive State*. Even the rude *Rocks*, the mossy *Caverns*, the irregular unwrought *Grotto's* and broken *Falls* of waters, with all the horrid graces of the *Wilderness* itself, as representing NATURE more, will be the more engaging, and appear with a magnificence beyond the mockery of princely gardens.[12]

Man's ideal landscape was no longer the manicured garden of the sixteenth and seventeenth centuries. Earlier styles had been of geometric design, including high walls, clipped bushes and patterns of low box hedges, an inheritance from Tudor, Dutch and French traditions. From the 1720s and 1730s, a leaning towards a more cultivated wilderness emerged, with classical temples an indispensable part of the environment, often set within woods. Specially created grottoes became popular, and grounds became dotted with statues. This trend led to the creation of the erotic landscape echoed in sexual writings as seen in the garden of Sir Francis Dashwood (see below). William Kent's favoured Palladian style (seen in the faithful interpretation of ancient architecture) would be displayed in erotica. *The Designs of Inigo Jones and Mr. William Kent* which depicts Kent's design of 'Merlin's Cave' was followed by a skittish poem, *Little Merlin's Cave*, a homage to Kent's garden project of the same name. In fact, a whole badinage developed around Kent's design and its title applying erotic connotations. The frontispiece of *Merryland Displayed* carries a picture, *Merlin's Cave*, which is repeated in Curll's publication of *Poems on Several Occasions* (also, see Figure 9).[13]

Simultaneously with the changes in landscapes at home came the broadening of the world-view. Accounts of 'new' lands and colonies were published in avidly read travelogues and fictional adventures.[14] Ned Ward wrote up his adventures in *A Trip to Jamaica* (1698), a popular pamphlet printed seven times in eighteen months, followed by *A Trip to New England* (1699). Defoe's *New Voyage Round the World* (1697) and *Robinson Crusoe* (1719) and Swift's *Gulliver's Travels* (1726) inspired many imitators. Utopian fiction frequently used the image of an ideal society as a form of social criticism, and particularly as a means of focusing on progressive ideas. These writings often redesigned social relations and were seen as a threat to the status quo.[15] Botanists made extensive voyages in search of botanical collections, discovering new species of plants, trees, birds and animals. Linnaeus, who undertook expeditions to northern Sweden, established a new sexual hierarchical cataloguing system of the animal and plant kingdom. Published travel journals also provided examples of alternative views on sexual behaviour and conjured up exotic utopian worlds as major travel expeditions were made to explore new countries and their inhabitants. Captain Cook explored uncharted territories in his voyages between 1768 and 1779, sailing the Pacific Ocean from the coasts of New Zealand, eastern Australia and the South Pacific. Cook related his opinions of the inhabitants of Tahiti in *A Journal of A Voyage Round the World In His Majesty's Ship ENDEAVOUR in the Year 1768, 1769, 1770 & 1771*:

> The women of Otahitee have agreeable features, are well-proportioned, sprightly and lascivious; neither do they esteem continence as a virtue, since almost every one of our crew procured temporary wives among them, who were easily retained during our stay.[16]

Travelogues, neoclassical revivalist publications, artistic depictions of the classical world and erotica were all part of the same cultural sphere. Books such as *The Villas of the Ancients* (1728), based partly on Pliny, and the ensuing James Stuart and Nicholas Revett's *Antiquities of Athens* (1762), helped to revive the interest in classical Greece. Both were arguing in favour of the original Greek form rather than its adulterated Roman style. The English gentleman was not only reading about Greece, but filling his garden with classical buildings. The Pantheon temple in Henry Hoare's gardens at Stourhead appears to have been modelled on Claude's picture, *Coast View of Delos with Aeneas*.[17] Erotic books, such as *The Worship of Priapus*, emerged as a direct result of this interest in the classical world.

All these developments – changes in landscape, travel writing and explorations of new worlds – had an obvious influence on developments in erotica. The extended agricultural allegory reflected a life steeped in a long tradition of rural living, closely connected to nature,[18] using metaphorical language already existing in literature and medicine. These explorations of foreign terrain and their ensuing effect on literature had an inevitable impact on the writing of erotic material.[19] Oceanographic and ethnographic scenic visions emerged to reflect developments in cartography, geography and ethnography. The authors of erotica emulated and assimilated utopian literature and travelogues into their narrative in an alternative portrayal of socio-sexual relations between men and women. Within these tales, analogies were made between the exploration of new territories and medical explorations of women's bodies.[20]

Geographical locations for sex in erotica were going through changes to reflect the growth in understanding of the external environment. The earlier erotic landscape had displayed the classical world of Ovid, with its Arcadia of nymphs and shepherds as seen in such tales as *New Atalantis for One Thousand Seven Hundred and Fifty-Eight*. These utopias reflected the earlier public reading tastes of the English gentleman and his classical education. Newer developments saw the introduction of the botanical garden, and reflected advances in science. By the late eighteenth century, the literary mode of the Greek and Romans had stretched to incorporate the bourgeois novel assimilating the new tastes for the extending middle-class reading audience. This readership was increasingly urban and the setting for erotica was not only the outdoor world of the pastoral but also the interior arcane world of the metropolitan family. However, rather than a complete shift in locations in erotica, there was movement to allow for the new settings of the domestic garden (and later the interior of the domestic middle-class home) to be enjoyed alongside the older, broader and more rural pastoral settings. The emphasis was more on their coexistence rather than substitution of one location for another.

Sexual landscapes

The agricultural landscape

Analogies between the body, nature and landscape were typical in descriptions of the body in the erotic writings of *Ερότοπολις, The Present State of Betty-land* (1684), *A New Description of Merryland* (1741) and *Merryland Display'd* (1741).[21] This erotica saw the creation of 'other worlds' as sexual utopias (Figure 11). These worlds were shaped through the use of metaphorical ribaldry in the terminology of botany and agriculture. In the creation of the sexual world, the agricultural terrain was defined as the female body, a mini-cosmos. Women were the earth itself, responsible for regeneration. Within this erotica, bodies became a euphemistic landscape; hills became breasts, caves became vaginas and shrubs became pubic hair.

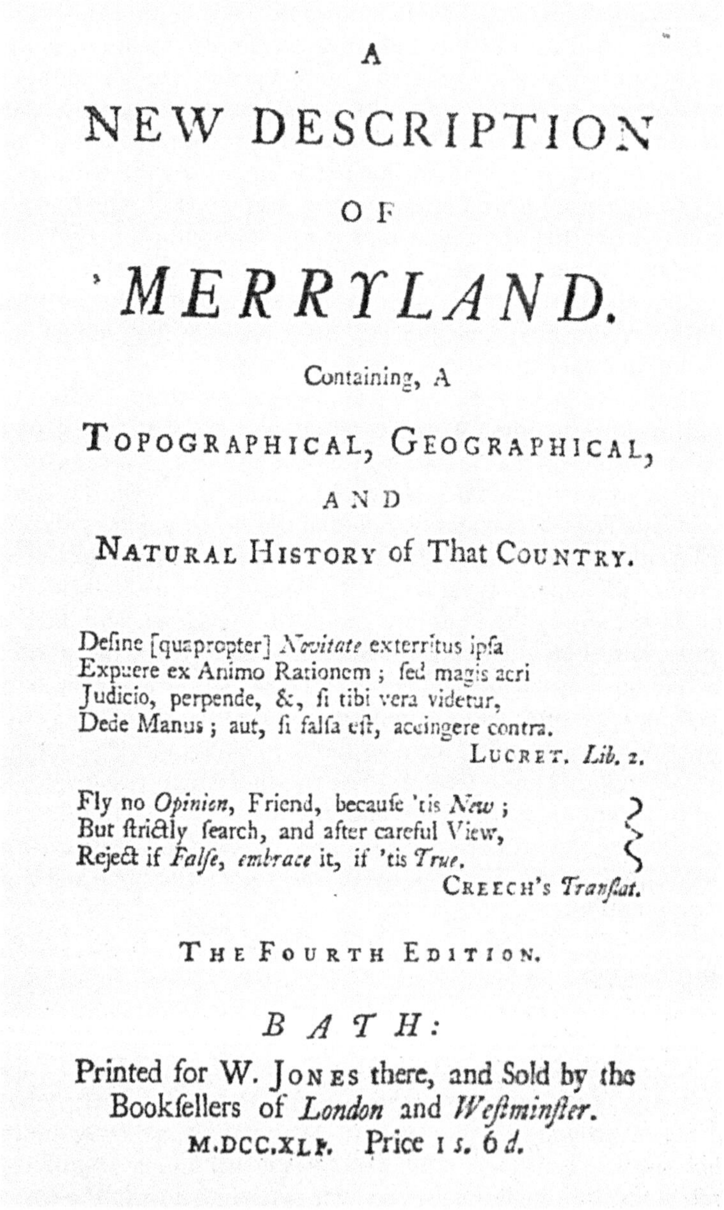

A

NEW DESCRIPTION

O F

'MERRYLAND.

Containing, A

TOPOGRAPHICAL, GEOGRAPHICAL,

A N D

NATURAL HISTORY of That COUNTRY.

Define [quapropter] *Novitate* exterritus ipfa
Expuere ex Animo Rationem ; fed magis acri
Judicio, perpende, &, fi tibi vera videtur,
Dede Manus ; aut, fi falfa eft, accingere contra.
                                        LUCRET. *Lib. 2.*

Fly no *Opinion*, Friend, becaufe 'tis *New* ;
But ftrictly fearch, and after careful View,
Reject if *Falfe*, *embrace* it, if 'tis *True*.
                                        CREECH's *Tranflat.*

THE FOURTH EDITION.

B A T H :

Printed for W. JONES there, and Sold by the
Bookfellers of *London* and *Weftminfter*.
M.DCC.XLF.   Price 1 *s.* 6 *d.*

Figure 11   A New Description of Merryland, 1741.

Marina Warner has identified this commonplace view of Universal Woman in *Monuments and Maidens* whereby 'The female form tends to be perceived as generic and universal, with symbolic overtones; the male as individual, even when it is being used to express a generalised idea'.[22] In the same way in erotica, the earth/'soyl'/nature would be used to describe Universal Sexual Woman. Woman was seen as nature itself, men protecting yet enjoying it. Boucé has argued that the 'earth' or 'nature' in this erotica appears passive, with seeds planted into yielding earth.[23] Yet this earth/soil is frequently active – it spreads diseases, it needs attention or it will become obstreperous, it swells and becomes threatening, and it can give trouble if irked. This nature can be hot in temperament and become demanding (sexually), men having to work hard to pacify and appease it. In this utopia, the Landscaped Body is the embodiment of Sexual Woman, with men as farmers who till and fertilise the soil/woman.

An example of the sexual landscape in utopian erotica can be seen in *Εροτόπολις, The Present State of Betty-land*. The author uses classical references to describe a world where 'The Planet which rules it is *Venus*'.[24] The reader is immersed in a place connected to sex and love, in which the landscape is used to define the corporeal.[25] Trees, shrubs, mountains, rivers, valleys become parts of the body. Sexual imagery is used to explain the effect women have on men: 'if a man make a hole in some part of the mould, and put but an inch of flesh in, it will raise such a flame in his body as would make him think Hell to be upon Earth'.[26] Warnings are given to the farmer who does not look after his land for 'if the husbandman be not very careful to tend it [the soil] and water it himself every night, once or twice a night, as they do Marjoram after Sunset, he will find a great deal of trouble all the year long'.[27] Women are depicted as possessing a high sexual drive. They are seen both to enjoy and need sex, and the deprivation of it makes them unhappy. Yet, a man must work hard if he is to satisfy his wife sexually. Men, with their 'Instruments of Agriculture',[28] need to be at the ready to till their soil and gratify its [woman's] needs. Throughout this scenario of the farmer tilling the soil, superficially men are seen as doing things actively to the soil [woman]. However, the soil retaliates if not satisfied, placing women in control.

A variety of characteristics is given to the landscape. It can be barren, fertile, hot, chalky, red and fiery. Women and their health are described through the guise of soil type. Description of colour of the soil is indicative of the woman's colouring and in turn, her colouring is indicative of her temperament:

for in some places you shall meet with a sandy mould which is generally very rank and very hot in its temperature, so it requires the greatest labour of all to manure it, sometimes you shall light upon a kind of white Chalk or marly kind of Soyl not so difficult to manure. ... sometimes you meet with a brown mould which is of two sorts, either light brown, or dark brown. Husbandmen generally take great delight in manuring either of these, for the Air is there generally wholesome, and not so much annoyed with morning and evening

Fogs and Vapours[29] as the former, besides that, the husbandman shall be sure to have his penny-worth out of them, for they will seldom lye fallow.[30]

Red-haired women are recognised for their hot tempers whereas white, sallow or pale women are easier to handle. However, Asian women are seen as the best choice as they do not suffer 'hysteria' or fits of fainting as the pale (presumably English) women do with their 'Fogs and Vapours'. African and Caribbean women are portrayed as being the most sexually voracious, with an insatiable lust. Advice is given to make sure one pays little and stays only for a short time, 'but if you meet with a black Soyl, be sure you take short Leases, and sit at an easie Rent, lest your back pay for the Tillage, for you must labour there night and day and all little enough'.[31]

Barrenness was ultimately thought to be the fault of the woman.[32] Yet contrary to the traditional view of infertile women as dried-up, desexualised old harridans (as seen in the Old Maid image in the early *Tatler* and *Spectator*), this literature depicts barren women as having a rapacious sexual appetite:

> If the Soyl be barren, all the dung in the world will never do it any good, yet the more barren it is, the more the Soyl cleave and gape for moisture ... the sands of Arabia are not so thirsty, and yet is there were a kind of witchcraft in the Soyl, there are thousands of Husbandmen so strangely besotted, that when they have hap'ned upon such a barren spot as this, yet they will not stick to lay out their whole stock upon it, tho they know it to be all to no purpose, whereby many Husbandmen come to ruine, not being able to pay their landlords.[33]

Women were blamed for the spread of venereal disease. Warnings were given to beware of women with genital crab lice wherein 'the mould being generally corse and rough, and consequently the ground either very morish, or very healthy, and then so full of Vermine withal, that there is no pleasure in the Tillage'.[34]

Overall, a celebration of nature is central to the theme, the intention being to link the sexual to the agricultural world. Female fertility is defined through physiological/topographical analogies. Mountains represent a swelling pregnant belly, the river the orifice for her bodily fluids (vaginal, urinal or menstrual). The representation of pregnancy is embodied in the earth and the seasons:

> the great River is over-look't by a great Mountain which (strange to tell at some seasons of the year) will swell at such a great rate that it is admirable to behold it, the swelling continues near 3/4 of a year, and then upon a sudden it falls as strangely again.[35]

Concerns about the cost of having children continually emerge in this erotica. Men desert their partners to avoid the cost of their impending offspring; 'the Husbandmen accompt the swelling of this Mountain very ominous, for it generally portends a very dear year: they that have not taken a Lease of their Farms, when they see this Mountain begin to swell, will run quite away for fear the law should make them stand to their Bargains.'[36]

The topographical landscape

Ερστόπολις was reprinted in *Potent Ally*, along with *A New Description of Merryland* (1741),[37] an updated and modernised version of *Ερστόπολις*.[38] This new description of Merryland parallels the themes and style of Bettyland but it has moved on from agricultural descriptions of the farmer and his land. The analogies are more reflective of the wider world setting of coasts and topography, with explicit anatomical terminology defining the female body. This time the analogy is extended to depict a woman's body as a whole continent, with its own government, religion, canals, tenures and coastal surveys. Merryland sits in 'a *low* Part of the Continent, bounded on the upper Side, or the Northward, by the little Mountain called MNSVNRS [Mons Venerus], on the East and West by COXASIN [left hip] and COXADEXT [right hip], and on the South or lower Part it lies open to the TERRA FIRMA.'[39] In the stance of a gynaecological exploration, Merryland and 'its Divisions and principal Places of Note' is investigated, with specific explorations of the clitoris and the hymen.[40]

The author raises doubts about the detectability of the hymen. In *Merryland*,

> Another part of the Country, often mentioned by Authors, is HYM [hymen], about which there has been great Controversies and Disputes among the Learned, some denying there was ever such a Place, others positively affirming to have seen it.[41]

This remark is intended not only as a quip about the apparent lack of available virgins, but as a comment about the contradiction of opinion which existed amongst physicians of the day.

Female agonophilia (women enjoying engaging in a pretend struggle before being overpowered by a man) is seen as part of the erotic foreplay. Persuasion and inducements of pleasure are outlined as the first plan of attack. Seduction is likened to the manoeuvring of a battle, using martial terminology to depict the combat:

> At the End of the great Canal toward the *Terra Firma*, are two Forts called LBA [labia], between which every one must necessarily pass, that goes up the Country, there being no other Road. The Fortifications are not very strong, tho' they have *Curtains, Hornworks,*[42] and *Ramparts;* they have indeed sometimes defended the Pass a pretty while, but were seldom or never known to hold out long against a close and vigorous Attack.[43]

This analogy, whereby attaining sexual intercourse is depicted as a battle, is frequently made in erotica. One poem, *The Petit Maître* (1749), suggests that women enjoy the struggle during sex, since 'This is the plain Reason, why most Women refuse to *surrender* upon Treaty, and why they delight so much in being storm'd'.[44]

Heterosexual activity is the main focus in eighteenth-century erotica. Sodomy is rarely discussed. However, the author of *Merryland* does touch on the subject, if only to dismiss the subject as being totally disagreeable: 'I shall leave the Affair of the *Antipodes* to those who have a *Taste* that Way; only shall observe, there are some People who very preposterously (as I think) give the Preference to the PDX [podex]'. Sodomy is considered a trait of foreigners; with the Dutch and Italians depicted as having a partiality for this practice, although the author expresses concern that the vice seems to have crept nearer home, 'and of late Years a few in *Great-Britain* have appeared not altogether adverse to it'.

Problems of having too many children are again a cause for concern in *Merryland*. It is an abundant terrain, yet its fecundity is a source of anxiety, 'The Country is generally fertile enough, where duly manured; and some Parts are so exceedingly fruitful as to bear two or three Crops at a time'. Again, barren women are advocated as a popular choice for a sexual partner. If sex could be obtained without the risk of being followed up by pregnancy, then an infertile woman would do nicely. Men therefore turn to infertile women to avoid father-ing children they cannot afford:

> they would chuse one of these barren Spots, rather than the more fertile ones; and indeed there is some Reason for it, People having by Experience several great Inconveniences by too fruitful a Crop. 'Tis a lamentable Thing for a Man to have too large a Crop, when his Circumstances can't afford Houses to keep it in, or Thatch to cover it.[45]

The stereotype of the 'dried-up old hag' used in other contemporary eighteenth-century literature is not coming into play in erotica. The sterile woman was seen to be a desirable sexual partner, a means to have sex while avoiding unwanted offspring. Various methods of contraception were dis-cussed, but the narrator points out that these practices were not necessarily acceptable to others: 'Some people invented ways of preventing the Seed taking Root or destroy it before it comes to maturity but such Practices are only used by Stealth, and not openly approved of; it is looked on as bad Practice, and we are told it was formerly punished by Death.'[46] Coitus interruptus, contracep-tion, abortion and infanticide were all well-trodden paths, but all had been dis-approved of by the Church.[47]

Venereal disease was also a constant fear. The author warns: 'The Climate is gen-erally warm and sometimes so very hot, that Strangers inconsiderately coming into it have suffered exceedingly; many have lost their Lives by it, some break out in Sores and ulcers difficult to be cured; and others, if they escape with their Lives, have lost a Member.'[48] For the protection against disease, the narrator advocates the use of condoms, detailing their description. He advises 'always to wear *proper cloathing*, of which they have a Sort that is very commodious, and peculiarly adapted to this Country; it is made of extraordinary fine thin Substance, and con-trived so as to be all of one Piece, and without a Seam, only about the Bottom it is generally bound round with a scarlet Ribbon for Ornament.'[49] Judging from the constant mention of genital lice, it would appear that the fear of catching them was also ever-present:[50] '*Cod* [cod-pieces] indeed are often found about the lower end of the great Canal, and *Crabs* in plenty on its Banks.'[51]

Masturbation figures as a sexual activity for the inhabitants of Merryland: 'They are vastly *ticklish*, and so fond of it, that when they can get no-body to please them that way, they will *tickle themselves*.' Incest, however, was considered too dangerous a taboo to be practised as 'to enter again in that Part they were born in, is looked on as an infamous Crime, and severely punishable by Law; yet some have been hardy enough to do it'.[52] Sexual positions and the enjoyment of variations do not seem to have changed over the years. Some liked their sex standing up, but dorsal sex seemed to be particularly popular. The farmer is described at work on his fields: 'then he sticks his Plough in it, and falls to labouring the Soil with all his Might, the Labourer being generally on his Knees: Some work standing; but the other way is the most common.'

The nautical landscape

The writers of erotica were quick to seize on any topical theme. Since oceanic explorations, and books about them, had become popular, erotica followed suit. *A Voyage to Lethe* (1741) saw Captain Samuel Cock makes a voyage in his ship the *Charming Sally*. In praise of the mind-broadening effects of such travels, he declares:

> I know not any thing that more enlarges the Mind of Man than Voyages: They are not only of absolute Use in opening a Commerce with our Fellow Inhabitants of the Globe, but by exhibiting a stupendous Variety of Heavens and Earth, Men and Beasts, Birds and Fishes, they shew the Deity in the most awful and striking Light.[53]

His voyage has been seen as an analogy of marriage[54] but from both the map (Figure 12) and the text it also appears to be the tour of courtship. This voyage could involve losing one's head in the 'Outlet of Reason', being made to look an idiot at 'Fools Cape', gaining optimism on the 'Cape of Good Hope' and finding 'Money', 'Lust' and 'Virtue', as seen in the islands of the same name. Alternatively, it might end in marriage, which contained its own pitfalls in 'Cuckoldom Bay', 'Extravagance Bank', 'Whirlpool of Adultery' and 'Henpeck'd Sand'. Finally, for those weary after this hard battle, there was the Outlet of Death into the Lake of Rest, a euphemism for ejaculation. The journey was not without its perils and could take a lifetime or no time at all, as 'Nothing can be more uncertain than the Time of performing this Voyage: I have known it run in twenty four Hours; sometimes it has taken up a Month; sometimes Years; and sometimes again, but very rarely, it requires the whole Life of Man.'[55] This journey potentially inflicts a wide range of emotions, as seen in the compass to Lethe, which is composed of Love (North), Hate (South), Joy (West) and Grief (East). The authors of erotica had found another seductive theme, taking on oceanic analogy as a tool to express the relationship between men and women.

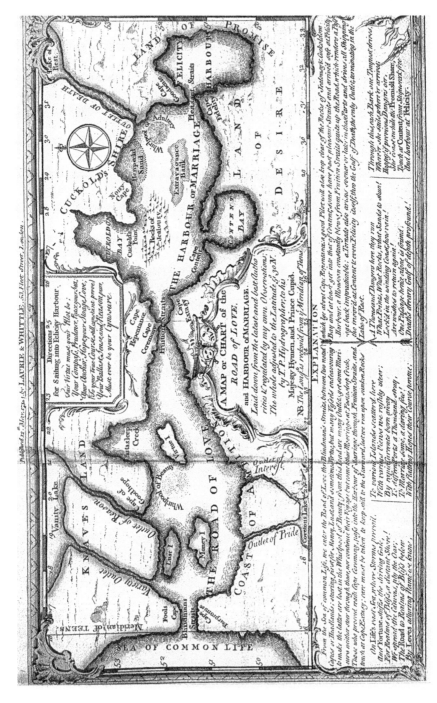

Figure 12   Anon, *A Map or Chart of the Road of Love*, in 'Captain Samuel Cock', *A Voyage to Lethe*, 1741.

Lethe was a popular topic in both mythology and contemporary writing. Lethe literally means oblivion, also known as both the river of forgetfulness, and one of the rivers on which the dead travelled on their way to Hades.[56] Around 1740, David Garrick wrote a short comic piece entitled *Lethe*.[57] Exploration influenced mainstream novels, which in turn affected erotic writings. *Voyage to Lethe* refers to Swift's *Gulliver's Travels*, 'My very good friend indeed Captain *Gulliver*, I am credibly inform'd was solicited some Years ago, by a very great Man, to oblige the learned World, with an accurate Journal to Lethe'.[58] The bound versions of *Voyage to Lethe* carried similar drawings undertaken on voyages round the Pacific, such as 'Monuments on Easter Island' (1744–97) made by William Hodges, draughtsman for James Cook on the *Endeavour*, although these were later additions to the text (Figure 13).[59] These covert messages contained in *Voyage to Lethe* would have been obvious to eighteenth-century readers. Indeed, the picture of Captain Sam Cock is none other than Cook himself (Figure 14).[60]

Nautical analogies were applied to the female body, the ship *Charming Sally* being a metaphor for a woman's body:

> She was of an admirable Dimension, being neither too large for Action, nor too small for making a Voyage with any tolerable Credit or Comfort: She had a most beautiful Slope from Stem to Stern; the one pleasing with an agreeable Jut, the other striking the Eye with all the Sweetness of Majesty; her Port Holes were all of due Aperture.[61]

This effort by the Captain to take care of his ship is virtually identical to the strivings of the Botanist to please his flowers, and the Husbandman to plough his land seen in other erotica described earlier. In these utopias, the stress is on how hard man must work to please a woman. The men might be cautious of women and unsure of their erratic emotions; nonetheless, they revered them. Nautical imagery would continue in later erotic descriptions, as seen in *Harris's List of Covent Garden Ladies for the Year 1788,* an almanac of London prostitutes: 'Miss H-ll-and, No. 2 York-Street, Queen Anne Street is described as 'a *first rate* ship' and 'tho' only seventeen and short, is very fat and corpulent'; the latter two being terms of admiration. The charge at this time was 'only' a guinea.[62]

The classical landscape

The recreation of a classical utopia can be seen in *New Atalantis for the Year One Thousand Seven Hundred and Fifty-Eight* (1758)[63] in one racy tale entitled 'An Introduction, Containing The Origin Of Love And Gallantry'. Set in two mythical islands near Cytherea, the first island, the Island of Shepherds, was populated by the act of tossing rocks over their shoulders (Figure 15): 'They soon procured a number of inhabitants by the stones they threw over their shoulders, being the manner the superior powers intended the human species should be propogated [sic] in this island'. This scene of procreation had been borrowed from Ovid's *Metamorphoses*. Its characters, Deucalion and Pyrrha, after consulting the oracle of Themis, repopulate the earth by throwing stones over their shoulders, the

Figure 13 'Land of the Dupees', *A Voyage to Lethe*. This was a later addition to the bound volume.

damp earth forming new bodies of men and women.[64] Pictures depicting this scene could be found in erotic books[65] and indicate the existence of a shared knowledge of this classical representation amongst the readers.

New erotica works were influenced by the neoclassical revival and fuelled by an increased curiosity about archaeological digs. Pompeii and Herculaneum were

Dodd del.   *Birrell sculp.*

CAPTAIN SAM COCK, F.R.S.

Figure 14   'Captain Sam Cock', ibid.

Figure 15   Le Cabinet D'Amour, '1700'. False imprint.

uncovered in 1738, stimulating further interest. Gentlemen who had conducted the Grand Tour brought back new ideas with them and formed societies to celebrate the classical world. Libertines such as Sir Francis Dashwood, who was later to establish the 'Knights of St. Francis' of Medmenham, also founded the Dilettanti Society in 1732/3 as a result of his interest in Italy,[66] and sponsored expeditions to Greece. Robert Wood (1717–71) visited Greece for the first time in 1742 and 1743, en route to Egypt and Syria. On the second trip in 1750, he was accompanied by John Bouverie (c. 1722–50) and James Dawkins (1722–57). Dawkins was another enthusiastic member of the Dilettanti, footing the bill for the cost of the expedition. The Dilettanti spread knowledge of the expeditions and their findings through their publishing activities including Stuart and Revett's *Antiquities of Athens* (1762). This contained spectacular drawings of their findings and was to play a decisive role in advancing the science of archaeology. In 1763, with the publication of *Marmora Oxoniensia*, Richard Chandler (1738–1810) came to the notice of the Dilettanti, who chose him as the leader of their first mission to Greece.[67] This Greek 'revival' owed much to the work of Johann Joachim Winckelmann (1717–68), one of the main advocates of the primacy of Greek art. Winckelmann's wrote about imitations of classical art, and produced a number of antiquaries' reports. Such publications further stimulated the growing interest in ancient cultures and their fertility rituals.

William Hamilton's discovery of Isternian phallic votive offerings led to the publication of another book of erotica, *An Account of the Remains of the Worship of Priapus* (1786)[68] by yet another member of the Dilettanti, Sir Richard Payne Knight (1750–1824).[69] The history of the book goes back to Hamilton's time spent in Naples as a diplomat. During his thirty-seven years as British envoy to the Neapolitan court of Ferdinand IV, Hamilton pursued activities as collector, connoisseur and scientific investigator. On his arrival in Naples, he had been present at the unearthing of the Temple of Isis at Pompeii. In a letter to Lord Palmerston dated 18 June 1765, he described the recovery of a statue at Pompeii, 'a Venus of white marble coming out of a bath and wringing her wet hair. What I thought was remarkable were that all her *tit-bits* such as *bubbies*, *mons veneris,* etc. are double gilt and the gold very well preserved, the rest of the marble is in its natural state.'[70] In 1769, Hamilton came across the disreputable publisher 'Baron' d'Hancarville whom he appointed to print his manuscripts on his vase collection. Unfortunately, after trying to raise money to publish pornography in an attempt to free himself from debt, d'Hancarville was expelled from Naples. Yet worse, he was still in possession of Hamilton's engraved plates of his collection. Hamilton was left trying to organise a syndicate where members pooled their cash in order to publish the book. There were further delays as not enough subscribers came forward to pay off d'Hancarville's creditors, and as a result, only a hundred copies of each volume were finally sent to London.[71] In 1775, Hamilton sent reports on his findings from his explorations at Pompeii to London's Society of Antiquities, which were read out at a series of their meetings. According to the Minute Book of the Society of the Dilettanti (1798–1815) on 6 March 1803, Hamilton had personally offered some papers[72] relating to Herculaneum to the Dilettanti Society but died before they transferred hands. Only a few fragments of the papers remain in the British Library.

Hamilton had discovered a curious ancient, yet still current, Italian custom of the worship of the phallus in the shape of St. Cosmo's great toe. The worshippers offered penis-shaped votives to ward off impotence and ensure fertility. Writing from Naples, Hamilton wrote to Banks in a letter dated 17 July 1781, 'I have actually discovered the Cult of Priapus in its full vigour, as in the days of the Greeks and Romans, at *Isternia* in *Abruzzo*.' He continued to explain the annual Fete of St. Cosmo's great toe and the votives, the latter representative of the phallus.

> I mean to send [to London] the *Ex voti* and faithful description of the annual fete of St Cosmo's great Toe, (for so the *Phallus* is here called, tho' it is precisely the same *thing*).[73]

These findings were recorded in *An Account of the Remains of the Worship of Priapus* (1786) which consists primarily of two sections: a letter by Hamilton reporting his findings; followed by a section by Payne Knight on 'The Discourse on the Worship of Priapus' commentating on Hamilton's report. In his letter dated 30 December 1781,[74] Hamilton relates how, on 27 September 1780 at Isternia, the Fete of St Cosmo (modern Priapus) was celebrated. Anyone who was impotent could find a remedy: 'Those who have an infirmity in any of their members, present themselves at the great Altar, and uncover the member affected … and the reverend Canon anoints it … . The Oil of St. Cosmo is in high repute for its invigorating quality, when the loins, and parts adjacent, are anointed with it.'[75] In his 'Discourse on the Worship of Priapus', Knight informs the readers about the veneration of the female genitalia:

> The Female Organs of Generation were revered as symbols of the generative powers of Nature or matter as the male were of the generative powers of God. They are usually represented emblematically, by the Shell, or *Concha Veneria*, which was therefore worn by devout persons of antiquity, as it still continues to be by pilgrims, and many of the common women of ITALY.[76]

The book was originally intended for private consumption, and the readership was limited to known gentlemen who shared an interest in such works. Members of the Dilettanti club who had backed Knight's expedition wanted control over the book's circulation. Sir Joseph Banks, acting on behalf of the Dilettanti society, regulated distribution to ensure only those entitled to receive a copy would do so. It may well have been the case that his intention was to restrict the book, but Hamilton experienced difficulties raising the money to publish his findings. Subscriptions were a well-known method of raising the funds necessary to cover the costs of publication, and by asking its own members to subscribe to a copy, the Dilettanti could cover the price of publishing. In the event, only eighty copies were to be circulated, Horace Walpole, Edward Gibbon, James Boswell, Edmund Malone, John Wilkes and the Duke of Portland being among the recipients. At the time, it was considered a highly erotic and subversive book; in 1808, T. J. Mathias pronounced it 'One of the most unbecoming and indecent treatises which ever disgraced the pen of a man who would be considered a scholar and a philosopher'.[77] In his book *Eros Revived*, Wagner suggests that

Knight was 'a romantic and a sensualist masquerading as a scholar'.[78] However, as a member himself, Knight was well known to the rest of the Dilettanti who were the main readership so it is likely they knew his credentials (or lack of them). Many of the Dilettanti themselves were virtuosi or amateur collectors, as indeed was Hamilton, so the question of his scholarship is unlikely to have been an issue.

As a member of the Dilettanti, Knight was circulating within a group of libertines known for their love of classicism and anti-Christian views. Knight was continuing the position of a long line of libertine men, which included Dashwood and Banks, his anti-clerical stance being part of this tradition. Although Dashwood would have been dead by the time the book was published, his ideas would have continued amongst his friends, he being the founding member of the Dilettanti. Considering the intention of the subtext and its condemnation of the over-zealous aspects of Christian morality, Rousseau has quite rightly stated that Knight's main purpose was 'enlightened paganism' not 'the creation of a sexual underworld'. He believes there is no reason to suspect Knight of any deeper or darker motives, and that the attack on him was indicative of a greater restriction on sexual morality towards the end of the eighteenth century.[79]

The theme of female fertility in *Worship Of Priapus* reflects the manifestation of eighteenth-century interest in female self-fertilisation.[80] It is part of a body of erotic writings playing out libertine concerns about female autonomy expressed in allusions to parthenogenesis and cuckoldry. Knight sarcastically refers to the sudden impregnation of 'many barren wives' after the religious festival of St. Cosmo as 'a miracle', which suggests their pregnancy was really a result of the women sleeping for two nights in the church near the friars and priests, while their husbands slept in the 'portici'. This attack on the Catholic clergy was in line with the anti-clerical stance taken in other works of erotica, which depicted sexually debauched priests, and echoes contemporary Protestant rhetoric.

John Camden Hotten, publisher of smutty works, reprinted the work in 1865 as a piece of pornography entitled *A Discourse on the Worship of Priapus*, and included the original plates depicting oral sex and sodomy. The drawings show images of genitalia as classical ruins (Figure 16). The erotic body, this time male, had become part of the archaeological landscape.

Archaeology and sex were closely aligned in the minds of both the libertine neo-classical revisionists and the public. An example of this can be seen in depictions of Emma Hamilton, her notorious affair with Horatio Nelson a source of much gossip. She inspired a series of paintings, sketches and cartoons depicting her posed in classical attitudes; Romney painted her as Medea and Circe (Figure 17); Cosway sketched her in a classical pose; Angelica Kauffmann depicted her as a Comic Muse (Figure 18); and Rowlandson made her into a cartoon life model (Figure 19). Emma was a popular figure of her day, her 'life story' turned into a racy memoir entitled *Memoirs of Lady Hamilton*.[81] In real life, Emma had been deposited with Hamilton, after the waning affections of Charles Greville, Hamilton's nephew. On her arrival in Naples in 1786, Hamilton was quite taken with her beauty. He wrote to Sir Joseph Banks: 'A beautiful plant called Emma has been transplanted here from

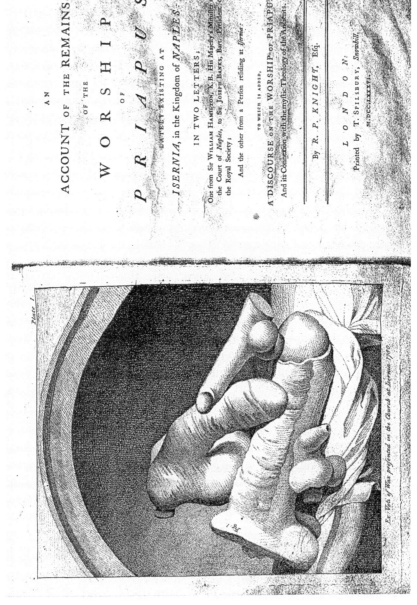

Figure 16 Frontispiece and title-page to *Ex: Voti of Wax presented in the Church at Isternia 1780* in Richard Payne Knight, *An Account of the Remains of the Worship of Priapus*, 1786.

Figure 17 Emma as Circe, by Romney.

Figure 18   Emma Lady Hamilton as the Comic Muse, an engraving after the portrait painted by Angelica Kauffmann, 1791.

England, or at least has not lost any of its beauty.'[82] The botanical metaphor was continuing to flourish alongside this interest in classicism.

By 1788, the amalgamation of all these metaphors, botanical, nautical and classical, culminated in a description in *Harris's List of Covent Garden Ladies for the Year 1788*, of a Miss L—st-r, of No. 6, Union Street, Oxford Road,

> Now arrived at the tempting age of nineteen, her imagination is filled with every luscious idea, *refined* sensibility, and *fierce desire* can unite, her form is majestic, tall and elegant ... [her] *Elysian font*, in the centre of a *black bewitching grove*, sup-

Figure 19   Thomas Rowlandson, *Lady Hxxxxxx Attitudes*.

ported by two pyramids white as alabaster, very delicate, as soft as turtle's down. At the *approach* of their *favourite lord* unfold, and for three guineas he is conducted to this *harbour* of never failing delight. Add to all this, she sings well, is a very chearful [sic] companion, and has only been in *life* nine months.[83]

This fondness for the classics in erotica would continue in depictions of the erotic garden.

The erotic garden

The body as a microcosm of the world was subdivided still further into the erotic garden. Within this vision, the broader topographical theme, as seen in the erotic landscape, contracted into the more diminutive corporeal garden. These grounds became a setting for further development of sexual imagery. This time the sexually pornographic world was placed in increasingly confined areas. Classical style buildings, porticoes, grottoes and statues were all important parts of the erotic garden, in both fictionalised accounts and in real gardens. These spaces provided an added dimension to social interaction and sexual negotiation. Moreover, they created a mood of secrecy where contrived sexual encounters took place in the world of the arcane garden. Whispered conversations were carried on behind hedges, hasty kisses were stolen in shady bowers and the ultimate gratification saw lovers entwined in secret temples or porticoes. Labyrinths and mazes completed the picture of intrigue and mystery. The intention was the creation of seclusion, a retreat into a more private sphere.

The eighteenth-century allegorical utopian garden had its history in the classics and was still largely connected to nature. But this nature had to some extent been 'tamed', it was a nature created by man. To this extent, erotica was in keeping with the themes and ideas expressed by designers of landscaped estates. The trend for laying out the grounds of one's country estate had become increasingly popular, and erotica followed some of the fashions. Woman's body as nature/cosmos/landscape became woman's body as a designer garden, reducing the expressions of the female form into a smaller, more reclusive space, while still connecting it to nature. Despite landscape gardeners' intention to recreate nature, they were nonetheless cultivating a 'look'. Emulating the gardener's work, which brought nature under man's control, the erotic garden brought sex under man's control. More specifically, the woman's body was being 'tamed' within the representation of the designed garden. In this erotica, the tiller of the farms (as seen in *Bettyland*) became the gardeners of the grounds. However, earlier gardeners' visions of the previous century, as seen in the carefully manicured gardens, with their walls, clipped hedges and contained atmosphere, were also cultivated in eighteenth-century erotica. Within erotica, the gardens were often locked, a place where female sexuality could be contained. This visual illustration had earlier depicted the cult of Mary and her virginity as 'a garden close-locked' inside 'a garden close-locked' (Figure 20).[84]

Figure 20   The Virgin Mary as 'a garden close-locked' inside 'a garden close-locked'. From
Livres Chants Royaux, fifteenth century.

These landscaped gardens became fashionable in bawdy and obscene writings. In *Voyage to Lethe*, Captain Cock's garden is a prime example of corporeal analogy as seen in his description of his manor at *Allcock*:

> I must own most singularly curious Shape, and situate withall in a very pleas-
> ant and fertile Part of the Country, being a long Neck of Land, shaded by a
> Grove of Trees, and supported by a couple of Hills,[85] impregnated according to
> the Virtuosi, with a white fort of Metal, which being liquify'd, is deem'd an
> Excellent Restorative. Its Figure towards the end is the Form of a large Nut;
> and there is an Aqueduct thro' it, that terminates in a *jette d'Eau,* as often as it
> is properly suppl'd with Water.[86]

In this version, the female body is displayed through erotic topiary.

By the second half of the eighteenth century, there was a shift in format to satisfy a more sophisticated audience. Although ribald allegories were still very much in circulation, the metalepsis became increasingly complex. In the mildly erotic *The Fruitshop* (1765), a connection is made between topographical descriptions, botanical metaphors and the Garden of Eden. The word 'fruitshop', we are told, comes from the French midwifery for a pregnant woman's being brought to bed: 'l'état de la femme deliverée de son fruit', or the state of a woman being delivered of her fruit. However, in the appendix, the author refers us to a 'fruit-shop' in St. James's Street where satisfaction seems guaranteed. Here the term is applied to a brothel, the fruit being the whores. The information acts as an advertisement to like-minded readers as to where they can find a decent brothel. Horticulture plays a large part in chapter 2, opening with a 'description of the garden [Eden] wherein the first fruit-tree stood', the fruit-tree a synonym for the penis.[87] The original edition of *The Fruit-Shop* carries a picture of a garden scene containing a tree standing before a classical temple, the tree designed as a phallus (Figure 21). A clergyman is holding an ass which is crushing a copy of the book *Tristram Shandy* (Figures 22 and 23).[88] In front of the clergyman a monkey is sitting on the Holy Bible squirting a syringe. Both the picture and the text are an attack on Laurence Sterne.[89] The author rails: 'You are displayed in our fron-tispiece, by way of a satirical gibbet'. The ass in the picture is referred to as 'the four-footed philosopher you cultivated an intimacy with at Lyons', a reference to Crébillon whom Sterne met in Paris in 1762 where they agreed to exchange specimens of their own pornography.[90] The author continues his tirade:

> you have reflected a disgrace on what, when properly supported, ought to be a
> respectable appellation, that of author; by running upon the world repeatedly,
> so many volumes of unconnected and slattern ribaldry; wherefore we exhibit
> you at full length, receiving ablutory chastisement, through what resembles
> your beloved slit of a French girl's petticoat.[91]

Sterne's marriage had turned sour and he had fallen in love with a French girl, Catherine Beranger de Fourmantelle, who was working as a singer in London and York.[92]

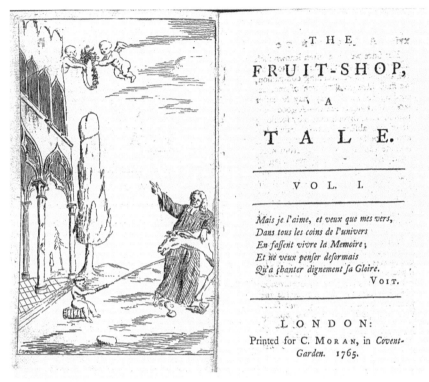

THE

FRUIT-SHOP,

A

T A L E.

VOL. I.

Mais je l'aime, et veux que mes vers,
Dans tous les coins de l'univers
En faffent vivre la Memoire;
Et ne veux penfer deformais
Qu'a chanter dignement fa Gloire.
                                    VOIT.

L O N D O N:
Printed for C. MORAN, in *Covent-*
Garden. 1765.

Figure 21   Frontispiece to *The Fruit-Shop, A Tale*, 1765.

Further jibes are directed at 'Sir Francis' [Sir Francis Dashwood], 'a wight [*sic*] gifted with such frequent uprisings of the standard of humanity, as would do honour to any officer of the guards, young templar, lieutenant of the navy, or profest fortune-hunter of whatever denomination'.[93] Apparently, Sir Francis's garden was put to good use, and 'has been a fertile source of a thousand different and celebrated conjectures, even among those who were the best qualified to devote themselves to profound researches',[94] a 'fertile source' presumably in the double sense as a breeding ground for scandal and a place of love-making. Indeed, the garden in the frontispiece might have been a reference to Dashwood's garden with its Greek temple and the monkey on the Bible the depictions of a shared select joke.[95] It has been suggested that Sterne might have been a visitor to Dashwood's gatherings.[96]

The gardens of the Dashwood estate were indeed designed as a utopia, a homage to classical love. At the entrance was a cave of Venus in the inside of which over a mossy couch was the inscription:

> Ite, agite, o juvenices; pariter fudate medullis
> Omnibus inter vos; non murmura vestra columbae,
> Brachia non hederae, non vincant oscula conchae.

THE

LIFE

AND

OPINIONS

OF

TRISTRAM SHANDY,
GENTLEMAN.

INCLUDING THE

SENTIMENTAL JOURNEY.

Ταράσσει τὸς Ἀνθρώπους ἰ τὰ Πράγματα, ἀλλὰ τὰ περὶ
τὰς Πραγμάτων, Δόγματα.

In FOUR VOLUMES.

VOL. I.

AMSTERDAM:
Printed for P. VAN SLAUKENBERG. 1771.
[Price Two Guineas, with a curious Set of Cuts.]

Figure 22   Frontispiece and title-page to Laurence Sterne, *The Life of Tristram Shandy*, 1771.

Figure 23   Ibid.

[Go into action, you youngsters; Put everything you've got
into it together, both of you; Let not doves outdo your cooings,
nor ivy your embraces, nor oysters your kisses.]

Many original porticoes and follies can still be found on the Dashwood estate.
Cockfights were held in the Temple of Apollo above the archway of which can
be found the motto of The Hellfire Club, 'Liberatati Amicatiaeque Sac' (Sacred
to Liberty and Friendship). The most recent, now late, Sir Francis Dashwood
believed the lake to have been in the shape of a swan,[97] the legs represented
by two small streams which are crossed by bridges of rough-knapped flints
designed by Revett. Revett's Cascade originally consisted of a mass of stone
boulders with retiring statue of Father Neptune at the centre with grottoes on
either side. However, it is more likely that Dashwood originally had the
garden designed in the topographical shape of a woman's body, the form most
suitably viewed from the top of the hill near Dashwood's family church.
Mannix relates the tale of a clergyman's visit, invited by Dashwood to view
the garden from the church tower:

> The clergyman cheerfully agreed and followed Francis to the top of the tower. He
> had just time to realise that he was gazing down at a garden elaborately designed
> to represent the body of a naked woman when Sir Francis gave a signal. Instantly
> a stream of water gushed from the shrubbery triangle while two fountains con-
> cealed in the flowerbeds shot streams of milky water into the air.[98]

The topography probably represented Leda and the Swan.[99] The best evidence of
its shape and form is given by Wilkes in *The Public Advertiser* for 2 June 1763, its
intention to make a sexual playground fairly obvious. He describes a remarkable
Temple where the entrance to it

> is the same Entrance by which we all come into the World, and the Door is
> what some idle Wits have called the Door of Life. It is reported that, on a
> late Visit to his Chancellor, Lord Bute particularly admired this Building
> and advised the noble Owner to lay out the £500 bequeathed to him by
> Lord Melcombe's Will, for an Erection, in a Paphian Column to stand at the
> Entrance, and it is said to be advised it to be made of Scottish pebbles ...
> and, at the Entrance to the Temple ... are two Urns sacred to the Ephesian
> Matron and to Potiphar's wife ... . You ascend to the Top of the Building,
> which is crowned with a particular Column, designed (I suppose) to repre-
> sent our former very upright State ... and is skirted with very pretty
> Underwood.[100]

The Temple of Venus, built in 1748, still stands on a mound where the original house stood. Beneath this is Venus's Parlour, which would appear to give
the female topographical tale credence. Further evidence can be seen in
William Hannan's picture, painted at that time, which hangs in Dashwood's

house and indicates the shape of a female body, with the triangle of trees representing the pudenda.

By the end of the eighteenth century, Erasmus Darwin would depict the erotic garden in *Botanic Garden*. Comprising of two poems, *The Loves of the Plants* (1789) and *The Economy of Vegetation* (1791), it was widely read and the poems well known, referred to in the letters of Horace Walpole, William Cowper, Walter Scott, Samuel Taylor Coleridge, William Wordsworth, Mrs Thrale, Percy Bysshe Shelley and William Godwin. *The Loves of the Plants* was initially published anonymously, and according to Darwin, written solely for money and to make botany agreeable to 'ladies and other unemploy'd scholars'. The poem is significant in that it brings together Linnaeus' sexual classification of plants and the social position, behaviour and functions of women; as Janet Browne notes: 'His version of Linnaeus' system therefore offers an opportunity to study the ways in which gender and views about gender relations were manifested in scientific practice'; Darwin gives 'the plant/woman the central role in characterizing the behaviour or story of each partnership, and the female personalities were allowed to carry the tone and impact of each stanza. The men – the stamens of Linnaeus' scheme – were not given the same attention or depth of characterization'.[101] According to Browne, the garden metaphor played an important role in the courtship between Darwin and Elizabeth Pole; in a poem addressed to her in 1775, Darwin, 'thinly disguised as a wood nymph from his botanic garden, begs that she should not proceed to lop any more trees in the garden'.[102]

This erotica shows how integral the garden had become as a sexual setting. The French writers had already employed the Arcadian setting as seen in *La Nuit Merveilleuse ou Le Nec Plus Ultra du Plaisir*.[103] This was translated into English as *The Voluptuous Night, or, The Non Plus Ultra of Pleasure* (1830). The Idyllic Elysian Garden is placed alongside the Garden of Love, which the amorous couple inhabit. The effect of kissing his lover transports the hero to the classical garden: 'I thought myself transported to the abode of the Gods, or that in the Garden of Imathontè. I was inhaling voluptuousness from the rosy mouth of the most enchanting of the Goddesses.'[104] A night promenade brings the lovers to an enchanting pavilion: 'We trembled as we entered. It was a sanctuary and that the sanctuary of love. The god took full possession of our knees – we lost every power and faculty but that of love.'[105] After making love, they take a stroll in the garden taking in its pleasures. The garden is conducive not merely to sex but to love and all its pleasures. The pavilion conceals inner apartments and is symbolic of the secrets of a woman's body. Once inside the house, the stairs and galleries become a 'labyrinth', the lovers passing through 'a dark narrow gallery'.[106] Everything is directed at creating the illusion of a Grecian Garden of Eden within the grotto or 'aerial grove', with its 'softened lustre', the 'coolness of water', the singing birds, 'green turf' and 'suspended garlands of flowers'.[107]

By the nineteenth century, full-blown analogies of female bodies as gardens had become commonplace. *The New Epicurean or The Delights of Sex facetiously and philosophically considered in graphic letters addressed to a young lady of quality* ('1740'; 1865)[108] stresses the importance of being protected from outside and a need for concealment. The grounds are spacious yet enclosed; to 'render these grounds more private, high walls extended like wings from either side of the house and joined the outer walls'. The description of the grounds suggests unexplored passages 'with umbrageous walks, alcoves, grottoes, fountains, and every adjunct that could add to their rustic beauty'. Seclusion and secrecy are evoked where a flourishing fruitfulness can be nurtured and sexual freedom enjoyed:

> In the open space, facing the secret apartment before alluded to, was spread out a fine lawn, embossed with beds of the choicest flowers, and in the centre, from a bouquet of maiden's blush roses, appeared a statue of Venus, in white marble at the end of every shady valley was a terminal figure of the god of gardens in his various forms; either bearded like the antique head of the Indian Bacchus; or soft and feminine as we see the lovely Antinous; or Hermaphroditic – the form of a lovely girl, with puerile attributes. In the fountains swam gold and silver fish, whilst rare crystals and spars glittered amidst mother o'pearl at the bottom of the basins.

Within this work, juxtaposing of open spaces and secret closed spaces makes assumptions about the body. The analogy is made obvious; the fine lawn represents the pubis and pubic hair, with the choicest of flowers being the vagina; the maiden's blush is a representation of the hymen and a symbolism for virginity and innocence; the allusion to secret places 'in shady valleys', symbolic of vaginal passages, is interrupted with the erect phallus of the garden god Bacchus, standing at the entrance to the Valley or vagina (since some of the figures of the garden are female we can presume this might be an allusion to female-with-female sex which comes later in the book); the fountains represent the ejaculations. We are informed that this is a garden of sex since the gardeners are allowed in on Mondays and Tuesdays only, 'the remaining four days being sacred to Venus and love'.[109] Concealed entrances give access to hidden erotic places shrouding the place in mystery, hinting at the pleasure therein: 'This garden had three massive doors in its walls, each fitted with a small lock made for the purpose, and all opened with a gold key, which never left my watch guard.'[110] Finally, even the furniture was sexualised, being 'in the French mode' (anything French being seen as infused with sex). The eroticisation of this terrain creates a unique location in which to place the plot and sets the scene for the delights which follow.

Conclusion

In fictional accounts, earlier utopian settings were pastoral and enjoyed the rural aspects of life. By the end of the century, it was obvious that writers of erotica had been influenced by the broadening world map. The neoclassical revival, mainstream fictional and factual travelogues, together with the interest in land-scaping estates and gardens would all influence new erotic utopias.

The importance of the garden as a focus of sexual pleasure is striking in eighteenth-century erotica. The idea that 'nature knows best' was a notion culled from classical philosophy, one that celebrated sexual activity. The publishers and writers of erotica such as Curll, Knight and Darwin were therefore reviving the equation between nature and sex in their neoclassical representations. The fictional landscape was Arcadian or pastoral, a sensual evocation of nature at its best; either free or wild, or both. The restraint of nature was condemned. Yet, in the real world, attempts were being made to recreate the Garden of Eden as an earthly paradise. The major preoccupation of landscape gardeners such as William Kent, 'Capability' Brown and Humphrey Repton was to reshape hills and lakes, moulding nature into patterns selected by man. These cultivated gardens would eventually become part of the new erotic utopias.

The gender relations inherent in this space were taken from descriptions of the natural world. The trope of the landscaped body varied according to which current influence was topical, whether it was the world of agriculture, anatomy, travel or archaeology. Within these worlds, a clearly defined set of gender rela-tions was drawn up which displayed sexual interactions between men and women. These images of women were closely linked to nature: women were the cosmos, men lived within. Characterisation of women showed less the modest nurturing side of nature than the wild and uncontrollable side. Images depicted women as passionate and sexually powerful (as nature). In the main, woman/landscape/ship/garden was revered and sex celebrated with sexual activ-ities mutually enjoyed. Men were their polar opposite, the controllers, the farmers and travellers within these unwieldy landscapes. This points to male anx-ieties felt about the enigma of female sexuality and their vulnerability in their ability to subjugate it. Nonetheless, the writers show an obvious interest in the pleasuring of women and such statements stand against the domestic ideology which identified women as non-sexual and passive. Women were depicted as rev-elling in sex and it was therefore in a man's interest to know how to satisfy them. When the male body was depicted as landscape, it was in the structured form of classical architecture. This rigid form points to a disciplined male body, one that is constructed and controlled. Again, this can be seen as the antithesis of the unrestrained 'natural' body of the female.

The changing shape of space in British landscape was paralleled in erotica, the structure of cultural and spatial views altering to fit different agendas. The interest in the early agricultural world showed woman/landscape as wild and abandoned nature simultaneously reflecting the rural perception of the sur-roundings. The interest in landscape gardening saw owners of large estates introducing major innovations to their properties, often in Arcadian fashion, with nude statues, erotic grottoes, fluid cascades and sensual waterfalls. As a result, English erotic material introduced similar features, with either the more tamed features of the landscaped garden's 'natural' look, or the private world of the walled garden (the latter being inherited from the previous centuries).

The erotic garden became more prevalent from the 1740s onwards. Although the macrocosmic utopia and botanical analogies continued right through the century, this form was used more in ribaldry rather than to arouse. The microcosmic world of interiors was increasingly called upon as a more suitable place for the erotic, eventually moving from the garden into the interior rooms, where parlours, secret closets and nunneries (the latter inherited from the French)[111] enabled the creation of a more stimulating and dangerous backdrop.

6
Anti-Catholic Erotica

This Hermaphrodite Order, [the Gilbertines] made up of both Sexes, did very soon bring forth Fruits worthy of itself; these holy Virgins having got almost all of them big Bellies ... . These Nuns to conceal from the World their Infamous Practices, made away secretly their Children; and this was the Reason, why at the time of the Reformation, so many Bones of Young Children were found buried in their Cloisters, and thrown into places where they ease Nature.

Gabriel D'Emiliane, *A Short History of Monastical Orders*[1]

The sexual activities of priests, female penitents, monks and nuns were to become a major preoccupation in a corpus of erotic anti-Catholic material during the long eighteenth century. A multiplicity of books and pamphlets describing their cavortings was published and reprinted, all taking up similar themes. Some of them addressed the debauched activities of priests; some focused on the seduction of young nuns by secular young men. This material provided many of the first basic elements that would be included as principal features of later English pornography.

This erotic sub-genre was a pivotal point in the development of erotic writing, bringing together sex and religion for the main purpose of arousing the reader. Although there is a long history of writings connecting sex and religion, its main focus had been the use of sex for attacking the Church. Earlier works had tended to use sexual accusations as ammunition in debates about the corruption of the Catholic Church whilst highlighting the hypocrisy and lasciviousness of the clergy. This was true of both seventeenth-century English works and of French material, the latter carrying its objective through to the eighteenth century.[2] Whereas earlier English eighteenth-century material had included a degree of sex among a welter of anti-clerical attacks, later pornographic anti-clerical works encouraged this sexual element to flourish, with its prime intention to cause sexual arousal. The topical material falls loosely into four categories: First was the anti-Catholic polemic, a specific response to home-grown fears about inveigling priests and the seduction of young innocent Protestant women. The seventeenth and early eighteenth centuries saw a surge of English denunciations of the Catholic clergy which employed venomous or satirical attacks in order to expose the sexual misdemeanours of priests, its primary function being as propaganda against the Catholics. The second category comprises English reports of French priests' trials. Catholic priests accused of seduction came under examination in court, and deputations about their sexual activities were transcribed and reported back to England, either verbatim or in greatly exaggerated form. Such reports ranged from what purported to be 'a true and accurate account' to blatant fabrication of sexual scenarios with notorious priests named as protagonists. In the English translations of the reports of the trials of Abbé des Rues and Father Girard (examined below), sex was brought even further to the forefront than in earlier attacks. Although written in the form of concern for the female penitent, the explicitness of the sexual details indicates an intention to arouse sexually. The third type of material can be seen in the nunnery tales, a spin-off from both the anti-Papist rhetoric and the trial reports written in the form of Gothic fiction. These stories explore sexual initiation of innocent young noviciates. The fourth type of material was French pornographic prose-style novels and their English translations.[3] This material, again purely fictional, made no apology for its blatant pornographic style. Not all this material fits neatly into categories. *Venus in the Cloister*, for example, overlaps the third and fourth categories. It fits into the former, as a nunnery tale, and the latter, in that it is French pornography yet still in dialogue form and has not yet developed into prose as in the later eighteenth-century nunnery tales or some of the French pornographic novels. Though it is also a nunnery tale, it is not over-concerned with the treatment of nuns, as with some of the examples of this genre. To some extent, there was a cross-over between all four sub-sets in the genre, in that the factual exposés of genuine seductions were frequently recounted in the same language as fictional descriptions of priests debauching young female penitents. This mix was confused still further by the fact that some erotic fabrications attempted verisimilitude by writing in documentary prose and adding factual footnotes.

French pornographic material was to profoundly influence the development of English pornographic material. A parallel can be seen between French attacks on the Church of Rome and English attacks on dissenters from the seventeenth century onwards in that they had shared primary aims; the objective was vilification of the religion rather than erotica for the sake of sex alone. Aggression towards dissenters came in the form of violence and sexual slander resulting from public fear, ignorance and resentment. This can be seen in the hostility shown to Quakers, Anabaptists and Methodists. Quakers were blamed during periods of economic hardship as they were the middlemen in the grain trade. Tales circulated of Anabaptists and Quakers cutting their enemies' throats, thereby fuelling violent public reaction. Methodist itinerant preachers were accused of seduction and became the butt of many a sexual jibe. Both Methodists and Quakers were accused of usurping the patriarchal role in the family. Mobs vandalised preaching-houses and even killed sectarians.[4] Erotica gave vent to this animosity targeting the dissenters, mainly in the form of caustic parodies, which carried descriptions of sexual encounters. This body of work has, to some extent, already been examined.[5] This chapter will therefore concentrate on the anti-Catholic material since it formed the bulk of the more obscene material. It was this material which most influenced the development of English pornography.

The material under study ranges from the raucous to the obscene. Some texts used satire or humour. Conversely, the more cutting anti-Papist rhetoric was often violent and aggressive. More importantly, a subtle shift is evident in anti-clerical sexual material available at different times through the late seventeenth and eighteenth centuries. Sex became the prime aim, the religious background reduced to a setting for sexual scenarios. Descriptions of sexual activities became extended, more detailed and at the forefront. An awareness developed of how religious anxieties could be channelled in material which would not only titil-late, but also excite in a more profound sexual way.

This was the beginning of the pattern of pain and pleasure most readily explored in flagellation, which would provide grounding for the later more extreme nineteenth-century sado-masochistic English pornography.[6] Although experiences of pain had been enjoyed in earlier defloration scenes, material in which flagellation occurred would expound on the themes of domination and submission. These elements included the unconsciousness of women during sexual activities; passive and aggressive mannerisms; positioning of the body; and flagellation. Early French convent erotica helped to instigate later English flagellation material. Most important to the English, however, was the threat of the convent to family life, and suggests why the family would become a central theme in later English erotica in the exploration of incest.[7]

English attitudes towards Catholics

> The *Licentious familiarities of Father N. with Mother N.* have been, these past thirty-eight years, the *scandal* of all *Provins*. It was begun by *magnificent treats*, which he caused to be fetched from town, for her, and her party; was continued by *presents of rings, watches, and looking glasses*, and all kinds of vanities, which were even laid on the Altar for her ...

> Anon, *The Nunns' Complaint against the Fryars*[8]

Such remarks were based on the real report made by the French nuns of St. Katherin's [*sic*] convent against their friars. It is an example of why the Catholic Church was perceived by the English Protestants as corrupt, hypocritical and tyrannical and thereby an acceptable target for sexual slander. Furthermore, the confessional was seen as a seduction ploy by English anti-Catholic writers and therefore provided yet further ammunition for attack. The confessional was believed to be particularly damaging since the confessor could influence the conduct of wives and daughters, inciting subversion of entire families. Much of eighteenth-century pornographic fiction was therefore in the form of confes-sions. The 'confessional technique' was one peculiar to our society from 1700 onwards and was a result of political, economic and technical revolution; 'confessions of the flesh' became increasingly popular with the need for self-examination. Although actual incidents of illicit sexual activity may not have fallen, the Counter-Reformation brought with it a new and more repressive attitude towards sexual expression.[9] But within English erotica, the attacks on both the confessional and the convent appear to be concentrated on protection of the Protestant family rather than calls for sexual repression. Indeed, within serious attacks on the priests and the convents, suppression of both male and female sexuality was seen as unnatural. More specifically, the enforced celibacy of priests and nuns was seen as an aberration since Protestants held that sex was necessary, but to be restricted within the realm of marriage. For them, the proper, and safest, environment for a young girl's upbringing was under the jurisdiction of her family.

Risqué anti-Catholic erotica developed in eighteenth-century England as a result of prevalent attitudes to the clergy. But where did anxieties about the Catholic religion come from? What were the tensions these beliefs provoked in the 'respectable' Protestant family? What were the influences that buttressed and reinforced English anti-Popery attacks? And how did these opinions become assimilated into an anti-clerical agenda within erotica? Before turning to the erotic material itself, an attempt must be made to answer these questions. We can then begin to see why there was such a ready English market for anti-Catholic erotica and the reasons for its formulaic style.

Protestant hostility can be traced to three main elements in the eighteenth century: political distrust, theological disagreement and popular fear.[10] The political perception was that Catholics could not be trusted in their allegiance to the Crown since they were first and foremost subject to the Pope. Since the Reformation, this principal anxiety was reinforced by Catholic plots against Elizabeth and the infamous Gunpowder Plot in 1605. National antagonism surged with the Jacobite rebellions of 1715 and 1745, and again in the Gordon Riots of 1780.[11] Theologically, Popery was seen as a perversion of true Christianity. Protestants viewed confessionals, penances and dispensations with disdain, as an easy way to dispose of guilt, an excuse for not following a truly virtuous path. Popular fears were fuelled by earlier persecutions by the Papists in the Inquisition with the burning of heretics and the use of the rack. Catholic proselytising was seen as an insidious threat, their tight control over education a way of brainwashing naive young minds. Most important in relation to erotic material, Protestants were at pains to emphasise the threat of priests and the hold they had over women. Priests were seen first to corrupt women spiritually, by turning them against the faith and submitting them to the authority of their confessors; and then to corrupt them bodily once they had broken their spiritual resistance. Furthermore, their encroachment on the family unit usurped the role of the husband and father, and thereby undermined his patriarchal authoritative role.

The press laboured to fuel antagonisms against Popery during the early eighteenth century. London newspapers and anti-Catholic pamphlets priced to be within reach of the lower-middling ranks and artisans gave detailed coverage of Catholic atrocities abroad.[12] Abundant contemporary evidence is available regarding other methods by which anti-Catholicism was passed on to the illiterate, such as through the spoken word, conversation, poems, sermon and pageants. Prints, cartoons and woodcuts would have reached many more. Foxe's *Book of Martyrs*,[13] with its images of tortured women and children, proved extremely popular during the eighteenth century. These pictures were used to expose the extent of the persecutions by the papists in the Inquisition, a sight to inflame the passions of all good Protestants. Writers and artists joined in the condemnation of the Catholics. Daniel Defoe wrote that Popery was 'the Hobgoblin, the Spectre with which the Nurse fright the Children, and entertain the old Women all over the Country'.[14] William Hogarth mocked Catholicism in his pictures. *Transubstantiation Satirized* (1735)[15] depicts baby Jesus fed into a huge machine, which churns out hosts made from his body. His *Calais Gate, or the Roast Beef of Old England* portrays a fat monk salivating over imported English beef while barefoot nuns inanely rejoice at having found an image in a skate-fish. Thomas Rowlandson joined in with his depictions of lascivious monks in *The Discovery*, and mainstream books were illustrated with lurid pictures as in *The Monk* (1796). Thus anti-Catholic images were widespread and permeated to the heart of English culture.

Visitors abroad fed back anecdotes about corrupt Roman Catholic practices, reinforcing anti-Catholic feeling in England. 'Popish superstition', such as relics, miracles and indulgences, instilled indignation in travellers.[16] Latin services were seen as a contrivance to maintain control over their Catholic following and to retain an air of mystery over their religion. Religious flagellation was viewed with particular contempt, one tourist remarking: 'One sees such processions, such penitents, and such nonsense, as is enough it give one ye gripes.'[17] English travellers showed their aversion to these practices through their bad behaviour, one defecating on the steps of the altar and another allowing his dog to jump on the priest during Mass and eat the host. On his visit to the Sistine Chapel, Sir Francis Dashwood was so disgusted at the spectacle of the penitents flogging themselves that he picked up a whip and commenced to whip them himself.[18] Reports of the lax morals of the Catholic clergy were related back to Britain. John Locke, in his account of his travels during 1675–79, painted a lubricious picture of Cardinal Bonzi, the Archbishop of Narbonne, whom he saw at Mass: 'He keeps a very fine mistress in the town, which some of the papists complain of, and hath some very fine boys in his train.' The sexual incontinence of French clerics was an issue for another British traveller who encountered the two orders of St. Augustine and St. Francis. He reported 'for courtship and toying with the wenches, you could easily believe that it had been a trade with which they had not been a little acquainted; of all men, when I am marryed, God keep my wife from them, till then, my neighbours'. Visiting the now infamous Loudain, Thomas Killigrew, the playwright, witnessed the sordid exorcisms by the friars on the nuns in the Ursuline convent, particularly noting one nun's outrageous behaviour as she tried to 'abuse the Frier, thrusting out her Tongue, & then catching him about the neck to have kist him'.[19]

Contemporary reports of convents show how and why erotica appropriated the nunnery as a suitable setting for unlicensed female sexual activities.

Nunneries were seen as hotbeds of vice, places where young girls were sexually corrupted. The convent therefore became another location in which to set lascivious tales. Indeed, England had its own long pedigree of tales about debauched nunneries. English medieval episcopal visitational records are full of examples of the various immodest cavorting of the nuns, with reports of them throwing parties, dancing with men and engaging musicians. After being entertained by wandering minstrels, one young nun ran off 'in apostasy cleaving to a harp player'.[20] Immorality was widespread, the records uncovering various priests' illicit affairs resulting in several pregnant nuns. After the Reformation, Catholic schools were illegal in England until 1778 and daughters of the Catholic families were often sent abroad to convent schools, such as the Benedictine nuns at Cambrai and the Augustinian Canonesses in Paris, where they benefited from a formal education and accomplishments well suited to the fashions of the day. In 1784, the Norfolk baronet, Sir William Jerningham, placed his fourteen-year-old daughter Charlotte at the Ursulines in Paris where Maria Fitzherbert, later mistress to the Prince Regent, was also educated.[21] Nunneries proved useful places to deposit young women from noble and gentry families in cases where there were many daughters to dower and sons had to be set up in the world.[22] Sometimes women were placed there against their will. Indeed, forced vocations were a real abuse in France, and, to a large extent, the English fantasy of life in the convent was based on French realities.[23] Writing in 1760, Denis Diderot[24] based his *La Religieuse* (*The Nun*) on a true contemporary case. He describes the life of a nun, Marguerite Delamarre, who unsuccessfully attempted to have her vows annulled on the grounds that she had been placed in a convent against her will. Priests and Catholic men made a real business of secreting young girls out of England to deposit them in convents abroad.[25] English Protestants saw this confinement of women as unnatural and perverse.[26] Mrs Montagu, in the Earl of Bath's party to Spa, wrote in 1763: 'We visited the Nunnerys in every town; Mrs. Carter constantly expressing the greatest abhorrence of their strict vows, and sequestered life ...'[27]

Such reports of corruption in the Catholic Church, and the specific issue of transgression, were to have a direct influence on the themes that would arise in fiction. Aphra Behn's *The Rover* (1677) describes tyrannical Roman Catholic relatives installing young girls in convents. By the end of the eighteenth century, Gothic novelists such as Ann Radcliffe were exploring depictions of sweet and dignified nuns in *Sicilian Romance* (1790) and conveying convent life as a moral and spiritual waste in *Romance of the Forest* (1791). Similar rhetoric resonated in Matthew Lewis's *The Monk* (1796), one of the most popular novels to depict nuns as victims of monasticism. His image of Sister Agnes, half-crazed in a dungeon clasping the decomposing body of her illegitimate daughter, was already common in convent exposés. This image would reverberate in erotic tales and more obscene fiction. Lax teachings, infamous doctrines and the commercial dealings of the Jesuits were particular favourites and were to become central themes in this thriving genre of erotica which demonstrated sexual disgrace and scandal within the Roman Catholic Church. Having looked at the anti-Catholic feelings in England, the following section will examine the propaganda which supported such enmity.

Anti-Papist propaganda

A genuine case of seduction

One English case of seduction by a priest came to light in *The ACCOUNT of the Seducing of Ann, the Daughter of Edward Ketelbey, of Ludlow, Gent. to the Popish religion*. Although not written as a piece of erotica, it highlights anxieties concerning sexually corrupt priests, arousing sufficient concern for the case to be presented to Parliament. Furthermore, it conveys just how seriously English Protestants took the threat of Catholic priests seducing their womenfolk. The pamphlet relates anecdotal evidence of the circumstances of a young girl who has been seduced into the Catholic religion through the wiles of a cunning priest.

> Mr. Ketelbey being often from home, particularly in the years 1696 and 1697 with his Wife and part of his Family, leaving only his Daughter, of the Age of Nineteen, and Servants at home, a Popish Family coming Strangers into the Town, and Living near him, obtained Leave of the Daughter to walk in the Garden being pleasant for Air, and by this means two young Ladies of that Family insinuating themselves into the Daughter's Acquaintance, with the assistance of one *Windsor*, a reputed Popish Priest, living with them, (who pretends to Practice Physick now, but in King *James* Reign shewed himself more open) Seduced her to the Popish religion; but Instructed her of what dangerous Consequence it might be if discovered, both the Seducer and Seduced being punishable with Death; which made her for a long time disown and forswear her Conversion to Popery.[28]

The language implies a sexual seduction, the girl complicit in the secret. The daughter exhibited changes in her manner, and her attitude and temperament altered after her conversion to the Catholic Church. Her mother, the first of the family to return to the country, found her daughter's humour changed since she had taken to 'disowning her Mother's Power and Authority over her, and denying to do several Things she Commanded without the Advice of her Friends, meaning the Papists that had Seduced her'. Although at first the concern here appears to be the girl's religious conversion, it turns out that the real danger is the loss of familial control. This occurs through the complete breakdown of the father's authority. On his return to the household, he found his daughter

> full of Equivocations and Lying Stories, and even denying that which seemed most apparent Truth, as to the Circumstances of her Change, the Method of

her Seduction, and the Persons who Seduced her, affirming that she was a very good Protestant, and gave out that there was nothing in it, but her Mother's Unkindness, who never Loved her from a Child, and Fondness to her Brother, which brought that Scandal and Reproach upon her of being a Papist, on purpose to deprive her of her Father's Favour.

Members of the family are set against each other, Ann flinging accusations of emotional indifference and parental neglect. Lies and secrets betray the collapse of the family relationship and emphasise the extent of moral decay which has filtered into their lives through interference from outside the home. The daughter is examined by the doctor: 'upon her Examination by the Doctor of the Parish, and other Protestant Divines, they thought her Stedfast therein'. This appears at face value to be an examination of her religious beliefs, but the lack of clarity leaves open the potential for double meaning. Although the examiner appears to be a doctor of divinity, through duplicity of language, there is an inference that he is examining the chasteness of her body as well as the purity of her religion. Both her bodily and religious virtue are synonymous, her hymen and her religious doctrine under suspicion of being broken. Her virginity is directly connected to her religion, the veracity of her story and her virtue directly dependent on her chastity. The story exemplifies the equation Protestants made between spiritual and sexual fidelity. If a woman was not spiritually trustworthy, she was unlikely to be physically faithful.

Spiritual corruption is therefore closely linked to sexual degeneration. This point is forced home in another piece of propaganda, *A True Account of the Unaccountable Dealings of Some Roman Catholick Missioners of this Nation. For Seducing Proselytes from the Simplicity of the Gospel to the Roman Mystery of Antiquity* (1703). In 'a particular Relation of a Gentlewoman lately seduced out of a *true Catholick Family*', the author uses the analogy of a whore and her activities in a comparison with the Catholic Church and its depravities:

> By this Way we know certainly, that *the Church of Rome* hath corrupted herself, is becoming of a faithful City and *Harlot*, hath committed *Fornication with the Kings of the Earth*, and is so full of *Abomination and Scandals*, that all Churches and People, which have any Sense of, and Concern for the Honour and Interest of our Lord and Saviour Jesus Christ, ought to *declare* against them.[29]

Moreover, the seduction of the pious female soul through '*Secret Suggestions* of Affrightment as well as Allurements' was provided as an example of the Catholic Church's potential for assault on female virtue. A further incitement was issued in *A Letter to a Missionary Priest* dated 23 August 1700, in which one young convert declared to her priest:

> I am constrained by an invisible Power, to make my Address to you. I have too long resisted its Motion ... if I have any Experience in the secret Conduct of

my own Soul or if I dare may speak my thoughts (Pardon me Sweet Jesus) I cannot submit to the Restraint he lays on me of not coming to see you.[30]

Sensually provocative expressions defined female converts as smitten lovers.[31] It is of little surprise that fathers and mothers were concerned about protecting their daughters' chastity when confronted with such passionate declarations.

This anti-Catholic rhetoric used submissive phraseologies of converts, themes of resisting, restraining and yielding. These expressions would be appropriated by erotica, which allowed for an exploration of another dimension of authority/control in dominant/submissive erotica. Primarily Protestant women were conveyed as modest and chaste, yet once violated they would yield to their base sexual impulses. A dual and contradictory image of woman reverberated in this depiction of the female convert;[32] one in which women were naturally chaste; another in which women were sexually insatiable.[33]

Calls for castration

As a result of the perceived threat posed by predatory priests, a whole collection of English anti-Papist tracts emerged calling for their castration.[34] In one 26-page pamphlet, *Reasons Humbly Offer'd for a Law to enact the Castration of Popish Ecclesiastics* (1700), priests are said to be better lovers than other men, their enthusiasm a result of their hitherto enforced celibacy. The priests, 'being pampered and restrained from the Marriage-Bed, must needs be more inclinable to Venery than other Men, and consequently more pleasing Companions to insatiable Women, and therefore the better fitted for the practice of *creeping into Houses, and leading captive silly Women, laden with divers Lusts'*.[35] Their greater virility is seen as a threat to Protestant manhood, playing on males' fears of cuckoldry. The author[36] accuses the priests of having

> an Opportunity of bringing to their Lure a buxom Wife, who perhaps had a sickly, weak, or absent Husband, a Green-sickness Daughter, or a wanton Maid; they would by the same Means become masters in a manner to all that belong'd to the Family, have the command of their Purses, know all their Secrets and improve all to the advantage of the See of *Rome*.[37]

Both serious and humorous attacks on priests and the Church continued in a deluge of pamphlets and books, including *A Full View of Popery, in a Satirical Account of the Lives of the Popes ... Written by a Learned Spanish Convert* (1704), *Popery Display'd: or, The Church of Rome Described in Her True Colours* (1713), *A Full and True Account of a Dreaded Fire that Lately Broke Out in the Pope's Breeches* (1713), *The Priest Gelded: Or, Popery At The Last Gasp Shewing* (1747), printing both new and older reworkings of earlier material; the latter, for example, contained much of the same material found in *Reasons Humbly Offer'd*.[38] Enforced celibacy is blamed for priests' sexual promiscuity. Forbidding priests to marry 'lays them under a Temptation peculiar to their Order'.[39] Secret communication with women provides the confessors with an opportunity to corrupt the penitents. They 'have an Advantage of knowing the

Inclinations, and of private Converse with Women by their auricular Confession, and by their pretended Power to give Pardon, have a Door open to persuade the committing of one Sin for expiating another; and accordingly improve it, by leading Captive silly Women'.[40] Women are again presented as innocent and gullible, yet culpable, as they are so easily subject to flattery. It was therefore better to allow them no contact with priests. It was advised 'that no Man ought to confess a Wife but her Husband, and that a Daughter ought to be confess'd by none but her Father'.[41] But far away the most secure method of prevention of such incidents altogether is gelding the potential offenders. 'The Castrating of Popish ecclesiastics will be so far from being a Loss to the Laics of *Great Britain*, that it will be the greatest friendship imaginable done to them.'[42]

Exposés of Catholic clergy

Anxieties surrounding corrupt Catholic clergy were apparent in lewd exposés of concupiscent clerics. *The Frauds of the Romish Monks and Priests* (1691) proved particularly popular,[43] reaching its fifth edition in 1725, to which a second volume, *Observations on a Journey to Italy*, was added. Amongst a vast array of other accusations, the author, said to be Gabriel D'Emiliane, attacked the priests for their treatment of female penitents, using explicit depictions of debauched priests. These allegations played on particular concerns around the confessional as a means of seduction:

> Indeed Auricular and Secret Confession, is the most commodious way the Priests have to lodge their Game; 'Tis there they put Women to the Question, and by this means accustoming them (by little and little) from their Youth up to speak with confidence of their secret Sins, they make them at length, lose that natural Shame-facedness, which otherwise they would be sensible of, in making the least mention of such filthiness.[44]

D'Emiliane followed this up with further lurid accounts of seduction, pregnancy and infanticide in *A Short History of Monastical Orders* (1693) in which the various sins of different religious orders are described.

Wagner attributes *The Frauds of the Romish Monks and Priests*[45] and *Observations on a Journey to Italy* to Antonio Gavin.[46] However, Ashbee refers to D'Emiliane as the author of these two books, as does the British Library Catalogue. Ashbee states that Quérard, in *La France Littéraire*, confused the work of Gavin with D'Emiliane.[47] *La France Littéraire* does indeed state that D'Emiliane was a pseudonym used by Gavin.[48] The French translation of the former book entitled *Ruses et Four-heries des Prêtres et des Moines*, carried the name D'Emiliane. D'Emiliane's *A Short History of Monastical Orders* contained an advertisement dated 3 February 1692, which points to D'Emiliane as the author. The advertisement announces: 'The Frauds of the Monks and Priests, set forth in Eight Letters lately written by a Gentleman in his Journey to *Italy* and Observations on Journey to *Naples* wherein the Frauds of the *Romish* Monks and Priests are farther discovered by the same author.' To complicate his identity further, Hoefer's *Nouvelle Bibliographie Universelle* claims that Gavin was the pseudonym of François-Michel Janiçon (1674–1730). However, Ashbee declares that Janiçon was in fact the translator rather than the author of Gavin's *Master-Key to Popery* (*Passe-Partout de L'Eglise Romaine; Ou Histoire des Tromperies des Prêtes et des Moines en Espagne, Traduit de L'Anglais*).[49] From the bibliographical details, there is a parallel to the life of Gavin. Janiçon's father allied himself to the Protestants. He himself joined the infantry and was stationed in Ireland. He settled in Holland and married a Dutch religious refugee. Gavin was born and educated in Spain, and became a priest in the Church of Rome at the age of twenty-three, abandoning Catholicism to join the Church of England in 1715. Soon after, rather than be put to death by the Inquisition, he disguised himself as an army officer and escaped to London. He was, according to his autobiographical sketch, received by Lord Stanhope, whom he knew from Zaragoza. He preached for three years at the chapel in Queen's Square, Westminster and then in Oxenden's chapel in the Haymarket. Eventually, he took up a curacy at Gowan, near Kilkenny and later, in Cork.[50]

Master-key to Popery relates women's own revelations about their corruption by priests. One young girl, Leonore, confessed the tale of her own seduction by a Franciscan friar. Even prior to the death of her mother and father, the family priest became master in their house, 'for my Father and Mother were entirely governed by him'.[51] After their death, all monies, bar a small part for her, were left to the priest. He declared, 'Your Patrimony is in my Hands, and you ought to obey me blindly in everything.' He seduced her, then abandoned her two months later, returning to the convent where he died. With no means of subsistence, she lived with an army officer for a while, until he had to move regiment, then decided to confess all and change her life. The subsequent father confessor was just as mercenary as the former. He both relieved her of her remaining jewels and forced her to submit to his desires with threats of the Inquisition. She admitted, 'I did converse unlawfully several times in the Church with him.'[52] Such tales of priests insinuating themselves into private households were often used to indicate their reptilian nature, epitomising the serpent in the Garden of Eden. This fear had been played out at other levels much earlier, for example in seventeenth-century theatre in Molière's *Tartuffe* (1664).

Not only were priests a problem but further sordid revelations proved that convents fostered sexual deviance:

> Many gentlemen send their daughter to the nunnery some of them as young as five or six years old, where they are educated till they are 15 years old. At 15 they receive the habit of a nun and begin their noviciate. They are flattered and given an easy life for fear that they might be dissatisfied and leave. Once their vows are taken, it all changes and they see they have lost the pleasures of the world. Then, minding nothing but to satisfy their passions, as well as they can, they abandon themselves to all sort of wickedness, and amorous intrigues.[53]

Evidence of corruption is provided through confessions of the young nun of SO (*sic*). This probably was a reference to the convent at St. Omer, which contained both a Jesuit monastery and its counterpart, The Institute of the Blessed Virgin.[54]

As a thirteen-year-old girl, the nun was tricked into the convent after she had been pursued by a suitor. Her father had lied, telling her that her lover had died. No longer caring about her fate, she took religious vows. She related how most of the nuns had a gallant or *devoto*, who came to visit at the grate. The nuns contrived to bring in a friar, one of the *devoti*, who serviced them all, and escaped only after 22 days, by which time three were pregnant. The girl found herself in the same state and mused, 'if I do continue in the convent, my big belly will discover me, and though one life shall be saved, I shall lose mine, by the rules of our order, and the dishonour of my family will be more publick'.[55]

Master-key to Popery was reissued in three volumes in as many years. It purported to be a book 'where only facts are related', which included various revelations including 'The Lives and Abominable Intrigues of Several Priests and Fryers of the Church of Rome', 'A Catalogue of Miracles wrought by the Consecrated Wafer' and 'Revelations of Three Nuns'. Gavin boasted: 'In less than two years, 5000 of my first and second volumes are dispersed among the Protestants of Great Britain and Ireland.'[56] The work was translated into French and published in abridged form in America.

Frequently, tales were lifted from an assortment of other books then mixed and matched as a new production. Some of the stories in *The Cloisters Laid Open* (Figure 24) come from Boccaccio, while others are taken from Gavin's *Master-key to Popery*. One adventure tells of a thirteen-year-old girl, Isabelle, seduced by a friar who uses religious doctrine as an excuse to have her undress. Isabelle confesses: 'He then told me, I must pull off my Shift too; for the Virgin and the Saints being all without Cloaths, would have nothing offered to them, but what was quite naked.'[57] He then proceeded to ravish her at the altar, offering her virginity to the Virgin Mary.

This erotic propaganda produced the motifs and attention to particular sexual details, which would be incorporated into later pornographic fiction. From these scenarios, anti-Catholic erotica would adopt special elements and develop them for its own use.

Religious flagellation

Another reason the English found to detest the French Catholic Church was its advocacy of flagellation as a penance. For Protestants, religious flagellation was another authorisation to commit sins and immediately absolve oneself. However, the relationship between religion and erotica was cemented in the activity of flagellation, the display of blood closely linked with both. Blood, pain and suffering had long been connected in a religious context, as seen in the shedding of blood in Christianity, in the crucifixion and in the sacraments. Furthermore, blood was prominent in religion when exemplifying sanctity. Martyrs had rapturous rhinorrhagia, saints showed signs of stigmata and icons of Mary wept blood. Caroline Walker Bynum argues that the premodern body was made up of some distinctly unscientific phenomena: 'stigmata, incorruptibility of the cadaver in death, mystical lactations and pregnancies, catatonic trances, ecstatic nosebleeds, miraculous inertia, eating

THE

Cloisters laid Open,

OR,

ADVENTURES

OF THE

PRIESTS and NUNS.

WITH

Some Account of CONFESSIONS, and the lewd Use they make of them.

Containing a Series of diverting STORIES.

ALSO,

The ADVENTURES of the BATH:

CONTAINING,

The Amours of THERESA and the DWARF, the Love Letters of the Count LUCIANO, and the Tragedy of the Baron CASANATTA.

LONDON:

Printed for MEANWELL, near Dutchey-Lane.
[Price Three Shillings.]

View the lascivious Priest, Religion's Jest!
By whom th'obedient Damsel is confest;
With whom she clears the long contracted Score
Of former Sins, and ticks with Heav'n for more.

Figure 24   Frontispiece and title-page to Anon., *The Cloisters Laid Open*, c. 1750–1800

pus, vision of bleeding hosts.'[58] Blood already carried erotic connotations[59] and therefore appropriation of flagellation by erotica was another method by which to display the bloodied body. Rudolph Bell, in *Holy Anorexia*, shows how ecstatic religious fantasies, humiliation and flagellation are closely entwined, the saints, even as children, indulging in a morbid enjoyment of self-mortification.[60] In confession, Catholics were encouraged to narrate detailed accounts of sexual thoughts, desires, lusts and perversions of the body. Deprivations of the body were used as a punishment, through fasting, mortification of the flesh and flagellation.

Incorporation of religious themes was significant in French anti-clerical erotica, which conjoined blood, ecstasy and flagellation for sexual purposes.[61] Inevitably, this influenced English interest in the subject. Reported tales of whipping nuns and flagellating penitents appeared to have had a peculiarly specific effect on the British imagination. One of the most popular was Abbé Boileau's *Historia flagellantum, de recto et perverso flagrorum usu apud Christianos* (the *History of the Flagellants, and of the Correct and Perverse Use of Rods among the Christians*) (Paris, 1700) (Figure 25). This was reprinted under various titles,

Figure 25 Abbé Boileau, *Historia flagellantum, de recto et perverso flagrorum usu apud Christianos*, 1700; translated as *History of the Flagellants, and of the Correct and perverse Use of Rods Among the Christians*, 1780.

including Jean Louis Lolme's *The History of the Flagellants* (1780) and *The Memorials of Human Superstition; Imitated from the Historia Flagellantium of the Abbé Boileau* (1785). In an address to the readers, the preface states:

> To the persons themselves who actually suffer from the injustice or wantonness of others, this performance will be of great service. Those, for instance, who smart under the lash of some insolent satirist, those who are disappointed in their expectations, those whose secrets have been betrayed, nay, even ladies, treacherously forsaken by those who had given them so many assurances of fidelity and external consistency, will find their misfortunes alleviated by reading the several instances in and facts related in this book.[62]

Although this purports to be a serious interpretation of flagellation, the author cannot resist including sexually revelatory material towards the last third of the book. The 'disciplines' are described as 'those voluntary Flagellations which the Penitents inflict upon themselves with their own hands; lashing their own backs, or posteriors, either with scourges or whips, or willow and birch rods'. The author believed this was not done in the past; it was a relatively new phenomenon.[63] He noted that the Penitents 'both inflict those Disciplines on themselves with their own hands, and receive the same from other persons, either with scourges, rods, or whip-cords'.

> All the Women (as the Writer of this Commentary has been told, when in Catholic countries) who make flagellation part of their religious exercises, whether they live in or out of Convents, use the lower discipline, as described above: their pious and merciful Confessors have suggested to them that the upper discipline may prove dangerous, and be the cause of hurting their breasts, especially when they mean to proceed in the holy exercise with unusual fervour and severity.[64]

Such penance had been made a Sacrament among the Catholics and the person involved had to feel satisfaction. Visions experienced by young flagellating nuns were common: 'Instances of revelations, like those of St. Bridget of Sweden, concerning the person of Jesus Christ and his suffering, are very frequent among nuns.'[65] The image of female noviciates in the bloom of youth, full of hot feverish passion, was one reiterated through erotic literature of the day. These depictions can be seen in the anti-Catholic erotic material discussed earlier and summarised in the author's assertion: 'To the mind of such of those unfortunate young Women as have once begun to indulge fancies of this kind, the image of their beloved Spouse is continually present ... and his flagellations, and other hardships which he was made to undergo, are, among other things, the objects of their tenderest concern.'[66] One particular anecdote of a Christian virgin conveyed the pleasure taken in pain, which he saw to be encouraged by the Catholic practice of self-mortification:

> This Virgin ... had formerly disguised herself in Man's clothes, and having assumed the name of Joseph, led for a while, a dissolute life. But she at last grieved so much for the abominable pleasures in which she had formerly indulged herself, that she could enjoy no rest, till, by the tortures she inflicted upon herself, she had largely made amends for them. Inebriated with the fervour of the Spirit, through the sweetness of the flesh of the Pascal lamb, she hated her own flesh, and would often cut from it, with a knife, pieces which were of no small size, which she afterwards hid underground, through modesty.[67]

Boileau's *Historia flagellantum* and its reprints in various guises define a historical trait in depth which would encourage the British interest in flagellation as a sexual activity. Such religious flagellation, seen to be spawned in France, was to be incorporated into English erotica. Two of the earlier examples which saw flagellation used for sexual purposes in a religious setting found their way to England through reports of the sexual misdemeanours of two French priests and would further fuel the English desire for more flagellation material.

French priests' trials

> What a Bustle is here
> About Madam *Cadiere*
> And *Girard* her Father confessor!
> Was every young Whore
> So Important before
> As this little Gypsy? God Bless Her.
> Anon, *Miss Cadiere's Case Very Handsomely Handled*[68]

The trials of two French priests would impact on English gossip, erotic writings and cultural attitudes. The scandals of these two men, Father des Rues and Father Girard, had their stories documented in erotic English reports during the 1720s and 1730s. Their trials were written up in reports, which frequently claimed to be factual exposés, 'translated from the French original'. In fact, they were often interspersed with the English narrators' opinions, with added salacious titbits. Edmund Curll was among the first of the publishers to recognise the value in these stories and was, at least in part, responsible for supplying the public with this particular lascivious reading matter. On 23 December 1725, in response to the Abbé des Rues case, he published *The Case of Seduction Being an Account of the late Proceedings at Paris, as well* Ecclesiastical; *as* Civil *Against the Reverent Abbé Claudius Nicholas des Rues for committing rapes on 133 Virgins* (Figure 26).[69] Translated by a Mr. Rogers, this was allegedly a transcript of the actual trial of the Abbé, the book selling for 2s 6d. The report explains the law on rape, describing two different types of rape – rape upon a virgin; and the rape of seduction, termed *raptum in parentes* (rape against the parents). Two provisos existed to establish that a crime had taken place. In the first type, the act must have been perpetrated on an innocent maiden. A rape could not be committed upon a woman who had been formerly debauched, even though she might now live chastely. Proof had to be provided that the woman was of honest behaviour and good fame and condition. In the second, there must be proof that the accused tried to entice the child away from her parents. The testimony of the victim was often doubted in these cases, implying an overlying misogyny as well as anti-Popery.

In France, numerous anecdotes circulated expressing doubt about certain women's chastity who had fallen victim to lascivious priests.[70] It was implicit that a priest could not be guilty without blame also being apportioned to the women. The narrator of *The Case of Seduction* provides this information in order to defend the actions of the Abbé, since he cites many instances where the deponents against the Abbé were already prostitutes. One example was the case of a mother who had offered her daughter to the Abbé for 600 livres, thus he could be charged with neither violence nor seduction. Contradictory evidence given by the daughter and her mother did not help their case. Another, Jeanne le Fort, a twenty-year-old tradesman's daughter, had already left her parents and therefore could not have been seduced away from them. Previous acts of lewdness were also proved against her throughout the proceedings.

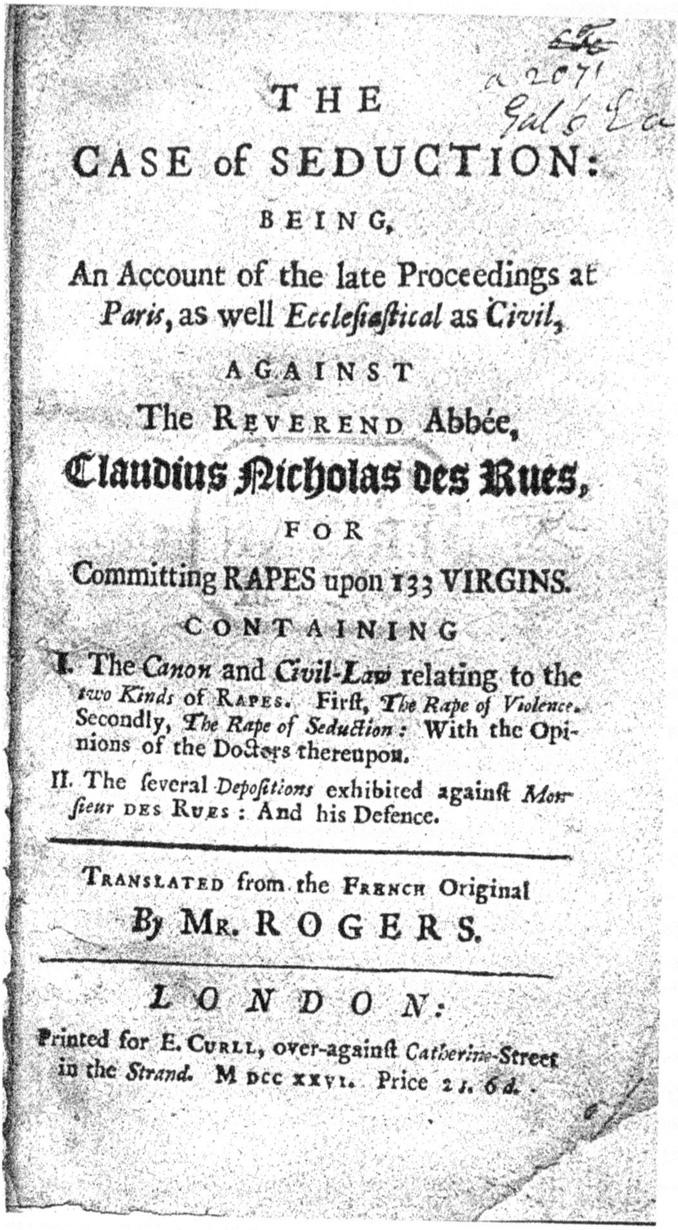

THE
CASE of SEDUCTION:

BEING,

An Account of the late Proceedings at
Paris, as well *Ecclesiastical* as *Civil*,

AGAINST

The REVEREND Abbée,

Claudius Nicholas des Rues,

FOR

Committing RAPES upon 133 VIRGINS.

CONTAINING

I. The *Canon* and *Civil-Law* relating to the
two Kinds of RAPES. First, *The Rape of Violence.*
Secondly, *The Rape of Seduction :* With the Opinions of the Doctors thereupon.

II. The several *Depositions* exhibited against *Monsieur* DES RUES : And his Defence.

TRANSLATED from the FRENCH Original
By MR. ROGERS.

LONDON:

Printed for E. CURLL, over-against *Catherine*-Street
in the *Strand.* M DCC XXVI.   Price 2 s. 6 d.

Figure 26   Title-page to Anon., *The Case of Seduction Being an Account of the late Proceedings
at Paris, as well Ecclesiastical; as Civil Against the Reverent Abbé Claudius Nicholas des Rues for
committing rapes on 133 Virgins*, 1726.

Des Rues' case was subsequently advertised when other clergymen were accused of similar misdemeanours. On hearing of a later case involving a Father Girard, Curll printed a rhyming couplet on the subject:

> Father Girard, by far, is by Des Rues out-done,
> One Hundred Virgins he seduc'd; Girard but one.[71]

Father John Baptist Girard's case excited a great deal of interest, as seen in the plethora of pamphlets which appeared at the time.[72] These accounts were all variations on the same theme, accusing John Baptist Girard of seducing Mary Catherine Cadière,[73] or of the latter's total fabrication of the seduction. Mary Cadière's brother had been a student at Girard's Jesuit college. Mary, then seventeen years old, had gone to Girard to confess. The constant reading of the pious lives of saints had upset her mind and, like the saints she read about, she too experienced visions. During the visits to the priest, which took place between December 1729 and June 1730, Mary became pregnant. She complied with Girard's wishes for the affair to be kept quiet, while he continued to have sex with her.[74] The case caused a considerable stir. Judgement was made in 1731 and Girard was acquitted, but people were curious as to the odd circumstances attending Girard's acquittal where 15 out of the 24 judges believed him guilty.

These reports contained elements prevalent in both earlier anti-Papist propaganda and later fictional pornographic works. First, they iterated the same warnings to Protestant men, which reflected underlying anxieties about women and their sexuality. Second, they portrayed women as hysterical, hallucinating and experiencing obscene visions, this being related to prevalent beliefs about uncontrollable female sexuality. Third, themes of submission and dominance emerged, flagellation and blood being introduced as part of these ritualised scenarios. These were, to a large extent, male attempts to control female sexual behaviour while subjecting the female body to humiliation through the exposure of blood (as seen in chapter 3). Finally, specific positioning of the body was important. Both A *Defence of F. John Baptist Girard*[75] and *The Case of Mary Katherine Cadière, Against the Jesuite Father John Baptist Girard*[76] side with the priest, charging Cadière with scheming and plotting. However, *The Case of Mrs. Mary Catherine Cadière, Against the Jesuit Father John Baptist Girard* voices popular fears about the loss of men's influence over their womenfolk:

> For we hope the following account of that young Lady's sad story will not only entertain the Reader's curiosity, but convey a most excellent and necessary lesson to every virtuous Fair one, every tender Husband, Parent and Brothers to every *British* Subject and true Protestant. Here they will see by what villainous and diabolical arts, the *Romish* Priests, but especially the Jesuits, usurp and maintain absolute domination over the Consciences as well as the Persons of their *Devotees* … here they will see what they may justly expect will be the fate of their Wives, their Daughters and their Sisters, should they for their sins be delivered up to the Infatuations of Popery and an

implicit Obedience to cunning and wicked Confessors, who will artfully worm themselves into the secrets of their Hearts and perniciously make use of that Advantage to ruin their Virtue.[77]

The *Tryal of Father John-Baptist Girard* related the furtive manoeuvrings of the supposedly chaste cleric:

It certainly reflected highly on the *Christian* Religion in general, that a Priest who assumed the Vocation of preaching *Christ* and the *Gospel*, and under that *Veil* gained everywhere Admittance, should have been guilty of seducing a *young Lady* eminently devoted to *Piety*, and whose innocence was rendered subservient to the *lustful* Inclinations of her *blind Guide*.[78]

The mental corruption of Cadière by Girard was seen as an important issue in the trial reports. She had become haunted by sexual thoughts, and troubled continually with obscene visions 'in which the secret Parts of both Sexes were exhibited to her, and the Horror of such unclean Thoughts as were thereby stirr'd up in her, put her into such violent Agonies, of which she often complain'd to Father *Girard*, who found new Excuses, and new Pretences of Piety, to sooth her Distractions'.[79] However, the minutes for the defence of Father John-Baptist Girard depict Cadière as an already hysterical woman given to ecstasies. Because of this, her Father Confessor and her companions nicknamed her *Catherine of Sienna* [sic], who was known for her ecstatic visions, a common theme in hagiography appropriated in this sub-genre of erotica.[80] Nonetheless, the prosecution denounced him for breathing evil spirits into Cadière, causing her to have fits and to faint, which effected hallucinations. The suggestions in these pamphlets alternated between depictions of Girard as the archetypal debauching priest and laying the blame on Cadière. The fault was not directly apportioned to her but on female nature, thereby denouncing all women at the same time as insensible, irrational, gullible and hysterical.

These trial reports were in fact erotic texts finding their voice. Sexually combative language was used to establish a relationship of dominance and submission. Girard demands, '*Will you not yield yourself up to me?* This was followed by a Kiss, in which breathing strongly on her, he so infected her, that she answered, *Holy Father, I will submit without reserve.*' The archetypes of male dominator and passive female are used. Girard is portrayed as an ardent lover and is 'gallant', Cadière's character is defined as the embodiment of innocence and modesty. He 'seizes', 'commands' and 'throws' her; she 'kneels', 'submits' and 'yields'. He is established as aggressive and controlling; she is conveyed as servile and easily governable. Taken to the extremes of passivity, she lies virtually unconscious while he has sex with her:

finding her one Day in Bed, he shut the door and locked it, then laying himself by her Side, put one of his Arms under her, with the other uncovered her, and while he kissed her so fast, that she had not time to speak, neither at those Times when he had once breathed on her had she the Power that his Hand wandered over all, even the most secret Parts of her Body, till fainting, she was no longer sensible of what he did; but when she came to herself, shew as but all too conscious of what had passed, feeling herself wet, and seeing the Posture in which he lay.[81]

Flagellation becomes the ultimate stage in her subordination as he commands Cadière to kneel, shifting the erotic content up a gear into sadomasochism. He introduces her to the 'Whip of Discipline' and to sodomy. After throwing her onto the bed, he 'did there what she was so innocent as not to conceive, tho' the natural Modesty of her Sex gave her Apprehensions of being very evil',[82] telling her it was 'a *New Way* to sublime Perfection'.[83] In the rare cases sodomy is alluded to in early pornographic works, it is viewed as abhorrent. It is shown here to convey the extremes of the priest's perversions and the lengths to which he will go to satisfy his abnormal voracious carnal desires.

The exploration of abortions, an abhorrence in the eyes of all good Christians, reinforced the image of the depraved priest and the extent to which they would go to hide their illicit activities. In one account, Girard becomes worried that Cadière might be pregnant and gives her a liquor he has brought to bring about a miscarriage. The results are graphically described in the style of a gothic horror tale: 'That the Effect of it was a great Flooding of Blood: That she not only inform'd him of it, but told him, she had something like a Piece of Flesh come from her; shew'd him the Pot; which he carried to the Window, and examined with great Attention.'[84] The Lady Abbess was called to give evidence, but on being asked the question '*If Miss Cadiere did not void a great deal of Blood?*' she was so confounded at the immodesty of the question she had to withdraw immediately.[85] Expositions of blood were explicit in these pornographic exposés and made with the obvious intention to shock. It has previously been suggested that abortions do not figure in pornography. De Walle, although recognising the usefulness of erotic material in shedding light on sexual practices in history, believes that herbs were used mainly to bring about menstruation rather than used as abortifacients, stating: 'Pornographic literature of the eighteenth century, an important source for the history of contraception, hardly ever mentioned abortion, and did not treat it as an option to avoid unwanted births.' [86] This perhaps needs modifying. As can be seen in these pornographic reports, the inclusion of abortion scenes was used during this period as a means of providing erotic images of blood emanating from the female body. Abortion is frequently mentioned in particular types of erotic tales, as seen in the nunnery tales below. However, it is reasonable to suggest that abortion scenes tended to be avoided in later eighteenth-century pornographic developments, such as flagellation material.[87]

Flagellation scenes in anti-Catholic material contained early erotic elements, such as positioning of the body, displays of blood and submissive and aggressive behaviour, which were to become crucial factors in later pornography, and would be used to distinct advantage in the fully-fledged flagellation material from the 1770s onwards.[88]

Another English pamphlet introduces flagellation; *The Case of Mary Katherine Cadière* shows the precise arranging of the body to show it at its submissive best.

> Ignorant as she was of His Design, she promised Secrecy: Whereupon he ordered her to get upon her Bed, and clapping a Cushion under her Elbows to raise her up a little, he gave her several lashes with the Discipline; after which he kiss'd the Place he had scourged, and then he made her get off the Bed and kneel before him, he told her, *That the gracious God was not satisfied, but she must strip herself naked before him.*[89]

A Compleat History of the Intrigues of Monks and Nuns (1746) contained the trials of both Des Rues and Girard.[90] Other salacious erotica emulated the sagas. *The Amours of Sainfroid and Eulalia* was a translation from the French version of the *Intrigues and Amours of a Jesuit and a Nun* and was influenced by the Girard-Cadière scandal.[91] De Sade was possibly influenced by the case in his cruellest chapters in *Justine*, as was the work *Les Amours de Sainfroid Jesuite*.[92] Even poems were made up about the case, as in 'Spiritual Fornication, a Burlesque Poem; wherein the Case of Miss *Cadiere* and Father *Girard* is merrily Display'd' and 'Miss *Cadiere's* Case very Handsomely Handled', carried in *The Ladies Miscellany* collection.[93]

Having examined the erotica based on priests' misdemeanours and its intent, the following section will look at the convent as a location for sex. The first section analyses the concept of spatial confinement as an important element in this sub-genre and acts as a link between the anti-Papist material examined above, and the nunnery tales which follow.

The convent

> Vows of Virginity should well be weigh'd;
> Too oft they're cancell'd, tho' in Convents made.[94]

Spatial confinement

French visitors commented on the English living in cells, boxes and cubicles, giving the impression of the towns having been turned into huge convents, with people becoming more inclined to privacy and isolation.[95] Cities were growing and more closed-in spaces were being constructed, particularly in London, whence the bulk of the erotica emanated. The location of the French setting of the convent for English erotica fitted well with this shift in attitudes[96] towards a desire for privacy, both physical and mental. Yet although privacy was considered important for self-reflection, spatial confinement was also equated with both sexual repression and expression.

Within this vision of the convent, spatial confinement became highly sexualised. In both factual and fictional accounts of the enclosure of nuns, an impression of private and confined space is conveyed through descriptions of cells, chapels and confessional boxes. Grates, grilles and partitions are seen as impediments to sexual fulfilment. In erotica, these were overcome by the use of underground tunnels, secret passages and knocked down walls. Accounts purporting to be factual exposés describe the lengths to which nuns would go to ensure access to their suitors. They would

> endeavour for Mony [*sic*] to corrupt the *Turn-Keys* and *Maid-Servants*, that have the Care of the Outward-Gates, to admit their *Gallants* at *Nights* by the Tower. Some have pluck'd away *whole Grates* from the Parlours; other have broke down Walls, or have made Passages underground; and it happens frequently enough, that by their Cunning, they get the Keys of the *Great Gate* of the Monastery from under the Lady Abbess's Pillow.[97]

An equation is made between the rejection of the Catholic religion and the means to sexual/spiritual freedom. Gates and keys offer well-known metonyms for the sexual act,[98] crossing material boundaries symbolic of the transgression into a woman's body. One close community of nuns, the Nuns of Bresse in Italy, decided to afford themselves the sexual pleasure of men by forging an easy access route to the outside world:

> quite weary of keeping their Vows of *Chastity*, agreed amongst themselves to admit their Loves into the Monastery, and having all bound themselves in an Oath of Secrecy, they wrought hard, to make a Passage Underground, under the Walls of their Enclosure, and which was to end in the House of a *young Gentleman*, who was one of the Plot. Their Undertaking has so good success, that the Nuns enjoyed the Gallants as often as they pleased.[99]

Excommunicated priests and dissatisfied nuns supplied descriptions of life within the confines of religious houses and thereby buttressed contemporary perceptions of convents as sexualised places: 'There are several narrow closets in the church, with a small iron grate: One side answers to the cloister, the other to the church; So the nun being on the inside, and father confessor on the outside, they hear one another.'[100] Another account reported: 'The Cordeliers were not satisfied with seeing the nuns at the grate, they made *secret and nocturnal* entries into the Garden and Monastery by the help of *false keys*, or *ladders of cord, and in baskets*.'[101] Sensual monastic grounds adorned with veiled greenery and running waters were so erotic that they could raise sexual feelings in those who spent time there:

> those very Places of Retirement, with their large Gardens, adorned with Walks and Shades, and many times watered by pleasant Fountains, or murmuring Streams, together with the idle Way of Living, seem to be accommodated to inspire them with amorous Sentiments, against which their Vows of Chastity, and the Rules of their Order, are so far from being Preservative, that they only act as Fuel to their Flames, and make them commit *Sin* with a higher *Relish*.[102]

These secret gardens screened behind cloister walls were part of the privatised erotic location, a repressed echo of the natural erotic gardens established in other erotica.[103] These ostensibly factual accounts raised issues about religious confinement and sexual repression, which were to be reflected in purely fictional tales of the convent.

Fictional nunnery tales

To date, the few examinations of convent erotica which have taken place have largely concentrated on the convent as a setting for lesbian sex.[104] Yet themes of confinement, sexual initiation and flagellation explored in anti-Papist rhetoric and the priests' trial reports, as seen above, reverberated in fictional nunnery tales.

The most notorious popular pornographic nunnery tale comes in the form of *Venus in the Cloister* (1725).[105] This could be had in a calf-bound volume of 184 pages for 3 shillings, but cheaper pamphlets such as *The Nun; Or, Memoirs of Angelique: An Interesting Tale* (1803), only 18 pages (complete with a picture of a nun baring her breasts) (Figure 27), could be had for a few pence. At least one original edition of *Venus in the Cloister* remains in the British Library together with a Xeroxed copy of the second edition, and six eighteenth-century French-language versions.

THE NUN;

OR,

MEMOIRS OF ANGELIQUE;

AN INTERESTING TALE.

ALSO

THE ADVENTURES OF

HENRY DE MONTMORENCY;

A TALE.

TO WHICH IS ADDED,

THE SURPRISING LIFE OF MRS. DHOLSON.

London:

PRINTED FOR TEGG AND CASTLEMAN,
Eccentric Book Warehouse,

NO. 122, ST. JOHN'S STREET, WEST SMITHFIELD,

Champante and Whitrow, Aldgate; T. Hughes, Paternoster-Row; Willmot and Hill, Borough; N. Rollason, Coventry; J. Belcher, Birmingham; B. Sellick, Bristol; T. Troughton, Liverpool; J. Mitchell, Newcastle; T. Brown, NorthStreet, Edinburgh; E. Peck, Lower Ousegate, York; T. Binns, Leeds; J. Dingle, Bury St. Edmund's; T. Brown, Bath; B. Dugdale, Dublin; M. Swindels, Manchester; J. Raw and J. Bush, Ipswich; J. Booth, Norwich; Collins and Fellows, Salisbury; and G. Wilkins, Derby.

T. Plummer, Printer, Seething-Lane;

THE NUN.

London. Published May 18 1803 by Tegg & Co.

Figure 27 Frontispiece and title-page to Anon., *The Nun; Or Memoirs Of Angelique: An Interesting Tale* (London, Tegg and Castleman, 1803).

The story-line follows the well-used device of dialogue form[106] to explore the sexual inauguration of Agnes, a young noviciate, by Angelica, a more sexually experienced nun. While in the nunnery, Angelica becomes sexually debauched and seduces young Agnes. A huge grate in the parlour separates the nuns from their secular visitors, providing a sense of further segregation from the outside world:

> These rooms are divided in the middle with an Iron Grate, so as to make two Apartments, the Inward and the Outward; and into the Inward the Nuns come, without coming out of their Inclosure, and the Visitors come into of the Outward by a Key, given through the Grate by the Portress at the entrance of the Monastery.[107]

Nuns are obliged to retire to their own cells for eight days once every year and have no contact with the rest of the community. Secret methods of communication enable seductions to take place. A hidden passage is revealed to Sister Agnes by her confessor, a route to their consummation.[108] Sex aids are introduced, such as the *Instrument of Glass* shown to Agnes by her confessors who assured her that 'there were above fifty of them in the House, and that every one, from the *Abbess* down to the last *Profest*, handled *them* [more] often than their *Beads*'. How these aids were used is not explained but they are obviously a sort of dildo.[109]

Flagellation is recognised as an activity that will sexually stimulate, even when applied as a penance. Although the portrayal of debauched convent life is generally comically light-hearted, attempts at verisimilitude interject in occasional footnotes. A description is given for the ignorant reader on the purpose and use of the scourge, 'a sort of Cat of Nine Tails with which they whip themselves in Monasteries'.[110] Agnes experiences ecstasy when whipping herself in self-mortification:

> Alas! my Zeal was indiscreet, I thought the more I laid on, the more I merited; my good plight of Health, and my Youth made me sensible of the least Stroke; so that at the Conclusion of this fine Exercise, I found my back Apartment all on Fire: I don't know whether I have not some Wound in those Parts, for I was altogether transported when I committed this so sensible an Outrage upon it.[111]

Echoing the flagellation scenario in the Cadière–Girard pamphlets, the position of the body is important, particularly the thighs. Angelica arranges Agnes so she can examine her flagellation wounds more closely: 'kneel down upon the Mattress, and hold down thy Head a little, that I may observe the Violence of thy Stripes!' Angelica commenting on Agnes's self-mortification declares: 'Sure one must have a great deal of Devotion for *the Mystery of Flagellation* thus to illuminate one's Thighs.'[112]

Other convent erotica would follow, most of it risqué, rather than pornographic, fiction. *Nunnery Tales Written by a Young Nobleman* (1727),[113] *The Nun; Or, Memoirs Of Angelique: An Interesting Tale* (1803)[114] and *The Nun in the*

Cloister or, the Amours, Intrigues and Adventures of the Marchioness of Beauville (1828)[115] all carry similar seduction plots. Within these tales, familiar rhetoric would be acted out: sexual initiation, secret vows, submissive entreaties and ecstatic visions. Women are deemed to be hysterical as a result of their fantasies. This established the image of the uncontrolled female religious body as a body of abandonment and resignation.

The early age of entrance into the convent is highlighted. All the girls come from the aristocratic or gentry class. In *Venus in the Cloister*, Angelica had been in the nunnery for seven years, having entered at thirteen years of age after she had been orphaned. Her parents' estate had been bequeathed to her brother leaving 'six of us without any other Support than what he promised us, which, according to his Humour, was to have been but very little'.[116] In 'The History of Bellardine and the Beautiful Cloretta', in *Nunnery Tales written by a Young Nobleman* (1727), the illegitimate daughter of a Jesuit and young lady of great quality is placed in a nunnery in order to cover up the affair of her parents and to prevent a public disgrace. In 'The History of Villaret and the Amiable Charlotta', another tale in the same book, Charlotta's rich father, unable to bear the thought of his daughter being sullied by another man, places her in a convent at fourteen years of age. *The Nun; Or, Memoirs Of Angelique: An Interesting Tale* (1803) condemns such enforced incarceration, emphasising the right of a woman to choose her own path:

> When the freedom of choice is taken from you, when you have no will of your own, you become degraded into a machine, the mere organ of another's sentiments, and cannot, in the nature of justice, be guilty for submitting to terms you had no power to refuse, or for resuming, on the very first opportunity, that natural right which had been rested from you.[117]

The oath the heroine has given is deemed not binding as she has been forced into it against her will. In *The Nun in the Cloister or, the Amours, Intrigues and Adventures of the Marchioness of Beauville* (1828) the young girl is placed in the nunnery at the age of seven, and thus unable to offer any resistance at all. The lack of freedom of choice for the girls is an important factor in the condemnation of the nunneries.

Two sorts of men are depicted in these nunnery tales: the young male paramours who use their charms in seduction and the evil monks who used their cunning. In *Nunnery Tales written by a Young Nobleman* (1727), Bellardine tricks his way into the convent in order to seduce Cloretta, where 'by a thousand soft Endearments, he soon brought her to a Forgetfulness of all Considerations, but such as served to heighten their mutual Raptures'.[118] Men are attacked for being deceitful, for their use of flattery and for employing any means possible in their seduction attempts: 'so difficult is it for Man [*sic*], skill'd as they are in the betraying Art, even to dissemble Love, when once they have gain'd a Gratification of that Passion.'[119] In another tale, the youthful suitor, Villaret, is assisted by a debauched older friar willing to help him seduce Charlotta, in exchange for a bag of money: 'If you could enjoy this sweet Girl, *said the old Hypocrite*, your Mind would doubtless be at peace.'[120]

Again, the abortion themes are reiterated. Lecherous older friars concoct abortifacients to give to the innocent pregnant young nuns, a theme no doubt influenced by the stories circulating in Europe of infants' bodies being found in wells and buried within monasteries.[121] Charlotta finds herself pregnant and is encouraged to drink an abortifacient

> composed of Herbs and Minerals, of so strong a nature that it could not fail of causing an immediate Abortion. It was with an infinite deal of difficulty he prevail'd on her to swallow it; but the Terrors of Death to which the Ecclesiastical Law condemn'd her, if discover'd, at last overcame all the Scruples of Conscience which pleaded hard within her to save the innocent unborn Product of Pleasure.[122]

Similarly, in *The Nun in the Cloister or, the Amours, Intrigues and Adventures of the Marchioness of Beauville* (1828) the older father confessor lusts after the heroine and concocts liquors to induce abortions.

Early erotic tales, which saw the death of the heroine, were more in the form of a caution to readers. Later stories appear in the form of racy novellas, allowing the heroine to live. These are more in the style of anti-Catholic libertine literature, using the convent as a licentious setting in which to explore sexual adventures. Although these plot-lines vary slightly, they all carry similar images of religious men and women which apply prevalent external values. Attitudes differed towards the sexually active in the religious community depending on their gender. Young noviciates are portrayed as innocent and gullible, and easily won through flattery, yet the writers are sympathetic to these women. In other erotica, licentious females are frequently portrayed as intimidating yet in this material carry no menace. Rather, a sentimentalised image of young nuns developed in which these women, incarcerated as they are, are naturally susceptible to the charms of young men. The nuns are allowed to indulge in sexual activities without moral judgement made on them, while the monks continue to be blamed for corruption and perversion. Women are portrayed as casualties of libertine convent life, an image that reflected Protestant perceptions of naive young girls corrupted by the Catholic religion. The monks, on the other hand, were seen as debauched, corrupt and frequently perverted, deflowerers of young virgins, infiltrating their virtue in order to violate their minds, bodies and souls. Innocent nuns were victims of corrupt lecherous priests. An age difference is also evident since the characters of the older monks and nuns are frequently debauched and perverted. As with the priests, older nuns, such as the mother superiors, are frequently seen as vicious, twisted and bitter old crones bent on the destruction of the pure young virginal souls and bodies. Young men are, however, seen as virile and attractive while simultaneously fickle and false.

Pedagogical themes through rites of passage are an integral part of this erotica. The texts relate to sexual initiation of girls at the onset of puberty. Two sorts of sexual images of women are revealed: passive receptors of sex where asinine girls undergo out-of-body experiences which 'transport' them so they are unconscious of what is taking place; and the women who actively seek sexual knowledge and experience through curiosity. Their fates vary from incarceration and death to sexual liberation and freedom. Some who transgressed the sexual barriers continued to be suppressed against their will and were murdered; others take control of their sexual destiny and break free. Physical, sexual and mental freedom is equated with rejection of the Catholic religion. Additional factors, such as rape scenes and cross-dressing, are introduced in this erotica to increase physical arousal. Throughout these accounts, marriage is seen as the most suitable form of occupation for a woman, the convent its antithesis.

French anti-clerical pornographic novels

France was at the forefront of the production of anti-Catholic material, and by the early eighteenth century had particularly well-advanced pornographic fiction compared to England. English publishers therefore picked from the supplies of material coming in from France, and either translated them or adapted them for English tastes. Although genuine trials and spurious reports based loosely around events and gossip would continue throughout the eighteenth century, a crystallisation of some of the elements can be seen in fictional anti-Catholic pornographic novels.

Two best-sellers dominated the French pornographic market,[123] *Histoire de Dom B...* (1741/2)[124] and *Thérèse Philosophe* (1748) (Figures 28–32),[125] both describing the sexual antics of the Catholics. The first, *Dom Bougre*, or 'The Master-Bugger', recounts tribadism, sodomy and incest and for its time was well advanced in its explicit depictions of vices of the clerics. Meanwhile, *Thérèse Philosophe* depicts an account entitled *Memoirs About the Affair Between Father Dirrag and Mademoiselle Eradice*, which readers would have recognised as anagrams of the names of Cadière and Girard from the incidents of 1729–31. The scandal was transformed into a fictional account and presented the series of sexual scenarios – masturbation, voyeurism and flagellation. Orgasms are represented as spiritual epiphanies. However, Thérèse is not the doomed victim of the early priests' or nunnery tales but is in control.[126] She explores the dangers of conception for women. In attempts to avoid pregnancy, she employs mutual masturbation and *coitus interruptus*. The dangers of pregnancy are also mentioned in the anti-Catholic material circulating in England. Nuns are depicted dying in childbirth, and children were certainly not a desirable part of the sexual relationship. Neither of these works was available in English until the nineteenth century, although the French versions could be obtained. According to Mendes, the earliest English translation of *Thérèse Philosophe* and *Histoire de Dom B...* appears to be c. 1800 and 1801 respectively.[127] Both these books are well known and have been discussed elsewhere,[128] but so far, little has been said about the earlier *Love in all its Shapes* (1734),[129] first published in France in 1696 as *Les Jésuits de la Maison Professe*.[130] The book enjoyed a great success, being reprinted several times during the eighteenth century, originally selling in England for one shilling for 58 pages. It was essentially a humorous yet titillating 'soft-core' pornographic work, which belonged to a long line of traditional French anti-clerical

Figure 28   Dom Bougre ou Le Portier des Chartreux, 1741.

Figure 29 Ibid.

Figure 30   Anon, *Thérèse Philosophe*, 1785.

Figure 31   Ibid.

Figure 32 Ibid.

works. One addition to the French original was the citing of a Father de la Rue (*sic*) as one of its main characters, alluding to the Abbé des Rues scandal in 1723. It purports to be a genuine account of the sexual adventures of the Jesuits, but is in fact a raucous, jocose satire depicting lecherous friars. In a work full of innuendoes, *double entendres* and racy cavorting, the Jesuits are attacked for their loose morals: 'It is no secret to the World, that the Order of *Jesuits*, as it is the most learn'd and subtle, so it is likewise the most loose and profligate, of all the Orders of the *Romish* Church.' The main character, Father de la Rue, uses the time-honoured confessional technique of seduction, and requests the girl to give up her maidenhead to him in penance for her sins. As in reports in the Girard case, priests are able to offer powders for abortion. Clotte, a pregnant servant, asked for help from Father *la Chaise* who kept a secret powder to 'make Lasses miscarry as had been venturing to take too much of the *Arbor Vitae*'.[131]

Adjectives applied in the English translation were to attain common usage. Particularly important would be 'snowy arms' and arms 'smoother than polish'd ivory'. Genitals are euphemistically renamed: the 'magick Rod', 'consecrate candle' and the 'charming Labyrinth'. The 'master-key', we discover, is the penis used to open the vagina, normally tightly closed. Flowers are recognised as an aphrodisiac as the Marchioness lay on 'Bed of white Satin ... holding in her Hand an infinite number of Flowers, which issued from her bosom'.[132] The sexual act is seen as an allegorical war: the Father-Guardian after having sex with the Marchioness 'came off with Honour from the Field of Battle', later with intents to '*besiege the Fort*' of the Marchioness, finding 'the TRENCHES *open* ... brought the lady to *capitulate* in form'.[133] Such erotica was not only providing its own particular descriptive language, but was also defining patterns and themes that would be woven within later stories. Fainting and voyeuristic themes, common elsewhere, were reiterated in *Love in all its Shapes*. Father *Bourdalou* ravishes 'a very pretty young Lady of Quality', his love-making enough to put the fair lady to swooning, as 'half-dying' she declares: 'O reverend Father what a difference do I find between you and ⸺ [her husband]. The Fair one could say no more, for a *Fainting* which is very common in Lovers.'[134] Peepholes were a speciality: as the Father-Guardian has sex with the Marchioness, the *Valet de Chambre* 'has seen *all the mystery* through a hole that was in the ceiling'.[135] Thus the scenarios in the earlier anti-Papist rhetoric and trial reports were copied in the fictional pornographic novels.

French pornography would influence John Cleland's *Memoirs of a Woman of Pleasure* (1749), which explored themes of both sexual initiation and flagellation. The terms 'nuns' and 'abbess' had become recognised terms for whores and their bawds. Cleland writes of the 'venerable mother Abbess herself!' in reference to Fanny Hill's brothel-keeper.[136] The language and motifs in these would in turn be used in later English pornographic works.

Conclusion

Late seventeenth-century antagonism against the Catholics was not merely based on conflict of religion but had become deeply imbedded in many aspects of

English culture. Society was steeped in novels, tracts, poems, pamphlets, prints and drawings which displayed antagonism to the Catholics. This enmity surfaced in erotic and pornographic depictions of the Catholic clergy. Earlier rhetoric had been in earnest and underpinned real concerns about the sexual threat of the priests, particularly the fear of them usurping the Protestant male's authority over his kin. Doubts about the Catholics and concerns about their untrustworthiness were pressed home in anti-Catholic tracts about seduction. This had the effect of inflating sexual tension, with Protestant anxieties erupting in erotic fantasies about priests' sexual misdemeanours. This anti-clerical erotica conveyed a certain set of images about male and female sexuality which held sway throughout the eighteenth century, with potent representations of male control and the ensuing powerlessness of the female victim. In reality, the cases against the two priests, des Rues and Girard, were discharged, but the long history of gossip and scandal caused by such reports was not so easily dismissed and would be reiterated time and time again in various other erotica as seen in the poems and novels.

In the trial reports and the nunnery tales, women are seen to be complicit in their own corruption. At the same time, women are represented as powerless, erratic and unable to control their emotions. They are depicted fainting, scream-ing and being 'transported', to show their modesty, weakness and gullibility, fre-quently passing out at their first experience of sex, subservient to men. However, in the more erotic and pornographic material, such as *The Nun in the Cloister or, the Amours, Intrigues and Adventures of the Marchioness of Beauville* and *Thérèse Philosophe*, the image of the more powerful libertine woman is displayed. They leave the confines of the convent for a life of sexual indulgence after having been 'enlightened' about life and sex.

The locations of the confessional and the walled convent were perfect back-drops to explore sexual excitement because they entailed much of what was 'secret' or 'hidden'. The setting of sexual activity as a private realm (confessional boxes, high walls of monasteries, communion with one's priest) heightened the sense of the 'forbidden'. A narrative created through the confessional or convent also gives us the added perspective of the voyeur, a watcher of that which is nor-mally shielded from public view. Although there was a move towards an increas-ingly private environment by the end of the eighteenth century, the world of secret locations in erotic literature had been established much earlier. Concealment evokes an element of danger of being discovered which accentu-ates the excitement. This secrecy involves promises and commitment between the parties where the women are generally subservient in the agreement. This private sexual space would be domesticated in later flagellation material and taken into the parlour, boudoir and bedroom.

English material differed from the French in that, rather than merely assailing the Church, it took the form of a defence of the English Protestant household. This was a result of underlying concerns about unlicensed female sexual activities and the perceived weakening of the reins of Protestant male authority. The fear that women could become subservient to any male other than those within the family, particularly a Catholic, was viewed with dread. In other words, while French pornography was rooted in politics, an attempt at subversion of the State and Church, in Britain it was a cultural development based on a deep-seated antagonism against the Catholics. This enmity surfaces in fears about female sexuality.

It has been suggested that the increasing aggressive tone used in pornography was a reaction against the increased suppression of sexuality.[137] Supposedly, by the turn of the nineteenth century, moral boundaries had tightened and restrictions on sexual practices were imposed. Pornography had to find a way to oppose contemporary morals and further transgress these new taboos. Thus, the argument goes, pornography moved towards an increasingly aggressive form. But this hypothesis implies too simple an explanation for the move towards aggression in the development of pornography. The early English language reports of the priest trials were already full of aggression. This highly charged rhetoric was also frequently sexually explicit. In addition, some new pornographic developments would maintain an element of humour. However, we can state categorically that *some* types of pornography were becoming more vicious in their treatment of women. This could be that authors were becoming more attuned to readers' fantasies and expanding choice, providing a broader variety of different forms of erotica to fulfil the demands of an expanding market, misogynists and sadists included. This wide variety of alternative methods of sexual excitement which pornographic material provided included mutual masturbation, tribadism, sodomy and flagellation not just vaginal and heterosexual penetrative sex.

More than any other material, early anti-Catholic erotica was particularly important to developments in other pornographic material and exerted a great influence on the long-term development of other erotica. Themes in the body of this material, sexual visions, blood, submission, flagellation and gothic terror would have a profound effect on the development of English pornography overall. Flagellation material was driven by religious erotica. Incest, albeit spiritual incest, is mentioned in the Girard case and implied a contact, in both a sexual and familial way. The trial reports therefore provided a set of themes and a form of language that were to provide a base for the later English pornographic novel.

7
Flagellation

> raising me on my knees, and making me kneel with them straddling
> wide, that tender part of me, naturally the province of pleasure, not
> pain, came in for its share of suffering: for now, eyeing it wistfully, he
> directed the rod so that the sharp ends of the twigs lighted there, so
> sensibly, that I could not help wincing, and writhing my limbs with
> pain;
>
> John Cleland, *Memoirs of a Woman of Pleasure* (1749)[1]

John Cleland's *Memoirs of a Woman of Pleasure* was a defining moment in English
erotica, not just in applying novelistic technique to erotica, but in recognising
that flagellation was a method to exploit English sexual fantasies (Figures 33 and
34). Fanny Hill's introduction to flagellation from Mr. Barville was both painful
and bloody. These flagellation scenes were to become common to erotica circulating in England in the eighteenth century.

Memoirs of a Woman of Pleasure was not the first piece of erotica to mention
flagellation as a sexual predilection. Flagellation had been mentioned in British
seventeenth-century erotica[2] and would prove of considerable interest in the
nineteenth century. It was also evident in French pornography, as seen in *Thérèse
Philosophe* (figures 35 and 36). By the late nineteenth century, the bibliographer
of erotica, Henry Spencer Ashbee, was to verify that

> no English bawdy book is free from descriptions of flagellation, and numerous
> separate plates exist, depicting whipping scenes; it has caused the separation
> of man and wife; the genteelest female schools have been made subservient to
> the passions of its votaries and formally it was spoken without reserve on the
> stage.[3]

So what had happened during the eighteenth century to establish flagellation
erotica as a new and potent form of fictional fantasy?

Few serious examinations of sexual flagellation in history (in any era) have
taken place, either looking at factual material or fiction.[4] The theme of flagellation, as with all other themes in erotica, was not an isolated image but one that

161

Figure 33   Fanny Hill flagellates Mr. Barville, in John Cleland, *Memoirs of a Woman of Pleasure*, 1766.

Figure 34   John Cleland, *Memoirs of a Woman of Pleasure*, 1776.

Figure 35   Anon, *Thérèse Philosophe*, 1785.

Figure 36 Ibid.

had been soaked up from English culture. Flogging was already prevalent in the household, in the school and in use as a corporal punishment.[5] It was advocated as a cure for impotence and was taking place as a sexual activity. These practices being played out in real life were absorbed in erotic literature, plays, poems, chapbooks, magazines and pornography. Erotica was not merely a fantastical whim but was wrought from flagellation practices in everyday life.

There was an emergence of a comprehensive new sub-genre of fictional flagellation pornography (in addition to the wealth of flagellation erotica already circulating) during the last quarter of the eighteenth century, which concentrated specifically on flagellation as a sexual predilection. This was a period when fully-fledged books on 'birch discipline' were honed in a way to give out specific signals, with the flagellatory narrative running throughout as a major theme. Although there is earlier evidence of flagellation as a sexual vice, as seen in Fanny Hill's experiences, these had been offered as a sideline to other more common sexual activities. Within this new sub-genre of English pornography, the domestic arena became a target for writers, moving flagellation from the French settings of the convent (although this area would continue to be explored) and placing scenes within a 'family' environment – the parlour and schoolroom. Furthermore, the relationships of the flagellants were domestic, involving mother/stepmother or governess. Both these factors, the settings and the relationships, linked sex to the home or its substitute, the boarding-school. This in turn introduced incestuous overtones to the scenes. Finally, in this material, exploration of erogenous zones was extended beyond the genitalia. Thighs, bellies, breasts, buttocks and plump forearms were all focused upon with as much interest as penises and vaginas. Although genitalia would obviously continue to play a part, they were less significant in this erotica. Overall, this chapter will show why this erotica emerged in the form it did, and how codes were developed to identify the flagellant.

Flogging in the household

Wife-beating in the eighteenth century was placed above the law, and men were allowed to beat their wives.[6] Imagery of the whipping of maid-servants and wives by masters and husbands circulated in trial reports, poems and plays. Seventeenth-century writers of erotic works make humorous references about the flogging of maid-servants in a pseudo-medical book, *Rare Verities* (1657).[7] An apology is made for its explicitness with jokes about potential ensuing punishment: 'For my part I expect no less then [*sic*] to be whipt by every squint-eyed fellow, worse then Dr. Gill lash'd his maids, Bumbgillion when

> He took up her smock
> And then whip'd her nock.[8]

The play *The Presbyterian Lash or Noctroff's Maid Whipt* (1661) makes the connection between flogging and sexual stimulation.[9] According to the title-page, it was acted out in the Great Room at the Pye Tavern by Noctroff the Priest and several of his Parishioners 'at the eating of a chine of Beefe'. In reference to Noctroff's activities, it declares: 'I warrant he thought that the tickling of the wench's buttocks with the rod would provoke her to lechery.'

THE

WORLD

TURNED

UPSIDE DOWN

OR THE

FOLLY OF MAN

EXEMPLIFIED

IN TWELVE COMICAL RELATIONS

UPON

UNCOMMON SUBJECTS

Illustrated with Twelve curious Cuts
Truly adapted to each Story

PRINTED AND SOLD IN LONDON

Figure 37   Anon, *The World Turned Upside Down, or the Folly Of Man*, 1647.

Early eighteenth-century chapbooks frequently carried themes of beatings, often inverting the matrimonial hierarchy, relating stories of women thrashing their husbands. Fears of women dominating men surfaced in *The World Turned Upside Down, or the Folly Of Man* in twelve satirical verses, illustrated by pictures of a woman birching her husband (Figure 37). Similarly, *Simple Simon's Misfortunes and his Wife Margery's Cruelty* depicts Simon's wife beating him. The tale relates how she 'snatched up Jobson's oaken staff of the table, and gave poor Simon such a clank on the noodle, as made the blood spin', and afterwards treated Jobson to a sound thrashing, whereupon she and her gossiping friends became 'as drunk as fishwomen'. This was particularly popular, with at least seven reprints between 1710 and 1825.[10] Bawdy songs about flogging were also popular. One lewd ditty of 1727, *Warning to Cuckolds*, described itself as 'a New Ballad on the Whipping-Club, held at Rings-End' and depicts a club where members have a penchant for the rod. Sung to the tune of 'Which No-body can deny, brave Boys', it ran,

> While on up her Heels in a moment is tripping,
> Another her Buttocks is decently stripping:
> And then She is fainting dismiss'd with a Whipping,
> Which No-body can deny, brave Boys, etc.[11]

Such songs, plays, chapbooks and poems all expressed the activities of flogging taking place in the home, a commonplace theme which would be woven into erotica.

Flogging as a school discipline

The practice of birching as a discipline common in public schools would be reflected in plays, mainstream novels and poems. Methods of preferred punishment at Eton College were eulogised in *The Opera of Il Penseroso* (1790). Advertised as 'A performance both vocal and instrumental as it is acted with authority, at the Royal Theatres of Eton & Westminster', the principal characters were Mr. Twigg-Him, Mr. Monitor and Miss Birch. Double entendres pepper the text in a celebration of the rod: 'our hero must be *unmasked*, that no *tender part* may *unfeelingly* be passed over; and that each *masterly stroke* in the *performance* may have its full *force* and *emphasis*, the more speedily to *draw tears*'.[12] Eton figures again in *All the Blocks! or, An Antidote to 'All the Talents'* in an attack on the government of the day:

> Give me the rod, I say, to whip the breeches
> of these vile Blocks – these folly-sucking leeches.[13]

Conduct literature for young boys warned of the dangers of being naughty, but sometimes reads like a disguised piece of erotic literature. One tiny pocketbook contains *The Adventures of a Whipping Top* (1780?) and is illustrated with 'Stories of many Bad Boys, who themselves deserve Whipping and Of Some Good Boys, who deserve Plum Cakes'. This curious piece appears in the guise of a boys' yarn, steering the youngsters towards improved behaviour. The author chastises 'that when naughty boys have been corrected for some time they continue very good till their parents, thinking they have left off being obstinate, leave off being servile and then they sink into their former naughtiness, and are obliged to undergo the same correction again which made them good before; these are bad boys to be compared to a silly *Top*, which must be well lashed before it can please you.'[14]

Fictional accounts of flogging reverberated in all types of literature. Henry Fielding's Mr. Thwackum in *Tom Jones* has recourse to the rod upon every occasion, and John Gay's verse in praise of *Molly Mog* an innkeeper's daughter at Oakingham in Berkshire 'lays it down as an undoubted maxim, that the delight of a schoolmaster is to use his whip'.

> The School-Boy's desire is a play-day,
> The Schoolmaster's joy is to flog,
> The milk-maid's delights are on May-day;
> But mine are on sweet Molly Mog.[15]

Faked correspondence on disciplining children was carried in various magazines throughout the eighteenth and nineteenth centuries, most expressly in the *Gentleman's Magazine* of the 1730s and the *Bon Ton* in the 1790s (both explored further below). Bogus correspondence relates the whipping of young girls, a topic which would continue through the nineteenth century, as seen in editions of the *Family Herald* and the *Englishwoman's Domestic Magazine* during the 1870s.

The curative powers of flagellation

Flagellation was seen not only as a means of punishment but also as a cure for impotence. One German doctor, Johann Heinrich Meibom (1590–1655), wrote about the curative powers of flagellation, particularly as an aid to erection and improving the circulation of blood. His essay, *De Flagrorum Usu in Re Veneria & Lumborum Renumque Officio* (1629) or 'On the Use of Rods in Venereal Matters and in the Office of the loins and Reins', was reprinted in English by Edmund Curll as *A Treatise of the Use of Flogging in Venereal Affairs* (1718). Meibom remarked,

> I further conclude, that *Strokes* upon the *Back* and *Loins*, as Parts appropriated for the Generating of the seed, and carrying it to the Genitals, warm and inflame those Parts, and contribute very much to the irritation of *Lechery*. From all which, it is no wonder that such shameless wretches, Victims of a detested appetite, such as we have mention'd, or others by too frequent a Repetition, the *Loins* and their vessels being drains have sought for a remedy by FLOGGING.[16]

The line demarcating medical literature and pornography was a fine one, and the boundaries shifted. Curll was subsequently prosecuted for the publication of

Meibom's medical work, the prosecutor believing it to be obscene. Yet Meibom's work was well known to the educated, and had already been rehashed in English translations of Sinibaldi's *Generanthropeiae* (1642). Alongside *A Treatise of the Use of Flogging*, Curll published *A Treatise of Hermaphrodites* featuring two women alternating masculine and feminine roles while indulging in flagellation. A voyeuristic manservant, Nicolini, watches them through a peephole. Barbarissa, seen as 'not so Masculine', has difficulties obtaining an 'erection of her Female Member' so her lover, Margureta, flogs her with a birch rod. In *The Honest Fellow, Or Reveller's Memorandum-Book* (1790), flagellation was again mentioned as a cure for impotence:

> Thence what desperate toil
> By flagellation, and the rage of blows,
> To rouse the VENUS loitering in his veins![17]

The advocates of the corporal discipline of children latched on to the curative powers of flogging as an example of its beneficial effects. One London letter purporting to be from 'A Female Advocator for Birch Discipline', dated 6 December in the *Bon Ton* December 1795 issue, wrote: 'We live in an age so dissolute, that if young girls are not kept under some sort of restraint, and punished when they deserve it, we shall see, by and bye [sic], nothing but women of the town parading our streets and public places.' She spells out the medicinal powers of the lash: 'Physicians strongly recommend to punish children with birch for faults which appear to proceed from a heavy or indolent disposition, as nothing tends more to promote the circulation of the blood than a good rod, made of new birch, and well applied to the posteriors.' She stresses the harmless nature of the rod: 'Birch breaks no bones, and therefore can do no great harm: and the harm it does is very trifling, when put in comparison to the evils it can prevent.'[18] Supporting medical opinion of the day, erotica such as *Venus School-Mistress* (see below) would take up the medical notion, also advocating the curative powers of flagellation.

Having looked at the use of the whip in the household, in schools, as a corporal punishment and as a cure for impotence, this next section will explore genuine reported instances of flagellation as a sexual predilection.

Flagellation as a sexual activity

One trial case of sexual flagellation which came to light uncovered the sexual activities of a group of middle- and lower middle-class young professional people in Norwich. They were found to be indulging in a variety of sexual experiments which included bisexual flagellation.[19] Samuel Self, a bookseller, and his wife, Sarah, finding themselves in debt took in another couple, Jane and Robert Morris, as lodgers. Meanwhile, Samuel Self was pressurising his 25-year-old friend, John Atmeare, to have sex with Sarah with the main aim of divorcing her while avoiding alimony. Self had wrongly banked on his wife not wanting to reveal the sexual activities in court. The description of group sex with four in a bed, group exhibitionism and flagellation came out: Samuel Self would put Jane Morris over his knee in the kitchen or on the upstairs bed and spank her naked buttocks. He also used rods and birches 'of which you had a great store or bundles' for the purpose of sexual pleasure. Various other sexual flagellation activities took place between others in the house.

Lawrence Stone, who uncovered the Norwich group, believes that pornography had a direct inspirational effect on their activities citing as evidence the available translations of French pornography in *The School of Venus* (1680), *Tullia and Octavia* (1684) and *Venus in the Cloister* (1692). He suggests that without pornography, it was unlikely that the group would have devised such activities, suggesting that the main source of information and influence was from the book trade. He supports his argument by pointing out that the group did not indulge in oral or anal sex, lesbianism or homosexuality. But no evidence exists that the group read any of this pornography. Tribadism is examined in *Venus in the Cloister* yet is not experimented with amongst the Norwich group.[20] Conversely, neither do group activities form part of any of the books, yet figure highly in real-life relations. Flagellation, although mentioned, is by no means a preoccupation in the pornography mentioned by Stone; *The School of Venus*[21] mentions flagellation only once, and then disparagingly:

> *Susanne:* They're those people whom you have to beat in order to get them interested. They strip naked in a large room and the girls take rods and beat them on the belly and all over until they see their yard growing erect. Then they throw down the rods, as if all this was nothing to run yards untie their own bellies and so take their pleasure.
> *Fanchon:* And such men can't manage an orgasm?
> *Susanne:* Of course they can, much more than the others. Afterwards it's impossible to restrain them.
> *Fanchon:* Even so, what a shocking thing it is when a girl is unlucky enough to have to whip her lover before he can get an erection![22]

The nuns indulge in only a taste of flagellation in *Venus in the Cloister*. There appears to be no extant copy of the book entitled *Tullia and Octavia*, so it is unlikely that Stone knew its contents.[23] His assertion therefore is hard to believe. It is more likely that sexual flagellation was already taking place and pornographic books merely reflected current trends. Flagellation was certainly not a new sexual practice, having been explored by the ancients[24] and it is just as likely that sexual practices already extant were explored in a new erotic fiction, the two then interacting with the development of pornography.

The *Bon Ton Magazine* for December 1792 reported that a club of 'Female Flagellants' met on a Thursday evening in Jermyn Street, London to indulge their own passions. Allegedly, the women were married and, having 'grown weary of wedlock in its accustomed form, and possibly impatient of that cold neglect and indifference which, after a certain term, becomes attendant upon Hymen, determined to excite, by adventurous application, those ecstasies which in the earlier period of marriage they had experienced'. About twelve women were involved in the group, six flogging the other half dozen. The chairwoman of the club gave each one a rod and began the proceedings herself.[25] It is, however, impossible to tell whether the *Bon Ton* was relating fact or fiction, although it was notorious for relating gossip. This eighteenth-century interest in flagellation was another sexual predilection which would be explored in depth in a new wave of fictional flagellation erotica which emerged in the form of a pornographic novella.

Flagellation pornography

The English interest in sexual flagellation surfaced in a new wave of pornographic fiction which emerged during the last quarter of the eighteenth century and ran into the nineteenth century. The flagellation theme was crystallised, the topic now becoming the main thrust of the whole story. The emergence of a new sub-genre can be seen with the publication of a plethora of pornographic novellas with titles such as *The Birchen Bouquet* (1770), *Exhibition of Female Flagellants* (1777) and *Venus School-Mistress, or Birchen Sports* (c.1808–10).[26] Dating the corpus of these flagellation novellas has led to confusion, many of them being attributed to the nineteenth rather than the eighteenth century, probably because of the extant reprints. Its clandestine nature has inevitably made it difficult to place and date the material and to identify publishers and authors. Pirate editions further complicate this process. However, with some investigation, the material can be pulled together into a body which was developing between 1770 and 1830. According to Ashbee, the original edition of *The Spirit of Flagellation; or The Memoirs of Mrs. Hinton, Who kept a School many years at Kensington*, appears by the costume prints to be c.1790, and according to a preface to *Exhibition of Female Flagellants* was reprinted by 'Mary Wilson' in 1827.[27] *Manon La Fouëtteuse, or the Quintessence of Birch Discipline* (c.1805),[28] often as with many others, mistakenly thought to be a late nineteenth-century original piece of flagellation pornography (usually referring to William Dugdale's[29] edition of 1860)[30] is in the early nineteenth century.[31] Court records for 1809 refer to the publisher, Edward Rich Junior, who was prosecuted for publishing the bestial *A Feast For All*, who had also published *Manon La Fouëtteuse, or the Quintessence of Birch Discipline* which included indecent postures of copulation.[32] Edward Rich was sentenced to two years hard labour in the House of Correction at Clerkenwell, including the pillory at Charing Cross. James Templar was also prosecuted for these. He also published *Venus School-Mistress*.[33] According to Ashbee, the *Birchen Bouquet* dates to 1770 or 1790, reprinted by George Cannon[34] in 1826 with engravings,[35] and printed again for 'George Tickler' (Dugdale) in 1860. Cannon was also responsible for *Element of Tuition* ('1794'), which had a prominent flagellation theme, printed around 1830, as did *The Bagnio Miscellany*,[36] published in 1830[37] by Cannon, containing 'the adventures of Miss Lais Lovecock as written by herself and what happened to her at Miss Twig's Academy'. Ashbee reported it to be 'a filthy and worthless book'. However, judging by the quantity of available material such books with central themes of flagellation would become increasingly popular and would remain so throughout the nineteenth century.

Kearney gives us two references for *Exhibition of Female Flagellants* (1777), both to be found in the Private Case at the British Library.[38] According to Kearney, one edition was published by Dugdale in c.1860: 'London. Printed at the Expense of Theresa Berkeley for the Benefit of Mary Wilson'; the other was one of a series of seven books reprinted by James Camden Hotten[39] in 1872 bearing the inscription 'Now first published from the authentic boudoir anecdotes, French and English, found in a Lady's Cabinet, printed for G. Peacock, 1777'. Other books in the Hotten series included a sequel to *Exhibition of Female Flagellants, Anecdotes and Lectures of the Female Flagellants for the Second Part with Tales* which is a collection of letters, tales and anecdotes, allegedly sent in to the editor from female readers of the first part. *Lady Bumtickler's Revels, Treatise of the Use of Flogging in Venereal Affairs, Madame Birchini's Dance, a Modern Tale, with Original Anecdotes collected in Fashionable Circles, by Lady Termagant Flaybum, Sublime of Flagellation in Letters from Lady Termagant Flaybum* and *Fashionable Lectures* were also included in a series Hotten facetiously entitled 'Library Illustrative of Social progress. From the Original editions collected by the late Henry Thomas Buckle, author of "A History of Civilisation in England"'. Ashbee responded that the books did not come from the collection of Buckle, but were in the possession of a 'well-known London collector' (himself).[40] Ashbee gives reference to three other editions of *Exhibition of Female Flagellants* apart from the Hotten version. First, the original edition, from which Hotten reprinted, containing a vignette of Cupid bound to a tree with a young girl preparing to whip him (no date mentioned) (figure 38); one 'printed at the expense of Theresa Berkley [*sic*] for the benefit of Mary Wilson by John Sudbury, 252 High Holborn,' dated 1793, but is in fact George Cannon's edition of c.1830 (on the frontispiece, this one contains a vignette of a hand brandishing a rod with a second title-page holding a lamp); and a third edition by Dugdale c. 1860 which contains a reprint of *The Cherub* (1792).[41] This is the correct dating for *The Cherub* as it was advertised in the *Bon Ton* for March 1792. It apologises for not being able to publish as promised: 'Interesting Extracts from the celebrated new pamphlet called THE CHERUB, or Guardian of Female Innocence – disclosing the treachery of Fortune Tellers, Boarding School, Milliners, and Apparent Women of Fashion – is unavoidably postponed'.[42]

Clear evidence points to the date of the original publications of *Exhibition of Female Flagellants* to being in the late eighteenth century. First, it is stylistically less developed than nineteenth-century flagellation pornography, although this can of course be faked. However, the content of the prose and the signals carried within it very much reflect the letters in the *Bon Ton* of the 1790s (see above), and so fits with other contemporary material. Second, Hotten was known for reprinting older books. The fourth volume in his series of seven books on flagellation was Meibom's *A Treatise of the Use of Flogging in Venereal Affairs*, the original written in 1626. Third, an earlier edition than Hotten's reprint of *Exhibition of Female Flagellants* is extant in the British Library. The preface states, 'this work was originally published about fifty years since and is now become so very scarce as seldom to be obtained'. According to Ashbee, Cannon's 1830 version carried this preface, thereby dating the original as far back as c.1780.[43] Furthermore, this edition states: 'Of the numerous books of this description formerly in circulation,

EXHIBITION

OF

FEMALE FLAGELLANTS

IN THE

Modest and Incontinent World.

Proving from Indubitable F A C T S,
That a Number of LADIES take a SECRET PLEASURE,
In W H I P P I N G their own,
AND CHILDREN COMMITTED TO THEIR CARE :
AND THAT THEIR P A S S I O N
FOR EXERCISING AND FEELING THE
P L E A S U R E OF A B I R C H - R O D,
FROM OBJECTS OF THEIR CHOICE,
OF BOTH SEXES,
IS TO THE FULL AS PREDOMINANT,
AS THAT OF MANKIND.

Now Firſt Publiſhed,
*From Authentic Anecdotes, French and English, found in a
Lady's Cabinet.*

LONDON:
Printed for G. Peacock, No. 66 Drury Lane.

MDCCLXXVII

Figure 38 Cupid with a birch. Frontispiece and title-page to Anon, *Exhibition of Female Flagellants in the Modest and Incontinent World*, reprint c. 1840.

only one is to be had at the present moment, namely, "The Spirit of Flagellation", reprinted by Miss Wilson in the year 1827 – all the rest are entirely out of print ...'. Miss Wilson is ascribed the title of 'Reviver of Erotic Literature in the present century' due to her reprints of old flagellatory material in a series of 'Birchen Classics'. According to Iain McCalman, 'Mary Wilson' was the pseudonym of Erasmus Perkins, who was editing, translating and publishing books on the 'philosophy of birch discipline' at the end of the 1820s.[44] This points to the date of at least one edition to around 1830 when Perkins was working in conjunction with Cannon.

Other historians agree with Ashbee. Iwan Bloch does not doubt its authenticity as an eighteenth-century source.[45] Peter Wagner gives the first publication dates of volume I and II of the series as 1777 and 1785 respectively.[46] One book entitled *Female Flagellants* is illustrated in a copy of Gillray's print *A Sale of English-Beauties, in the East Indies* dated 1786 (figure 2), and is likely to be the same book, so it must have existed by this time. Furthermore, Lady Termagant Flaybum mentioned in the titles of both the fifth and sixth books, *Madame Birchini's Dance ... by Lady Termagant Flaybum* and *Sublime of Flagellation in Letters from Lady Termagant Flaybum,* was a popular eighteenth-century character, indicating that these two books in Hotten's series might also have been from an eighteenth-century original. Roxana Termagant could be seen in *The Drury Lane Journal* and was the pseudonym for Bonnell Thornton (1724–68), a journalist who also wrote for *The Connoisseur*. Gillray's personified the figure in his sketch of *Lady Termagant Flaybum Going to Give her Step-Son a Taste of her Desert after Dinner* (Figure 39). His print bears the inscription 25 May 1786 by W. Holland, who was connected to 'George Peacock', the name of the publisher which appears on the title-pages of the *Exhibition of Female Flagellants*. This print also carried the address at 66 Drury Lane. Ashbee stated he was uncertain whether the name of George Peacock was real or assumed: 'At all events, he must have been associated or in partnership with W. Holland, both at 66, Drury Lane and 50 Oxford Street.'[47] Finally, the seventh book of the Hotten series, *Fashionable Lectures*, might too have been a reprint of an earlier work. The names of the harlots included recognisable eighteenth-century prostitutes. If Hotten had wanted to publish a new money-spinner, it is more likely he would have used the names of current whores, particularly since these books were used as a form of advertising for flagellatory services and the brothels that provided them (see below).

The connection between Peacock and Holland, as with most clandestine operators, is a complicated one, but links can be made. The series of works on flagellation are said to be published for G. Peacock and sold at 66 Drury Lane from

LADY TERMAGANT FLAYBUM going to give her STEP SON a tule of her DESERT after Dinner
A Scene performed every day near Grosvenor Square to the annoyance of the neighbourhood.

Figure 39 James Gillray, *Lady Termagant Flaybum*, 1786.

1777 to 1785. William Holland is listed as having operated from that address between 1782 and 1786 and from 50 Oxford Street between 1782 and 1803.[48] A William (as opposed to George) Peacock is registered as having operated with William Holland from 18 Salisbury Square, listed as a pocket book-maker, stationer and book-binder.[49] Trade Committee Minutes also list a certain Peacock (no initials given, but presumably William) as having operated from 18 Salisbury Square.[50] Another list states that William Peacock was operating at that address between 1778 and 1861, and '& Sons' to his trade between 1801 and 1809.[51] George might have been one of his sons. Also, a George Peacock was operating as a master bookbinder in York between 1776 and 1809, who might have collaborated with Holland. In any event, there was obviously a family of Peacocks working in the book trade in league with Holland, suggesting that George Peacock was the original producer of *Exhibition of Female Flagellants*.

Venus School-Mistress: or Birchen Sports ('1788') was allegedly written by a well-known flagellant, Theresa Berkeley, and published by Mary Wilson, the two women's names which were given as the publishers of *Exhibition of Female Flagellants* and various other flagellation erotica (see above).[52] Ashbee believed the book was based on the authentic memoirs of Theresa Berkeley which were destroyed, and suggests the book was first published c.1808–10. He notes three other editions: one c.1820; Cannon's edition c.1830 to which a preface by 'Mary Wilson' was added (see above); and Dugdale's edition c.1860. He does not believe it could have been published before 1805 because of the references made to *Manon la Fouëtteuse* (see below) which was published after that date.[53]

This emergence of this flagellation material during the last quarter of the eighteenth century reflected an increasing interest with flagellation as a sexual theme. Having looked at some of the problems with dating and identifying the publishers and authors of this flagellation material, the next section will identify the themes that emerge in the flagellation fiction and how the flagellant came to be identified.

Themes in flagellation fiction

Common story-lines or scenarios emerged in pornographic flagellation novellas which ran through most of the plots. Certain motifs would be used as signals which became essential to this sub-genre. First, the importance of blood, evident in earlier erotica,[54] was further emphasised in this new material. Blood on the skin, particularly white skin, became a focal point. Second, the location changed. Early flagellation scenes were played out in Catholic convents and monasteries. This setting would gradually be eclipsed by the more domestic interiors of the home and its substitute, the boarding school. Third, the positioning of the body was important. Attention to details of particular favourable positions led to descriptions of flagellants lying over laps, bending over sofas and crouching over stools. Fourth, the relationship between the flagellants became more disciplinarian and incestuous. The flagellants were either governesses with their pupils, or mothers/stepmothers/aunts with their young relations. Fifth, a dress code emerged, which identified the sexual fetish of the wearer – purple gloves and nosegays being especially significant.

Throughout all the flagellation stories, the focus was on the particular body parts which were of interest to the flagellant – the thighs, buttocks and forearms. Earlier attempts at presenting flagellation in erotica had come from French adaptations or translations and were frequently set in a religious location, as seen in *Venus in the Cloister* and *Tryal of Father Girard*.[55] With the new English setting, the location of the scenes became domestic and thereby tinged with incest.

So far, little work has been undertaken to investigate the motifs which signified the eighteenth-century flagellant. The next section will concentrate on two main flagellation novellas, *Exhibition of Female Flagellants* and *Venus School-Mistress*, and compare them with a contemporary magazine, the *Bon Ton*, to provide an insight into the nature of flagellation material at this time. It will show how erotic perceptions about the sexual role of the female flagellant in erotica were hewn from English culture (as explored above). It will draw out the themes current in flagellation material exemplifying both its coded signals and its incestuous nature to understand how the flagellants identified themselves and others.

Blood

The display of blood became an essential ingredient in flagellation material. This is explored in *Exhibition of Female Flagellants*, a collection of anecdotes in prose, mainly made up of conversation between two young women, Flirtilla and Clarissa. The interest is focused on the blooded buttocks as a governess disciplines her pupil:

> she commands her to lye across her lap, or to mount on her maid's shoulders, and then with the loveliest hands imaginable removes every impediment from the whimpering lady's b———e, who all the time, with tears, and entreaties of the sweetest kind implores her dear mother or governess, to pardon her; all which the lovely disciplinarian listens to with the utmost delight, running over with rapture at the same time those white, angelic orbs, that in a few minutes she crimsons as deep as the finest rose, with a well-exercised and elegantly-handed rod!

The severity of whippings under the hand of Lady Caroline were displayed at some length as one witness comments, 'but I soon understood she carried her passion to greater lengths with others – particularly Ma'emoiselle B., who has been whipped by her till the blood has been near starting'.[56]

The preface to *Venus School-Mistress: or Birchen Sports* supplies an extract from the correspondence of a gentleman living at the time who was an ardent follower of the birching school confirming the contemporary erotic delight experienced through the sight of blood:

> In my experience I have known personally several ladies of high rank who had an extraordinary passion for administering the rod, and that too with

merciless severity. I knew too the wife of a clergyman, young and pretty, who carried the taste to excess. I have known only one who liked receiving it, and she was quite of the lowest order; when excited by drink, she would allow herself to be birched until her bottom was utterly raw, and the rod saturated with blood, she crying out during the operation 'harder! harder!' and blaspheming if it was not well laid on.

In one letter, a customer wrote to stipulate the sort of chastisement they required and how much they were prepared to pay:

1. To be well secured to the horse with the chains I bring.
2. One pound for the first drawn blood.
3. Two pounds if the blood runs down to the heels.
4. Three pounds if it reaches the heels.
5. Four pounds if it flows on the floor.
6. Five pounds if you cause me to faint away.

These displays of blood were at the core of the flagellatory descriptions, in this case simultaneously acting as advertising material for the type of services which could be obtained at Theresa Berkeley's brothel. [57]

Governesses and boarding schools

The themes of blood are linked to the governess character. Boarding schools became a prime location for sexual action in flagellation erotica, along with private parlours and the nursery. To a large extent, these specific locations would overtake the nunneries as an erotic backdrop for flagellation, although cloister novels would remain popular. The dominatrix in these fantasies was frequently a teacher or governess. In *Exhibition of Female Flagellants,* one Miss L, a 'votary to birch-discipline', the daughter of a clergyman, opened a boarding school enabling her to indulge her particular fantasies, whipping sometimes a dozen girls a day: 'Her pleasure was to cut them, and generally whipped till the blood would come.'[58] In another tale, blood is connected to sexual fervour. The heroine Flirtilla alludes to her blood rising, '[I] felt her [the governess's] soft angelic hand catch hold of my arm to bring me to the sopha [*sic*], my blood mantled within me as if I had been in a fever … . I was whipped by this lovely woman, not only then, but several times since.'[59]

The positioning of the body and gradual revealing of certain parts of the body were a particular development in flagellation material which saw a concentration on the buttocks, thighs and plump forearms. There was much 'lifting of shifts', 'lowering of breeches' and 'tucking of shirts', as seen in one anecdote which relays the positions and preparation involved in the disciplining of a young boy; the flagellator:

laid him across her lap, and after removing his shirt above his waist, made use of all the tricks she had heard gentlemen were fond of who loved the rod, such as settling him on her knee, handling his b————e, at the same time pulling his breeches lower, tucking in his shirt, and talking of the ladies who spare the rod and spoil the child, bidding him at the same time prepare for something delicious from her hand, for nothing was half so pleasing to her as exercising the rod on a bold boy's b————e.[60]

Children were obvious sexual fodder in this material, the flagellators viewing both young boys and girls as a source of sexual pleasure. The relationship between the couples was often familial. One Miss B————ge————n, who was 'a corpulent but handsome woman', 'passionately fond of the exercise'[61] took pleasure in whipping her young nephew:

and instantly stretched him along the sopha where she whipped him with a severity I had never seen before; and what amazed me was, the boy would not acknowledge himself in error to the last; and arose with more pleasure in his countenance than anguish.[62]

The flagellant and recipient are frequently depicted within an affectionate relationship. If the participants were not related, then the roles of governess and pupil were played out with the dominant partner taking on the persona of governess. In *Exhibition of Female Flagellants*, Clarissa takes the leading role. 'She instantly, by desire, assumed the character of Flirtilla's Governess and having stretched her on the bed, with some seemingly reluctant struggles on the part of Flirtilla, she uncovered to the waist the plumpest, fairest, and most beautiful posteriors that ever charmed mankind.'[63] A particular interest in buttocks is keenly accentuated in this erotica. Also, flagellation activities are frequently between women. After the above scene, Miss B., the subservient partner, takes on the role of naughty child:

I could not conceive what she was at till she dropped to her knees, implored, with streaming eyes (for she absolutely cried), forgiveness from her dear aunt for insulting her, and declaring she would never offend me again. All the time she was on her knees she was kissing my hand with greater ecstasy than it had ever been kissed before.[64]

Although in much earlier material, tribadism and submission are explored in parts of the story, in *Exhibition of Female Flagellants* they become central themes.

The vocabulary and style of these erotic books reflected the expressions, terminology and debates being carried in racy magazines. In 1788, the same year *The Times* was deliberating on school discipline, the *Rambler's Magazine* jovially related stories of whippings given by governesses which left pupils sore for a week. One letter from a young girl describes how the magazine was smuggled into her school.[65] This appears to have started a flurry of letters on school discipline, which was to continue for the next decade. In an interchange of letters in the *Bon Ton* during the 1790s, recommendations on the merits of such punishment asserted that a good flogging could stimulate the blood. The practice was further exposed in a letter to the *Bon Ton* magazine dated March 1792, when one writer disparages the punishments taking place at a boarding-school near Parsons Green:

> whenever one of the Mademoiselles offend their Mistress so, as to deserve the calling of a third power, or, to speak more plainly, to need the application of any instrument with which nature has not already provided her, the young lady is conducted into a closet, set apart chiefly for that purpose, where they immediately proceed to action, after the following manner.[66]

In another letter to *Bon Ton* for March 1794, on 'the Utility of Birch Discipline', a 'Miss Birch' wrote:

> I have kept school, though not above two and twenty years, these four years, and have been under the necessity to use the rod almost every day; and though I tickle my pupils very smartly, I assure you, that in an hour after the whipping they are as gay and as full of play, as if they had not felt the rod.[67]

At the same time, she points out the propitious medicinal qualities of flogging (a notion propounded by Meibom), declaring that a good flogging 'promotes the circulation of the blood in dull children, and will fetch out, often, talents that would, otherwise, have remained concealed, perhaps forever'.[68]

In *Venus School-Mistress*, Berkeley experienced her first taste of flogging in school. A fresh stock of canes was steadily replenished by a male employee 'bringing every Monday a regular supply of birch broom for the use of the school, which he cut fresh from the trees'. Other instruments kept by this particular school-mistress included not only the birch but a more violent instrument: 'She used as a kind of cat-o'nine tails, or rather o'sixty tails, for it had about sixty lashes to it, of the length of the arm. It was made of thin slips of parchment, which had been first moistened, and closely twisted, with five knots at the end.'[69] Theresa Berkeley describes herself as having 'a particular itch for flogging',[70] this predilection coming from the surprising sights to which she had been subjected as a child. *Venus School-Mistress* also incorporates Meibom's medical notion, one governess confiding: 'I have very much afflicted at times with rheumatism in my backside, and suffer a great deal from it – the physician has prescribed the use of birch – will you do me the favour to give me a good whipping with this rod?' Although, of course, we can see the intention of the governess, the ruse has to be based on a known medical conception of the day. Indeed, in the footnotes, the writer states: 'I have flogged many gentleman with birch for the same complaint, who preferred it to flesh brushes.'[71]

Incestuous mothers and stepmothers

In flagellation erotica, mothers and stepmothers figure prominently. The scenes not only carry paedophiliac overtones, but also hint at incestuous relationships. In *Exhibition of Female Flagellants*, stepmothers are seen to beat their stepchildren, the material carrying sexual connotations. One tale relates a mother and her maid who flagellate the young son. They 'instantly unbuttoned his breeches, and let them down to his knees; and having placed him across his mother's lap, and the women holding his legs, his mother whipped him till the twigs flew about the room'.[72] Tales of daughters receiving a flogging are also prevalent:

> The mother did not say a sentence in reply, but instantly left the room, and returning in less than a minute, with a neat rod in her hand, she commanded Miss to lie across her lap, who instantly, with disdain pictured in her countenance, complied.[73]

The picture of the maternal despot appears to have been a popular one. She reappears again in a sham letter written to the *Bon Ton* magazine of January 1796. 'Rebecca Rantipole' claimed she was under the torture of floggings from her tyrannical stepmother: 'I hope you insert this Mr Editor – though I must expect to feel the birch for it, when my mother reads it – because, I am persuaded that in the end reflection and her natural goodness will prevail, and cause her to treat us with more humanity.'[74] These letters purported to come from members of the public but were more likely an editorial hoax. In *Venus School-Mistress*, Theresa Berkeley refers to the birch as the most popular method of punishment for children, both her mother and her teaching partner at their boarding school staunch supporters of its use:

> My mother, as well as her sweet partner, were great advocates for the use of the rod, never adopting any other mode of punishment, as the generality of the children's parents prefers that kind of correction, indeed by far the best, as no sort of injury to the child can result from it, particularly when the birch is green, so it has been late adopted in many schools for boys and girls instead of canes.[75]

Tribadism, incest and discipline were all played out within 'safe' relationships in the security of parlours or schoolrooms. Earlier occasional expeditions into flagellation scenarios had identified specific titbits to stimulate the flagellant. These themes became accentuated and elongated with additions of incest to create a new form of fully-fledged flagellation pornography. The creation of specific symbols and codes saw an obsession with clothing (the 'tucking in' of shifts, the 'pulling down' of breeches) and a focus on positions of the body (lying over sofas, stools and laps) thereby exposing the buttocks. The crimson blood on lily-white buttocks was all-important; the redder the blood and the whiter the flesh, the more provocative the image. The most significant factor in all these new elements was the refocusing of the object of desire, which saw a shift from the genitalia to the buttocks and thighs. These areas defined the *raison d'être* for the flagellant. Furthermore, a particular type of dress emphasising a particular class of women, from the elite or upper-middling sort, would also become a necessary part of this material. The image of this character was identifiably the strict disciplinarian, the controlled female. This added to the excitement when she invariably collapsed in a frenzy of uncontrolled sexual abandonment.

Dress

The women in flagellation erotica were depicted as strong and forceful. Their authority often lay in the awe inspired by their delicate costume and elegant manner. Female apparel was described in great detail in this sub-genre, the mothers and governesses notable for their elite style. The quality of beauty and refinement was summed up in Lady Caroline's description to Flirtilla in *Exhibition of Female Flagellants*: 'Mrs. E was of the first order of beauty; has a fine noble person, fine turned limbs, good skin, fine blue eyes, as brilliant as Venus', and when not ruffled by passion, was certainly very captivating', but most importantly, 'If she but stepped across the room, she discovered uncommon dignity and elegance, and every motion expressed the *Je ne scai* [sic] *quoi* an elegant French woman is so idolized for'.[76] Expensive jewellery and high orna-mentation played a central role in creating a character. Flirtilla, who was about to be spanked by Lady Caroline, 'idolized Lady Caroline's hand and arm, could not bear to see it hold the rod without the ornaments of pearls, bracelets, a wedding and diamond rings'. Even details about her shoes became important: 'her legs and feet which were elegantly formed, were as beautifully embellished with the neatest silk shoes and brilliant buckles of the first fashion.'[77]

Venus School-Mistress and the *Bon Ton* magazine show a similar interest in details of dress and elegance. Theresa Berkeley uses the same French phrase as was used in *Female Flagellants*. One attractive woman is described as 'elegantly formed and rather pretty; she had that *je ne sais quoi*, so captivating in French women'.[78] A fondness for French elegance was also admitted by the author of a letter entitled 'The French Governess' printed in the *Bon Ton* magazine in November 1791. While expounding upon the merits of flogging children, he confessed his admiration for a young French governess as 'every motion of her expresses that *je ne sais quoi* an elegant French woman is so idolised for'. Again, a measured interest for her couture is revealed: 'she was in a white dress, with a very broad blue sash, her hair dressed all over in curls, with a very broad chignon behind – very high on the left side of her bosom, she wore a most enormous bouquet of natural flowers.'[79] This fixation on dress brought with it recurring motifs, most notably, those of purple gloves and nosegays.

Gloves

A curious fetish for gloves appeared in the letters printed in the *Bon Ton* magazine in the June 1792 edition. A letter headed 'A Singular Propensity' signed by Amicus, castigated the flogging of children. He had witnessed a Mrs. James flogging her daughter, Sophia, 'which seemed to be laid on with uncommon vigour of arm', merely for not mending her purple gloves. The scene went on for quarter of an hour and, as he listened, he was astonished to hear Mrs. James confess to her sister how much joy she had received from the situation, and astounded when the sister added: 'if she was her daughter, she would flog her every day of the week; for she knew of no greater delight than that of whipping a full-grown girl'.[80] Such letters divulging an obsession with gloves became a curious yet popular phenomenon and such accessories were to make an impact in various guises.

Purple gloves were a particular favourite. They were used to signify power of the wearer and more emphatically to denote sexual experience in whipping. In a letter dated July 1792, the same Mrs. James and Sophia used purple gloves as a sort of dress code, a symbol of the flagellator: 'After we had been a few minutes seated in the carriage, Mrs. James took a new pair of purple gloves out of her pocket, and pulling off the white ones she had on, began drawing them on her arms: this did not escape the notice of the sister, who turning to Sophia, asked her where the pair of purple mitts were, which she had given her to mend.'[81] In the case of flagellation, it was the dominant partner who donned the purple gloves. The changing out of 'ordinary' white gloves to the purple gloves of flagellation was also indication of a shift from the business of everyday life into a sexual performance. Readers would have been aware of the code implicit in these letters, a shared knowledge existing between readers and magazine.

Kid gloves play a part in another anecdote told in the *Bon Ton,* in November 1795. In one particular episode witnessed by the author through an open front door, a neighbour is described disciplining two daughters, Molly and Louisa. Turning to the youngest, the neighbour demanded: 'And you, Miss; give me my purple kid mitts out of that drawer and tell Molly to come up to my bedroom ... . When she had received the mitts, she drew them on her arms, fastening them up so tight that they looked almost like her skin.' Molly endured a beating, attempting to protect herself the while, 'For her skin was almost as white as the white kid gloves she had on, and which she held on her backside to save the strokes.'[82] White, a symbol of purity, was closely associated with sexual innocence in flagellation material, descriptions of white flesh fronting the literature.

In February 1796, another advocator of the birch, 'Old Maid, from Cow-Cross', wrote in to the *Bon Ton* magazine to complain of the degeneracy of the youth of the day positing the example of a friend who became stepmother to two daughters. She and her friend were sitting in her friend's dressing-room before dinner, when, as

> she was drawing on a new pair of purple kid gloves, she happened to burst one of them; and taking them off, she desired her eldest step-daughter, a beautiful girl of sixteen, to sew up the rent, which miss most insolently refused.

The young girl retorted that there were maids enough in the house and that she had an aversion to purple gloves. Assisting her friend, the Old Maid dragged the girl to the sofa and 'pulled up her petticoats and pinned her shift to her shoulders'. She made a huge rod 'out of the broom' and 'when she had done, she drew on her purple gloves' and began to whip her stepdaughter. The stepmother inquired: 'Have you had enough to cure your aversion to purple gloves?'[83]

Nosegays

Nosegays became another erotic symbol of the flagellant which indicated a woman's sexual predilection. *Exhibition of Female Flagellants* described one female flagellant's manner of dress: 'Very high on the left side of her bosom she wore an enormous bouquet of natural flowers, which had a beautiful effect.' Another, Miss G., confessed: 'I am passionately fond of them – their sweetest perfume excites in me the most exquisite sensations.' Her lover 'delighted in seeing her dressed with a very large one'. She knew of many gentlemen 'who were equally as fond of them as his lordship, and delighted in seeing their favourite ladies dressed with them; that the larger and fuller they are, the greater their influences, especially when worn very high on the left side, the luxurious mode of wearing them'.[84]

Nosegays as symbols of flagellatory inclinations were not confined to erotic books, but were recognised by gentlemen's magazines. The *Bon Ton* magazine for November 1791 published a letter from 'A. Rambler' who described the actions taken to entice an admired French governess: 'as she is extremely fond of flowers, I got my flower-garden enlarged and stocked with the most beautiful flowers that could be had.' A. Rambler follows her, secretly watching her make up a birch in the garden: 'She, however, stopped in the shrubbery and seeing her cut some twigs from a birch tree, I retreated behind some trees unperceived; when she had got a large bundle of them, she bound them up in a rod with a ribbon, as she seemed to be in a great passion.' She went upstairs to the room where she sat with her pupils and commenced flogging the young girl who had scratched her brother all over in a fit of temper.[85]

The theme of nosegays is reiterated in the alleged memoirs of Theresa Berkeley as she describes a Miss Smart 'with her face nearly buried in her monstrous bouquet',[86] while flogging a young girl. Theresa relates how her mother and Miss Smart looked out for such pleasures and went in search of similar experiences, 'when, after partaking of some refreshment, they both set off for Ranelagh, with their monstrous brooms in their bosoms, in search of further adventures'. Nosegays are a prominent feature in all the works examined here and acted as both a signal to others in search of similar persuasion and an enticement and stimulant. Men took pleasure in the women wearing nosegays:

> Miss Smart told me that they had often gratified that gentleman in that manner, whose propensity was to enjoy a woman, while another was engaged in a severe whipping to some wicked young girl, provided he was convinced that she really deserved the chastisement, and that he took singular pleasure in having them dressed in white, with a large nosegay in their bosom.[87]

Theresa noticed that whenever she wore a nosegay, her lover was always smelling it: 'I discovered that he was passionately fond of seeing me with a very large one: he would frequently bring me one, and then help me fasten it to my bosom.'[88] The next three pages are taken up with descriptions of the delights of her nosegay.

The mistresses themselves had special relationships with both those in authority above them and with their pupils, and this was bound by flowers, particularly nosegays. One mistress, a widow, 'received very often from one of the trustees of the school, an old friend of hers, and a consummate libertine, a large *bouquet* of costly flowers'. She also founded her relationships with a particular pupil through flowers and 'would sometimes make her favourite girl or myself wear it, though on *certain* occasions she would wear it herself'. Depictions of a female network that had been formed were shown through the protagonist's displays of favouritism, delegation and subjugation to the whip:

> One day that she had received a most beautiful one, almost as big as a broom, she insisted on my wearing it, and would tie it herself to my bosom, which she did so high, that the flowers shaded almost the left side of my face – that is the way, said she, a young girl should wear a nosegay.[89]

The left-hand side was known to be the sinister side in heraldry[90] but more likely this was also the accepted fashion.

Theresa herself experienced sensations through flowers which overwhelmed her. After she has scourged her first male youth of thirteen, the scent of the flowers and the ferocity of the flogging make her weak with lust.

> I remained for a few minutes in a kind of lascivious stupor, and confess that I felt that day such *sensations* as I had never experienced before – perhaps, too, the luxurious fragrance of my bouquet might have contributed to excite them, for I kept smelling at it all the time I scourged him.[91]

The same stimulating effect brought on by the floral scent was noticeable in another governess who approached Theresa:

> Then she began kissing me again, and smelling at my nosegay, or rather my sweet broom, the scent of which seemed to augment her lust: she passed her hands all over my body, and in fact acted with me as men do with women to excite their desire before they enjoy them.

The 'Bouquet de Luxe' appears to be the largest nosegay one could acquire and has explicit sexual connotations. The *bouquet de luxe* are otherwise known as 'nosegays of lechery',[92] so called on account of their supposed influence in venereal enjoyments.[93] Nosegays were therefore yet another symbol used in flagellation material. It was one signifier amongst many others which included elegant dress, purple gloves and incestuous relationships.

Conclusion

Flagellation was a common spectacle in the eighteenth century, as seen in household corrections dispensed to wives and servants, the enforcement of school discipline and public punishments meted out by the courts. Discussions on the merits and demerits of flogging in magazines and newspapers were buttress by both medical promulgations and Protestant antagonism to Catholic Church penances. Flagellation thereby became yet another prominent contemporary issue embraced by erotica and imbued with a sexual element. But this was developed in English erotica and undertaken in a specific way, with certain conservative elements incorporated, and other more radical ideas omitted.

English flagellation erotica began to explore settings apart from the convent (although this would continue), particularly domestic backdrops. The family (or pseudo-family in the case of the boarding school) became the centre of this erotic world. The characters of mother/stepmother/governess were all conservative figures as displayed by their refined style of dress. Yet although the sex is comfortable and 'safe', dangerous elements lay in the very conservative and familial nature of the characters. Closely linked to representations of the 'household' or its alternative, the school, these sheltered settings for a childhood-related fantasy introduced the taboo of incestuous relationships.

The confined settings worked to create intimacy. Sexual flagellation did not happen in wide agrarian or pelagic settings (as seen in chapter 5) in either French or English erotica, but remained within the enclosed private spaces of the domestic household and the claustrophobic boarding school. The construction of these intimate areas, removed from the public arena, suggests the need for a constriction in the mental scenery. Confinement and enclosed spaces became increasingly important in defining the erotic. Furthermore, rigidity and discipline began to figure as an added *frisson*. This idea is supported by the themes of chastisement, correction and control conveyed in all the flagellation material. However, just as the Catholics had deemed the nunnery a proper place for a girl's education, so the Protestants had deemed the patriarchal family. It was therefore inevitable that this area would be used as a target for attack, just as the monasteries had been in France. In this, the more pornographic material was attacking the most vulnerable area of the restrictive dominant morality, one which highlighted the constrained and sexually continent patriarchal family. Just as the writers of French erotica had an understanding how an attack on the Church would be perceived as erotic, the English writers comprehended that an attack on the highly prized family could lead to a new erotic threat. Furthermore, as flogging became less public and more 'hidden', erotica took the opportunity, once again, to expose what was meant to be hidden in polite society.

Within flagellation material, there was a distinct emphasis on displaying mounds of white flesh and a certain focusing on particular body parts. During the latter part of the seventeenth and early eighteenth century, breasts and vaginas, particularly virginal ones, were the main source of erotic enjoyment. However, although breasts and vaginas would continue to figure well into the nineteenth century, by the 1770s, a new interest arrived with the introduction of flagellation material which placed the focus firmly on buttocks, thighs and the forearm; thus the main pleasure spot was no longer always the genitalia. Within this material, although coitus did take place, it did not invariably happen.

8
Conclusion

London was deluged with new erotica during the eighteenth century with an increase in the type of format in which it could be bought and a wider circulation to the country. English erotic fiction, salacious reports of French priests' trials, short Gothic seduction stories, suggestive poems, bawdy chapbooks, scandal sheets and French pornography could be bought in forms cheap enough for the middling and even for the lower ranks. These social groups were not averse to spending their money on reading material which included erotic and obscene books. Although it is obvious that greater access would have been possible for the richer gentleman, working men who liked such books could, and would, purchase them. Nor is there any reason to suppose that women could not also lay their hands on erotic material. It would appear from prostitutes' memoirs that pornography was kept in brothels for perusal by clients so the women themselves would certainly have had access to it. Mistresses of gentlemen would also have read their lovers' pornographic books. Those from the lower classes, such as servants buying it for their masters, would have known the content of such clandestine books. Although the greatest circulation and availability was in London (with Edinburgh, Bath and Dublin publishing the occasional racy memoir or erotic book), material spread throughout the country through hawkers, subscriptions and visitors returning from London. We can therefore see that the conventional assumption that erotica was contained within a readership of elite richer gentlemen needs to be reassessed. Without doubt, women, the lower classes and country folk would know about, see and have access to erotica in many different formats.

A specifically English erotica developed during the eighteenth century which ran the gamut from slightly risqué to the illegally obscene. The euphemistic implicative erotic material was more 'permissible' and allowed for sex to be discussed within the public realm, although some of the more graphic work in this category was published under assumed names. Blatantly obscene material remained clandestine because of its prosecutionable content. However, the mixing of the erotic with the non-erotic in contemporary books shows how the sexual was integrated into a wide variety of discourses, both public and private. Pornography was not yet relegated to the back shelf.

Cultural influences

Erotica contained not only the subject of sex, but just about every other popular topic which was being discussed in eighteenth-century society. Erotica discussed superstition, botany, medicine, regeneration, folklore, electricity and religion. Non-sexual topics current elsewhere were turned into sexual themes. Definitions of sexuality arranged themselves within new contexts, aligning themselves with new contemporary topics. This is most evident in the erotica that responded to the new sciences and that which was written as a result of anti-Catholicism. Mapping these various cultural threads in erotica has to be undertaken with caution. Although certain topics emerged at specific times, some themes existing in the eighteenth century can be traced back to earlier material. Without reading all erotica from the earliest times, the emergence of any one theme is difficult to trace with certainty. One thing we can say is that the production of erotic material rapidly increased, along with other types of material, and encompassed discussion on a wide range of subjects.

Any attempt at a broad chronological overview should be approached tentatively since its study is dependent on material still extant. No doubt much of the material has been lost to us forever, particularly the ephemera. The more likely material to survive is the hardbound and, being more expensive, this might reflect tastes particular to the wealthier reader. Great tranches of erotica material might yet emerge which could significantly add to this picture.[1] With these cautions in mind, erotica can be placed in a basic time frame which helps to understand the development of material circulating during the eighteenth century.

First, during the seventeenth century and throughout the eighteenth, the humoral notions about the body continued to be in evidence in erotica. These consisted of ancient medical beliefs and folklore which were expressed through discussion on, and displays of, bodily fluids. These can be seen in French originals, such as *Histoire de Dom B*; in translations of French books, such as *Dialogue between a Married Lady*; and in English erotica, such as *The Palace Miscellany* and *A New Atlantis for the Year One Thousand Seven Hundred and Fifty-Eight*.

Second, from at least the beginning of the century, English anti-Papist rhetoric incorporated an increasingly strong sexual current in its accounts of tales of priests' and nuns' sexual misdemeanours. Encouraged by the popularity of French pornography such as *Venus in the Cloister*, the 1720s and 1730s saw the emergence of obscene English-language descriptions of priests' sexual activities, which were presented as sexually graphic factual accounts. The grandiloquence of early anti-Catholic rhetoric was left behind in concentration on supplying what was essentially pornographic material. In other words, this material was written with the prime intent to arouse sexually, unlike the earlier material where the main focus had been attacking Catholics, using sexual accusations as the best means to do so; the latter was a means to an end; the former an end in itself. Pornography was finding its voice.

Third, during the 1730s and 1740s, there was a proliferation of Curll's productions based on agricultural metaphors and classical allusions (*New Description of*

Merryland, Merryland Displayed, Pandora's Box, The Rape of Adonis). Around this time, scientific themes were explored; during the 1730s, botanical metaphors became popular, followed by satires on reproduction in the 1750s, and electrical metaphors in the 1770s. The only English original fictional obscene book published up until then was Cleland's *Memoirs of a Woman of Pleasure* in 1749.

Fourth, the final flourish of the eighteenth century can be seen in the flagellation material of the 1770s, the importance of which should not be underestimated, since it moved erotica into another realm, with a fictional sexual exploration of a monolithic theme of a particular predilection as its main theme. Racy poems were prevalent throughout every single decade of the century, and these would remain popular, found in bound-book form and in single sheets.

Perceptions of female and male sexuality

The erotic body was not viewed in a single way within erotica but through a multiplicity of diverse lenses. These variations can be seen in depictions of the humoral body, the landscaped body, the reproductive body, the botanical body, the electric body, the religious body and the body of the secular flagellant.

Male and female sexuality can be seen in erotica in the ever-widening range of characters being depicted: whores and rakes were to be found in brothels; virgins waited in family homes to be seduced by libertine rascals; gullible virtuous nuns found their introduction into libidinous abandonment through secular paramours or villainous priests; the refined élite flagellants were found in parlours and in boarding schools disciplining their young charges; while the morally unencumbered rustic peasants continued to occupy the Arcadian landscapes free from guilt. Each of these images presents a complex view about sexualities which were current in the eighteenth century.

Female sexuality

Some notions are expressed routinely throughout much of the erotica, for example, the notion of an essential female lasciviousness.[2] Women were believed to be connected to nature. As such, they were seen as unrestrained and powerful and therefore were perceived as both irrational and threatening. This notion was expressly exemplified in depictions of the female humoral body which was the epitome of sexual abandonment. Despite being embarrassing and 'uncivilised' because of its uncontrolled expression of bodily fluids, it was nonetheless pleasurable since it could not be 'spent' or exhausted. Women were frequently depicted as taking control of their own destinies which included licentious liberation. The landscaped female was depicted as wild, unpredictable and unruly echoing the uncontrollable force of the humoral female body. Efforts were directed at 'taming'/controlling this nature/female body.

Two prominent images initially appear at odds with the sexually voracious image: the nun and the flagellant. The innocent female *religieuse* differs from the other images in that she is portrayed as submissive, gullible and a victim. Therefore, she is non-threatening, as she wields no power. However, once introduced to sex, she became as lascivious as the other images. The female flagellant is depicted as dominant, elegant and refined, whilst being familial and domesticated. Although a disciplinarian, the excitement now rests not in her continued lasciviousness but in catching a glimpse of her gradual unravelling, as her sexual fervour pushes through her disciplined exterior. This image exemplifies the contriving of the writers; in their search for heightened excitement, they make the female figure even more tantalising.

Male sexuality

The most prominent image of masculinity was one of self-possession and self-control, the polar opposite of its female comparative. The male humoral body was depicted as a cauldron of energetic fluids which were to be released only in a controlled way. When they were copious and frequent, through excess ejaculations, men became enfeebled, weakened or died, a 'spent force'. The male 'scientific' body was seen as the principal force for reproduction (the 'tree of life' of the botanical metaphor, or the 'spark of life' of the electrical metaphor) or, conversely in satire, was made completely redundant (as in Hill's erotica), echoing male fear of female autonomy. The landscaped framework depicted sexual men as controllers/cultivators, as farmers or gardeners (and occasionally seafarers) attempting to conquer the unruly force of female sexuality. When in the rare instance the male body was defined as part of a landscape, it was in the rigid disciplined form of classical buildings, as in *The Worship of Priapus,* as opposed to the free-flowing nature of the female landscape.

The two obvious representations which do not mesh with this self-possessed image are the religious male body, which was undisciplined and antagonistic; and the male flagellatory body, which was undisciplined and needed to be controlled. In an area of writing where one would imagine it in man's interest to depict himself as powerful, why did these images exist in erotica? In answering this, we need to place the body within its location. The image of the male religious body was not a Protestant one but the body of a Catholic. This could therefore be defined not only as undisciplined but as abhorrent. With the flagellatory body, flagellation was connected with children and related to childhood fantasy. Children, along with women, were conventionally classed as inferior so this image was permissible. Alternatively, it was sometimes connected with older people, usually older impotent men.

The main themes of sexuality

Certain overriding themes were prominent through nearly all the erotica around these sexualities. Women were seen to sap men's strength and were continually portrayed as exhausting their partners. They were frequently conveyed as sexually indomitable, occasionally troublesome, but more usually threatening. Assumptions about female sexual unassailability fostered male anxieties, resulting in accusations of nymphomania and female adultery. Because of the perceived threat caused by their women's sexual capacity and natural lasciviousness, continuous attempts were made to overcome and control female sexuality.

Making love to a woman was frequently compared to going into battle. Images of female containment point to male anxieties about the needs to restrain women and command power. Nonetheless, most scenarios describing sexual activities between men and women, did so within the context of a loving relationship between a couple who mutually enjoyed sex.

Women were presented as both passive and assertive, sometimes within the same works, sometimes within the same female character. Both demeanours were deemed attractive; a faithful wife was desired, but so was a lusty wench. Despite the female body being shown as having weak resolve in humoral terms, they possessed an underlying force which gushed out making them strong and enduring. Men, despite their control and power within the sexual hierarchy, were often seen as less energetic sexually and easier to weaken. Apportioned significance of bodily fluids saw sperm deemed more important than vaginal fluid; it was thought there was less of it and it was more 'precious'. Despite this, men's and women's genitalia were deemed equally important and revered (or mocked) in similar terms.

The agricultural, scientific and anti-Catholic material share concerns about reproduction, its cost (in monetary or moral terms), how to prevent it and how to procure abortions. Although prominent in earlier material, anxieties around contraception and venereal disease are not prominent in eighteenth-century flagellation pornography from the late eighteenth century onward. This indicates recognition by writers that expression of worries was not conducive to sexual pleasure. The focus should be on unencumbered sex.

The development of English pornography

For the development of English pornographic material, the writers recognised the need for certain elements if they were to provide the maximum pleasure principle. This was increasingly geared towards solitary reading. The writers saw a need to develop new and diverse methods to fulfil specifically English whims. Fresh techniques in erotic writing were therefore introduced which stimulated the pornographic imagination and allowed for the expression of a new form of sexual fantasy. These can be seen in diversification in location and the multiplicity of sexual interests being provided. New elements were added; claustrophobia, submission, domination, blood, flagellation and incest would turn a merely erotic work into pornography for sexual gratification.

Location

Writers of erotica saw a need to expand upon the intimate setting which had already occurred in seventeenth-century French pornography. The smaller confined areas in which sex was conveyed were further developed, running alongside the open rurally spaced locations. These settings reflected different modes of living: the transition from open to enclosed spaces, from agricultural to urban, and in certain aspects from public to private. This was a very broad yet subtle development alongside the more bucolic literature. In attempts to provide a more pornographic world, the use of private space was developed.[3] Confined spaces proved more appropriate settings for the exploration of sexual action as seen in the extended use of secluded grottoes, secret niches and labyrinthine pathways, the small enclosed gardens of monasteries and private estates, and the cells of the walled convent.

The development of English pornography was not merely about regurgitating the French material (although this was also happening), but about developing a style and taste catering for the peculiar English preferences. The major development in English pornography can be seen in flagellation material, which shifted sexual action into the genteel family home. Parlours, drawing rooms, nurseries and schoolrooms became prime locations for the exploration of the incest theme, the inclusion of the family unit being integral to this development.

Obviously, there was overlap within these themes. Broad Arcadian landscapes ran parallel with smaller spaces hewn from the neoclassical English garden. Convents were used for both early French pornographic material, but also in later Gothic non-explicit erotica. Overall, there was a comprehensive elaboration in the depictions of sexual action in enclosed spaces, most noticeably in flagellation pornography. Furthermore, there was a subtle shift to a sophisticated domesticity, reflecting the growth of urban spaces and the importance of the family.

The diversification of sexual interests

Different approaches were being tried in an attempt to establish the best way to produce sexual excitement for the reader. Part of this entailed playing with language and speech patterns. For example, submissive female entreaties were common during the eighteenth century. But by the nineteenth century, cursing obscenities began to be routine in the more pornographic material. The increasing use of fictional prose form added realism to pornography. Sexual acts were no longer under the guise of flowery language but became more lurid and described at length. Furthermore, sexual subject matter developed and became increasingly diversified. The early interest in maidenheads, with the occasional diversions into abortion scenes, gave way to polymorphous experimentation, including tribadism, group sex and flagellation. Blood and genital fluids were described at length. From the 1770s onwards, the English took the themes presented in the French convent pornography as a sideline to new lengths. Flagellation became the new obsession, with whole books dedicated to the main theme of birching.

The exposure of blood in earlier material was explored in depth in flagellation pornography. In the case of the eighteenth-century flagellatory body, the bodily fluid most frequently exposed was female blood, usually displayed on the woman's white skin. This was initially a move into exposing the secret part of the female body. As yet, male blood was not so frequently exposed, as his body was still seen to be contained, and thereby controlled. Flagellation material also explored alternatives to genitalia as the focus of sexual joy. Other body parts were also targeted with a concentration on the buttocks and thighs. Although these had been mentioned as desirable subject matter in earlier material, they were now highlighted and repeatedly inspected. As pornography developed in the nineteenth century, further transgression into the body saw development in descriptions of oral and anal sex. The emphasis would be placed on perceived degenerate sexual acts, but in the eighteenth century it was as yet merely the occasional foray into sodomy and dildo use.

An interest in genteel women developed in pornography in the latter part of the eighteenth century, which also saw the rise of the middle classes. Many of the descriptions of the female characters in flagellation material were of women of higher rank, perhaps pandering to the taste of the males of this new social group, or to fantasies of plebeian men for women of a higher social status. Their manner of dress and their social standing were frequently described at length. The fact that they were also described as mothers, stepmothers or governesses, and given a role as head of the middle-class family is significant. The gradual revealing of the licentious nature of such a woman would reflect the process of the transgression of the family moral values.

Ultimately, it was the anti-Catholic erotica that provided the springboard for the development of more private pornographic themes. On the whole, earlier English erotica had portrayed women as sexually on equal terms with men but the anti-Catholic material stands out for its depictions of women in submissive victim roles. Women have become so passive during sex that they are frequently unconscious during the sexual act. This particular locus provided mental boundaries defined within tiny convent cells, claustrophobic corridors and walled gardens. The setting of the convent was crucial, not only in the establishment towards the private, 'hidden' and secret space, but also in providing a stimulus for the breaking of one of the biggest taboos, that of sex within the religious 'family'. English flagellation material would take this idea from the convent into the home of the middle-class nuclear family.

Incest was to be the spur into depravity associated with dangerous sex, increasingly to become a strong element in pornography. What had been castigated at the beginning of the century was to be explored by the end of it. Flagellation had moved on from the 'spiritual' incest of the religious family to incest between female relatives. No longer were the father confessors responsible for debauchery and corruption of the innocent, but one's own mother, aunt or governess. By the nineteenth century, this was taken still further in incest material in which images of the protective father would give way to those of the insatiable paternal rapist.

Radicalism versus conservatism

The significance of eighteenth-century erotica lies not with how radical the writers were, but how conservative. Although some of the erotic threads emitted radical opinions about sex and other issues (to be expected in pornography), other elements were more contained and upheld mainstream ideas. Wagner has pointed to the importance of literary pornography as a vehicle of revolutionary thought in the Age of Enlightenment,[4] but English erotica and pornography often carried traditional beliefs. In relation to medical theories, erotica often retained old folklore views and rejected new scientific revelations. Traditional taboo beliefs about blood, the importance of female chastity, reproduction, marriage and the family, and anti-Catholicism were very conventional themes in eighteenth-century English culture. For example, in some of the works, the writers continued to incorporate themes on the importance of female chastity and advocate marriage as the best form of sexual expression. Not only did erotica continue to validate ancient humoral notions on the necessity of conservation of sperm, but it mocked new scientific theories on reproduction and electricity through satire as seen in *Arbor Vitae, History of the Frutex Vulvaria, Lucina Sine Concubitu, The Electric Eel, The Torpedo*, and so on.

As regards religion, it harboured the same grudges as contained elsewhere in society. It also expressed the same old fears of cuckoldry. Whereas Darnton's findings about the radical influence of cheap pornography on the French Revolution might well be true, in England no such crisis was to take place. Although political skirmishes would be effected through pornography (such as Wilkes' *Essay on Women*) and stabs at the establishment through satirical jibes at the Royal Society, English erotica was less revolutionary. What had worked for French pornography was the use of the convent or religious setting. As a Catholic country, its most sacred institution was the Church. Transgression of sacred boundaries through the use of religious institutions as a backdrop to sexual debauchery was specifically a Catholic country's pornography. England's writers saw the attraction of such transgressions, particularly in the light of the English anti-Catholic stance. But the very fact that England was anti-Catholic meant that the religious transgression would not be so acute and the sexual tension not so intense. The shock value would therefore not be so great since it reinforced beliefs about the Catholics which were already present. For Protestant England, the family was the sacred institution; the shock value would therefore lie in the secular, in the transgression of family values and the inner sanctum of the home. Flagellation material perfected this move. Erotic action in this material was located in the respectable family home or school which meant that its transgression would be more shocking. The violation of the home as an institution, and the breach of the moral values of the family, was a natural progression from the violation of the monastery/convent and religious values. The move with flagellation material into the parlour, nursery or schoolroom provided a move into the secret or 'private' world of the family. This is where the radical nature of pornography can be seen, in the development of incestuous material with its corruption of family values, an attack on the ideology of the family.

Appendix: A Note on Sources

My interest in erotica developed after encountering the work of Victorian bibliophile, Henry Spencer Ashbee. Under the pseudonym 'Pisanus Fraxi',[1] he wrote a meticulous bibliography of erotica in three volumes, *Index Librorum Prohibitorum, Centuria Librorum Absconditorum* and *Catena Librorum Tacendorum*.[2] This work is not a catalogue of his own collection of erotic works as some people think, but a bibliography of those books known to him at the time. Many of these are held in the British Library, bequeathed from Ashbee's own collection. This is now housed in the 'Private Case' collection, and I have used this and other erotica, in the British Library and elsewhere, for the basis of this book. Unfortunately, some of the erotic books Ashbee mentions no longer exist. Luckily, Ashbee left copious annotations of many of these works, and we can at least gain some insight into their contents. The other two major bibliographical works I have used are *Registrum Librorum Eroticorum* (1936)[3] compiled by Alfred Rose under the pseudonym of 'Rolfe S. Reade'; although valuable as a reference source, it is not so interesting or comprehensive as Ashbee's compilation; and Patrick Kearney's *The Private Case*,[4] invaluable to any serious researcher of erotica.

I have had to be selective in my use of texts, and in choosing my focus. I have concentrated mainly on texts written in the English language, since my object is to look at the development of English erotica, although part of its development involves the influence of French erotica. Many of the texts in the Private Case are written in French and I have chosen in the main to avoid these, but include the English translations of French originals, which would have been more widely understood and therefore accessible to a larger audience. Some of the French books I have read so as to compare content with the English translations. I have not been able to include *all* the writings of any one particular sub-genre but have elected to give prime examples of the topic displayed in any one erotic strand.

I have looked at over 500 pieces from the British Library collection, including duplicates[5] and other editions of the same book to look for variations; I have read all the eighteenth-century English works listed by Kearney as being in the Private Case, and all eighteenth-century English erotic books referred to in both Rose's and Ashbee's bibliographies where they were still extant. Obviously, the bibliographies overlap but Ashbee leads to other works extant which are not in the Private Case but in the ordinary catalogue. I have included some fifty pieces from the seventeenth and nineteenth century (about half from each) to use in comparison. I have chosen the material in the British Library since it is the largest collection of English erotica of which I am aware and, until now, has still not been subjected to an extensive critical study. Since the categorising of the Private Case material took place during the nineteenth century, distinctions about the material were based on Victorian values, and were not necessarily the same as those made either now, or in the eighteenth century. Classifying material in this way gives a misleading notion that a definitive clear picture of 'pornography' existed during the eighteenth century, which is not the case (see below). Furthermore, the destruction of books by various libraries on grounds of duplication and/or for moral reasons frequently makes it difficult to estimate exactly how popular a book was since we have no real way of knowing exactly how many editions it went through.

Other collections of erotica exist, such as the Bodleian's, some of their holdings being duplicates of those in the British Library. The Vatican's *Index Librorum Prohibitorum*, allegedly with the largest collection of books (around 25,000 volumes and 100,000 prints) is 'forbidden' to Catholics, and not open to the general public. Occasionally, erotic books or pamphlets were found in other libraries such as the Pierpont Morgan library in New York, but the head librarian believed the main small collection of erotica which they did possess, has since been disposed of. Dubious sources[6] indicated that the Huntington Library in San Marino held a collection of erotica but they had no knowledge of such a collection. However, erotic material does exist in their library (at least two copies were found in the Huntington Library of the same material deemed 'private' by the British Library) although it is not segregated into a 'collection', indicating that the categorisation of such material is fairly arbitrary. Caches of erotica no doubt lie hidden amongst the vast catalogues of more acceptable material. Other sources exist which still segregate material deemed too uncivilised for public eyes, such as the *L'Enfer* at the Bibliothèque Nationale in Paris, the 'Cherry Case' at the Armed Forces Medical Library, and Dr Alfred C. Kinsey's held at Indiana University's Institute for Sex Research.

Notes

Introduction

1 See chapter 1. Peter Wagner, *Eros Revived: Erotica of the Enlightenment in England and America* (London, Secker & Warburg, 1988); Lynn Hunt (ed.), *The Invention of Pornography: Obscenity and the Origins of Modernity, 1500–1800* (New York, Zone Books, 1993).
2 See Robert Darnton, *The Forbidden Best-Sellers of Pre-Revolutionary France* (London, HarperCollins, 1997).
3 Lesley Hall undertakes a similar exploration for the nineteenth and twentieth centuries.
4 For further examples of his work, see below.

Chapter 1

1 Peter Wagner, *Eros Revived: Erotica of the Enlightenment in England and America* (London, Secker & Warburg, 1988), p. 7; Lynn Hunt (ed.), *The Invention of Pornography: Obscenity and the Origins of Modernity, 1500–1800* (New York, Zone Books, 1993), p. 10; Patrick Kearney, *The History of Erotica* (London, Macmillan, 1982), p. 7; Dorelies Kraakman, 'A Historical History of Sexual Knowledge for Girls in French Erotic Fiction, 1750–1840', *Journal of the History of Sexuality*, Vol. 4, No. 4 (1994), pp. 517–48; Maurice Charney, *Sexual Fiction* (Iowa, Kendall Hunt Publishing Company, 1981). Also see Steven Marcus, *The Other Victorians. A Study of Sexuality and Pornography in Mid-Nineteenth Century England* (New York, Basic, 1964).
2 Walter Kendrick, *The Secret Museum: Pornography in Modern Culture* (New York, Penguin, 1987).
3 This has been successfully undertaken by Robert Darnton with French erotica and Peter Wagner with English erotica. See Robert Darnton, 'The High Enlightenment and the Low-Life of Literature in Pre-Revolutionary France', *Past and Present*, No. 51 (1971), pp. 81–115; also see his *The Literary Underground of the Old Regime* (Cambridge, Mass, Harvard University Press, 1982); Robert Darnton and Daniel Roche (eds.), *The Press during the French Revolution* (Berkeley, Berkeley University Press, 1989); and Wagner, *Eros Revived*.
4 Vernon A. Rosario, *The Erotic Imagination. French Histories of Perversity* (Oxford, Oxford University Press, 1997).
5 'One would make no mistake in calling you a pornographer ...', Athenaeus' *Deipnosophistae*, Vol. 13, Section 567b. I would like to thank Colin Annis, librarian at the Institute of Classical Studies Library, for these references and translation.
6 Some writers see pornography as a tool of female oppression and as such, are against it. For examples of this reasoning, see Catherine A. Mackinnon, *Only Words* (Cambridge, Cambridge University Press, 1993); and Andrea Dworkin, *Pornography: Men Possessing Women* (London, Women's Press, 1981).
7 Hunt, *The Invention of Pornography*, p. 10.
8 Jean Marie Goulemot, *Forbidden Texts. Erotic Literature and its Readers in Eighteenth-Century France* (Cambridge, Polity Press, 1994), p. 62.
9 Wagner, *Eros Revived*, p. 6.
10 For list of bibliographers of erotica, see Appendix on 'Sources' below.
11 Legman points out that no erotic bibliographies exclude or differentiate between pseudo-medical texts, chapbooks, bawdy songsters or pornography; all come within

the confines of erotica. Some differentiation can be seen within the audience of such materials. G. Legman, *The Horn Book. Studies in Erotic Folklore and Bibliography* (London, Jonathan Cape, 1970).

12 Roger Thompson, *Unfit for Modest Ears* (London, Macmillan, 1979).

13 However, even the legal definition would find difficulty in pinning down which books it should apply to, and this boundary is by no means clear-cut. The pattern of censorship sometimes appears somewhat arbitrary. For a fuller examination of censorship, including a literary survey, see chapter 2.

14 David Loth, *The Erotic in Literature* (London, Secker & Warburg, 1962), p. 8.

15 David Foxon, *Libertine Literature in England 1660–1745* (New York, University Books, 1965), p. 47.

16 Lisa Z. Sigel, 'Name Your Pleasure: The Transformation of Sexual Language in Nineteenth-Century Pornography', *Journal of the History of Sexuality*, Vol. 9, No. 4 (October 2000), pp. 395–419.

17 In *New Atalantis for the Year 1758*, Rocforia demands foreplay, declaring 'I never let any male suppliant approach the shrine of my Mecca, but after proper adoration paid; such as the burning incense, repeated genufluxions [sic], alternate kissing of the two collateral columns, (white as Parisian marble) which leads to the blissful altar, veiled from the vulgar eyes with the fringe of Venus'. On *New Atlantis*, see chapter 3.

18 See chapter 3.

19 The fear of prosecution, while a possibility, is not really feasible, since many had continued to publish after and despite prosecution during the first half of the century, Edmund Curll being one example.

20 Michel Foucault, *The History of Sexuality*, Vol. I, *An Introduction* (London, Penguin, 1976), p. 34. But also see Colin Jones and Roy Porter (eds.), *Reassessing Foucault. Power, Medicine and the Body* (London and New York, Routledge, 1994) for a criticism of Foucault for his neglect of class and gender issues.

21 Lawrence Stone, *The Family, Sex and Marriage in England 1500–1800* (London, Weidenfeld and Nicolson, 1977), pp. 149–72, 339. Stone went on to consolidate this work in a trilogy on courting, sex and divorce in *Roads to Divorce: England, 1530–1987* (Oxford, Oxford University Press, 1990); *Uncertain Unions, Marriage in England, 1660–1753* (Oxford, Oxford University Press, 1992); and *Broken Lives, Separation and Divorce in England 1660–1857* (Oxford, Oxford University Press, 1993).

22 Paul-Gabriel Boucé (ed.), *Sexuality in Eighteenth-Century Britain* (Manchester, Manchester University Press, 1982); G. S. Rousseau and Roy Porter (eds.), *Sexual Underworlds of the Enlightenment* (Manchester, Manchester University Press, 1987); Robert Purks Maccubbin (ed.), *'Tis Nature's Fault. Unauthorised Sexuality during the Enlightenment* (Cambridge, Cambridge University Press, 1987); Roy Porter and Mikuláš Teich (eds.), *Sexual Knowledge and Sexual Science. The History of Attitudes to Sexuality* (Cambridge, Cambridge University Press, 1994); John C. Fout (ed.), *Forbidden History. The State, Society and the Regulation of Sexuality in Modern Europe* (Chicago, Chicago University Press, 1990). Michael Mason has helped review the notion of 'eighteenth-century libertinism versus Victorian repression', questioning traditional clichés; *The Making of Victorian Sexuality* (Oxford, Oxford University Press, 1994); Franz X. Eder, Lesley Hall and Gert Hekma (eds.), *National Histories, Sexual Cultures in Europe* (Manchester, Manchester University Press, 1999); Kim M. Phillips and Barry Reay (eds.), *Sexualities in History* (London, Routledge, 2002).

23 The wide variety of studies revealing women in British history includes Alice Clark, *Working Life of Women in the Seventeenth Century* (1919, reprint, London, Routledge and Kegan Paul, 1982), Ivy Pinchbeck, *Women Workers and the Industrial Revolution, 1750–1850* (1930, reprint, London, Virago, 1981); Louise Tilly and Joan Scott, *Women, Work, and Family* (New York, Holt, Rinehart and Winston, 1978); Mary Prior (ed.), *Women in English Society, 1500–1800* (London, Methuen & Co., 1985); Anne Laurence, *Women in England 1500–1760. A Social History* (London, Weidenfeld and Nicolson,

1994); and Olwen Hufton, *The Prospect Before Her. A History of Women in Western Europe* (London, Fontana Press, 1997).

24 Martha Vicinus, 'Who is Sylvia? On the Loss of Sexual Paradigms', in Vicinus, 'Sexuality and Power. A Review of Current Work in the History of Sexuality', *Feminist Studies*, Vol. 8, No. 1 (1982), pp. 133–56.

25 Joan W. Scott, 'A Useful Category of Historical Analysis', *American Historical Review*, Vol. 91, No. 5 (1986), pp. 1053–75. Also see Scott, 'Deconstructing Equality-versus-Difference: Or, the Uses of Poststructuralist Theory for Feminism', *Feminist Studies*, Vol. 14, No. 1 (1988), pp. 33–49; and Mary Poovey, 'Feminism and Deconstruction', *Feminist Studies*, Vol. 14, No. 1 (1988), pp. 51–63.

26 Judith Butler, *Gender Trouble, Feminism and the Subversion of Identity* (London, Routledge, 1990), especially pp. 1–34. Also see Denise Riley, *Am I that Name? Feminism and the Category of 'Women' in History* (New York, Macmillan, 1988).

27 Judith M. Bennett, 'Feminism and History', *Gender and History*, Vol. 1, No. 3 (1989), pp. 251–72.

28 Leonore Davidoff and Catherine Hall, *Family Fortunes: Men and Women of the English Middle-Class, 1780–1850* (London, Routledge, 1987).

29 Anna Clark, *Struggle for the Breeches. Gender and the Making of the British Working Class* (London, Rivers Oram Press, 1995), pp. 42–62.

30 Amanda Vickery, *The Gentleman's Daughter. Women's Lives in Georgian England* (New Haven, Conn., Yale University Press, 1998); Robert Shoemaker, *Gender in English Society, 1650–1850. The Emergence of Separate Spheres?* (London, Longman, 1998). Also for a summary of current debates in women's history, see Amanda Vickery, 'Golden Age to Separate Spheres? A Review of the Categories and Chronology of English Women's History', *Historical Journal*, Vol. 32, No. 2 (1993), pp. 383–414.

31 Penelope Corfield, 'History and the Challenge of Gender History', *Rethinking History*, Vol. 1, No. 3 (1997), pp. 241–58.

32 Edward Shorter, *A History of Women's Bodies* (New York, Basic Books, 1982).

33 Clark, *Struggle for the Breeches*.

34 Tim Hitchcock, *English Sexualities, 1700–1800* (London, Macmillan, 1997), p. 2; and his 'Redefining Sex in Eighteenth-Century England', *History Workshop Journal*, No. 41 (1996), pp. 72–90.

35 Randolph Trumbach, *Sex and the Gender Revolution. Heterosexuality and the Third Gender in Enlightenment London* (Chicago and London, University of Chicago Press, 1998), p. 429.

Chapter 2

1 This had been true of non-erotic books, including political and religious attacks made in writings during the seventeenth century but throughout the eighteenth century prosecution was increasingly aimed at books of a sexual nature. See chapter 3.

2 Edmund Curll published an account of Lord Audley's sodomy and adultery trial in 1707.

3 See chapter 7 on 'Flagellation'.

4 Such advertisements are valuable to the scholar attempting to identify the dates of the books.

5 The majority of works listed in Kearney's *The Private Case* are foreign, mostly French.

6 For example, nine copies of *Venus dans le Cloître*, seventeen editions of *Thérèse Philosophe*, and forty-six copies of *Satyra Sotadica* (or *L'Académie des Dames*), and this is only Kearney's listings. Many 'Private Case' books have since been 'demoted' to the ordinary catalogue where more editions lie.

7 David Foxon, *Libertine Literature in England 1660–1745* (New York, University Books, 1965), p. 5. Apparently this book retained its popularity – my Italian friend recalls her father kept a copy in his library in Rome in the 1950s.

8   Patrick Kearney, *The History of Erotica* (London, Macmillan, 1982), p. 24.

9   Kearney attributes *La Puttana Errante* to Niccolò Franco (1515–70); it is often incorrectly ascribed to Aretino.

10 James Maidment, who reprinted it in Edinburgh in 1836, attributes the translation to Sir Roger L'Estrange, but cites no evidence. Sir Roger was surveyor of the printing presses and licensor of the press; in other words, the man in charge of censorship. He is also attributed as translator of *Letters from a Portuguese Nun*; see Raymond Mortimer (ed.), *Letters from a Portuguese Nun* (London, Hamish Hamilton, 1956), p. 12.

11 See chapter 4 on the electrical eel in erotica in the 1770s.

12 Giovanni Battista Marini, *Difesa dell' Adone* (Venetia, G. Scaglia, 1629), IX, pp. 48–51.

13 Kearney attributes the work to Antonio Vignale; it is sometimes falsely ascribed to Giovanni Battista Marini.

14 Armando Marchi, 'Obscene Literature in Eighteenth-century Italy: an Historical and Bibliographical Note', in Robert Perks Maccubbin (ed.), *'Tis Natures Fault: Unauthorised Sexuality during the Enlightenment* (Cambridge, Cambridge University Press, 1987), pp. 244–60.

15 All themes to be explored in later chapters.

16 Not to be confused with Captain Alexander Smith, *The School of Venus, or Cupid Restor'd to Sight* (London, J. Morphew, 1716); or *The School of Venus: or, The Lady's Miscellany* (London, Curll, 1739), though this might have been the publishers' intention.

17 Donald Thomas's preface to Michel Millot and Jean L'Ange, *The School of Venus* (London, Panther Books Limited, 1972).

18 For a history of the book, see Kearney, *History of Erotica*, pp. 34–46; and Foxon, *Libertine Literature*, pp. 38–51.

19 See Peter Wagner, 'Anti-Catholic Erotica in Eighteenth Century England', in Peter Wagner (ed.), *Erotica and the Enlightenment* (Frankfurt, Peter Lang, 1991), pp. 166–209. However, Donald Thomas states that an English translation was available the same year it was first published in France. See *A Long Time Burning. A History of Literary Censorship in England* (London, Routledge and Kegan Paul, 1969), p. 19. It would therefore have been available to an English audience much earlier than the date of Curll's prosecution. In fact, the English translation was advertised in Henry Rhodes, *Term Catalogue* for Easter 1683.

20 Anon, *The Whore's Rhetorick* (London, George Shell, 1683), p. 171.

21 Thomas's introduction to *The School of Venus*, p. 20.

22 Lawrence Stone points to the increasing importance of the nuclear family in *The Family, Sex and Marriage in England 1500–1800* (London, Weidenfeld & Nicolson, 1977). See chapter 1.

23 See chapter 1 for Wagner's comments on taboo.

24 Incest will be explored in chapters 6 and 7, material which introduces corruption of daughters by priests and sexual mother-figures respectively.

25 Foxon, *Libertine Literature*, p. 41. Foxon points to later copies being recorded but which cannot be found; *Delights of the Nuptial Bed, or a Lady's Academy in Dialogues* (printed 'in the island of Paphos', the dedication signed 'Philadelphia, May 1806' with eight plates); *Delights of the Nuptial Bed Laid Open in Luscious Dialogues*. Translated from an original manuscript (Printed in the island of Paphos, Cannon, c.1830); *The Bedfellows; Or Young Misses Manual* (London, Dickinson, c.1820).

26 *L'Académie des Dames, ou Le Meurius Français Entretiens Galas* (A Cythère, Chez l'Amour, au Palais des Graces, 1793), p. 25.

27 Kearney probably means the pornographic fiction form here, since he acknowledges the other erotic works produced at this time. Kearney, *The History of Erotic Literature*, p. 53.

28 Wagner, *Eros Revived*, p. 234. Other editions include *Life and Adventures of Father Silas* (London, private edition, 1907) and *The Lascivious Monk* (Malborough, Venus Classic, 1993).

29   Jean-Marie Goulemot, *Forbidden Texts. Erotic Literature and its Readers in Eighteenth-Century France* (Cambridge, Polity Press, 1994).

30   Foxon classes *Memoirs of a Woman of Pleasure* as the first original English pornography when Britain became an exporter, not just an importer of such material; Foxon, *Libertine Literature*, p. 45.

31   Records of Stationers' Company 1688 contain receipts from the accounts of one investigator of the book trade, Henry Hills, showing where obscene books could be purchased; Foxon, *Libertine Literature*, p. 11.

32   *The Times*, 20 August 1788.

33   H. R. Plomer, *Dictionary of Printers 1726–1775* (Oxford, Oxford University Press, 1932). Also see Ellic Howe, *A List of London Bookbinders, 1648–1815* (London, Bibliographical Society, 1950); John Pendred, *The Earliest Directory of the Book Trade, 1795* (London, Bibliographical Society, 1955); Charles Ramsden, *London Bookbinders, 1789–1840* (London, B. T. Batsford, 1956); Phillip A. Brown, *London Publishers and Printers, c. 1800–1870* (London, British Library Board, 1982).

34   Pat Rogers on 'Publishers and Booksellers' in Gerald Newman (ed.), *Britain in the Hanoverian Age, 1714–1837* (New York and London, Garland Publishing Inc., 1997), pp. 573–75.

35   Cheryl Turner, *Living By The Pen. Women Writers in the Eighteenth Century* (London, Routledge, 1992), p. 86.

36   Robin Myers and Michael Harris (eds.), *Spreading the Word. The Distribution Networks of Print 1550–1850* (Winchester, St. Paul's Bibliographies, 1990), p. vii.

37   Pat Rogers, *Grub Street: Studies in a Subculture* (London, Methuen, 1972). Also see his revision in *Hacks & Dunces, Pope, Swift and Grub Street* (London, Methuen, 1980).

38   Turner, *Living by the Pen*, p. 88.

39   G. S. Rousseau, *Enlightenment Borders* (Manchester, Manchester University Press, 1991), pp. 265–8. G. S. Rousseau and Roy Porter (eds.), *Sexual Underworlds of the Enlightenment*; Roy Porter and Marie Mulvey Roberts (eds.), *Literature and Medicine During the Eighteenth Century* (London, Routledge, 1993).

40   Michael Harris, 'A Few Shillings for Small Books: the Experience of a Flying Stationer in the Eighteenth Century', in Myers and Harris (eds.), *Spreading the Word*, pp. 83–108.

41   SP 35/11/14, f. 33, 25 January 1717/18.

42   Ralph Straus, *The Unspeakable Curll* (London, Chapman & Hall, 1927), p. 14.

43   I have found only one such copy of *Arbor Vitae* in cheap sheet form, the majority of copies of the verse and prose found in the more enduring form of hard-back books. However, many other forms of titillating penny sheets and bawdy verse are extant in sheet form, collected in books of tracts in the British Library.

44   Many editions exist by various publishers. Curll first published it in 1718, followed by a second edition in 1721, and another in 1732 – *The Ladies Miscellany* (London, Curll, 1732).

45   Both themes explored in chapter 4.

46   Some manuscripts of erotic poetry remain but these are few. See Legman, *The Horn Book*, pp. 78–135. Even less evidence exists of any manuscripts of erotic prose.

47   On Curll's publications, see Straus, *The Unspeakable Curll*; and see below.

48   *A New Miscellany of Original Poems*. Translation and imitations. By the most Eminnent [*sic*] Hands Viz. Mr. Prior, Mr. Pope, Mr. Hughes, Mr. Harcourt, Lady M. W. M. [Mary Wortley Montagu], Mrs Manley, & Co. Now first published from their Respective Manuscripts (London, T. Jauncy, 1720).

49   Straus, *The Unspeakable Curll*, pp. 21, 44–7, 50–1.

50   Plomer, *Dictionary of Printers 1726–1775*.

51   Paula McDowell, *The Women of Grub Street. Press, Politics and Gender in the London Literary Marketplace 1678–1730* (Oxford, Oxford University Press, 1998), pp. 38, 43.

52 Pat Rogers on 'Publishers and Booksellers' in Newman (ed.), *Britain in the Hanoverian Age, 1714–1837*, pp. 573–5.

53 McDowell, *Women of Grub Street*, p. 294.

54 Ibid., p. 26.

55 Tim Merriman, Esq., *The St. James's Miscellany Or The Citizens Amusement Being A New And Curious Collection Of Many Amorous Tales Humorous Poems, Diverting Epitaphs, Pleasant Epigrams, and Delightful Songs, etc...* . (London, printed and sold by T. Payne, at the Crown in Paternoster Row, T. Ashley, in St. Pauls Church-yard, A. Dodd without Temple Bar. E Nutt at the Royal Exchange, and by the Bookseller of London and Westminster, n.d.).

56 McDowell, *Women of Grub Street*, p. 56.

57 Straus, *The Unspeakable Curll*, pp. 65–6.

58 In 1784, one French woman, Madame Charmet, wrote to her suppliers about Turgot's *Oeuvres Posthumes* commentating on the power and energy of the book, displaying knowledge of the trade and ability to recognise a best-seller. A female bookbinder was found by the Parisian police in 1800 with 200 unbound copies of Piron's *Oeuvres badines,* an eighteenth-century poetry book illustrated with erotic engravings; Darnton, *The Forbidden Best-Sellers*, p. 37; Lynn Hunt, *The Invention of Pornography: Obscenity and the Origins of Modernity, 1500–1800* (New York, Zone Books, 1990), p. 18.

59 Foxon, *Libertine Literature*, pp. 16–17.

60 Ibid., p. 16.

61 Paul-Gabriel Boucé, 'The Secret Sex Nexus: Sex and Literature in Eighteenth Century Britain', in Alan Bold (ed.), *The Sexual Dimension in Literature* (London, Vision Press, 1983), p. 71.

62 C. Y. Ferdinand, 'Local Distribution Networks in Eighteenth-century England', in Myers and Harris (eds.), *Spreading the Word*, pp. 131–49.

63 Quoted by Tessa Watt, 'Publisher, Pedlar, Pot-Poet: The Changing Character of the Broadside Trade, 1550–1640', in ibid., pp. 61–81.

64 D. F. McKenzie, 'Trading Places? England 1689-France 1789', in Haydn T. Mason, *The Darnton Debate. Books and Revolution in the Eighteenth Century* (Oxford, Voltaire Foundation, 1999), pp. 1–24.

65 The editor of the *British Magazine* wrote his own erotic prose. See chapter 4.

66 'An Odd Letter From a Country Correspondent', *British Magazine*, Vol. 4, June (1749), p. 232.

67 This remark would indicate that scandal sheets were common reading material made available in coffee-shops.

68 John Feather, 'The Country Book Trade in Books', in Myers and Harris (eds.), *Spreading the Word*, pp. 165–83.

69 The printer was probably Elizabeth Brice.

70 Ian Maxted, 'Single Sheets from a Country Town: the Example of Exeter', in Myers and Harris (eds.), *Spreading the Word*, pp. 109–29.

71 Kearney, *History of Erotic Literature*, pp. 53–100. Also see Foxon, *Libertine Literature*; and Randolph Trumbach, 'Erotic Fantasy and Male Libertinism in Enlightenment England', in Hunt (ed.), *Invention of Pornography*, p. 253.

72 Margaret Spufford, *Small Books and Pleasant Histories. Popular Fiction and its Readership in Seventeenth-Century England* (Cambridge, Cambridge University Press, 1981), p. 62.

73 Hitchcock, *English Sexualities*, pp. 10, 13, 40.

74 Darnton, *The Forbidden Best-Sellers*, pp. 107, 110, 111, 184–97.

75 Goulemot, *Forbidden Texts*, p. 17.

76 Despite mentioning the Beggar's Benison five times, Wagner's only source is an edition of the above book edited by Alan Bold (who, according to Wagner, is 'not a great stickler for bibliographical detail'). Wagner is at least tentative in his assertions, qualifying his statements with 'if the records are to be believed'. However, Karen

Harvey, in her PhD thesis, uses the records as the main basis for her evidence of male readership of erotic works yet provides no evidence of the veracity of the minutes or proof of existence of the society. G. Legman was probably the first to mention the eighteenth-century Beggar's Benison, referring to the *Supplement to the Records* printed in 1892; but although he believes the society to have existed, he suggests the book was a parody/plagiarism of other writings. Wagner, *Eros Revived*, p. 58; Karen Harvey, 'Representations of Bodies and Sexual Difference In Eighteenth-Century English Erotica' (PhD Thesis, London, RHBNC, 1999); G. Legman, *The Horn Book: Studies in Erotic Folklore* (London, Jonathan Cape, 1970), pp. 142–3.

77 Anon, *Supplement To The Historical Portion Of The 'Records Of The Most Ancient And Puissant Order Of The Beggar's Benison And Merryland, Anstruther', Being An Account Of The Proceedings At The Meeting Of The Society, Together With Excerpts, Stories, Bon-Mots, Speeches, And Songs Delivered Thereat* (Anstruther, printed for private distribution, 1892).

78 *Beggar's Benison*, pp. 13–14.

79 Wagner has suggested that the manuscript existed in the early 1730s. See Peter Wagner's introduction to *Fanny Hill or Memoirs of a Woman of Pleasure* (London, Penguin, 1985), pp. 7–30.

80 See Kearney, *The Private Case*, p. 290.

81 Ibid.; Jad Adams, *Madder Music, Stronger Wine: The Life of Ernest Dowson* (London, I. B. Tauris, 2000), pp. 125–6, 145–7,150, 154–5, 160–5; G. A. Cevasco (ed.), *The 1890s. An Encyclopaedia of British Literature, Art, and Culture* (London & New York, Garland Publishing, Inc., 1993), pp. 562–3.

82 With thanks to Dr. Norman H. Reid at the University of St. Andrews University Library, and Jilly Boid at the Artefact Museum of St. Andrews University for their assistance in providing me with the manuscripts and artefacts for viewing.

83 The importance of which I only recently uncovered; see below.

84 All correspondence quoted below is held at St. Andrews library, MS. 38351.

85 For the main biographies of Sir Francis Dashwood, see Donald McCormack, *The Hell-fire Club* (Norwich, Jarrolds, 1958); Daniel P. Mannix, *The Hell-Fire Club* (London, New English Library, 1962); Betty Kemp, *Sir Francis Dashwood* (London, Macmillan, 1967); Geoffrey Ashe, *The Hell-Fire Club. A History of Anti-Morality* (1974; reprint Stroud, Sutton Publishing, 2000); Eric Towers, *Dashwood. The Man and The Myth* (London, Crucible, 1986); Sir Francis Dashwood, *The Dashwoods of West Wycombe* (London, Aurum Press, 1987).

86 An inventory was taken of the books in the library at that time, a copy exists in Sir Francis Dashwood's private papers. I would like to express my gratitude to the late Sir Francis Dashwood for allowing me the time to examine the private papers kept at West Wycombe.

87 See Walpole's *Memoirs of the Reign of George III* (London, Lawrence and Bullen, 1894), Vol. I, pp. 246–9.

88 Sir Francis Dashwood, private papers.

89 Dashwood, *The Dashwoods of West Wycombe*, p. 19.

90 Some of the portraits, including that of Dashwood, now hang at Brookes's Club in St. James' Street. Other portraits of Dashwood's set, including members of the Divan Club, hang in the hall at the Dashwood home in West Wycombe.

91 For a fuller discussion of this book, and problems with costs, see chapter 5.

92 The case has been discussed at length by most of Wilkes's biographers. See Charles Chenevix Trench, *Portrait of a Patriot. A Biography of John Wilkes* (London, Blackwood, 1962); and more recently, Peter D. G. Thomas, *John Wilkes, A Friend to Liberty* (Oxford, Clarendon, 1996).

93 Ashbee, Vol. 1, p. 202.

94 Walpole, *Memoirs of King George III*, Vol. I, p. 310.

95 *Gentleman's Magazine* 1763, Vol. 33, p. 526.

96 *Gentleman's Magazine* 1763, Vol. 34, p. 580.

97 Thomas Hamilton, *New Crazy Tales* (Mulbery Hill, printed at Crazy Castle, 1783).

98 According to Wagner, Swift owned classical erotica of Lucian, Terence, Virgil, Ovid, Suetonius, Rabelais, La Fontaine, Voltaire and Bussy-Rabutin. Sterne had licentious novels of Crébillon, Le Sage, Marquis d'Argens, Voltaire and numerous 'chroniques scandaleuses'. He also owned paramedical works on sexology, midwifery, venereal diseases and classical erotica in French translation. Wagner, *Eros Revived*, pp. 3–4.

99 J. Paul Hunter, *Before Novels: the Cultural Contexts of Eighteenth Century English Fiction* (New York, Norton, 1990).

100 Alan Booth, 'The Memory of the Liberty of the Press: the Suppression of Radical Writing in the 1790s', in Paul Hyland and Neil Sammells (eds.), *Writing and Censorship in Britain* (London, Routledge, 1992), pp. 106–22.

101 David Cressy, *Literacy and the Social Order: Reading and Writing in Tudor and Stuart England* (Cambridge, Cambridge University Press), pp. 45–6; also see R. A. Houston, *Literacy in Early Modern Europe: Culture and Education, 1500–1800* (London, Longman, 1988).

102 For a discussion on the problem of defining and assessing literacy, see R. S. Schofield, 'The Measurement of Literacy in Pre-Industrial England', in J. R. Goody (ed.), *Literacy in Traditional Societies* (Cambridge, Cambridge University Press, 1968), pp. 311–25.

103 Quoted by Tessa Watt, 'Publisher, Pedlar, Pot-Poet: The Changing Character of the Broadside Trade, 1550–1640', in Myers and Harris (eds.), *Spreading the Word*, pp. 61–81.

104 See chapter 6.

105 William Cobbett, *The Progress of a Plough-Boy to a Seat in Parliament As Exemplified in the History of the Life of William Cobbett* (reprint: London, Faber and Faber, 1933), p. 13.

106 Michael Harris, 'A Few Shillings for Small Books: the Experience of a Flying Stationer in the Eighteenth Century', in Myers and Harris (eds.), *Spreading the Word*, pp. 83–108.

107 R. M. Wiles, *Serial Publication in England Before 1750* (Cambridge, Cambridge University Press, 1957), pp. 7–8.

108 See the introduction to Paul Hyland (ed.), Ned Ward, *The London Spy* (reprint: East Lansing, Mich., Colleagues Press, 1993), pp. xi–xxviii.

109 Teresia Phillips was an eighteenth-century British courtesan who brought out her memoirs relating her various intrigues. No doubt inspired by the success of Ms. Phillips, Charlotte Charke brought out her own memoirs entitled *A Narrative of the Life of Mrs. Charlotte Charke* (1755). Daughter of the poet Colley Cibber, she embarked on a life on the stage playing roles at the Drury Lane theatre. She gained a reputation as a wastrel and a troublemaker. Down on her luck, she worked as a strolling player, sold sausages and wrote novels, including *The Lover's Treat, The Mercer* and *Henry Dumont*. She frequently disguised herself as a man, both on and off stage, and formed 'female friendships'. See Fidelis Morgan, *The Well-Known Trouble Maker. A Life of Charlotte Charke* (London, Faber and Faber, 1988).

110 Wiles, *Serial Publication ...*, pp. 63, 143; Emma Donoghue, *Passions between Women* (London, Scarlet Press, 1993), p. 13.

111 At least one sheet exists in the BL.

112 A few historians have mentioned female readers (cited above and below), but mainly as an aside.

113 Anon, *Merryland Displayed* (London, Curll, 1741), p. 5.

114 Henry Fielding, *Shamela* (Oxford, Oxford University Press, 1980), p. 344.

115 *Rare Verities. The Cabinet of Venus Unlocked and Her Secrets laid open* (London, P. Brigg, 1657). This continued to be popular during the eighteenth century.

116 *A New Atlantis for the Year One Thousand Seven Hundred and Fifty-Eight* (2nd edn., London, M. Thrush, 1758), p. 52.

117 Jan Fergus, 'Provincial Servants' Reading in Late Eighteenth Century', in J. Raven, H. Small and N. Tadmor (eds.), *The Practices and Representation of Reading in England* (Cambridge, Cambridge University Press, 1996), pp. 202–25.
118 Stone, *The Family, Sex and Marriage*, p. 394.
119 Mary Lyons (ed.), *The Memoirs of Mrs. Leeson* (Dublin, The Lilliput Press, 1995), pp. 154, 170.
120 Foxon, *Libertine Literature*, p. 6.
121 In 1805, the Vice Society used the case of Baptisa Bertazzi, who was sentenced to six months for selling obscene prints in a girls' school, as a defence against its detractors; Edward J. Bristow, *Vice and Vigilance. Purity Movements in Britain since 1700* (London, Macmillan, 1977), pp. 42–3.
122 Iain McCalman, *Radical Underworlds. Prophets, Revolutionaries and Pornographers in London 1795–1840* (Oxford, Oxford University Press, 1988), p. 213.
123 Copies of *Lucina Sine Concubitu* exist in the Private Case in the BL. See chapter 3.
124 Darnton groups François de Baculard d'Arnaud's *Le Canapé* with other French pornography such as *Histoire de Dom B* and *Thérèse Philosophe*; Darnton, *Forbidden Best-Sellers*, p. 87.
125 Stella Tillyard, *Aristocrats. Caroline, Emily, Louisa and Sarah Lennox 1740–1832* (London, Vintage, 1995), pp. 19–20, 39, 172, 238, 263, 351.
126 Roy Porter and Lesley Hall, *Facts of Life. The Creation of Sexual Knowledge in Britain, 1650–1950* (New Haven, Conn., and London, Yale University Press, 1995), pp. 6–7.
127 See above.
128 Where authors are known, they are indicated throughout the body of the work.
129 See Kearney, *The Private Case*, p. 319.
130 Rousseau, *Enlightenment Borders*, p. 299. For an examination of Hill's work, see chapter 4.
131 For a fuller account and assessment of other versions of *Essay on Woman*, see Ashbee, Vol. I, pp, 198–236; Kearney, *A History of Erotic Literature*, pp. 70–4.
132 See Cheryl Turner's examination of women writers in her *Living by the Pen. Woman Writers in the Eighteenth Century* (London, Routledge, 1992).
133 G. J. Barker-Benfield, *The Culture of Sensibility. Sex and Society in Eighteenth-Century Britain* (Chicago, University of Chicago Press, 1992), p. xix.
134 Ros Ballaster, *Seductive Forms: Women's Amatory Fiction from 1684 to 1740* (Oxford, Clarendon Press, 1992).
135 Katherine Rogers, *Feminism in the Eighteenth Century* (Hemel Hempstead, Harvester Press, 1982), p. 22.
136 McDowell, *Women of Grub Street*, p. 294.
137 Thomas, *A Long Time Burning*, p. 88.
138 Lyons (ed.), *The Memoirs of Mrs. Leeson*, p. xvi.
139 Turner, *Living By the Pen*, p. 88.
140 The Licensing Act of 1662 should have been renewed in 1679 but lapsed, although the printing of seditious, blasphemous and obscene books was still punishable under common law. The Licensing Act was renewed in 1685 and again in 1693 but the House of Commons refused to renew it again in 1695. For a listed chronology of censorship at this time, see Hyland and Sammells (eds.), *Writing and Censorship*, pp. 16–17.
141 C. H. Rolph, *Books in the Dock* (London, André Deutsch, 1969); Christopher Hill, 'Censorship and English Literature', in *Collected Essays, Vol. I. Writing and Revolution in Seventeenth Century England* (Brighton, Harvester Press, 1985).
142 Foxon, *Libertine Literature*, p. 11.
143 Alec Craig, *The Banned Books of England* (London, Allen & Unwin, 1962), p. 25; State Trials XVII, p. 157.
144 Translation by Albertus Magnus; see Straus, *The Unspeakable Curll*, p. 101.
145 Translated by George Sewell, 'a physician', p. 103.
146 PRO, SP, 35/55/102.

147 25 marks (£16 13s 4d) fine each for publishing *Venus in the Cloister* and *Treatise of the Use of Flogging*, plus 20 marks for Ker's *Memoirs*, which he had published throughout the long-drawn out trial, plus the pillory.

148 State Trials XVII, pp. 153–60; and John Strange, 'Reports of Adjudged Cases in the Courts of Chancery Kings Bench', 1755, quoted in Straus, *The Unspeakable Curll*, p. 121 and Thomas, *A Long Time Burning*, p. 83.

149 Lord John Fortescue, *Reports of Select Cases* (London, 1748), p. 100.

150 Alison Shell, 'Catholic Texts and Anti-Catholic Prejudice in the Seventeenth Century Book Trade', in Robin Myers and Michael Harris (eds.), *Censorship and the Control of Print in England and France 1600–1910* (Winchester, St. Paul's Bibliographies, 1992), pp. 33–57.

151 PRO, SP, 35/55/102.

152 For more on Woolston, see William H. Trapnell, *Thomas Woolston. Madman & Deist?* (Bristol, Thoemmes Press, 1994).

153 Porter and Hall, *The Facts of Life*, p. 82.

154 PRO, SP, 44/83/456, 458, 460.

155 Along with Curll, Leake was responsible for other erotica, such as *A New Description of Merryland* published at Pope's Head in Rose Street, Covent Garden in 1741. With their usual sense of irony, they dedicated the book to George Cheyne MD, the book being a semi-pornographic anatomical description.

156 PRO, SP, 44/83/462.

157 PRO, SP, 44/183/463.

158 PRO, KB, 28/176/19.

159 PRO, KB, 28/176/20.

160 PRO, KB, 28/176/21.

161 PRO, KB, 28/176/21.

162 See Joanna Innes, 'Politics and Morals. The Reformation of Manners Movement in Later Eighteenth-Century England', in Eckhart Hellmuth (ed.), *The Transformation of Political Culture: England and Germany in the Late Eighteenth Century* (London, Oxford University Press, 1990), pp. 57–118.

163 PRO, KB, 28/347/4. The majority of the following accusations were in the same vein.

164 PRO, KB, 28/347/5.

165 PRO, KB, 28/353/6.

166 PRO, KB, 28/368/18.

167 Thomas, *A Long Time Burning*, p. 77.

168 PRO, KB, 28/387/2; KB. 28/428/22. State Trials XVII, p. 157.

169 PRO, KB, 28/387/2.

170 PRO, KB, 28/391/12.

171 PRO, KB, 28/391/13.

172 Hunt, *The Invention of Pornography*, pp. 9–45, 301–39.

173 M. J. D. Roberts, 'The Society for the Suppression of Vice and its Early Critics, 1802–1812', *The Historical Journal*, Vol. 26, No. 1 (1983), pp. 159–76.

Chapter 3

1 Anon, *A New Atalantis for the Year One Thousand Seven Hundred and Fifty-Eight* (2nd edn., London, M. Thrush, 1758), p. 67.

2 The intermingling of food, drink and sex was to become a common theme in pornography, an extension of shared sensual pleasure.

3 Tissot refers to, and agrees with, Hippocrates. S.A.A.D. Tissot MD, *Onanism; or a Treatise upon the Disorders produced by Masturbation, or the Dangerous Effects of Secret Excessive Venery* (London, B. Thomas, 1766), p. 57. The first French edition came out in 1760, the English translation reaching the British audiences in 1766.

4 This applies to the works examined in this chapter. However, the erotic body was changeable and would mutate at different times. For example, at certain times, it might be a scientific body. See chapter 4.

5 See Helen King's chapter on 'green sickness' in her *Hippocrates' Women. Reading the Female Body in Ancient Greece* (London, Routledge, 1998), pp. 188–204.

6 Thomas Laqueur, *Making Sex. Body and Gender from the Greeks to Freud* (Cambridge, Mass., Harvard University Press, 1992); Caroline Bynum, 'The Body of Christ in the Later Middle Ages', *Renaissance Quarterly*, Vol. 39, No. 3 (1986), pp. 399–439.

7 Excess discharge of bodily fluids was harmful to the health of both women (through excess menstrual discharge) and men (through excess emission of semen). See below.

8 See 'Blood and Codpieces: Masculinity in the Early Modern German Town', in Lyndal Roper, *Oedipus and the Devil. Witchcraft, Sexuality and Religion in Early Modern Europe* (London, Routledge, 1994), pp. 107–24.

9 James Thorpe (ed.), *Rochester's Poems on Several Occasions* (Princeton, New Jersey, Princeton University Press, 1950); Jonathan Sawday, *The Body Emblazoned. Dissection and the Human Body in Renaissance Culture* (London, Routledge, 1995), p. 245.

10 See Judith Butler, 'Subversive Bodily Acts', in *Gender Trouble. Feminism and the Subversion of Identity* (London, Routledge, 1990), pp. 79–141; Peter Stallybrass, 'Patriarchal Territories', in Margaret W. Ferguson, Maureen Quilligan and Nancy J. Vickers (eds.), *Rewriting the Renaissance* (Chicago, Chicago University Press, 1986), pp. 123–42.

11 Gail Kern Paster, *The Body Embarrassed, Drama and the Disciplines of Shame in Early Modern England* (Ithaca, NY, Cornell University Press, 1993).

12 Norbert Elias, *The Civilising Process. Sociogenetic and Psychogenetic Investigations* (Oxford, Basil Blackwell, 1982).

13 Paster, *The Body Embarrassed*, p. 7.

14 Etienne van de Walle, 'Flowers and Fruits: Two Thousand Years of Menstrual Regulation', *Journal of Interdisciplinary History*, Vol. 18, No. 2 (1997), pp. 183–203.

15 Patricia Crawford, 'Attitudes to Menstruation in Seventeenth-Century England', *Past and Present*, No. 91 (1981), pp. 47–73.

16 Keith Thomas, *Religion and the Decline of Magic* (Harmondsworth, Penguin, 1971), p. 649.

17 Robert Burton, *Anatomy of Melancholy* I. iii. 2 (4) [1.414–19], quoted in N. H. Keeble (ed.), *The Cultural Identity of Seventeenth Century Women* (London, Routledge, 1994), pp. 35–7.

18 Roy Porter and Dorothy Porter, *In Sickness and in Health* (London, Fourth Estate, 1988), pp. 51, 83.

19 Ibid., p. 14.

20 Porter and Hall, *Facts of Life*, pp. 36, 298.

21 Wagner, *Eros Revived*, p. 11.

22 Roy Porter has already thoroughly examined the impact of *Aristotle's Master-piece* and Venette's *The Mysteries of Conjugal Love Reveal'd* in Porter and Hall, *Facts of Life*, pp. 33–90.

23 See section on readers in chapter 2.

24 *Rare Verities, The Cabinet of Venus Unlocked and her Secrets Laid Open* (London. P. Brigg, 1657), p. 24.

25 Ibid., p. 58.

26 Anon, *Aristotle's Master-piece, Or the Secrets of Generation* (London, J. How, 1690), p. 71.

27 Ibid, p. 88.

28 Anon, *The Palace Miscellany* (London, J. Dormer, 1732). Price one shilling and six-pence.

29 As late as 1895, the American Consuelo Vanderbilt, recently married to the Duke of Marlborough, was subjected on her first meeting with the Dowager Duchess, to 'an embarrassing inspection of my person'. Judith Schneid Lewis, *In the Family Way*.

Childbearing in the Aristocracy 1760–1860 (New Brunswick, Rutgers University Press, 1986), p. 60.

30   See Laura Gowing's work on sexual slander in her 'Gender and Language of Insult in Early Modern London', *History Workshop*, No. 35 (1993), pp. 1–21; and 'Language, Power and the Law: Women's Slander Litigation in Early Modern London', in Jenny Kermode and Garthine Walker (eds.), *Women, Crime and the Courts in Early Modern England*. Also see Vivien Jones (ed.), *Women in the Eighteenth Century. Construction of Femininity* (London, Routledge, 1990); Margaret Sommerville, *Sex and Subjugation. Attitudes in Early-Modern Society* (London, Arnold, 1995).

31   There has been a tendency to emphasise the importance of sexual virtue for women's honour but not for men's. New evidence suggests that men's honour was less different from women's than originally supposed and their honour could also involve their sexual reputation; Elizabeth A. Foyster, *Manhood in Early Modern England. Honour, Sex and Marriage* (London, Longman, 1999); David Turner, '"Nothing So Secret Shall Be Revealed": The Scandalous Life of Robert Folkes', in Tim Hitchcock and Michèle Cohen (eds.), *English Masculinities, 1600–1800* (London, Longman, 1999).

32   J. Donnison, *Midwives and Medical Men* (London, Heinemann, 1977); Helen Rodnite Lemay, 'Anthonius Guainerius and Medieval Gynaecology', in Julius Kirschner and Suzanne Wemple (eds.), *Women of the Medieval World* (London, Blackwell, 1885), pp. 317–34; Roy Porter (ed.), *Lay Patients and Practitioners. Lay Perceptions of Medicine in Pre-Industrial Society* (Cambridge, Cambridge University Press, 1985).

33   Trumbach relates the eighteenth-century tale of Elizabeth Canning who had allegedly been raped, whereupon a midwife was called in to establish her virginity. Trumbach, *Sex and the Gender Revolution*, pp. 148–9.

34   Akhito Suzuki, 'Reading Signs of Pregnancy in the Eighteenth and Nineteenth Centuries', in Yasuo Otsuka, Shizu Sakai and Shigehisa Kuriyama (eds.), *Medicine and History of the Body* (Tokyo, Isiyaku EuroAmerica, 1999), pp. 313–26.

35   Roy Porter, 'A Touch of Danger: the Man-Midwife as Sexual Predator', in Rousseau and Porter (eds.), *Sexual Underworlds*, pp. 206–32.

36   Bloch was among the first to describe the Victorian 'defloration mania' in the 1920s; David Loth also refers to the Victorian defloration mania, although he recognises that this interest in virgins was evident earlier. Simpson and Trumbach provide ample evidence of the reality of defloration of young girls in the eighteenth century. Iwan Bloch, *Sexual Life in England. Past and Present* (reprint: London, Arco, 1958); Loth, *The Erotic in Literature*, p. 182; Anthony E. Simpson, 'Vulnerability and the Age of Female Consent', in Rousseau and Porter (eds.), *Sexual Underworlds*, pp. 181–205; Trumbach, *Sex and the Gender Revolution*, pp. 212–18.

37   Anon, *Dialogue between a Married Lady and a Maid* (London, n.p., 1740), p. 18.

38   *Dialogue …* , p. 33.

39   Tassie Williams, 'Female Fraud: Counterfeit Maidenheads in the Eighteenth Century', *Journal of the History of Sexuality*, Vol. 6, No. 41 (1996), pp. 518–48.

40   'By A Monk Of The Order Of St. Francis', *Nocturnal Revels, Or, The History Of King's-Palace and Other Modern Nunneries Containing Their Mysteries, Devotions And Sacrifices. Comprising Also, The Ancient And Present State Of Promiscuous Gallantry* (London, M. Goadby, 1779), pp. 49–51. Possibly written by a member of Dashwood's libertine group, the book is full of gossip about notorious rakes. Published under the name of Goadby, it describes the West End brothel, Mrs Goadby's, in Berwick Street, Soho. The book was translated into French as *Les Sérails de Londres* (1801); Ashbee, Vol. I, p. 321. Mannix appears to believe Hayes's account book to be genuine but I have found no evidence of it elsewhere.

41   Mannix, *The Hell-Fire Club*, p. 33.

42   George Selwyn (1719–56) was another member of Dashwood's infamous Medmenham Hell-Fire Club.

43   *Nocturnal Revels*, p. 164.

44   John Cleland, *Memoirs of a Woman of Pleasure* (London, George Fenton, 1749), Vol. II, p. 120.

45   Anon, *Kitty's Attalantis for the Year 1766* (London, J. Harrison, 1766), pp. 20–1.

46   For a background on venereal disease, see Linda E. Merians (ed.), *The Secret Malady. Venereal Disease in Eighteenth-Century Britain and France* (Lexington, University Press of Kentucky, 1996).

47   *Bon Ton*, Vol. 3, March 1793, pp. 21–2.

48   Keith Thomas, 'The Double Standard', *Journal of History of Ideas*, No. 20 (1959), pp. 195–216.

49   Jones, *Women in the Eighteenth Century*, p. 46.

50   Ruth Bernard Yeazell, *Fictions of Modesty: Women and Courtship in the English Novel* (Chicago, Chicago University Press, 1990). Also see Felicity Nussbaum, 'The Empire of Love. The Veil and the Blush of Romance', in Felicity Nussbaum (ed.), *Torrid Zones. Maternity, Sexuality and Empire in Eighteenth Century Narratives* (Baltimore, Johns Hopkins University Press, 1995), pp. 114–34.

51   Charlotte Lennox, *The Female Quixote* (reprint: London, Pandora, 1986), pp. 8, 34, 42, 161.

52   Mary Wollstonecraft, *Vindication of the Rights of Woman* (1792; reprint London, Penguin, 1988), p. 174.

53   Richard Polwhele, *The Unsex'd Females* (London, Cadell & Davies, 1798), p. 13.

54   Anon, *The Whore's Rhetorick* (London, George Shell, 1683), p. 121.

55   Delarivier Manley, *Secret Memoirs and Manners of Several Persons of Quality of both Sexes. From the New Atalantis, an Island in the Mediteranean* (1709; reprinted, London, Penguin, 1992), p. 235.

56   *Dialogue ...*, pp. 6–7.

57   Cleland, *Woman of Pleasure*, p. 69.

58   Anon, *The Joys of Hymen, or the Conjugal Directory* (London, D. Davis, 1768).

59   Rosa Matilda, *Confessions of the Nun of St. Omer* (London, D. N. Shury, 1805), p. 185.

60   Flagellation was another method to place blood on display and use it for sexual purposes. See chapter 7.

61   *Rare Verities*, p. 43.

62   For a more detailed account of reproduction and medical opinion, see the section on John Hill in chapter 4.

63   Quoted in Vernon A. Rosario, *The Erotic Imagination. French Histories of Perversity* (Oxford, Oxford University Press, 1997), p. 17.

64   James quoted in 'The Secret Nexus', p. 79.

65   Under 'Vagina and its Disorders', in Robert James, *Medicinal Dictionary*, Vol. III (London, T. Osbourne, 1745).

66   James Clifford (ed.), *Dr Campbell's Diary of a Visit to England in 1775* (Cambridge, Cambridge University Press, 1947), p. 69. Referenced in Porter and Porter, *In Sickness and In Health*, p. 51.

67   According to Wagner, thought to be written by Balthazar Beckers (or Bekkers); however, this has now been contested by Michael Stolberg, who suggests John Marten might been the author. Stolberg also argues that the date previously assumed by historians of 1710 is incorrect. I have used Stolberg's date although the BL catalogue gives a date (including question mark) as 1710[?]. This edition has since been destroyed. I have used the eighth edition: *Onania; or the Heinous Sin of Self-pollution, and All Its Frightful Consequences in both Sexes Considered with Spiritual and Physical Advice to Those Who Have Already Injured Themselves by this Abominable Practice and Seasonable Admonition to the Youth of the Nation of Both sexes* (8th edn., London, Thomas Crouch, 1723). See Peter Wagner, 'The Veil of Medicine and Morality: Some Pornographic Aspects of the *Onania*', *Eighteenth-Century Studies*, Vol. 6 (1983), pp. 179–84; Robert H. MacDonald, 'The Frightful Consequences of Onania', *Journal of the History of Ideas*, No. 28 (1967), pp. 423–31; Michael Stolberg, 'Self-Pollution, Moral Reform, and the Venereal Trade: Notes on the Sources and Historical Content of *Onania* (1716)', *Journal of the History of Sexuality*, Vol. 9, No. 1–2 (January/April 2000), pp. 37–61.

68 Stone, *The Family, Sex and Marriage*, p. 320.

69 F. J. Barker-Benfield, *The Horrors of the Half-Known Life* (New York, HarperColophon, 1976).

70 Ludmilla Jordanova, 'The Popularisation of Medicine: Tissot and Onanism', in her *Nature Displayed. Gender, Science and Medicine 1700–1820* (London, Longman, 1999), pp. 103–17; also see the chapter on 'Masturbation in the Enlightenment', Porter and Hall, *Facts of Life*, pp. 91–105. I have found at least four English-language copies listed in the British Library catalogue, one from 1766, two from 1772, and one from 1781, the latter being a fifth edition. Unfortunately, only two from 1772 survive, the two other editions having been destroyed, and possibly others not carried in the catalogue.

71 Tissot, *Onanism*, p. 24.

72 According to Vern and Bonnie Bullough, Tissot's views were widely accepted. Vern L. and Bonnie Bullough, *Sexual Attitudes* (London: Prometheus Books, 1995), p. 71.

73 Tissot, *Onanism*, pp. 41–2.

74 Paul-Gabriel Boucé, 'Imagination, Pregnant Women and Monsters, in Eighteenth-Century England and France', in Rousseau and Porter (eds.), *Sexual Underworlds*, pp. 86–100.

75 *Critical Review*, Vol. 18 (1760), pp. 304–5.

76 Little is known about Bienville, except that he may have lived in Holland for most of his life and that he wrote several other scientific works including two treatises defending smallpox inoculation – no biographical materials have been found. Rousseau cites various French editions, two in 1771; one in 1772, 1778 and 1784; a French edition appeared as 'Published in London', 1789; and two English translations for 1775 and c.1840; G. S. Rousseau, 'Nymphomania, Bienville and the Rise of Erotic Sensibility', in Boucé, *Sexuality in Eighteenth-Century Britain*, pp. 95–119. I have found eight French-language copies and three English copies in the British Library catalogue, one for 1775 and two for 1840, the former of which I have used. Another English language copy for 1766 has been destroyed. There is also one Italian and one German edition for 1760.

77 M. D. T. Bienville, *Nymphomania, or a Dissertation Concerning the Furor Uterinus* (London, J. Bew, 1775), p. 36.

78 Ibid., p. 74.

79 Ibid., p. 50.

80 *Dialogue ...*, pp. 12–13.

81 Jane Sharp, *The Compleat Midwife's Companion: or the Art of Midwifery Improv'd* (London, Simon Miller, 1671), p. 36.

82 Ibid., p. 13.

83 Attributed to Jacques Charles Gervaise de Latouche, *Histoire de Dom B...* (London, n.p., 1743) saw various translations into English which, according to Kearney, date as far back as the French original; Kearney, *The Private Case*, p. 193. Reprint and rework-ings of this book appeared under various titles including *Dom Bougre* (i.e. Master Bugger), *Portier des Chartreux, Mémoires de Saturnin Histoire de Gouberdon*, and later translations such as *The Life and Adventures of Uncle Silas* (London, private edition, 1907 – although the BL Catalogue states that the imprint is false and it was printed in Paris) and *The Lascivious Monk* (Marlborough, Venus Classic, 1993).

84 *The Life and Adventures of Uncle Silas*, based on the original 1742, pp. 30–1.

85 Hunt mentions the latter and Rosario describes both books. Hunt (ed.), *The Invention of Pornography*, p. 324; Rosario, *The Erotic Imagination*, p. 31.

86 Harris's *List Of Covent Garden Ladies, Or Man Of Pleasure's Kalander For The Year 1788* (London, H. Ranger, 1788), pp. 24, 32.

87 *Dialogue*, p. 16.

88 Ibid., p. 8.

89 Ibid., p. 17.

90 *A New Atalantis for the Year One Thousand Seven Hundred and Fifty-Eight*, pp. 78–81.

91 Despite containing no anatomical detail, John Armstrong's *Economy of Love* was a popular sex guide manual written in idealised verse in 1736; Roy Porter, *Facts of Life*, p. 82.

92 *A New Atalantis*, p. 83.

93 Ibid., pp. 83–4.

94 Ibid., p. 86.

95 Ibid., p. 104.

96 Anon, *The Secret History of Pandora's Box containing i) Homer's descriptions of the Cave of the Nymphs explained, ii) the methods that Jupiter took to get into the Sanctuary* (London, T. Cooper, 1742), pp. 30–2.

97 Ibid., p. 35.

98 Ibid., p. 23.

99 'Timothy Touchit, Esq', *La Souricière Or The Mouse-trap* (London, J. Parsons, 1794) described itself as 'A Facetious and sentimental excursion through part of Austrian Flanders and France being a divertisement for both sexes', a skit on Sterne's *The Sentimental Journey*.

100 'Let the bloat King tempt you again to bed/Pinch wanton on your cheek; call you his mouse' [*Hamlet*, III.iv.183]: 'Mouse' could be seen as a substitute for pudenda – 'she has got a *Mause* of *Wedge* – Let's Bone her' [*Select Trials from 1724 to 1732*]: 'The women or harlots taken up for assault or night-brawls were there [in Wood-Street Compter] called Mice.' [R. King's *Mod. London Spy* 1781]. 'Mousetrap' could also refer to matrimony as in 'the Parson's Mouse-trap'. See *OED*, Eric Partridge, *A Dictionary of the Underworld* (London, Routledge & Kegan Paul, 1950) and Captain Francis Grose, *A Dictionary of Buckish Slang, University Wit, and Pickpocket Eloquence* (London, C. Chappel, 1811; reprinted London, Senate, 1994).

101 *La Souricière*, p. 23.

102 In Scotland, Daniel McLauchlan, the author, was accused of drinking, swearing and singing obscene songs, and later imprisoned in England as the author of *An Essay*. The Church ex-communicated McLauchlan in 1737. See Wagner, *Eros Revived*, p. 60.

103 'Philosarchus' (i.e. Daniel McLauchlan), *An Essay Upon Improving and Adding to the Strength of Great- Britain and Ireland by Fornication* (London, n.p., 1735), p. 35.

104 The Beggar's Benison artefacts contain five medals, some bearing the inscription, 'Be Fruitful and Multiply'. It is possible that McLauchlan was a member of the association but so far, I have been unable positively to connect him.

105 Ibid., p. 18. Such botanical references were common in erotica: see my article in the Appendix.

106 Anon, *An Address of Thanks from the Society of Rakes, To the Pious Author of 'An Essay upon Improving and adding to the Strength of Great Britain and Ireland by Fornication'* together with an *Epistle to the Reverend 'Philosarchus', Minister of Scotland* (Edinburgh, Alan Ramsay, 1735).

107 This was a translation of *De Secretis Mulierum*. Laqueur, *Making Sex*, p. 257.

108 Terry Castle, *The Female Thermometer. Eighteenth Century Culture and the Invention of the Uncanny* (Oxford, Oxford University Press, 1995), pp. 16, 21.

109 Ibid., pp. 23–5.

110 See Valerie Fildes, *Breasts, Bottles and Babies: A History of Infant Feeding* (Edinburgh, Edinburgh University Press, 1986).

111 Buchan quoted by Ruth Perry, 'Colonising the Breast: Sexuality and Maternity in Eighteenth-Century England', *Journal of History of Sexuality*, Vol. 2, No. 2 (1991), pp. 204–34. Also see Londa Schiebinger, 'Why Mammals Are Called Mammals', in her *Nature's Body. Sexual Politics and the Making of Modern Science* (London, Pandora, 1993), pp. 40–74; Marilyn Yalom, *A History of the Breast* (London, Pandora, 1998).

112 Anon, *The Whore's Rhetorick*, p. 138.

113 *Rare Verities*, p. 28.

114   Anon, *Exhibition of Female Flagellants, Part Two* (1788; repr. London, Dugdale, 1872), p. 14. See chapter 7.

115   *A New Atalantis*, p. 58.

116   'Theresa Berkeley', *Venus Schoolmistress: or Birchen Sports* (London, 'Mary Wilson', 1788). See chapter 8.

117   *Venus Schoolmistress*, pp. ix–x.

118   *A New Atalantis*, p. 56.

119   While not the *only* male blood seen in erotica, flagellation was one of the main ways in which male blood was exposed in a sexual way. See chapter 7.

Chapter 4

1   Anon, *Arbor Vitae Or, The Natural History of the Tree of Life* (London: W. James, 1732).

2   For an example of a mixture of new electrical metaphors and older botanical ones in erotica, see *Teague-Root Display'd*, examined below.

3   Brian Easlea, *Science and Sexual Oppression: Patriarchal Confrontation with Women and Nature* (London, Weidenfeld and Nicolson, 1981).

4   Carolyn Merchant, *The Death of Nature: Women, Ecology and the Scientific Revolution* (San Francisco, Harper & Row, 1980), p. 6.

5   Although this scientific change was reflected within *some* erotica, as seen in that examined here, it was not conveyed in all of it. The organic conception of the world, woman as nature/earth continued to prevail, particularly in seventeenth- and early eighteenth-century material. See chapter 5.

6   Ludmilla Jordanova, *Sexual Visions. Images of Gender in Science and Medicine between the Eighteenth and Nineteenth Centuries* (London, Harvester Wheatsheaf, 1989). Also see her *Nature Displayed*. See chapter 3.

7   Evelyn Fox Keller, *Secrets of Life, Secrets of Death. Essays on Language, Gender and Science* (London, Routledge, 1992). Also see Evelyn Fox Keller, *Reflections on Gender and Science* (New Haven, Conn.,Yale University Press, 1985).

8   Thomas Laqueur, *Making Sex. Body and Gender from the Greeks to Freud* (Cambridge, Mass., Harvard University Press, 1992), p. 5.

9   Ibid., p. vii.

10   William Harvey, *Disputations Touching the Generation of Animals* (1653) quoted by Laqueur, *Making Sex*, p. 67.

11   Angus McLaren, 'The Pleasures of Procreation: Traditional and Bio-medical Theories of Conception', in W. F. Bynum and Roy Porter (eds.), *William Hunter and the Eighteenth Century Medical World* (Cambridge, Cambridge University Press, 1985), pp. 323–42.

12   Quoted by Laqueur, *Making Sex*, p. 161.

13   See her chapter on 'The Weaker Seed', in Nancy Tuana, *The Less Noble Sex. Scientific, Religious and Philosophical Conceptions of Woman's Nature* (Bloomington and Indianapolis, Indiana University Press, 1983), pp. 130–52.

14   Generation was the term used in connection with biological investigations into the existence of animal and plant matter.

15   Joseph Needham, *History of Embryology* (Cambridge, Cambridge University Press, 1959); Roy Porter (ed.), *Cambridge Illustrated History of Medicine* (Cambridge, Cambridge University Press, 1996), pp. 154–73; Roy Porter, *The Greatest Benefit to Mankind. A Medical History of Humanity from Antiquity to the Present* (London, HarperCollins, 1997), pp. 211–32.

16   For a history of the Royal Society, see T. Sprat, *The History of the Royal Society in the Eighteenth Century of London, for the Improving of Natural Knowledge* (London, Routledge, 1959); D. Stimson, *Scientists and Amateurs: A History of the Royal Society* (New York, Greenwood, 1968); Larry Stewart, *The Rise of Public Science. Rhetoric,*

Technology, and Natural Philosophy in Newtonian Britain, 1660–1750 (Cambridge, Cambridge University Press, 1992); Dwight Atkinson, *Scientific Discourse in Sociohistorical Context. The Philosophical Transactions of the Royal Society of London 1675–1975* (Mahwah, NJ and London, Lawrence Erlbaum, 1999), pp. 16–34.

17 A twopenny sheet on *The Natural History of Arbor Vitae, or Tree of Life* (London, printed for the Company of Gardeners, 1732) is held in a collection of tracts in the BL (816 m 19).

18 Julie Peakman, 'Medicine, the Body and the Botanical Metaphor in Erotica', in Kurt Bayertz and Roy Porter, *From Physico-Theology to Bio-Technology. Essays in the Social and Cultural History of Biosciences* (Atlanta, GA, Amsterdam, 1998), pp.197–223.

19 See chapter 2 for circulation of ballads and cheap reading material.

20 Richard Bradley, *Dictionarum Botanicum* (1728), Carl Linnaeus, *Praelidia Sponsaliorum Plantarum* (1729) and Phillip Miller, *Catalogus Plantarum Officinalium* (1730) were all exciting interest during this time.

21 E. Guhl and W. Koner, *The Greeks, Their Life and Customs* (London, Senate Editions, 1994), pp. 3–4.

22 Londa Schiebinger cites John Fraley, *Gamete and Spires: Ideas about Sexual Reproduction, 1750–1914* (Baltimore, Johns Hopkins University Press, 1982); Londa Schiebinger, 'The Private Life of Plants: Sexual Politics in Carl Linnaeus and Erasmus Darwin', in Marina Benjamin (ed.), *Science and Sensibility: Gender and Scientific Enquiry 1780–1945* (Oxford, Basil Blackwell, 1991), p. 126. Also see Londa Schiebinger, *The Mind has No Sex. Women in the Origins of Modern Science* (Cambridge, Mass., Harvard University Press, 1989).

23 Londa Schiebinger, *Nature's Body: Sexual Politics and the Making of the Modern Science* (London, Pandora, 1993), pp. 4, 37.

24 Carl Linnaeus, *System of Nature; a general system of nature through the three grand kingdoms of Animal, Vegetable and Minerals* (1802 edition); original *System Naturae* (1735).

25 Quoted in Schiebinger, *Nature's Body*, p. 19.

26 Mary Wollstonecraft, *Vindication of the Rights of Woman* (1792). A proponent of free love, Mary fell in love with Henry Fuseli who was already married. According to the DNB, she got rid of her previously slovenly habits of dress in order to please him and then proposed to stay in his house in order to be near him. Mrs. Fuseli forbade her in the house, and she went to Paris to get over him. She later met Gilbert Imlay, a captain in the American army, and gave birth to their daughter, Fanny. Marriage was unimportant to her. She also lived with William Godwin before their marriage.

27 Schiebinger, 'The Private Life of Plants', p. 134.

28 See Roger Thompson, *Unfit for Modest Ears* (London, Macmillan, 1979); and Ralph Straus, *The Unspeakable Curll* (London, Chapman and Hall, 1927).

29 Wagner, *Eros Revived*, pp. 192–3.

30 Anon [thought to be by Thomas Stretser], *Abor Vitae* (London, E. Curll, 1741).

31 Ibid., pp. 2–4.

32 John Gascoigne, *Joseph Banks and the English Enlightenment; Useful Knowledge and Polite Culture* (Cambridge, Cambridge University Press, 1994). See chapter 3, 'From Virtuoso to Botanist'.

33 A French translator and dramatist, he wrote satirical plays with evocative titles such as 'Love's a Jest', 'The Loves of Mars and Venus' and 'The Temple of Love', the latter performed at the Haymarket in 1706, as well as editing *Gentleman's Journal or the Monthly Miscellany*. He had gone to the house with a woman named Mary Roberts after calling in at White's chocolate-house. The brothel-keeper and her daughter were committed to Newgate to await the inquest. Roberts alleged that he had been taken ill while still in the coach, but speculation surrounded the incident. NDB see Trial at the Old Bailey, 23 April 1718; Motteux is mentioned in Addison's *Spectator*, 21 March 1711, 30 January 1712, No. 288.

34 *Arbor Vitae*, pp. 6–7.

35   We find Dr. Misaubin, along with Dr. Rock, in Hogarth's *The Harlot's Progress,* Plate 5, shown as money-grabbing quacks haggling while Moll dies of VD in front of them. On the floor lies an advert for an 'anodyne' (pain-killing) necklace bought to cure syphilis and on the coal shuttle lies the remnants of Dr. Rock's unsuccessful pills (or Moll's teeth, according to Wagner, 'Satire on doctors in Hogarth's work', fallen out as a result of taking Mercury on his advice). Hogarth was well known for his fastidious authenticity of his interiors. The doctor's office in *Marriage à la Mode,* Plate III, is said to be that of Misaubin at 96 St. Martin's Lane, Westminster. See Sean Shesgreen (ed.), *Engravings by Hogarth* (New York, Dover, 1975), p. xx.

36   Anon, *Wisdom Revealed; Or The Tree Of Life, discover'd and describ'd. By a Studious enquirer into the mysteries of Nature. To which is added The Crab-Tree: or; Sylvia Discover'd* (London, W. Shaw, 1732).

37   Vincent Miller (London, M. Cooper, 1752).

38   James Perry [?], *Mimosa or, A Sensitive Plant* [London, W. Sandwich, 1779]. A POEM dedicated to Mr. Banks [i.e. Joseph Banks] and Addressed to Kitt Frederick, Duchess of Queensbury, Elect. Price one shilling and sixpence.

39   John Cleland, *Memoirs of a Woman of Pleasure* (Wordsworth Classics, Herts, 1993), p. 192.

40   *The Designs of Inigo Jones and Mr. William Kent* (London, J. Vardy, 1744).

41   A known pseudonym for one of Curll's hacks.

42   'Philogynes Clitorides', *Natural History of the Frutex Vulvaria, Or Flowering Shrub* (London, W. James, 1732), p. 6.

43   *Natural History of the Frutex Vulvaria,* p. 7.

44   Ibid., pp. 7–8.

45   Ibid., p. 14.

46   Roy Porter, *Health for Sale 1650–1850* (Manchester, Manchester University Press, 1989); see chapter 6, 'Quacks and Sex: Pioneering or Anxiety Making?'.

47   *Natural History of the Frutex Vulvaria,* p. 12.

48   Ibid., p. 13.

49   'Mr. Woolaston' is a reference to William Wollaston whose work is discussed in more detail below.

50   'Dr. Abraham Johnson', *Lucina Sine Concubitu* (London, M. Cooper, 1750), p. 11.

51   William Harvey, *The Works of William Harvey* (London, Sydenham Society, 1847), quoted in Elizabeth B. Gasking, *Investigations into Generation, 1651–1828* (London, Hutchinson, 1967), p. 19.

52   The tracts will be examined in detail below.

53   According to Rousseau, Hill took to calling himself 'Sir' after 1774, receiving the order of Vasa from the King of Sweden.

54   J. Donnison, *Midwives and Medical Men. A History of Inter-professional Rivalries and Women's Rights* (London, Heinemann Educational, 1977); Roy Porter, 'A Touch of Danger: The Man Mid-wife as Sexual Predator', in Rousseau and Porter (eds.), *Sexual Underworlds,* pp. 206–32; Adrian Wilson, 'Participant or Patient? Seventeenth-Century Childbirth From the Mother's Point of View', in Roy Porter (ed.), *Lay Patients and Practitioners. Lay Perceptions of Medicine in Pre-Industrial Society* (Cambridge, Cambridge University Press, 1985), pp. 129–44.

55   'The Ront', his play, was hissed off stage. He squabbled with the comedian Woodward, and made venomous attacks on Garrick. Garrick responded thus: 'For physic and farce, his equal there scarce is His farces are physic, his physic a farce is.' (*DNB*)

56   Wagner, p. 219.

57   Anon [John Hill], *Letters From The Inspector to a Lady* (London, M. Cooper, 1752).

58   G. S. Rousseau, 'The Much Maligned Doctor', *Journal of American Medical Association,* No. 8 (1960); G. S. Rousseau (ed.), *The Letters and Papers of Sir John Hill 1714–75* (New York, AMS Press Inc., 1982); G. S. Rousseau and David Haycock,

'Voices Calling for Reform: The Royal Society in the Mid-Eighteenth century – Martin Folkes, John Hill, and William Stukeley', *History of Science*, Vol. 37, No. 118 (1999), pp. 377–406.

59 John Hill, *Exotic Botany Illustrated In Thirty-Five Figures Of Curious And Elegant Plants: Explaining The Sexual System And Tending To Give Some New Lights Into The Vegetable Philosophy* (London, printed at the expense of the author, 1759). This book is illustrated with impressive detailed paintings of the flowers it describes, prefaced with a letter (dated 18 January 1759) to the Earl of Northumberland who first cultivated the plants in Britain.

60 John Hill, *The Sleep of Plants and Cause of Motion in the Sensitive Plant Explain'd* (London, R. Baldwin, 1757).

61 *Lucina Sine Concubitu* was published both as a chapbook (which can be found in the British Library) and as an article in *British Magazine*, March 1750 (of which Hill was editor).

62 *Lucina Sine Concubitu*, p. 1.

63 Ibid., pp. 10–11.

64 William Wollaston, *Religion of Nature Delineated* (London, privately printed, 1722), p. 65. The copy used here was owned by Thomas Birch, who inscribed on 9 June 1764, 'This is one of the few copies printed off for private use, the first edition not being published until September 1724'. The sixth edition (1738) is prefaced by his life story.

65 William H. Trapnell, *Thomas Woolston. Madman or Deist* (Bristol, Thoemmes Press, 1994), p. 34.

66 See chapter 2. Curll was prosecuted for obscene libel for his publication of *Venus in the Cloister*.

67 Thomas Woolston, *The Moderator Between An Infidel and an Apostate* (London, n.p., 1725), p. 66.

68 This had not been translated earlier because of regard for propriety and fear of the mention of sexual parts in vulgar words, Latin expressions even used in the translations. Gasking, *On Generation*, p. 52.

69 *Lucina Sine Concubitu*, p. 13.

70 Londa Schiebinger, 'Gender and Natural History', in N. Jardine, J. A. Secord and E. C. Spary (eds.), *Culture of Natural History* (Cambridge, Cambridge University Press, 1996), pp. 163–77.

71 *Lucina Sine Concubitu*, pp. 15–16.

72 Ibid., p. 19.

73 The playwright Edward Ravenscroft had touched on the idea in *The London Cuckolds* (1681), where Wiseacres, an alderman, takes an innocent country wife in the belief that she will be a virgin and remain sexually innocent. Thomas Day (1748–89) would later try this Pygmalion-style scheme, attempting to educate a foundling girl as his perfect wife over whom he had absolute command.

74 *Lucina Sine Concubitu*, p. 37.

75 Ibid., p. 38.

76 John Gascoigne, *Joseph Banks and the English Enlightenment. Useful Knowledge and Polite Culture* (Cambridge, Cambridge University Press, 1994), p. 52.

77 *The Art of Hatching and Bringing up Domestic Fowls by Means of Artificial Heat*. 'An abstract of Réaumur's work communicated to the Royal Society January last by Mr. Trembley translated from the French' (Dublin, George Faulkner, 1750), p. 4.

78 Ibid., p. 12.

79 'Richard Roe', *A Letter To Dr. Abraham Johnson, On The Subject Of His New Scheme For The Propagation Of The Human Species: In Which Another Method Of Obtaining That Great End, More Adequate To The Sentiments Of The Ladies, Is Proposed; And The Reflections That Author Has Cast Upon The Royal Society Of London Are Answered* (London, M. Cooper, 1750), p. 13. Price one shilling.

80 *A Letter*, pp. 18–20.

81   Eagle-stones were hollow stones composed of several crusts, having a loose stone within, which were supposed at one time to be found in eagles' nests, to which medicinal values were attributed. *Brewer's Dictionary of Phrase and Fable*.

82   *A Letter*, pp. 25–6.

83   Angus McLaren, *Reproduction Rituals. The Perception of Fertility in England from the Sixteenth Century to the Nineteenth Century* (London, Methuen, 1984).

84   *A Letter*, pp. 25–6.

85   This is also probably Hill, according to the BL Catalogue. Indeed, the article itself suggests the possibility that both writers are one and the same.

86   Anon [Hill], *A Dissertation On Royal Societies In Three Letters* from a nobleman on his Travels, to a Person of Distinction in *Sclavonia, Containing An Account of an Assembly of a Royal Academy of Sciences at Paris. A Description Of A Meeting Of A Royal Society In London And A Coffee-House Conversation. With Explanatory Notes.* (London, John Doughty, 1750). Price one shilling.

87   Rousseau and Haycock, 'Voices Calling for Reform'.

88   'A Description of a Meeting of a Royal Society in London and a Coffee-House Conversation', in *A Dissertation On Royal Societies*, pp. 32–5.

89   In a footnote he adds: 'A Coffee-House in *Covent Garden*, where the People who esteem themselves wiser than the rest of the Company, are separated from them by a Curtain.'

90   Stewart, *The Rise of Public Science*, pp. 144–51.

91   *The Gentleman's Magazine*, Vol. 16 (1746), p. 270.

92   *British Magazine*, February 1750 (London, C. Corbett, 1750).

93   *British Magazine*, May 1750, p. 216.

94   'By Lucretia Lovejoy, Sister to Adam Strong, Author of the Electrical Eel', *An Elegy On The Lamented Death Of The Electrical Eel; Or Gymotus Electricus With The Lapidary Inscription As Placed On A Superb Erection At The Expense Of The Countess Of H—— And Chevalier-Madame D'eon De Beaumont* (London, Fielding and Walker, 1777). Price one shilling and sixpence.

95   A list of lectures is given in *The Principles of Natural Philosophy Explain'd and Illustrated by Experiments in a course of such lectures to be perform'd at Mr Fuller's academy In Lottsbury, near the Royal-Exchange* (By J. Robertson, FRS, 1745). The charge for the whole lecture course was two guineas. This was addressed to gentlemen attending the course and included lectures on mechanics, hydrostatics, pneumatics, optics and astronomy.

96   See above the section on Hill's *A Description of a Meeting of a Royal Society in London* (London, John Doughty, 1750).

97   Quoted from *Statical Essays* in Edwin Clarke and L. S. Jacyna, *Nineteenth Century Origins of Neuroscientific Concepts* (Los Angeles, University of California Press, 1987), pp. 160–1.

98   Although elected to the Royal Society in 1751, he was in fact an artist (evidence of the diversification of these virtuosi), Martin Folkes, David Garrick and Samuel Foote being among his first sitters. In his attack on Benjamin Franklin on the question of whether lightning conductors should be round or pointed at the top, he was supported by George III, who declared the experiments as insufficient to convince the apple-woman in Covent Garden. *DNB*.

99   Benjamin Wilson, *An Essay Towards An Explication Of The Phenomena of Electricity Deduced From The Aether Of Sir Isaac Newton. Contained in Three Papers which were read before The Royal-Society* (London, C. Davis and M. Cooper, 1746), p. 4. Price 1s. 6d.

100   Ibid., p. 10.

101   William Watson MD, *Account of the Experiments made by a Gentleman of the Royal Society in order to discover whether the ELECTRICAL POWER could be sensible at great distances etc. on Electrical Power* (London, C. Davis, 1748), p. 2.

102   Teague being the name for Irishmen, renowned for their sexual energy.

103   Anon, *Teague-Root Display'd Being Some Useful And Important Discoveries Tending To Illustrate The Doctrine Of Electricity In A Letter From Paddy Strong-Cock, Fellow of Drury-Lane, and Professor of Natural Philosophy in M. KING's College, Covent-Garden, to W—M W—N* [William Watson] *F.R.S. Author of the late Pamphlet on that SUBJECT* (London, W. Webb, 1746), pp. 8–12.

104   Anon, *Teague-Root Display'd*, p. 15.

105   Ibid., p. 19.

106   Ibid., p. 14.

107   Ibid., p. 14.

108   'Vincent Miller', *The Man-Plant, Or Schemes for Increasing and Improving the British Breed* (London, M. Cooper, 1752), p. 17. Price one shilling.

109   Ibid., p. 19.

110   See chapter 3.

111   Before the invention of the Leyden Jar in 1745, electricity could be produced by friction only, mainly from the friction machine invented by Otto von Guericke (1606–86), Clarke and Jacyna, *Neuroscientific Concepts*, p. 163.

112   'Adam Strong' (James Perry), *The Electrical Eel, or Gymnotus Electricus* (London, J. Bew, 1777) and Anon, *The Torpedo; A Poem* (London, Fielding and Walker, 1777). Copies of both sold for 2s 6d, singular poem from 1s 6d.

113   Danniel Owen Madden has provided hand-written annotations at the back of the book dated 185? (the end of the date has been cut off). He dates the book c.1770. Sarah Lennox (1745–1826) had been at various stages of her life at the centre of the tittle-tattle as a result of her various intrigues and general misbehaviour. During an increasingly unhappy marriage, in 1768, she bore an illegitimate daughter, so giving her detractors ammunition. From there on, she was a continuing source of trouble for her family and a subject of public gossip, her reputation in tatters at twenty-four years of age. Sir William Gordon was cited in the divorce trial during 1769. She eventually married Colonel George Napier. See Stella Tillyard, *Aristocrats: Caroline, Emily, Louisa and Sarah Lennox 1740–1832* (London, Chatto & Windus, 1994).

114   See I. M. Davies, *The Harlot and the Statesman. The Story of Elizabeth Armistead & Charles James Fox* (Bourne End, The Kensal Press, 1986), pp. 50–1.

115   During 1770 a flurry of such books were written about her as a result of their affair. The servants of her husband, the Earl of Grosvenor, had burst into a lodging house in St. Albans and 'found the Duke of C. sitting on the bed-side along Lady G – with his waistcoat loose, and the lady with her Dresden unbuttoned, and her breasts wholly exposed'. Anon, *The Trial of his R. H the D. of C. with Lady Harriet G——R* [Grosvenor], *July 5th 1770 for Criminal Conversation with Lady Harriet G——R* (London, John Walker, 1770). Price 1s 6d. Also see *Genuine Copies of the Love Letter and Cards which Passed Between an Illustrious Personage and a Noble Lady During the Course of a Case Amour* (London, L. Browning, 1770); 'A Civilian', *Free Thoughts on Seduction, Adultery and Divorce with Reflections on Gallantry of Princes, particularly those of the Blood-Royal of England Occasioned by The Late Intrigue between His Royal Highness the Duke of Cumberland, and Henrietta, Wife of the Right Honourable Richard Lord Grosvenor, Also Remarks on the Trial; at Law, Between his Lordship and his Royal Highness in Consequence of that Illicit amour* (London, J. Bell, 1771).

116   'The author will be found in this Elegy, to have cast his eye on Gray's Elegy of the Church-yard, and tho' parodies of solemn subjects are serious things, yet he trusts he hath used the elegiac bard to his advantage, and the entertainment of his readers.' 'Lucretia Lovejoy', 'sister to Adam Strong', *An Elegy On the Lamented Death of the Electrical Eel; Or Gymotus Electricus*, p. 3.

117   A skit on the pagoda at Kew which Bute had erected in 1763.

118   Chevalier d'Eon came to England in 1752 on political business on behalf of Louis XVI, adopting female dress during the 1760s. A friend of John Wilkes and Sir Francis Dashwood, d'Eon mixed in élite libertine circles and was a popular figure. D'Eon's

lack of sexual contact with other parties of either sex made interpretation of his sexuality more difficult and bets were laid on his gender. Right up until after his death, it was thought he was a woman dressed as a man. Gary Kates, *Monsieur d'Eon Is a Woman* (London, HarperCollins, 1995).

119 Anon, *The Old Serpent's Reply to the Electrical Eel* (London, M. Smith, 1777).

Chapter 5

1 Anon, *A New Description of Merryland* (London, E. Curll, 1741), p. 15. This and *Merryland Displayed* were probably written by one of Curll's hacks, Thomas Stretser, the author of the prose version of *Arbor Vitae*.

2 This microcosmic view of the world sprang from Plato's *Timaeus*.

3 Leonard Barkan, *Nature's Work Of Art: The Human Body as Image of the World* (New Haven, Conn., Yale University Press, 1975), p. 2.

4 Barkan, *Nature's Work Of Art*, p. 4.

5 Robert Erickson, '"The Books of Generation": Some Observations on the Style of the British Midwife Books, 1671–1764', in Paul Gabriel Boucé (ed.), *Sexuality in Eighteenth-Century Britain* (Manchester, Manchester University Press, 1982), pp. 74–94.

6 Jane Sharp, *The Midwives Book, or the Whole Art of Midwifery Discovered Directing Childbearing Women How to Behave Themselves in Their Conception, Breeding, Bearing and Children* (London, Simon Miller, 1671), pp. 40–2.

7 See chapter 4, particularly with reference to Merchant and Jordanova.

8 Peter Laslett, *The World We Have Lost* (London, Methuen, 1965); Peter Mathias, *The First Industrial Nation, 1700–1914* (London, Methuen, 1969); E. P. Thompson, *The Making of the English Working Class* (Harmondsworth, Penguin, 1968); Roy Porter, *English Society in the Eighteenth Century* (London, Penguin, 1982).

9 W. G. Hoskins, *The Making of the English Landscape* (London, Hodder and Stoughton, 1955).

10 Tobias Smollett, *Travels Through France and Italy* (1766), Letter 36.

11 For a history of landscape and gardening, see Christopher Hussey, *English Gardens and Landscapes, 1700–1750* (London, Country Life, 1967); Christopher Thacker, *The History of Gardens* (London, Croom Helm, 1979); Ann Bermingham, *Landscape and Ideology. The English Rustic Tradition* (Berkeley and Los Angeles, California University Press, 1986); Tom Williams, *Polite Landscapes. Gardens and Society in Eighteenth-century England* (Stroud, Alan Sutton, 1995).

12 Anthony Ashley Cooper, *The Moralists* (London, 1709).

13 See *The Designs of Inigo Jones and Mr. William Kent* (London, J. Vardy, 1744).

14 Geoff Ward (ed.), *Romantic Literature. From 1790–1830* (London, Bloomsbury, 1993), pp. 235–6.

15 Claeys states that such tracts were seen as 'potentially corrosive of the entire social order'. Darnton provides a French example, *L'An 2440* (1771), a futuristic utopian fantasy which plays with the idea of a revolutionary upheaval; Gregory Claeys (ed.), *Utopias of the British Enlightenment* (Cambridge, Cambridge University Press, 1994), p. viii; Darnton, 'Utopian Fantasy', *The Forbidden Best-Sellers*, pp. 115–36.

16 Captain James Cook, *A Journal of A Voyage Round the World In His Majesty's Ship ENDEAVOUR in the Year 1768, 1769, 1770 & 1771* (London, T. Beckett & P.A. Dettont, 1771), p. 46.

17 Ibid., p. 32.

18 Mikuláš Teich, Roy Porter and Bo Gustafsson (eds.), *Nature and Society in Historical Context* (Cambridge, Cambridge University Press, 1993); N. Jardine, J. A. Secord and E. C. Spary (eds.), *Cultures of Natural History* (Cambridge, Cambridge University Press, 1996).

19 Ward, *Romantic Literature*, p. 235.

20 Boucé has already recognised the connection between erotica and the development of the sciences such as topography, cartography, geography, obstetrics and botany; Paul Gabriel Boucé, 'Chronic and Pelagic Metaphorization in Eighteenth Century English Erotica', *Eighteenth Century Life*, No. 9 (1984–5), pp. 202–16.

21 Curll published *Merryland Display'd* as a mock critique of *A New Description of Merryland*, in an attempt to cash in on further sales and publicity. Curll published at least two editions of *Merryland Display'd* in 1741, and by the same date, seven editions of *New Description of Merryland* had appeared. *Merryland Display'd* states that *New Description of Merryland* was published October last (1740) and in three months went through seven editions it was so popular 'besides some Thousands of pirated Copies that were sold in the Town and Country'. This would indicate that such erotica was not restricted to town nor difficult to obtain in the country.

22 Marina Warner, *Monuments and Maidens: The Allegory of the Female Form* (London, Vintage, 1996).

23 Boucé, 'Chronic and Pelagic Metaphorization'.

24 Charles Cotton, Ερότοπόλις, *The Present State of Betty-land* (London, Thomas Fox, 1684), p. 3. This was later reprinted in *Potent Ally: Or Succours from Merryland* (London, E. Curll, 1741) which also contained *Armour. An Imitation of the Splendid Shilling, ΚΥΝΔΥΜΟΓΕΝΙΑ, A Tale of the Story of Pandora, Horace's Inter Vitae & Co, Natural History of the Frutex Vulvaria, Arborvitae*, and *Consummation, Or The Rape of Adonis*. The same year Curll published two other books in the series, one *New Description of Merryland. Containing a Topographical, Geographical and Natural History of that Country* ('Bath', 'W. Jones', 1741), initially publishing under a pseudonym, admitting he and Leake were the publishers in a later edition; and *Merryland Display'd: Or Plagiarism, Ignorance and Impudence Detected* ('Paris', Printed by Direction of the Author, 1741).

25 Body as an expression of society, as in the body-politic, was to become a much used metaphor by the second half of the eighteenth century and a full-blown analogy by the nineteenth. Venereal disease was seen as systematic decay of a generally disease-ridden and corrupt society: See Judith R. Walkowitz, *City of Dreadful Delight* (London, Virago Press, 1992).

26 Ερότοπολις, p. 6.

27 Ibid., p. 7.

28 Ibid., p. 15.

29 Women were frequently believed to be suffering from 'the vapours' as evident in anything from *The Spectator* (1711) to Defoe's *Moll Flanders* (1722).

30 Ερότοπολις, pp. 9–10.

31 Ibid., p. 10.

32 McLaren, *Reproductive Rituals*, p. 38.

33 Ibid., p. 9.

34 Ερότοπολις, pp. 23–4.

35 Ibid., p. 14.

36 Ibid., p. 14. This section was cut from the later version reprinted in Potent Alley, although little else of the original is changed.

37 'Roger Pheuquewell' [Thomas Stretser?], *A New Description of Merryland* (London, J. Leake and E. Curll, 1741). Price 1s 6d. Although the name is connected to the libertine club, Beggar's Benison, in their title 'The Ancient and most Puissant Order of the Beggar's Benison and Merryland', and was possibly a reference to their activities, I have found no positive evidence to connect the book directly to the group. 'Merryland' was, however, an obvious well-known topical joke.

38 Straus, *The Unspeakable Curll*, pp. 308–14.

39 Ibid., p. 3. *A New Description of Merryland* was dedicated to Mr George Cheyne MD, in order to 'do Justice to your great Abilities, both as a Physician and Philosopher, to describe your amiable genteel Address, and polite Behaviour, and your generous

Contempt of Money, and Abhorrence of Adulation, with the rest of your Christian Virtues'. Cheyne had been elected as a fellow of the Royal Society in 1701 and, as well as medical subjects, occupied himself with science, philosophy and theology. After leading a more sedate life while he wrote *Philosophical Principles of Natural Religion* (1705), he moved to London and livened up, his free-living and indulgent life-style ballooning him to 32 stone in weight. He was a well liked figure as a result of his wit and repartee and *The English Malady* (1733), a treatise on the nervous condition, spleen vapours and lowness of spirits, proved to be a more popular book.

40   See chapter 3 for descriptions of the clitoris in medical handbooks and other erotica.
41   Ibid., p. 17.
42   Horn Work meant cuckold-making.
43   *A New Description of Merryland*, p. 15.
44   See John Aitkins, *Sex in Literature: Vol. IV. High Noon: The Seventeenth and Eighteenth Centuries* (London, John Calder, 1982), p. 91.
45   *A New Description of Merryland*, pp. 12–13.
46   Ibid., p. 13.
47   Lawrence Stone, *The Family, Sex and Marriage in England 1500–1800* (London, Penguin, 1990), p. 262; Keith Thomas, *Religion and Decline of Magic* (London, Penguin, 1991), pp. 223, 760. Henry Coley in the 1690s was said to be selling astrological signs at four shillings each to servant girls as a contraceptive.
48   Ibid., pp. 7–8.
49   Evidence of these eighteenth-century condoms, complete with silk ribbon, can be seen in the British Museum (not on show). Although Lawrence Stone suggests that condoms appear only in the late seventeenth century, there is new evidence to prove they were in use prior to 1647. A recent archaeological dig of Dudley Castle's latrines has shown that similar condoms made from animal membrane were widely used at the castle during the Civil War. Standardisation of the product indicates that there was a highly professionalised manufacturing of condoms. See Stone, *The Family, Sex and Marriage*, p. 266; David Gaimster, Peter Boland, Steve Linnard and Caroline Cartwright, 'The Archaeology of Private Life: the Dudley Castle Condoms', *Post-Medieval Archaeology*, Vol. 30 (1996), pp. 129–42.
50   Linda E. Merians (ed.), *The Secret Malady. Venereal Disease in Eighteenth-Century Britain and France* (Lexington, University of Kentucky Press, 1996).
51   *A New Description of Merryland*, p. 23.
52   *Ibid.*, p. 19.
53   'Captain Samuel Cock', *A Voyage To Lethe* (London, J. Conybeare, 1741), p. 1.
54   Aitkins, *Sex in Literature*, pp. 96–101.
55   *Lethe*, p. 9.
56   *New Larousse Encyclopaedia of Mythology* (Twickenham, Hamlyn Publishing Group, 1985), pp. 132, 165; Abraham H. Lass, David Kiremidjian and Ruth M. Goldstein (eds.), *The Wordsworth Dictionary of Classical and Literary Allusion* (Ware, Wordsworth Editions, 1987), p. 131.
57   Christopher Hibbert, *The Personal History of Samuel Johnson* (London, Pimlico, 1998), p. 50.
58   *Lethe*, p. 2.
59   Other pictures include 'The Dog' (1784) and Rowlandson's 'Love in a Tub, Cure for a Cold' (1802).
60   The title has obviously been purposely changed from James Cook to Samuel Cock with the intention of an additional pun for the reader.
61   Ibid., p. 10.
62   *Harris's List of Covent Garden Ladies for the Year 1788*, pp. 17–18.
63   *A New Atalantis for the Year One Thousand Seven Hundred and Fifty-Eight*.
64   See Mary M. Innes (trans.), Ovid, *Metamorphoses* (London, Penguin, 1961), pp. 42–3.

65 *New Atalantis,* p. 10. This picture was attached to one edition of *Cabinet D'Amour* in the British Library. PC 30 a 19.

66 See chapter 2.

67 G. Tolias, *British Travellers in Greece, 1759–1820* (London, Foundation of Hellenic Culture, 1995).

68 Richard Payne Knight, *An Account of the Remains Of The Worship Of Priapus, Lately Existing At Isternia, In The Kingdom Of Naples In Two Letters; One From Sir William Hamilton, K.B. His Majesty's Minister At The Court Of Naples, To Sir Joseph Banks, Bart. President Of The Royal Society; And The Other From A Person Residing At Isternia: To Which Is Added, A Discourse On The Worship Of Priapus, And Its Connection With The Mystic Theology Of The Ancients* (London, T. Spilsbury, 1786), p. 11.

69 Richard Payne Knight was a poet as well as an archaeologist, lived for a long time in Naples visiting Herculaneum and Pompeii, where his large fortune enabled him to collect antiquities which he bequeathed to the British Museum. See Ashbee, Vol. 1, p. 10.

70 J. Ward-Perkins and A. Claridge, *Pompeii AD 79. Treasures from the National Archaeological Museum, Naples and the Pompeii Antiquarium, Italy,* cat. no. 218. Quoted in Ian Jenkins, '"Contemporary Minds": Sir William's Affair with Antiquity', Ian Jenkins and Kim Sloan (eds.), *Vases & Volcanoes* (London, British Museum Press, 1996), pp. 40–64. Also see Kim Sloan, '"Observations on the Kingdom of Naples": William Hamilton's Career' in ibid., pp. 24–39.

71 Ibid., pp. 48–9.

72 These were the memoirs of Padre Antonio Piaggio on the papyri he had found in a town just outside Herculaneum.

73 Letter from William Hamilton, Naples, 17 July 1781 to Joseph Banks, London. British Library Add, MS 34 048, ff. 12–14. Quoted in Giancarlo Carabelli, *In The Image of Priapus* (London, Duckworth, 1996), p. 2.

74 In fact, the original 'Letter from Isternia', which was used as Hamilton's main source, was by an engineer Andrea Pigonati. Jenkins and Sloan (eds.), *Vases & Volcanoes,* p. 73.

75 Knight, *Worship Of Priapus,* p. 11.

76 Ibid., p. 47.

77 Ashbee, Vol. I, p. 5.

78 Wagner, *Eros Revived,* p. 269.

79 G. S. Rousseau, 'The Sorrows of Priapus: Anticlericalism, Homosocial Desire, and Richard Payne Knight', in Rousseau and Porter (eds.), *Sexual Underworlds of the Enlightenment,* pp. 101–53.

80 Giancarlo Carabelli, *In The Image of Priapus* (London, Duckworth, 1996), pp. 21–2. Also see chapter 4.

81 Anon, *Memoirs of Lady Hamilton with Illustrative Anecdotes of Many of Her Most Particular Friends and Distinguished Contemporaries* (London, Henry Colburn, 1815).

82 BL Add MS 34.048, f. 30.

83 *Harris's List of Covent Garden Ladies for the Year 1788,* pp. 16–17.

84 The same representation of a closed garden representing virginity can be seen in the religious erotica in the following chapter. See Andrew Cunningham, 'The Culture of Gardens', in N. Jardine, J. A. Secord and E. C. Spary (eds.), *Cultures of Natural History* (Cambridge, Cambridge University Press, 1996), pp. 38–56.

85 A couple of hills as breasts had already been used in the frontispiece for *A New Description of Merryland.*

86 *A Voyage to Lethe,* p. 8.

87 *The Fruit-shop, A Tale Vol. I* (London, C. Moran, 1765), p. 19. A second edition was printed in 1766 for J. Harrison, near Covent Garden.

88 *Tristram Shandy* had been brought out in a version containing pornographic prints.

89 Ashbee, Vol. III, p. 108.

90 Jean-Jacques Mayoux, 'Laurence Sterne' in John Traugott (ed.), *Laurence Sterne. A Collection of Critical Essays* (New Jersey, Spectrum, 1968), p. 108. Crébillon is most famous for *Le Sopha* (1742).

91 *The Fruit-Shop*, p. i–iii.

92 Yoseloff, *Laurence Sterne*, pp. 75–85.

93 *The Fruit-Shop*, p. 99.

94 Ibid., p. 22.

95 Dashwood was said to have given fake communion to Lady Wortley Montagu's monkey in the chapel. Daniel P. Mannix, *The Hell-Fire Club* (London, New English Library, 1962), p. 56.

96 McCormick lists Sterne amongst the possible members of the order of St. Francis; Donald McCormick, *The Hell-Fire Club* (Whitefriars, Jarrolds, 1958), pp. 195–8.

97 Dashwood, *The Dashwoods of West Wycombe*, p. 223.

98 The recently deceased Sir Francis Dashwood dismissed the idea as fantasy invented by Mannix, although there is plenty of evidence of the popularity of this topographical form as indicated in the erotica mentioned above. Mannix also states that Dashwood hollowed out a tiny cave in a little hill which he called the Cave of Trophonius. The cave is possibly similar to the one as seen in the image of Merryland, to which Dashwood more than likely had access, although I can find no evidence of it in his library records. Dan Cruickshank has recently given credence to the idea that the West Wycombe estate was designed in the shape of a female body; Mannix, *The Hell-Fire Club*, p. 5; *The Times*, Monday, 17 April 2000, p. 8.

99 The garden has since been redesigned and no longer retains its original form.

100 *The Public Advertiser*, 2 June 1763, p. 2, col. a/b.

101 Janet Browne, 'Botany for Gentlemen. Erasmus Darwin and *The Loves of the Plants*', *Isis*, No. 80 (1989), pp. 593–612.

102 Ibid.

103 *La Nuit Merveilleuse ou Le Nec Plus Ultra du Plaisir* (n.p., n.p., n.d.).

104 Ibid., p. 23.

105 Ibid., p. 33.

106 Ibid., pp. 46, 49.

107 Ibid., pp. 49–50.

108 'Thomas Longtool', *The New Epicurean or The Delights of Sex Facetiously and Philosophically Considered in Graphic Letters Addressed To A Young Lady Of Quality* (London, n.p., '1740'). According to Ashbee, this was in fact originally published by W. Dugdale in 1865, and reprinted by Edward Sellon in 1875; Ashbee, Vol. I, pp. 314–19. Price £1 11s 6d.

109 *New Epicurean*, p. 5.

110 Ibid., p. 5.

111 For examples, see chapters 6 and 7.

Chapter 6

1 Gabriel D'Emiliane, *A Short History of Monastical Orders* (London, Robert Clarvell, 1693), pp. 133–4.

2 See Wagner, Hunt and Darnton in chapter 1. All point to the French anti-Catholic pornographic material as having a prime objective of attacking the Church and State.

3 Both 'pornographic' and 'novel' are anachronisms used here to assist the twenty-first century reader in identifying the type and style of material.

4 For further information on minorities, see J. D. Walsh, 'Methodism and the Mob in the Eighteenth Century', in G. J. Cuming and D. Baker (eds.), *Popular Belief and Practice, Studies on Church History*, Vol. VIII (Cambridge, Cambridge University Press, 1972); B. Reay, *The Quakers and the English Revolution* (Hounslow, Temple Smith,

1985), pp. 81–100; D. Hempton, *Methodism and Politics in British Society, 1750–1850* (London, Hutchinson, 1984); H. R. Trevor-Roper, *Religion, the Reformation, and Social Change* (London, Macmillan, 1967).

5 Space prevents a detailed examination of this work. Few of the books or pamphlets form part of the definitive bibliographies of erotica mentioned in chapter 1. For a summary, see Albert M. Lyles, *Methodism Mocked. The Satirical Reaction to Methodism in the Eighteenth Century* (London, The Epworth Press, 1960); Roger Thompson, *Unfit for Modest Ears. A Study of Pornographic, Obscene and Bawdy Works Written or Published in England in the Second Half of the Seventeenth Century* (London and Basingstoke, Macmillan, 1979), pp. 40–56; Peter Wagner, *Eros Revived: Erotica of the Enlightenment in England and America* (London, Secker & Warburg, 1988), pp. 59–72.

6 See chapter 7.

7 See chapter 7 on mothers and stepmothers in flagellation material.

8 Anon, *The Nunns' Complaint against the Fryars being the Charge Given into the Court of France by the Nunns of St. Katherin, Near Provins, in France, against the Father Cordeliers their confessours [sic]. Several times printed in France, and now faithfully done into English* (London, E.H. and Robert Pawlett, 1676. Reprint by Alfred Harper Free Press Office, 1865), p. 81.

9 Stephen Haliczer, *Sexuality in the Confessional* (Oxford, Oxford University Press, 1996), p. 149.

10 See Linda Colley, *Britons. Forging the Nation 1707–1837* (New Haven, Conn., Yale University Press, 1992), p. 54. For examples of contemporary anti-Catholic diatribes, see Anon, *The Present Danger of Popery* (London, J. Howe & B. Bragg, 1703); E. Gibson (ed.), *A Preservative against Popery*, 3 vols. (London, n.p., 1738).

11 G. Rudé, 'The Gordon Riots: a study of the rioters and their victims', *TRHS*, 5th Series, Vol. VI (Cambridge, Cambridge University Press, 1956), pp. 93–114.

12 Colin Haydon, *Anti-Catholicism in the Eighteenth Century, 1714–80* (Manchester, Manchester University Press, 1993), p. 38.

13 First published in 1563, *The Book of Martyrs: Containing an Account of the Sufferings and Death of the Protestant in the reign of Mary the First. Illustrated with Copper Plates* wrote history through an essentially Protestant bias and remained popular until the end of the nineteenth century.

14 Haydon, *Anti-Catholicism*, p. 43.

15 Hogarth, 'Transubstantiation Satirized', 1735, BM, DPD 3446 (plate 8).

16 Jeremy Black, *The British and The Grand Tour* (Stroud, Alan Sutton, 1992).

17 Jeremy Black, *The Grand Tour* (London, Croom Helm, 1985), p. 243.

18 Daniel P. Mannix, *The Hell-Fire Club* (London, The New English Library, 1959), pp. 11–13. According to Mannix, his tutor wrote about the incident.

19 John Locke, *Travels in France 1675–1679*; Peter Heylyn, *A Full Relation of Two Journeys; the One into the Main-Land of France; the Other into Some of the Adjacent Islands* (1656); Thomas Killigrew, letter of 7 December 1635, all quoted in John Lough, *France Observed in the Seventeenth Century by British Travellers* (Stockfield, Oriel Press, 1985), pp. 185–7, 190.

20 Graciela S. Daichman, 'Misconduct in the Medieval Nunnery: Fact not Fiction', in Lynda L. Coon, Katherine J. Haldane and Elisabeth W. Sommer (eds.), *That Gentle Strength, Historical Perspectives on Women in Christianity* (Charlottesville and London, University of Virginia Press, 1990), pp. 97–117.

21 Mark Bence-Jones, *The Catholic Families* (London, Constable, 1992), p. 42.

22 Derek Baker (ed.), *Medieval Women* (Oxford, Basil Blackwell, 1978); Eileen Power, *Medieval Women* (Cambridge, Cambridge University Press, 1975), pp. 89–99; Eileen Power, *Medieval English Nunneries c. 1275 to 1535* (New York, Biblo and Tansen, 1964).

23 Katherine Rogers, 'Fantasy and Reality in Fictional Convents of the Eighteenth Century', *Comparative Literature Studies*, Vol. 22, No. 3 (1985), pp. 227–315.

24 Diderot was imprisoned for writing pornography in 1749.

25 See Marie B. Rowlands, 'Recusant Women 1560–1640', in Mary Prior (ed.), *Women in English Society 1500–1800* (London, Routledge, 1985), pp. 150–80, particularly p. 167.

26 There was a substantial number of Catholics and Anglicans who advocated the superiority of the married state over virginity, religious duties of householders and the necessity for parents to catechise their children. See Margo Dodd, 'Humanists, Puritans and the Spiritualized Household', *Church History*, No. 49 (1980), pp. 18–34.

27 Black, *The Grand Tour*, p. 239.

28 Anon, *The Account of the Seducing of Ann, the Daughter of Edward Ketelbey, of Ludlow, Gent. to the Popish religion. With some very Extraordinary Passages relating thereto PARTICULARLY, Of the gross Prevarications, and insolent Boldness of the two Popish Bishops Leyborn and Gifford in the Management of it … presented to the Lords Spiritual and Temporal and Commons, now Assembled in Parliament* (London, J. Nutt, 1700).

29 Mr. Edward Stephens, *A True Account of the Unaccountable Dealings of Some Roman Catholick Missioners of this Nation. For Seducing Proselytes from the Simplicity of the Gospel to the Roman Mystery of Antiquity* (London, J. Downing, 1703), p. 13.

30 'Socrates Christianus', *A Letter to a Missionary Priest, concerning the Qualifications requisite for that Service, and the usual Performance thereof, and the Authority by which he acts in the Service he's employed in and his Performance of it* (n.p., n.p., n.d.).

31 Narratives expressed by converts were similar to those expressed in the writings of female saints about their love of Christ. See the writings of St. Theresa of Avila in Kieran Kavanaugh and Otilio Rodriguez (trans.), *The Collected Work of St. Theresa of Avila* (Washington, Province of Discalced Carmelites, 1976); Rudolph Bell, *Holy Anorexia* (Chicago, Chigaco University Press, 1985).

32 This notion would also carry through in depictions of young nuns. See 'Fictional nunnery tales' below.

33 See chapter 3.

34 This material has been classified as erotica by bibliographers and historians including Ashbee and Wagner.

35 'Petition to Parliament', *Reasons Humbly offer'd for a Law to enact the Castration of Popish Ecclesiastics, As the best way to prevent th [sic] Growth of Popery in England* (London, A. Baldwin, 1700), p. 8.

36 Although Wagner's bibliography suggests Edward Ravenscroft, the well-known British playwright, as the author, I have been unable to locate any other source confirming this; Wagner, *Eros Revived*, p. 447. Ravenscroft wrote many plays including *The Careless Lovers* (1673) and *The London Cuckolds* (1681), the latter being his greatest hit playing with great acclaim to London audiences in the eighteenth century.

37 *Reasons Humbly offer'd*, p. 8. The same material here was also reprinted in the British Library copy of *The Priest Gelded: Or, Popery At The Last Gasp Shewing* (London, A. McCulloh, 1747), p. 14.

38 Cipriano de Valera, *A Full View of Popery, in a Satirical Account of the Lives of the Popes … Written by a Learned Spanish Convert* (London, Bernard Lintott, 1704); Anon, *Popery Display'd: or, The Church of Rome Described in Her True Colours* (London, Joseph Downing, 1713); Anon, *A Full and True Account of a Dreaded Fire that Lately Broke Out in the Pope's Breeches* (London, J. Baker, 1713); Anon, *The Artifices of the Romish Priests* (London, M. Cooper, 1745); Anon, *The Priest Gelded: Or, Popery At The Last Gasp Shewing* (London, M'Culloh, 1747).

39 Anon, *The Priest Gelded: Or, Popery At The Last Gasp Shewing*, p. 6.

40 Ibid, p. 7.

41 Ibid. pp. 14–18.

42 Ibid, p. 27.

43 Fifteen copies of the book are extant in the British Library alone; four for 1691, 1704, 1710, 1712–16, 1721, 1725, 1727, 1817, 1821, 1827, 1865 and a French version Paris, 1845.

44   Gabriel D'Emiliane, *The Frauds of the Romish Monks and Priests* (London, R. Wilkin, D. Midwinter, A. Bettesworth, B. Motte and J. Lacy, 1725, fifth edition), p. 332. This edition includes *Observations on a Journey to Italy*.

45   Translated as *Histoire des Tromperies des Prêtres et Moines de L'Eglise Romaine* and *Ruses et Four-heries des Prêtres et des Moines*.

46   Wagner, *Eros Revived*, p. 78.

47   Ashbee, Vol. II, pp. 114, 122–8.

48   *La France Littéraire* (Paris, 1823).

49   The sub-title of *Master-Key to Popery* translates as 'History of the Frauds of the Priests and Monks in Spain'. However, Ashbee states that Janiçon lived between 1674 and 1730 which if he was one and the same as Gavin, would have made him an unlikely seventeen-year-old author of *Frauds of the Romish Monk*.

50   These events are recorded in both his own autobiographical sketch in the front of *Master-Key* and in *DNB*.

51   Antonio Gavin, *Master-Key to Popery* (Dublin, J. Walthoe, 1724), p. 31. The *DNB* declares *Master-Key* to be 'a farrago of lies and libels, interspersed with indecent tales', although Ashbee believed the accounts to be true, stating, 'It is full of anecdotes and curious information concerning the church of Rome, for the most part from personal knowledge, and is on this account the more remarkable'; Ashbee, Vol. II, pp. 112–20.

52   Gavin, *Master-Key to Popery*, p. 34.

53   Ibid., p. 51.

54   Both were known to teach English children, the latter developing from its founding in 1609 by Mary Ward and her ten companions who accompanied her English and Flemish pupils to mass and sacraments. Bence-Jones, *The Catholic Families*, p. 42; Mary Prior, *Women in English Society*, p. 169. St. Omer would be used as a setting for 'Rosa Matilda', *Confessions of the Nun of St. Omer* (1805); see chapter 3.

55   Gavin, *Master-Key*, p. 56.

56   *DNB*.

57   Anon, *The Cloisters Laid Open, Or Adventures of the Priests and Nuns* (London, Meanwell, n.d.), pp. 37–8. Price 3 shillings. Wagner dates this as being published between 1750 and 1800.

58   Caroline Walker Bynum, 'The Female Body and Religious Practice in the Later Middle Ages', in Michael Feher, Ramona Nadaff, and Nadia Tazi (eds.), *Fragments of a History of the Human Body, Part One* (New York, Zone Press, 1989), p. 171.

59   See chapter 3.

60   Rudolph M. Bell, *Holy Anorexia* (Chicago, University of Chicago Press, 1985).

61   See *Venus in the Cloister* and *The Case of Mary Katherine Cadière* below.

62   Jean Louis DeLolme, *The Memorials Of Human Superstition; Imitated From The Historia Flagellantium* Abbé Boileau, Doctor of The Sorbonne, Canon of the Holy Chapel, &c (3rd edition: London, n.p., 1785). This material had been taken from Boileau's *Historia Flagellantium Vindicata* (1732), p. 14.

63   Ibid., p. 7.

64   Ibid., p. 21.

65   Ibid., p. 107.

66   Ibid., p.108.

67   Jean Louis Lolme, *The History of the Flagellants* (London, n.p., 1780), pp. 103–4.

68   Anon, *Miss Cadiere's Case Very Handsomely Handled* in *The Ladies Miscellany* (London, W. Hinton, 1751).

69   Anon, *The Case of Seduction Being an Account of the late Proceedings at Paris, as well Ecclesiastical; as Civil Against the Reverent Abbé Claudius Nicholas des Rues for committing rapes on 133 Virgins* (London, E. Curll, 1726).

70   Arlette Farge, *Subversive Words. Public Opinion in Eighteenth-Century France* (London, Polity Press, 1994), pp. 68–9.

71   *The Unspeakable Curll*, p. 227.

72 Anon, *The Case of Mary Katherine Cadière, Against the Jesuite Father John Baptist Girard* (London, J Critchley, 1731); Anon, *The Case of Mrs. Mary Catherine Cadière Against the Jesuit Father John Baptist Girard* (London, J Roberts, 1732); Anon, *A Defence of F. John Baptist Girard* (London, J. Roberts 1732); Anon, *A Compleat Translation of the Memorial of the Jesuit Father John Baptist Girard* (London, J. Millan, 1732); Anon, *A Compleat Translation of the Sequel of the Proceedings of Mary Catherine Cadière* (London, J. Millan, 1732). These pamphlets sold for between 6d and 1s 6d, most of them 1 shilling.

73 Sterne kept books on the Cadière-Giraud case; Wagner, *Eros Revived*, pp. 3–4, 75.

74 See Ashbee, Vol. III, pp. 225–53 for an extended synopsis of the case.

75 Anon, *A Defence of F. John Baptist Girard* (London, J. Roberts, 1732).

76 Anon, *The Case of Mary Katherine Cadière* (London, J. Critchley, 1731).

77 Anon, *The Case of Mrs. Mary Catherine Cadière* (London, J. Roberts, 1732).

78 Anon, *Tryal of Father John-Baptist Girard Cadière* (London, J. Isted, T. Astley, E. Nutt, A. Dod and J. Jollifre, 1732), p. iv.

79 Ibid., p. 8.

80 Ibid., p. 10.

81 Ibid., p. 8.

82 Ibid., p. 9.

83 Ibid., p. 9.

84 *Tryal of Father John-Baptist Girard*, p. 9.

85 Ibid., p. 25.

86 Etienne van de Walle, 'Flowers and Fruits: Two Thousand Years of Menstrual Regulation', *Journal of Interdisciplinary History*, Vol. 18, No. 2 (1997), pp. 183–203.

87 See chapter 7.

88 See chapter 7.

89 *The Case of Mary Katherine Cadière*, p. 12.

90 Ashbee, Vol. II, pp. 423–4.

91 *Les Amours de Sanfroid Jesuite, et D'Eulalie Fille Devote* (A La Haye chez I. Van der Kloot, 1729) was followed with further editions in 1743, 1748 and 1760. Ashbee believes there to be little doubt that it is based on the Girard-Cadière case. Despite the fact that the proceedings of the trial were not published until 1731, there were undoubtedly gossip in Toulon arising from the trial in 1728. Ashbee, Vol. I, pp. 64–70.

92 Ashbee, Vol. II, p. 253.

93 Anon, *The Ladies Miscellany* (London, Curll, 1732), p. 14. Cheaper versions of the poem 'Spiritual Fornication' were printed separately as seen in one 28-page pamphlet written under the pseudonym 'Jeremy Jingle', to which were prefixed 'several curious copper-plates, done from the *French* originals' (2nd edition, London, H. Cook, 1732), price sixpence.

94 A couplet from Samuel Garth quoted in Straus, *The Unspeakable Curll*, p. 99. Garth (1661–1719) was a physician, poet and a member of the Kit-Cat Club. Known for his burlesque poem, *The Dispensary*, which satirised the apothecaries, he was praised by Pope. *DNB*.

95 Paul Langford, 'British Politeness and the Progress of Western Manners: An Eighteenth-Century Enigma', *Transactions of the Royal Historical Society*, Vol. 7 (Cambridge, Cambridge University Press, 1997), pp. 53–72.

96 According to Charles Taylor, the origins of modern identity and this awakening of individualism can be located in the move towards 'inwardness' in the rise of the Protestant Reformation. Charles Taylor, *Sources of the Self. The Making of the Modern Identity* (Cambridge, Cambridge University Press, 1989), p. 2.

97 D'Emiliane, *Frauds of Romish Monks and Priests*, p. 122.

98 John Florio's Italian-English dictionary from the 1590s reads: 'To locke with a key: but nowe adaies abusively used for *fottere*'; Bette Talvachhia, *Taking Positions. On the Erotic in Renaissance Culture* (Princeton, Princeton University Press, 1999), p. 43.

99 D'Emiliane, *Frauds of Romish Monks and Priests*, Vol. II, p. 131.

100 Gavin, *Master-Key to Popery*, p. 43.

101 Nuns were given presents such as ribbons, watches, looking glasses and seals, and the priests sent them amorous letters declaring their passion. The Fathers were declared unfit to govern the nuns as charged in the court of France by the nuns of St. Katherin [*sic*], near Provins, in France, against the Father Cordeliers their confessors. *The Nunns Complaints Against The Fryars* (London, E.H. and Robert Pawlett, 1676. Reprint by Alfred Harper Free Press Office, 1865), p. 34. This was reprinted several times in France, and 'faithfully done into English'.

102 *The Priest Gelded: Or, Popery At The Last Gasp Shewing*, pp. 10–11.

103 See chapter 5.

104 Dorelies Kraakman, 'Reading Pornography Anew: A Critical History of Sexual Knowledge for Girls in French Erotic Fiction, 1750–1840', *Journal of the History of Sexuality*, Vol. 4, No 4 (1994), pp. 517–48; Christopher Rivers, 'Safe Sex: The Prophylactic Walls of the Cloister in the French Libertine Convent Novel of the Eighteenth Century', *Journal of the History of Sexuality*, Vol. 5, No. 3 (1995), pp. 381–402; Emma Donoghue, *Passions Between Women* (London, Scarlet Press, 1993), pp. 222–32.

105 See chapter 2 for bibliographical details, evidence of its popularity and details surrounding its publication.

106 This device had been used in *L'Escole des Filles* (1655) and *L'Académie des Dames* (1680). See chapter 2.

107 *Venus in the Cloister*, p. 23.

108 Ibid., p. 55.

109 Ibid., pp. 54–5.

110 Ibid., p. 6.

111 *Venus in the Cloister*, pp. 20–1.

112 Ibid., p. 21.

113 Anon, *Nunnery Tales Written by a Young Nobleman* (London, n.p., 1727), 'translated from his French'.

114 Anon, *The Nun; Or, Memoirs Of Angelique: An Interesting Tale* (London, Tegg and Castleman, 1803).

115 Anon, *The Nun in the Cloister or, The Amours, Intrigues and Adventures of the Marchioness of Beauville* (London, W. Dugdale, 1828).

116 *Venus in the Cloister*, p. 28.

117 *The Nun; Or Memoirs Of Angelique*, p. 9.

118 *Nunnery Tales Written by a Young Nobleman*, p. 33.

119 Ibid., p. 38.

120 Ibid., p. 64.

121 See above; D'Emiliane, *A Short History of Monastical Orders*.

122 *Nunnery Tales written by a Young Nobleman*, p. 91.

123 See Darnton, *Forbidden Best-Sellers*, pp. 63–4.

124 Attributed to Jacques Charles Gervaise de Latouche and Nourry. Many reprints and reworkings of this book came out with various titles including *Dom Bougre, Portier des Chartreux, Mémoires de Saturnin*, and *Histoire de Gouberdon*. English editions were introduced, *The Life and Adventures of Father Silas Shovewell* (London, printed for the booksellers, 1801), 2 vols; *The History of Father Saturnin* alias *Don BXXX* (London, Mary Fisher, c. 1827), 2 vols., another under the same title in 1836. See Peter Mendes, *Clandestine Erotic Fiction in English 1800–1930* (Aldershot, Scholar Press, 1998), p.153. Yet another version is held at the British Library under the title *Life and Adventures of Father Silas* (Private edition, London, '1907', c.1930).

125 Attributed to both Jean-Baptiste de Boyer d'Argens and d'Arles de Montigny. Darnton, p. 65.

126 See Katherine Norberg, 'The Libertine Whore: Prostitution in French Pornography from Margot to Juliette', in Lynn Hunt (ed.), *The Invention of Pornography: Obscenity and the Origins of Modernity, 1500–1800* (New York, Zone Books, 1993), pp. 225–52.

127 Mendes, *Clandestine Erotic Fiction*, pp. 326, 153.

128 Darnton, *The Forbidden Best-Sellers*; Hunt (ed.), *The Invention of Pornography*.

129 Anon, *Love in All its Shapes: Or the Way of A Man with A Woman. Illustrated in the various Practices of the Jesuits of the Maison Professe at Paris with diverse Ladies of Quality and Fashion at the Court of France* (London, the author, 1734).

130 Wagner, *Eros Revived*, p. 82; Kearney, *The Private Case*, p. 211.

131 *Love in All its Shapes*, p. 49. The botanical term was assimilated by other categories of erotica, such as the bawdy poems and prose shown in the earlier chapter.

132 *Love in All its Shapes*, pp. 30, 44 and 20, 22, 23. See chapter 7 for the importance of flowers in flagellation material.

133 Ibid., pp. 24, 32–4. Martial terminology was common and has already been mentioned in chapter 5 in depictions of Merryland.

134 Ibid., p. 13.

135 Ibid., p. 34.

136 Cleland's *Memoirs of a Woman of Pleasure* (London, G. Fenton, 1749), p. 35.

137 For arguments on this subject, see chapter 1.

Chapter 7

1 John Cleland, *Memoirs of a Woman of Pleasure* (London, G. Fenton, 1749), Vol. II, pp. 155–6. Plates depicting flagellation were incorporated into the book.

2 For example, *The Wandering Whore* (1660) refers to men who need flogging in order to gain an erection and 'needs be whipt to raise lechery and cause a standing P——'; John Garfield was charged with writing both this and *The Ladies Champion* (1660–1); Anon, *The Wandering Whore* (London, 1660–63; reprint: New York, Garland, 1986), part III, p. 9; Thompson, *Unfit for Modest Ears*, p. 65.

3 Ashbee, Vol. I, p. xli.

4 Although sexologists and a handful of historians have mentioned flagellation as a sexual activity (discussed below), the only comprehensive study to date is by Ian Gibson, *The English Vice. Beating, Sex and Shame in Victorian England and After* (London, Duckworth, 1978). Also see Julie Peakman, 'Initiation, Defloration and Flagellation: Sexual Propensities in *Memoirs of a Woman of Pleasure*', in Patsy Fowler and Alan Jackson (eds.), *This Launch into the Wide World: Essays on Fanny Hill* (New York, AMS Press, 2003); Julie Peakman, 'Bodily Anxieties in Enlightenment Sex Literature', *Voltaire Studies*, forthcoming.

5 For an exploration of factual incidents of flagellation, see Julie Peakman, *Sexual Behaviour in Eighteenth-Century England* (London, Atlantic, forthcoming).

6 Anna Clark, 'Humanity or Justice? Wife-beating and the Law in the Eighteenth and Nineteenth Centuries', in Carol Smart (ed.), *Regulating Womanhood. Historical Essays on Marriage, Motherhood and Sexuality* (London, Routledge, 1992), pp. 187–206; A. Simpson, *Biographical Dictionary of Common Law* (London, Butterworth, 1984), p. 88; Peter Wagner, 'The Discourse on Sex – or Sex as Discourse. Eighteenth-century and paramedical erotica', in G. S. Rousseau and Roy Porter (eds.), *Sexual Underworlds of the Enlightenment* (Manchester, Manchester University Press, 1987), pp. 48–68.

7 Anon, *Rare Verities*.

8 Nock, 'the breech, or posterior', 'the female pudenda'; Eric Partridge, *Dictionary of the Underworld* (London, Routledge, 1950).

9 Francis Kirkman, *The Presbyterian Lash or Noctroff's Maid Whipt* (London, 'Printed for the use of Mr. Noctroff's friends, and are to be told at the Pye at Aldgate', 1661). 'Noctroff' was Zachary Crofton (d. 1672), a nonconformist divine who obtained the

vicarage of St. Botolph, Aldgate. He had a hasty temper and prejudiced views, which saw him imprisoned for maintaining that the Solemn League and Covenant were still binding upon the English nation. He published many tracts and sermons including 'Altar Worship, or Bowing to the Communion Table Considered ... ' (1661). See *DNB*.

10 Anon, *Simple Simon's Misfortunes and his Wife Margery's Cruelty which Began The Very next Morning after their Marriage* (London, 1710?). Extant editions in the BL include 1750 [?], 1780[?], 1800[?], 1820 and 1825.

11 Anon, *Warning to Cuckolds* (London, n.p., 1727).

12 Anon, *The Opera of Il Penseroso* (London, n.p., 1790?). BL catalogue dates it as 1790 although there is neither date nor publisher inscribed on the pamphlet.

13 'Flagellum' (i.e. Samuel William Henry Ireland), *All the Blocks! Or, An Antidote to 'All the Talents'* (London, Mathews and Leigh, 1807), pp. 1–2. This was a response to James Sayer, *All the Talents; Or a Few Rockets Let Off at Celebrated Ministry* (London, J. J. Stockdale, 1807).

14 'Written by Itself', *The Adventures of a Whipping Top. Illustrated with Stories of many Bad Boys, who themselves deserve Whipping and Of Some Good Boys, who deserve Plum Cakes* (London, n.p., n.d.), p. 24. The BL catalogue suggests the date as 1780[?]. Price three-pence.

15 Jean Louis Lolme, *The History of the Flagellants* (London, G. Robinson, 1783), pp. 70, 77.

16 John Henry Meibomius, *A Treatise Of the Use of Flogging in Venereal Affairs: Also of the Office of the Loins and Reins* (London, E. Curll, 1718), p. 34.

17 'Bumper All Right, Esq.', *The Honest Fellow, Or Reveller's Memorandum-Book*, (London, n.p., 1790), p. 30. Price 4s 4d.

18 *Bon Ton*, December 1795, pp. 375–6.

19 Lawrence Stone, 'Libertine Sexuality in Post-Restoration England: Group Sex and Flagellation among the Middling Sort in Norwich in 1706–07', *Journal of the History of Sexuality*, Vol. 2, No. 4 (1992), pp. 525–51.

20 Tribadism is also evident in the French original of *School of Venus, L'Escole des Filles*, but most of it omitted in the extant English translation. See Foxon, *Libertine Literature*, p. 41.

21 First published in Paris in 1655, *L'Echolle des Filles*, the French version was widely available in England by 1668. We do not know from when it was available in English, but there is evidence of prosecutions in 1688 brought against publishers who sold the English edition. Perhaps the crackdown explains the absence of an eighteenth-century translation in the BL, although five French editions exist. See chapter 2 for further information on publication details and prosecutions.

22 Michel Millot and Jean L'Ange (trans. Donald Thomas), *The School of Venus* (London, Panther Books Limited, 1972), pp. 128–9.

23 Although it would appear to be a derivative of *Dialogue Between a Married Lady and her Maid* (the characters being of the same name), no assumptions can be made that it is the same story-line. Frequently translations or adaptations were made which added or omitted particular sexual practices. See chapter 2.

24 According to Plutarch, erotic flagellation was practised at the festival of Aphrodite Anosia in Thessaly; Hans Licht, *Sexual Life in Ancient Greece* (London, Constable, 1931), pp. 130, 503. Also see whippings and sodomising of young boys; flagellation and castration in the legend of Attis (Ovid's *Fasti*) and the cult of the Mighty Mother in Otto Kiefer, *Sexual Life in Ancient Rome* (London, Constable, 1994), pp. 72–3, 126–7.

25 *Bon Ton Magazine*, December 1792, pp. 359–96.

26 See Julie Peakman, 'Flagellation in the Eighteenth Century', MA Dissertation, RHBNC, 1992.

27 *The Spirit of Flagellation* (London, Mary Wilson, n.d.). Ashbee points to three different editions: one by Cannon in 1827; one by E. Dyer in 1852; and c. 1870. Ashbee, Vol. III, pp. 238–9.

28 *Manon La Fouëtteuse, or the Quintessence of Birch Discipline*, 'Translated from the French by Rebecca Birch, late teacher at Mrs. Busby's Young Ladies Boarding School' (London, Society of Vice, n.d.). This is Dugdale's reprint of 1860. Rose mentions an edition by Cannon, c. 1830 in his *Registrum Librorum Eroticorum*, and dates the first edition c. 1805.

29 William Dugdale (1800–68) was born in Stockport in 1800. He was implicated in 1819 in the Cato Street conspiracy, was frequently jailed and died in the House of Correction on 11 November 1868. He conducted his business from 23 Russell Court, Drury, at 3 Wynch Street; at 5, 16, and 37 Holywell Street and at 44 Wynch Street under the aliases Turner, Smith, Young and Brown. See Ashbee, Vol. I, p. 127.

30 Mendes lists editions of *The Quintessence of Birch Discipline* as from 1883 (with a false imprint of 1870). Yet later, he points to an edition of *Manon la Fouëtteuse*, c. 1805 remarking 'Though probably written in French, it seems to have been published solely in this English translation', citing *Margot, the Birching Beauty* (1905) as the title of the English translation. There appears to be no connection made between the earlier *The Quintessence of Birch Discipline* and *Manon la Fouëtteuse*; Mendes, *Clandestine Erotic Fiction*, pp. 158, 368.

31 Ashbee dates it between 1805 and 1810.

32 PRO, KB, 28/428/22.

33 Mendes, *Clandestine Erotic Fiction*, p. 426.

34 George Cannon was an ex-lawyer's clerk who became a publisher of obscene books. Based at Ryder's Court in Leicester Square in Maiden Lane, later moving to 2 May's Building at St. Martin's Lane. He carried out his business from 1815 until he died in 1854. See Ashbee, Vol. I, p. 114.

35 Ashbee, Vol. III, p. 242.

36 *The Bagnio Miscellany* (London, John Jones, '1792'). This edition is 1870, the imprint being false.

37 See Ashbee, Vol. 1, p. 113.

38 Kearney, *The Private Case*, p. 177.

39 James Hotten (1832–73) began his small publishing business in a shop at 151b Piccadilly. An avid collector of erotica, he delighted in being regarded as a respectable publisher whilst publishing obscene material. He also reprinted other eighteenth-century erotica such as Knight's *Worship of Priapus* (see Chapter 5). See Ashbee, Vol. I, pp. 249–56.

40 Now in the collection of the author of this book.

41 Ashbee, Vol. 1, pp. 238–45.

42 *Bon Ton*, March 1792, p. 1.

43 I have examined both extant editions in the BL. The BL catalogue gives the date of the earliest copy of *Exhibition of Female Flagellants* (London, n.p., n.d.). as c.1840. This copy carries 'The Cherub' which is referred to by Kearney as the Dugdale reprint c.1860. However, it also carries the preface mentioned by Ashbee which Cannon's edition carried and also carries the vignette of the cupid mentioned as being in the original. It appears to be earlier than 1860 both from its binding and its prints, although, of course, the prints could have been earlier then added to a later edition.

44 Iain McCalman, *Radical Underworld. Prophets, Revolutionaries, and Pornographers in London 1795–1840* (Oxford, Oxford University Press, 1988), p. 204.

45 Iwan Bloch, *Sex Life in England* (New York, Panurge Press, 1934), pp. 191–239.

46 Wagner, 'The Discourse on Sex', p. 52.

47 Ashbee, Vol. I, pp. 374–5.

48 Ian Maxted, *The London Book Trades, 1775–1800* (Gresham, Old Woking Press, 1977). Holland was also not unknown for pushing subversive books having been fined £100 and imprisoned for selling Paine's 'Letter to the Addresses, 16 Feb 1793'.

49 Charles Ramsden, *London Bookbinders, 1780–1840* (London, B.T. Batsford, 1956), pp. 113, 173.

50 Ellic Howe, *A List of London Bookbinders, 1648–1815* (London, Bibliographical Society, 1950), p. 75.

51 Phillip A. Brown, *London Publishers and Printers c. 1800–1870* (London British Library Board, 1982).

52 See above on pseudonym for Erasmus Perkins. Theresa Berkeley, *Venus School-Mistress: or Birchen Sports* (London, 'Mary Wilson', '1788'). The edition I have used is a reprint of 1917, the only extant edition in the British Library. Mendes notes an 1810 edition of *Venus School-Mistress* published by Edward Rich still extant at the Library of Trinity College, Oxford; Peter Mendes, *Clandestine Erotic Fiction in English 1800–1930. A Bibliographical Study* (London, Scolar Press, 1993), p. 426.

53 Ashbee, Vol. I, pp. xlv, 397.

54 See chapter 3.

55 See chapter 6.

56 *Female Flagellants*, pp. 8, 33–4.

57 *Venus School-Mistress*, pp. xii, xvi.

58 Anon, *Exhibition of Female Flagellants* (London, n.p., '1775'), p. 53. The edition used in this examination is the Hotten.

59 *Female Flagellants*, p. 14.

60 Ibid., p. 28.

61 Ibid., p. 8.

62 Ibid., pp. 9–10.

63 Ibid., p. 17.

64 Ibid., pp. 11–12.

65 Although this might have been an editorial hoax, McCalman provides evidence that Cannon used this method to attract readers. See chapter 2; Anon, *The Rambler's Magazine Or, The Annals of Gallantry, Glee, Pleasure, and the Bon Ton* (London, 'Printed for the Author', n.d.). Vol. VI, No. 25 (1788).

66 *Bon Ton*, March 1792, pp. 3–34.

67 *Bon Ton*, March 1794, pp. 3–35.

68 Ibid.

69 *Venus School-Mistress*, pp. 20–1.

70 Ibid., p. 9.

71 Ibid., p. 24.

72 *Female Flagellants*, p. 23.

73 Ibid., p. 24.

74 *Bon Ton*, January 1796, pp. 399–444.

75 *Venus School-Mistress*, pp. 6–7.

76 *Female Flagellants*, p. 21.

77 Ibid., p. 31.

78 *Venus School-Mistress*, p. 4.

79 *Bon Ton*, November 1791, pp. 323–56.

80 *Bon Ton*, June 1792, pp. 119–52.

81 *Bon Ton*, July 1792, pp. 158–95.

82 *Bon Ton*, November 1795, pp. 319–56.

83 *Bon Ton*, February 1796, pp. 439–76.

84 *Female Flagellants*, p. 48.

85 *Bon Ton*, November 1791, pp. 323–56.

86 *Venus School-Mistress*, p. 14.

87 Ibid., pp. 15–16.

88 Ibid., p. 27.

89 Ibid., pp. 21–2.

90 Brewer's *Dictionary of Phrase and Fable*, p. 1037.

91 *Venus School-Mistress*, p. 23.

92 Ibid., pp. 45–6.

93   Certain flowers were alleged to have certain aphrodisiac effects and moss roses signify
     voluptuous love; Brewer's *Dictionary of Phrase and Fable*, p. 965.

Chapter 8

1   Only approximately half of the material I have studied has been included here. A
    second study is intended and should add to the framework established in this book.
2   This conclusion fits well with Sarah Todd's work on the seventeenth-century ballads:
    Sarah Annice Todd, 'The Representation of Aggression in the Seventeenth-Century
    English Broadside Ballad', PhD Thesis, University of Wales, Aberystwyth, 1998.
3   Within this discussion, 'public' space does not necessarily mean in the street or parks as
    opposed to the 'private' of the home. Rather private indicates 'hidden', 'enclosed' and
    'secret', rather than necessarily merely the private sphere of domesticity. Although sex
    was conveyed as taking place in boudoirs, dressing-rooms and bedrooms, activities were
    also seen to take place in public places such as taverns, gardens, carriages and streets.
    But these spaces were 'privatised' in the sense they were confined by walls, curtains or
    hedges, not being open wide unconfined places. 'Enclosed' is therefore not necessarily
    synonymous with 'private', nor 'open' with 'public'.
4   See Peter Wagner's introduction to *Fanny Hill or Memoirs of a Woman of Pleasure*
    (London, Penguin, 1985), p. 17.

Appendix

1   Ashbee's pseudonym was revealed in a discreet notice of his death in 1901 appearing in
    the *Annuaire de la Société des Amis des Livres*, a society of which Ashbee had been the
    principal foreign member. See preface by G. Legman, *Bibliography of Forbidden Books*
    (London, Jonathan Cape, 1970), pp. 18–23. Also see Ian Gibson, *The Erotomaniac: The
    Secret Life of Henry Spencer Ashbee* (London, Faber & Faber, 2001).
2   Pisanus Fraxi [Henry Spencer Ashbee], *Index Librorum Prohibitorum, Centuria Librorum
    Absconditorum* and *Catena Librorum Tacendorum* (London, privately printed, 1877),
    reprinted as *Bibliography of Forbidden Books* (New York, Jack Brussel, 1962).
3   Alfred Rose, *Register of Erotic Books* (reprint; New York, Jack Brussel, 1965).
4   Patrick Kearney, *The Private Case. An Annotated Bibliography of the Private Case Erotic
    Collection in the British (Museum) Library* (London, Jay Landesman, 1981).
5   Sometimes duplicates would lead to another collection of erotica in a differently bound
    book.
6   Ralph Ginzburg, *An Unhurried View of Erotica* (London, Secker & Warburg, 1959), p. 105.

Bibliography*

Primary sources

'Adam Strong' [James Perry], *The Electrical Eel, or Gymnotus Electricus* (London, J. Bew, 1777).

'Aristotle', *Aristotle's Master-piece* (London, D.P., 1710).

'Bumper All Right, Esq.', *The Honest Fellow, Or Reveller's Memorandum-Book*, (London, n.p., 1790).

'Captain Samuel Cock', *A Voyage To Lethe* (London, J. Conybeare, 1741).

'Chevalier Plant Amour' [François Bruys], *The Art of Knowing Women, Or the Female Sex Dissected* (London, n.p., 1730).

'Flagellum' (Samuel William Henry Ireland), *All the Blocks! Or, An Antidote to 'All the Talents'* (London, Mathews and Leigh, 1807).

'Jeremy Jingle', *Spiritual Fornication* (2nd edition, London, H. Cook, 1732).

'Lucretia Lovejoy, Sister to Adam Strong', *An Elegy On The Lamented Death Of The Electrical Eel; Or Gymotus Electricus With The Lapidary Inscription As Placed On A Superb Erection At The Expense Of The Countess Of H—— And Chevalier-Madame D'Eon De Beaumont* (London, Fielding and Walker, 1777).

'Petition to Parliament', *Reasons Humbly offer'd for a Law to enact the Castration of Popish Ecclesiatics, As the best way to prevent th* [sic] *Growth of Popery in England* (London, A. Baldwin, 1700).

'Philogynes Clitorides', *Natural History of the Frutex Vulvaria, Or Flowering Shrub* (London, W. James, 1732).

'Roger Pheuquewell' [Thomas Strester?], *A New Description of Merryland* (London, J. Leake and E. Curll, 1741).

'Socrates Christianus', *A Letter to a Missionary Priest, concerning the Qualifications requisite for that Service, and the usual Performance thereof, and the Authority by which he acts in the Service he's employed in and his Performance of it* (n.p., n.p., n.d.).

'Theresa Berkeley', *Venus School-Mistress: or Birchen Sports* ('Reprinted from the edition of 1788, with a Preface by Mary Wilson'; reprint c. 1917).

'Thomas Longtool', *The New Epicurean, or The Delights of Sex Facetiously and Philosophically Considered in Graphic Letters Addressed To A Young Lady Of Quality* (London, n.p., 1740).

'Timothy Touchit, Esq', *La Sourcière, Or The Mouse-trap* (London, J. Parsons, 1794)

'Vincent Miller', *The Man-Plant, Or Schemes for Increasing and Improving the British Breed* (London, M. Cooper, 1752).

'Written by Itself', *The Adventures of a Whipping Top. Illustrated with Stories of many Bad Boys, who themselves deserve Whipping and Of Some Good Boys, who deserve Plum Cakes* (London, n.p., n.d.).

Anon [Daniel McLauchlan], *An Essay Upon Improving and Adding to the Strength of Great-Britain and Ireland by Fornication* (London, n.p., 1735).

Anon [Ferrante Pallavicino], *The Whore's Rhetorick* (London, George Shell, 1683).

Anon [James Perry], *Mimosa, or a Sensitive Plant* (London, W. Sandwich, 1779).

Anon [Jean-Baptiste Argens], *Thérèse Philosophe, ou Mémoirs pour Servir à L'Histoire de P. Dirrag & de Mademoiselle Eradice* (À La Haye, n.p., c. 1750).

Anon [John Hill], *Letters From The Inspector to a Lady* (London, M. Cooper, 1752).

Anon [Michel Millot], *L'Eschole des Filles Ou La Philosophe des Dames* ('Imprimé à Fribourg,; Chez Roger Bon Temps, L'An 1668'). False Imprint.

---

* I have listed only the books referred to in the book rather than all 500 and more pieces of material investigated. For a fuller list of erotica, see the bibliographies mentioned in chapter 1.

Anon [Nicolas Chorier], *Aloisiæ Sigeæ Toletanæ, Satyra Sotadica de Arcanis Amoris et Veneris* (n.p., n.p., c. 1665).

Anon [Nicolas Chorier], *Satyra Sotadica. L'Académie des Dames.* L'Académie des Dames (c.1659 or 1660).

Anon [Nicolas Chorier], *L'Académie des Dames* ('À Venise, Pierre Arretin'Amsterdam? c. 1690).

Anon [Nicolas Chorier], *L'Académie des Dames, ou Le Meurius Français Entretiens Galas* (A Cythère, Chez l'Amour, au Palais des Graces, 1793).

Anon [Sinibaldus], *Rare Verities. The Cabinet of Venus Unlocked and her Secrets Laid Open* (London. P. Briggs, 1657).

Anon, *Genuine Copies of the Love Letter and Cards which Passed Between an Illustrious Personage and a Noble Lady During the Course of a Case Amour* (London, L. Browning, 1770).

Anon, *The Joys of Hymen, or the Conjugal Directory* (London, D. Davis, 1768).

Anon, [François de Baculard d'Arnaud?], *Le Canapé* ('Londres, 1742': Brussels, 1868).

Anon, [Hill, John?], *A Dissertation On Royal Societies In Three Letters* from a nobleman on his Travels, to a Person of Distinction in *Sclavonia, Containing An Account of an Assembly of a Royal Academy of Sciences at Paris. A Description Of A Meeting Of A Royal Society In London And A Coffee-House Conversation. With Explanatory Notes* (London, John Doughty, 1750).

Anon, [John Hill?], *A Dissertation on Royal Societies. Occasion'd by the late pamphlets of Dr. Abraham Johnson, and Dr. Richard Roe, on the Propagation of the Human Species,* British Magazine (March 1750).

'D'Abraham Johnson', *Lucina Sine Concubitu* (London, M. Cooper, 1750).

Anon [Millot Michel and Jean L'Ange; trans. Donald Thomas], *The School of Venus* (London, Panther Books Limited, 1972).

Anon, 'A Monk Of The Order Of St. Frances', *Nocturnal Revels, Or, The History Of King's-Palace and Other Modern Nunneries Containing Their Mysteries, Devotions And Sacrifices. Comprising Also, The Ancient And Present State Of Promiscuous Gallantry* (London, M. Goadby, 1779).

Anon, *A Flaming Whip for Lechery; or the Whoremongers Speculum* (London, Eliz. Harris, 1700)

Anon, *A Compleat Translation of the Memorial of the Jesuit Father John Baptist Girard* (London, J. Millan, 1732).

Anon, *A Compleat Translation of the Sequel of the Proceedings of Mary Catherine Cadière* (London, J. Millan, 1732).

Anon, *A Complete Collection of Songs,* (London, James Ridgeway, 1788).

Anon, *A Defence of F. John Baptist Girard* (London, J. Roberts, 1732).

Anon, *A Full and True Account of a Dreaded Fire that Lately Broke Out in the Pope's Breeches* (London, J. Baker, 1713).

Anon, *A New Atalantis for the Year One Thousand Seven Hundred and Fifty-Eight* (2nd edn., London, M. Thrush, 1758).

Anon, *A New Miscellany of Original Poems* (London, T. Jauncy, 1720).

Anon, *An Address of Thanks from the Society of Rakes, To the Pious Author of 'An Essay upon Improving and Adding to the Strength of Great Britain and Ireland by Fornication'* (Edinburgh, Alan Ramsay, 1735).

Anon, *An Appeal to Humanity in an Account of the Life and Cruel Actions of Elizabeth Brownrigg* (London, Harrison and Ward, 1767).

Anon, *Arbor Vitae, or the Natural History of the Tree of Life* (London, W. James, 1732).

Anon, *Armour. An Imitation of the Splendid Shilling, ΚΥΝΔΥΜΟΓΕΝΙΑ in Potent Ally.*

Anon, *Compleat History of the Intrigues of the Priests and Nuns* (London, Richard Adams, 1746).

Anon, *Consumation, Or the Rape of Adonis* (London, E. Curll, 1741).

Anon, *Delights of the Nuptial Bed, or a Lady's Academy in Dialogues* (Printed 'in the island of Paphos', 'Philadelphia, May 1806'; London, Cannon, c.1830).

Anon, *Dialogue between a Married Lady and a Maid*, (London, n.p., 1740).

Anon, *Elements of Tuition* ('London, George Peacock, 1794'; London, Edward Avery?, c. 1880).

Anon, *Exhibition of Female Flagellants* (London, n.p., n.d).

Anon, *Exhibition of Female Flagellants in the Modest and Incontinent World* ('London, George Peacock, 1777'; repr. London, J. C. Hotten, 1872).

—— *Part the Second. Exhibition of Female Flagellants in the Modest and Incontinent World* ('London, George Peacock, 1785'; repr. London, J. C. Hotten, 1872).

Also part of the above Hotten seven-part collection of reprints:

—— *Lady Bumtickler's Revels*

—— *A Treastise on the Use of Flogging in Venereal Affairs*

—— *Madame Birchini's Dance*

—— *Sublime of Flagellation*

—— *Fashonable Lectures*

Anon, *Festival of Ancareon [sic]: being a complete collection of Songs by Captain Morris* (London, James Ridgeway, 1788).

Anon, *Festival of Love* (London, M. Smith, c. 1770).

Anon, *Harris's List Of Covent Garden Ladies Or Man Of Pleasure's Kalander For The Year 1788* (London, H. Ranger, 1788).

Anon, *Hilaria* (London, Printed for the author, 1798).

Anon [attributed to both Jacques Charles Gervaise de Latouche and Nourry], *Histoire de Dom B... Portier des Chartreux* ('À Rome, Philotanus'; London, c. 1745).

—— *Histoire de Gouberdon ... Portier des Chartreux*, ('À Rome, 1776').

—— *Histoire de Dom B* (London, n.p., 1743).

—— *The History of Father Saturnin* (London, Mary Fisher, c. 1827), 2 vols.

—— *The Life and Adventures of Father Silas Shovewell* (London, Printed for the Booksellers, 1801), 2 vols.

—— *The Life and Adventures of Father Silas* ('based on the original 1742', London, n.p., '1907').

—— *The Lascivious Monk* (Malborough, Venus Classic, 1993).

'A Civilian', *Free Thoughts on Seduction, Adultery and Divorce with Reflections on Gallantry of Princes, particularly those of the Blood-Royal of England Occasioned by The Late Intrigue between His Royal Highness the Duke of Cumberland, and Henrietta, Wife of the Right Honourable Richard Lord Grosvenor, Also Remarks on the Trial; at Law, Between his Lordship and his Royal Highness in Consequence of that Illicit amour* (London, J. Bell, 1771).

Anon, *Horace's Inter Vitae & Co.* in *Potent Ally*.

Anon, *Jésuites de la Maison Professe* (À Lions, Jean Montos, 1760).

Anon, *Kick Him Jenny. A Tale* (London, W. France, 1737).

Anon, *Kitty's Attalantis for the Year 1766* (London, J. Harrison, 1766).

Anon, *L'Arétin d'Augustin Carrache, ou Recueil de Postures Érotiques D'Après Les Gravures á L'Eau par cet Artiste Célèbre* ('À La Nouvelle Cythère'; Paris, Pierre Didot, 1798).

Anon, *La Nuit Merveilleuse ou Le Nec Plus Ultra du Plaisir* (n.p, n.p., n.d.).

Anon, *Les Amours de Sanfroid Jesuite, et D'Eulalie Fille Devote* (A La Haye chez I. Van der Kloot, 1729).

Anon, *Little Merlin's Cave* (London, T. Read, 1737).

Anon, *Love in All its Shapes: Or the Way of A Man with A Woman* (London, The Author, 1734).

Anon, *Manon La Fouëtteuse, or the Quintessence of Birch Discipline* (London, 'Society of Vice', n.d., c. 1805).

Anon, *Memoirs of Lady Hamilton with Illustrative Anecdotes of Many of Her Most Particular Friends and Distinguished Contemporaries* (London, Henry Colburn, 1815).

Anon, *Merryland Displayed: Or Plagiarism, Ignorance, And Impudence, Detected Being Observations Upon A Pamphlet Entitled A New Description Of Merryland* (London, E. Curll, 1741).

Anon, *Miss Cadiere's Case Very Handsomely Handled* in *The Ladies Miscellany* (London, W. Hinton, 1751).

Anon, *New Description of Merryland. Containing a Topographical, Geographical and Natural History of that Country* ('Bath', 'W. Jones', 1741).

Anon, *Nunnery Tales Written by a Young Nobleman* (London, n.p., 1727).

Anon, *Onania; or the Heinous Sin of Self-Pollution and All its Frightful Consequences in both Sexes Consider'd with Spiritual and Physical Advice to those Who Have Already Injur'd Themselves by This Abominable Practice, And Seasonable Admonition to The youth of the Nation of Both sexes and Those Whose Tuition They Are Under, Whether Parents, Guardians, Masters, or Mistresses* (London, Printed by E. Rumball for T. Crouch, 1723).

Anon, *Pleasures that Please* (London, W. Holland, 1789).

Anon, *Polly Peachum's Jests* (London, J Roberts, 1727).

Anon, *Popery Display'd: or, The Church of Rome Described in Her True Colours* (London, Joseph Downing, 1713).

Anon, *Potent Ally: Or Succours from Merryland* (London, E. Curll, 1741).

Anon, *Records Of The Most Ancient And Puissant Order Of The Beggar's Benison And Merryland, Anstruther'* ('Anstruther', Printed for Private Distribution, 1892).

Anon, *Simon's Misfortunes and his Wife Margery's Cruelty which Began The Very next Morning after their Marriage* (London, 1710?).

Anon, *Supplement To The Historical Portion Of The 'Records Of The Most Ancient And Puissant Order Of The Beggar's Benison And Merryland, Anstruther' Being An Account Of The Proceedings At The Meeting Of The Society, Together With Excerpts, Stories, Bon-Mots, Speeches, And Songs Delivered Thereat* ('Anstruther', Printed for Private Distribution 1892).

Anon, *Teague-Root Display'd. Being Some Useful And Important Discoveries Tending To Illustrate The Doctrine Of Electricity In A Letter From Paddy Strong-Cock, Fellow of Drury-Lane, and Professor of Natural Philosophy in M. KING's College, Covent-Garden, to W---M W---N* [William Watson] *F.R.S. Author of the late Pamphlet on that SUBJECT* (London, W. Webb, 1746).

Anon, *The Account of the Seducing of Ann, the Daughter Edward Ketelbey, of Ludlow, Gent. To the Popish religion. With some very Extraordinary Passages relating thereto PARTICULARLY, Of the gross Prevarications, and insolent Boldness of the two Popish Bishops Leyborn and Gifford in the Management of it, ...presented to the Lords Spiritual and Temporal and Commons, now Assembled in Parliament* (London, J. Nutt, 1700).

Anon, *The Artifices of the Romish Priests* (London, M. Cooper, 1745).

Anon, *The Bagnio Miscellany,* (London, John Jones, 1792).

Anon, *The Bedfellows; or Young Misses Manual* (London, Dickinson, c.1820).

Anon, *The Benefit of School Discipline* (London, R. Minors, 1741).

Anon, *The Birchen Bouquet, Or Curious and Original Anecdotes of Ladies fond of Administering the Birch Discipline* ('Birchington-on-Sea', 1881) [from original 1770 or 1790; reprint London, Edward Avery?].

Anon, *The Cabinet of Venus* including *The Voluptuous Night* and *The Cardinal's Amours* (London, Erotica-Bibliomaniac Society, 1896).

Anon, *The Case of Mary Katherine Cadière, Against the Jesuite Father John Baptist Girard* (London, J Critchley, 1731).

Anon, *The Case of Mrs. Mary Catherine Cadière Against the Father John Baptist Girard* (London, J Roberts, 1732).

Anon, *The Case of Seduction Being an Account of the late Proceedings at Paris, as well Ecclesiastical; as Civil Against the Reverent Abbé Claudius Nicholas des Rues for committing rapes on 133 Virgins* (London, E. Curll, 1726).

Anon, *The Cloisters Laid Open, Or Adventures of the Priests and Nuns* (London, Meanwell, n.d.).

Anon, *The Fruit-shop, A Tale* (London, C. Moran, 1765).

Anon, *The Ladies Miscellany* (London, Curll, 1732).

Anon, *The Nun in the Cloister or, The Amours, Intrigues and Adventures of the Marchioness of Beauville* (London, W. Dugdale, 1828).

Anon, *The Nun; Or, Memoirs Of Angelique: An Interesting Tale* (London, Tegg and Castleman, 1803).

Anon, *The Nunns' Complaint against the Fryars being the Charge Given into the Court of France by the Nunns of St. Katherin, Near Provins, in France, against the Father Cordeliers their confessours [sic]*. (London, E.H. and Robert Pawlett, 1676. Reprint by Alfred Harper Free Press Office 1865).

Anon, *The Old Serpent's Reply to the Electrical Eel* (London, M. Smith, 1777).

Anon, *The Opera of ll Penseroso* (London, n.p., 1790?).

Anon, *The Palace Miscellany* (London, J. Dormer, 1732).

Anon, *The Present Danger of Popery* (London, J. Howe & B. Bragg, 1703).

Anon, *The Priest Gelded: Or, Popery At The Last Gasp Shewing* (London, A. McCulloh, 1747).

Anon, *The Principles of Natural Philosophy Explain'd and Illustrated by Experiments in a course of such lectures to be perform'd at Mr Fuller's academy In Lottsbury, near the Royal-Exchange* (By J. Robertson, FRS, 1745).

Anon, *The Rambler's Magazine Or, The Annals of Gallantry, Glee, Pleasure, and the Bon Ton* (London, 'Printed for the Author', n.d.). Vol. VI, No. 25 (1788).

Anon, *The School of Venus: or, The Lady's Miscellany* (London, Curll, 1739).

Anon, *The Secret History of Pandora's Box* (London, T. Cooper, 1742).

Anon, *The Spirit of Flagellation* (London, Mary Wilson, n.d.).

Anon, *The Torpedo; A Poem* (London, Fielding and Walker, 1777).

Anon, *The Trial of his R. H the D. of C. with Lady Harriet G---R* [Grosvenor], *July 5th 1770 for Criminal Conversation with Lady Harriet G---R* (London, John Walker, 1770).

Anon, *The Voluptuous Night, Or The Non Plus Ultra for Pleasure* ('London, Sarah Brown, 1830').

Anon, *The Wandering Whore* (London, 1660–1663; reprint: New York, Garland, 1986).

Anon, *The Whole Proceeding on the King's Commission of the Peace, Oyer and Terminer, and Gaol Delivery for the City of London; Old Bailey* No. VII, Part I (London, J. Wilkins, 1767).

Anon, *The World Turned Upside Down, or the Folly Of Man* (London, n.p., 1647).

Anon, *Tryal of Father John-Baptist Girard Cadiere* (London, J. Isted, T. Astley, E. Nutt, A. Dod and J. Jollifre, 1732).

Anon, *Venus dans Le Cloître* (À Cologne, Jacques Durand, 1702).

Anon, *Venus in the Cloister: or the Nun in her Smock* (London, Edmund Curll, 1725).

Anon, *Warning to Cuckolds*, (London, n.p., 1727).

Anon, *Wisdom Revealed, Or the Tree of Life Discover'd and Describ'd* (London, W. Shaw, 1732).

Anon., *A New Description of Merryland* (London, Curll, 1741).

Anon., *New Collection of Trials for Adultery, Or General History of Modern Gallantry and Divorces* (London, Printed for the Proprietors, 1799).

Alcoforado, Mariana, *Letters from a Portuguese Nun* (1667; reprint, London, Hamish Hamilton, 1956).

Armstrong, John, *Economy of Love* (London, n.p., 1736).

Athenaeus, *Deipnosophistae* (Athena, Zacharopoulous, 1979), Vol. 13.

Bienville, M. D. T., *Nymphomania or a Dissertation Concerning the Furor Uterinus* (London, J. Bew, 1775).

Boileau, Jacques, *Historia Flagellantium Vindicata* (Amsterdam, n.p., 1732).

Brownrigg, Elizabeth, *Genuine and Authentic Account of the Life, Trial and Execution of Elizabeth Brownrigg who was executed for the Barbarous Murder of Mary Clifford. Together with the Sufferings of Mary Mitchell and Mary Jones* (London, R. Richards, 1767).

Cadogan, William, *An Essay Upon Nursing* (London, n.p., 1748).

Cleland, John, *Memoirs of a Woman of Pleasure* (London, George Fenton, 1749).

Cleland, John, *Memoirs of a Woman of Pleasure* (London, n.p., 1766).

Cobbett, William, *The Progress of a Plough-Boy to a Seat in Parliament As Exemplified in the History of the Life of William Cobbett* (reprint: London, Faber and Faber, 1933).

Coffey, Charles, *The Boarding-School; or the Sham Captain. An Opera. As it is Perform'd at the Theatre-Royal in Drury-Lane By His Majesty Servant's* (London, J. Watts, 1732).

Cook, Captain James, *A Journal of A Voyage Round the World In His Majesty's Ship ENDEAV-OUR in the Year 1768, 1769, 1770 & 1771* (London, T. Beckett & P.A. Dettont, 1771).

Cooper, Anthony Asley, *The Moralist* (London, n.p., 1709).

Cotton, Charles, Ερoτόπoλις, *The Present State of Betty-land,* (London, Thomas Fox, 1684).

D'Emiliane, Gabriel, *A Short History of Monastical Orders* (London, Robert Clarvell, 1693).

D'Emiliane, Gabriel, *The Frauds of the Romish Monks and Priests* (London, R. Wilkin, D. Midwinter, A. Bettesworth, B. Motte, and J. Lacy, 1725, fifth edition).

Davenport, John, *Aphrodisiacs and Anti-Aphrodisiacs* ('London, Privately Printed, 1869'; London, J. C. Hotten, 1873).

Defoe, Daniel, *Moll Flanders* (1722; reprint, London, Penguin, 1989).

Delolme, J. D., *The History of the Flagellants* (London, G. Robinson, 1783).

———— *Memorials Of Human Superstition; Imitated From The Historia Flagellantium*, Abbé Boileau, Doctor of The Sorbonne, Canon of the Holy Chapel, &c (3rd edition: London, n.p., 1785).

Fielding, Henry, *Shamela* (Oxford, Oxford University Press, 1980).

Fielding, Henry, *The Female Husband* (London, M. Cooper, 1746).

Fortescue, Lord John, *Reports of Select Cases* (London, 1748).

Foxe, John, *The Book of Martyrs: Containing an Account of the Sufferings and Death of the Protestant in the reign of Mary the First. Illustrated with Copper Plates* (n.p., n.p. n.d.).

Franco, Niccolò, *Puttana Errante* (London?, c. 1750.).

Franco, Niccolò, *Puttana Errante* (n.p., n.p., n.d.).

Fuller, William, *Mr. William Fuller's Trip to Bridewell* (London, n.p., 1703).

Gavin, Antonio, *Master-Key to Popery* (Dublin, J. Walthoe, 1724).

Gibson, E. (ed.), *A Preservative against Popery*, 3 vols. (London, n.p., 1738).

Gill, Chrisopher (ed.), Plato, *Timaeus* (Bristol, Classical Press, 1980).

Hamilton, Thomas, *New Crazy Tales, Or Ludicrous Stories* (Mulbery Hill, Printed at Crazy Castle, 1783).

———— *Monstrous Good Things!! Humorous Tales in Verse* (Mulbery Hill, Printed at Crazy Castle, 1785).

———— *Select Poems on Several Occasions* (London, n.p. 1824).

Harvey, William, *The Works of William Harvey*, Trans. R. Willis. Sydenham Society, London, 1847.

'Richard Roe' [John Hill?], *A Letter To Dr. Abraham Johnson(1750), On the Subject of his new Scheme for the Propagation of the human species: In Which Another Method of obtaining that great End, more adequate to the Sentiments of the Ladies, is proposed; and The Reflections that Author has cast upon The Royal Society of London are answered.* (London, M. Cooper, 1750).

Hill, John, *Exotic Botany Illustrated In Thirty-Five Figures Of Curious And Elegant Plants: Explaining The Sexual System And Tending To Give Some New Lights Into The Vegetable Philosophy* (London, Printed at the Expense of the Author, 1759).

Hill, John, *The Sleep of Plants and Cause of Motion in the Sensitive Plant Explain'd* (London, R. Baldwin, 1757).

James, Robert, *Medicinal Dictionary* (reprint; London, T. Osbourne, 1745).

Kirkman, Francis, *The Presbyterian Lash or Noctroff's Maid Whipt* (London, 'Printed for the use of Mr. Noctroff's friends, and are to be told at the Pye at Aldgate', 1661).

Knight, R. P., *The Landscape* (London, n.p.1794).

Knight, Richard Payne, *An Account Of The Worship Of Priapus, Lately Existing At Isternia, In The Kingdom Of Naples In Two Letters; One From Sir William Hamilton, K.B. His Majesty's Minister At The Court Of Naples, To Sir Joseph Banks, Bart. President Of The Royal Society; And The Other From A Person Residing At Isternia: To Which Is Added, A Discourse On The Worship Of Priapus, And Its Connection With The Mystic Theology Of The Ancients* (London, T. Spilsbury, 1785).

Lennox, Charlotte, *The Female Quixote* (reprint: London, Pandora, 1986).

Lyons, Mary (ed.), *The Memoirs of Mrs. Leeson* (reprint; Dublin, The Lilliput Press, 1995).

Manley, Delarivier, *Secret Memoirs and Manners of Several Persons of Quality of both Sexes. From the New Atalantis, an Island in the* Mediteranean (1709; reprinted, London, Penguin, 1992).

Marini, Giovanni Battista, *Difesa dell' Adone* (Venetia, G. Scaglia, 1629), Vol. IX.

Matilda, Rosa, *Confessions of the Nun of St. Omer* (London, D. N. Shury, 1805).

Meibomius, John Henry, *A Treatise Of the Use of Flogging In Venereal Affairs: Also of the Office of the Loins and Reins* (London, E. Curll, 1718).

Merriman, Tim, Esq., *The St. James's Miscellany Or The Citizens Amusement Being A New And Curious Collection Of Many Amorous Tales Humorous Poems, Diverting Epitaphs, Pleasant Epigrams, and Delightful Songs, etc...* (London. Printed and sold by T. Payne, at the Crown in Pater-noster Row, T. Ashley, in St. Pauls Church-yard, A. Dodd without Temple Bar. E Nutt at the Royal Exchange, and by the Bookseller of London and Westminster, n.d.).

Morris, A.D., 'Sir John Hill MA-MD Apothecary, Botanist, etc in *Proceedings of the Royal Society of Medicine*, May 1730.

Murphy, Arthur, *Doctor Bobadil's Monopoly Occasioned by an Unhappy Accident He met with at Ranelagh last Summer* (London, W. Owen, 1752).

Polwhele, Richard, *The Unsex'd Females* (London, Cadnell & Davies, 1798).

Ravenscroft, Edward, *The London Cuckolds* (London, n.p., 1682).

Ravenscroft, Edward, *The Careless Lovers* (London, n.p., 1673).

Rhodes, Henry, *Term Catalogue* for Easter 1683 (London, n.p. 1683).

Rochester, Earl of, *Rochester's Poems On Several Occasions* (reprint; Princeton New Jersey, Princeton University Press, 1950).

Rousseau, Jean-Jacques, *Confessions* (reprint; London Everyman, 1931).

Rousseau, Jean-Jacques, *Emile* (reprint; Harmondsworth, Penguin, 1991).

Sharp, Jane, *The Midwives Book, or the Whole Art of Midwifery Discovered Directing Childbearing Women How to Behave Themselves in Their Conception, Breeding, Bearing and Children* (London, Simon Miller, 1671).

Sinibaldus, J. B., *Geneanthropeia* (Rome, n.p., 1642).

Smith, Captain Alexander, *The School of Venus, or Cupid Restor'd to Sight* (London, J. Morphew, 1716).

Smollett, Tobias, *Travels Through France and Italy* (London, R. Baldwin, 1766).

Stanhope, Philip Henry Earl, *History of England* (Leipzig, Bernard Tauchnitz, 1870).

Stephens, Edward, *A True Account of the Unaccountable Dealings of Some Roman Catholick Missioners Of this Nation. For Seducing Proselytes from the Simplicity of the Gospel to the Roman Mystery of Antiquity* (London, J. Downing, 1703).

Sterne, Laurence *The Life and Opinions of Tristram Shandy* (Amsterdam, P. Van Slaukenberg, 1771).

Tissot, S.A.A.D., M.D., *Onanism; or a Treatise upon the Disorders produced by Masturbation, or the Dangerous Effects of Secret Excessive Venery* (London, B. Thomas, 1766).

The Art of Hatching and Bringing up Domestic Fowls by Means of Artificial Heat. 'An abstract of Réaumur's work communicated to the Royal Society January last by Mr. Trembley translated from the French' (Dublin, George Faulkner, 1750).

The Designs of Inigo Jones and Mr. William Kent (London, J. Vardy, 1744).

Valera, Cipriano de, *A Full View of Popery, in a Satirical Account of the Lives of the Popes ... Written by a Learned Spanish Convent* (London, Bernard Lintott, 1704).

Venette, N., *The Pleasures of Conjugal-Love Explain'd* (London, P. Meighan, n.d.).

Vignale, Antonio [falsey ascribed to Chevalier Marino], *The Why and The Wherefore* (London, J. Lamb, 1765).

Ward, Edward, *A Riddle of a Paradoxical Character of an Hairy Monster (London, A Moore,* c. 1725*).*

Ward, Ned [Hyland, Paul (ed.)], *The London Spy* (reprint from 4th edition of 1709; East Lansing, Colleagues Press, 1993).

Walpole, Horace, *Memoirs of the Reign of George III* (London, Lawrence and Bullen, 1894).

Watson, William, FRS., *Experiments and Observations Tending To Illustrate the Nature and Properties of Electricity*. 'In one LETTER to Martin Folkes, Esq, President and Two to the Royal Society' (London, Jacob Ilive, 1745).

Watson, William, MD, *Account of the Experiments made by a Gentleman of the Royal Society in order to discover whether the ELECTRICAL POWER could be sensible at great distances etc. on Electrical Power* (London, C Davis, 1748).

White, John, *First Century of Scandalous, Malignant Priests* (London, George Miller, 1643).

Wilson, Benjamin, *An Essay Towards An Explication Of The Phenomena of Electricity Deduced From The Aether Of Sir Isaac Newton. Contained in Three Papers which were read before The Royal-Society* (London, C Davis and M. Cooper, 1746).

Wollaston, William, *Religion of Nature Delineated* (London, privately printed, 1722).

Wollstonecraft, Mary, *The Vindication of the Rights of Women* (1792: reprint, London, Penguin, 1988).

Woolston, Thomas, *The Moderator, Between and An Infidel and an Apostate* (London, n.p., 1725).

Secondary sources

Adams, Jad, *Madder Music, Stronger Wine: The Life of Ernest Dowson* (London, I. B. Tauris, 2000).

Aitkins, John, *Sex in Literature: Vol. IV. High Noon: The Seventeenth and Eighteenth Centuries* (John Calder, London. 1982).

Aston, John (ed.), *Chapbooks of the Eighteenth Century* (1882 reprint, London, Skoob Books Publishing Ltd, n.d.).

Baker, Derek (ed.), *Medieval Women* (Oxford, Basil Blackwell, 1978).

Ballaster, Ros, *Seductive Forms: Women's Amatory Fiction from 1684 to 1740* (Oxford, Clarenden Press, 1992).

Barkan, Leonard, *Nature's Work Of Art; The Human Body as Image of the World* (New Haven, Conn., Yale University Press, 1975)..

Barker-Benfield, F. J., *The Horrors of the Half-Known Life* (New York, Harper Colophon, 1976).

Barker-Benfield, G. J., *The Culture of Sensibility. Sex and Society in Eighteenth-Century Britain* (Chicago, University of Chicago Press, 1992).

Bell, Rudolph M., *Holy Anorexia* (Chicago, Chigaco University Press, 1985).

Bence-Jones, Mark, *The Catholic Families* (London, Constable, 1992).

Bennett, Judith M., 'Feminism and History', *Gender and History*, Vol. 1, No. 3 (1989), pp. 251–72.

Bermingham, Ann, *Landscape and Ideology. The English Rustic Tradition* (Berkeley and Los Angeles, California University Press, 1986).

Black, Jeremy, *The British and The Grand Tour* (Stroud, Alan Sutton, 1992).

Black, Jeremy, *The Grand Tour* (London, Croom Helm, 1985).

Bloch, Iwan, *Sex Life in England* (New York, Panurge Press, 1934).

Bonfield, L., R. M. Smith and K. Wrightson (eds.), *The World We Have Gained. Histories of Population and Social Structure* (Oxford, Oxford University Press, 1986).

Booth, Alan, 'The Memory of the Liberty of the Press: The Suppression of Radical Writing in the 1790s', in Paul Hyland and Neil Sammells (eds.), *Writing and Censorship in Britain* (London, Routledge, 1992), pp. 106–122.

Boucé, Paul-Gabriel (ed.), *Sexuality in Eighteenth-Century Britain* (Manchester, Manchester University Press, 1982).

Boucé, Paul-Gabriel, 'The Secret Sex Nexus: Sex and Literature in Eighteenth Century Britain', in Alan Bold (ed.), *The Sexual Dimension in Literature* (London, Vision Press Ltd, 1983).

Boucé, Paul Gabriel, 'Chronic and Pelagic Metaphorization in Eighteenth Century English Erotica', *Eighteenth Century Life*, No. 9, 1984–5, pp. 202–16.

Brewer, John, *The Pleasures of the Imagination. English Culture in the Eighteenth Century* (London, HarperCollins, 1997)

Bristow, Edward J., *Vice and Vigilance. Purity Movements in Britain since 1700* (London, Macmillan, 1977).

Bryant, Julius, *Marble Hill House* (London, English Heritage, 1994).

Brown, Phillip A., *London Publishers and Printers, c. 1800–1870* (London British Library Board, 1982).

Browne, Janet, 'Botany for Gentlemen. Erasmus Darwin and *The Loves of the Plants*', *Isis*, No. 80 (1989), pp. 593–612.

Bullough, Vern L. and Bonnie, *Sexual Attitudes* (London: Prometheus Books, 1995).

Butler, Judith, *Gender Trouble, Feminism and the Subversion of Identity* (London, Routledge, 1990).

Bynum, Caroline Walker, 'The Female Body and Religious Practice in the Later Middle Ages', in Michael Feher, Ramona Nadaff, and Nadia Tazi (eds.), *Fragments of a History of the Human Body, Part One* (New York, Zone Press, 1989).

Bynum, Caroline, 'The Body of Christ in Later Middle Ages', *Renaissance Quarterly*, Vol. 39, No. 3 (1986).

Bynum, W. F. and Roy Porter (eds.), *William Hunter and the Eighteenth Century Medical World* (Cambridge, Cambridge University Press, 1985).

Carabelli, Giancarlo, *In The Image of Priapus* (London, Duckworth, 1996), p. 2.

Castle, Terry, *The Female Thermometer. Eighteenth Century Culture and the Invention of the Uncanny* (Oxford, Oxford University, 1995).

Cevasco, A., (ed.), *The 1890s. An Encyclopaedia of British Literature, Art, and Culture* (London & New York, Garland Publishing, Inc., 1993).

Charney, Maurice, *Sexual Fiction* (Iowa, Kendall Hunt Publishing Company, 1981).

Claeys, Gregory, (ed.), *Utopias of the British Enlightenment* (Cambridge University Press, 1994).

Clark, Alice, *Working Life of Women in the Seventeenth Century* (1919, reprint, London, Routledge and Kegan Paul, 1982).

Clark, Anna, 'Humanity or Justice? Wife-beating and the Law in Eighteenth and Nineteenth Centuries', in Carol Smart (ed.), *Regulating Womanhood. Historical Essays on Marriage, Motherhood and Sexuality* (London, Routledge, 1992), pp. 187–206.

Clark, Anna, *Struggle for the Breeches. Gender and the Making of the British Working Class* (London, Rivers Oram Press, 1995).

Clarke, Edwin, and L. S. Jacyna, *Nineteenth Century Origins of Neuroscientific Concepts*, (Los Angeles, University of California Press, 1987).

Colley, Linda, *Britons. Forging the Nation 1707–1837* (New Haven, Conn., Yale University Press, 1992).

Cooper, Rev. Wm. M., *History of the Rod* (London, William Reeves Bookseller, 1870).

Corfield, Penelope, 'History and the Challenge of Gender History', *Rethinking History*, Vol. 1, No. 3 (1997), pp. 241–58.

Craig, Alec, *The Banned Books of England* (London, Allen & Unwin, 1962).

Crawford, Patricia, 'Attitudes to Menstruation in Seventeenth-Century England', *Past and Present*, No. 91 (1981), pp. 47–73.

Cressy, David, *Literacy and the Social Order: Reading and writing in Tudor and Stuart England* (Cambridge, Cambridge University Press).

Daichman, Graciela S., 'Misconduct in the Medieval Nunnery: Fact not Fiction', in Lynda L. Coon, Katherine J. Haldane, and Elisabeth W. Sommer (eds.), *That Gentle Strength, Historical Perspectives on Women in Christianity* (Charlottesville and London, University of Virginia Press, 1990), pp. 97–117.

Darnton, Robert and Daniel Roche (eds.), *The Press During the French Revolution* (Berkeley, Berkeley University Press, 1989).

Darnton, Robert, 'The High Enlightenment and the Low-Life of literature in Pre-Revolutionary France', *Past and Present*, No. 51 (1971), pp. 81–115.

Darnton, Robert, *The Forbidden Best-Sellers of Pre-Revolutionary France* (London, HarperCollins, 1997).

Darnton, Robert, *The Great Cat Massacre* (London, Allen Lane, 1984).

Darnton, Robert, *The Literary Underground of the Old Regime* (Cambridge, Mass: Harvard University Press, 1982).

Dashwood, Sir Francis, *The Dashwoods of West Wycombe* (London, Aurum Press, 1987).

Davidoff, Leonore, and Catherine Hall, *Family Fortunes: Men and Women of the English Middle-Class, 1780–1850* (London, Routledge, 1987).

Davies, I. M., *The Harlot and the Statesman. The Story of Elizabeth Armistead & Charles James Fox* (Bourne End, The Kensal Press, 1986).

Denison, Cara D., Evelyn J. Phimister and Stephanie Wiles, *Gainsborough to Ruskin. British Landscapes and Watercolours from the Morgan Library* (New York, Pierpoint Morgan Library, 1994).

Dodd, Margo, 'Humanists, Puritans and the Spiritualized Household', *Church History*, No. 49 (1980), pp. 18–34.

Donnison, J., *Midwives and Medical Men. A History of Inter-professional Rivalries and Women's Rights* (London, Heinemann Educational Books, 1977).

Donoghue, Emma, *Passions Between Women* (London, Scarlet Press, 1993).

Dworkin, Andrea, *Pornography: Men Possessing Women* (London, Women's Press, 1981).

Easlea, Brian, *Science and Sexual Oppression: Patriarchy Confrontation with Women and Nature,* (Weidenfeld and Nicolson, 1981).

Eder, Franz X., Lesley Hall and Gert Hekma (eds.), *National Histories, Sexual Cultures in Europe* (Manchester, Manchester University Press, 1999);

Elias, Norbert, *The Civilising Process: Sociogenetic and Psychogenetic Investigations* (Oxford, Basil Blackwell, 1982).

Farge, Arlette, *Subversive Words. Public Opinion in Eighteenth-Century France* (London, Polity Press, 1994).

Fergus, Jan, 'Provincial Servants' Reading in Late Eighteenth Century', in J. Raven, H. Small and N. Tadmor (eds.), *The Practices and Representation of Reading in England* (Cambridge, Cambridge University, 1996), pp. 202–25.

Fildes, Valerie, *Breasts, Bottle and Babies: A History of Infant Feeding* (Edinburgh, Edinburgh University Press, 1986).

Foucault, Michel, *The History of Sexuality, Vol. I, An Introduction* (London, Penguin, 1976).

Fout, John C. (ed.), *Forbidden History. The State, Society and the Regulation of Sexuality in Modern Europe* (Chicago, Chicago University Press, 1990).

Fox Keller, Evelyn, *Reflections on Gender and Science* (New Haven, Conn.,Yale University Press, 1985).

Fox Keller, Evelyn, *Secrets of Life, Secrets of Death. Essays on Language, Gender and Science* (London, Routledge, 1992).

Foxon, David, *Libertine Literature in England 1660–1745* (New York, University Books, 1965).

Foyster, Elizabeth A., *Manhood in Early Modern England. Honour, Sex and Marriage* (London, Longman, 1999).

Gaimster, David, Peter Boland, Steve Linnard and Caroline Cartwright, 'The Archaeology of Private Life: the Dudley Castle Condoms', *Post-Medieval Archaeology*, Vol. 30 (1996), pp. 129–42.

Gascoigne, John, *Joseph Banks and the Enlightenment. Useful Knowledge and Polite Culture* (Cambridge, Cambridge University Press, 1994).

Gasking, Elizabeth B., *Investigations into Generation, 1651–1828* (Hutchinson, London, 1967).

Gay, Peter, *The Education of the Senses*, Vol. 1 of *The Bourgeois Experience: Victoria to Freud* (New York, Oxford University Press, 1984).

Gibson, Ian, *The English Vice. Beating, Sex and Shame in Victorian England and After* (London, Duckworth, 1978).

Gibson, Ian, *The Erotomaniac: The Secret Life of Henry Spencer Ashbee* (London, Faber & Faber, 2001).

Ginzburg, Ralph, *An Unhurried View of Erotica* (London, Secker & Warburg, 1959).

Goulemot, Jean Marie, *Forbidden Texts. Erotic Literature and its Readers in Eighteenth-Century France* (Cambridge, Polity Press, 1994).

Gowing, Laura, 'Gender and Language of Insult in Early Modern London', *History Workshop*, No. 35 (1993), pp. 1–21.

Guhl, E. and W. Koner, *The Greeks, Their Life and Customs,* Senate Editions, 1994).

Haliczer, Stephen, *Sexuality in the Confessional* (Oxford, Oxford University Press, 1996).

Hamilton, Adrian, *The Infamous Essay on Woman, or John Wilkes Seated Between Vice and Virtue* (London, André Deutsch, 1972).

Harvey, Karen, 'Representations of Bodies and Sexual Difference In Eighteenth-Century English Erotica' (PhD Thesis, London, RHBNC, 1999).

Haydon, Colin, *Anti-Catholicism in the Eighteenth Century, 1714–80,* (Manchester, Manchester University Press, 1993).

Hempton, D., *Methodism and Politics in British Society, 1750–1850* (London, Hutchinson, 1984).

Henderson, Anthony, 'Female Prostitution in London, 1730–1830' (PhD Thesis, London, RHBNC 1992).

Hibbert, Christopher, *The Personal History of Samuel Johnson* (London, Pimlico, 1998).

Hill, Christopher, 'Censorship and English Literature', in *Collected Essays, Vol. I. Writing and Revolution in Seventeenth Century England* (Brighton, Harvester, 1985).

Hitchcock, Tim, *English Sexualities, 1700–1800* (London, Macmillan, 1997).

Hitchcock, Tim, 'Redefining Sex in Eighteenth-Century England', *History Workshop Journal*, No. 41 (1996), pp. 72–90.

Hoskins, W. G., *The Making of the English Landscape* (London, Hodder and Stoughton, 1955).

Houston, R. A, *Literacy in Early Modern Europe: Culture and Education, 1500–1800* (London, Longman, 1988).

Howe, Ellic, *A List of London Bookbinders, 1648–1815* (London, Bibliographical Society, 1950).

Hufton, Olwen, *The Prospect Before Her. A History of Women in Western Europe* (London, Fontana Press, 1997).

Hunt, Lynn, (ed.), *The Invention of Pornography: Obscenity and the Origins of Modernity, 1500–1800* (New York, Zone Books, 1993).

Hunter, J. Paul, *Before Novels: the Cultural Contexts of Eighteenth Century English Fiction* (New York, Norton, 1990).

Hussey, Christopher, *English Gardens and Landscapes, 1700–1750* (London, Country Life, 1967),

Hyland, Paul and Neil Sammells (eds.), *Writing and Censorship in Britain* (London, Routledge, 1992).

Innes, Joanna, 'Politics and Morals. The Reformation of Manners Movement in Later Eighteenth-Century England', in Eckhart Hellmuth (ed.), *The Transformation of Political Culture: England and Germany in the Late Eighteenth Century* (London, Oxford University Press, 1990), pp. 57–118.

Innes, Mary M. (trans.), Ovid, *Metamorphoses* (London, Penguin, 1961).

Jardine, N., J. A. Secord and E. C. Spary (eds.), *Cultures of Natural History* (Cambridge, Cambridge University Press, 1996).

Jenkins, Ian, and Kim Sloan (eds.), *Vases & Volcanoes* (London, British Museum Press, 1996).

Jones, Colin and Roy Porter (eds.), *Reassessing Foucault. Power, Medicine and the Body* (London and New York, Routledge, 1994)

Jones, Vivien (ed.), *Women in the Eighteenth Century. Constructions of Femininity* (London, Routledge, 1990).

Jordanova, Ludmilla, *Nature Displayed. Gender, Science and Medicine 1760–1820* (London, Longman, 1999).

Jordanova, Ludmilla, *Sexual Visions; Images of Gender in Science and Medicine between the Eighteenth and Nineteenth Centuries* (London, Harvester Wheatsheaf, 1989).

Kearney, Patrick, *The History of Erotica* (London, Macmillan, 1982).

Keeble, N. H. (ed.), *The Cultural Identity of Seventeenth Century Women* (London, Routledge, 1994).

Kemp, Betty, *Sir Francis Dashwood* (London, Macmillan, 1967).

Kendrick, Walter, *The Secret Museum: Pornography in Modern Culture* (New York, Penguin, 1987).

Kermode, Jenny and Garthine Walker (eds.), *Women, Crime and the Courts in Early Modern England* (London, University College Press, 1994).

Kiefer, Otto, *Sexual Life in Ancient Rome* (London, Constable, 1994).

Kieran Kavanaugh and Otilio Rodriguez (trans.), *The Collected Work of St. Theresa of Avila* (Washington, Province of Discalced Carmelites, 1976).

King, Helen, *Hippocrates' Women. Reading the Female Body in Ancient Greece* (London, Routledge, 1998).

Kraakman, Dorelies, 'A Historical History of Sexual Knowledge for Girls in French Erotic Fiction, 1750–1840', *Journal of the History of Sexuality*, Vol. 4, No. 4 (1994), pp. 517–48.

Kraakman, Dorelies, 'Reading Pornography Anew: A Critical History of Sexual Knowledge for Girls in French Erotic Fiction, 1750–1840', *Journal of the History of Sexuality*, Vol. 4, No. 4 (1994), pp. 517–48.

Langford, Paul, 'British Politeness and the Progress of Western Manners: An Eighteenth-Century Enigma', *Transactions of the Royal Historical Society*, Vol. 7 (Cambridge, Cambridge University Press, 1997), pp. 53–72.

Laqueur, Thomas, *Making Sex. Body and Gender from the Greeks to Freud* (Cambridge Mass., Harvard University Press, 1992).

Laqueur, T. and C. Gallagher (eds.), *The Making of the Modern Body, Sexuality and Society in the Nineteenth Century* (Berkeley, University of California Press, 1987).

Laslett, Peter, *The World We Have Lost* (London, Methuen, 1965).

Laurence, Anne, *Women in England 1500–1760. A Social History* (London, Weidenfeld and Nicolson, 1994).

Legman, G., *The Horn Book: Studies in Erotic Folklore* (London, Jonathan Cape, 1970).

Lewis, Judith Schneid, *In the Family Way. Childbearing in the Aristocracy 1760–1860* (New Brunswick, Rutgers University Press, 1986).

Licht, Hans, *Sexual Life in Ancient Greece* (London, Constable, 1931).

Lindsay, Lord, *Lives of the Lindsays: or a Memoir of the Houses of Crawford and Blacarres* (London, John Murray, 1849).

Loth, David, *The Erotic in Literature* (London, Secker & Warburg, 1962).

Lough, John, *French Travellers in the Seventeenth Century by British Travellers* (London, Oriel Press, 1985).

Lyles, Albert M., *Methodism Mocked. The Satirical Reaction to Methodism in the Eighteenth Century* (London, The Epworth Press, 1960).

Maccubbin, Robert Purks, (ed.), *'Tis Nature's Fault. Unauthorised Sexuality during the Enlightenment* (Cambridge, Cambridge University Press, 1987).

MacKinnon, Catherine A., *Only Words* (Cambridge, Cambridge University Press, 1993).

Mannix, Daniel P., *The Hell-Fire Club* (London, New English Library, 1962).

Marshall, Tim, *Murdering to Dissect. Grave-Robbing, Frankenstein and the Anatomy of Literature* (Manchester, Manchester University Press, 1995).

Mason, Michael, *The Making of Victorian Sexuality* (Oxford, Oxford University Press, 1994).

Mathias, Peter, *The First Industrial Nation 1700–1914* (London, Methuen, 1969).

Maxted, Ian, *The London Book Trades, 1775–1800* (Old Woking Press, Gresham, 1977).

Mayoux, Jean-Jacques, 'Laurence Sterne', in John Traugott (ed.), *Laurence Sterne. A Collection of Critical Essays* (New Jersey, Spectrum, 1968).

McCalman, Iain, *Radical Underworld. Prophets, Revolutionaries, and Pornographers in London 1795–1840* (Oxford, Oxford University Press, 1988).

McCormack, Donald, The *Hellfire Club* (Norwich, Jarrolds, 1958).

McDowell, Paula, *The Women of Grub Street. Press, Politics and Gender in the London Literary Marketplace 1678–1730* (Oxford, Oxford University Press, 1998).

McKenzie, D. F., 'Trading Places? England 1689-France 1789', in Haydn T. Mason, *The Darnton Debate. Books and Revolution in the Eighteenth Century* (Oxford, Voltaire Foundation, 1999), pp. 1–24.

McLaren, Angus, 'The Pleasures of Procreation: Traditional and Bio-medical Theories of Conception', in W. F. Bynum and Roy Porter (eds.), *William Hunter and the Eighteenth Century Medical World* (Cambridge, Cambridge University Press, 1985), pp. 323–42.

McLaren, Angus, *Reproduction Rituals. The Perception of Fertility in England from the Sixteenth Century to the Nineteenth Century* (London, Methuen, 1984).

McLynn, Frank, *Crime & Punishment in Eighteenth-Century England* (Oxford, Oxford University Press, 1991).

Merchant, Carolyn, *The Death of Nature: Women, Ecology and the Scientific Revolution* (San Francisco, Harper & Row, 1980).

Merians, Linda E. (ed.), *The Secret Malady. Venereal Disease in Eighteenth-Century Britain and France* (Kentucky, University Press of Kentucky, 1996).

Morgan, Fidelis, *The Well-Known Trouble Maker. A Life of Charlotte Charke* (London, Faber and Faber, 1988).

Moulton, Ian Frederick, *Before Pornography. Erotic Writings in Early Modern England* (Oxford, Oxford University Press, 2000).

Myers, Robin, and Michael Harris (eds.), *Spreading the Word. The Distribution Networks of Print 1550–1850* (Winchester, St. Paul's Bibliographies, 1990).

Needham, Joseph, *History of Embryology* (Cambridge, Cambridge University Press, 1959).

Nelson, James G., *Publisher to the Decadents. Leonard Smithers in the Careers of Beardsley, Wilde, Dowson* (High Wycombe, Rivendale Press, 2000).

Norberg, Katherine, 'The Libertine Whore: Prostitution in French Pornography from Margot to Juliette', in Hunt, *The Invention of Pornography*, pp. 225–52.

Nussbaum, Felicity (ed.), *Torrid Zones. Maternity, Sexuality and Empire in Eighteenth Century Narratives* (Baltimore, Johns Hopkins University Press, 1995).

Paster, Gail Kern, *The Body Embarrassed, Drama and the Disciplines of Shame in Early Modern England* (Ithaca, Cornell University Press, 1993).

Peakman, Julie, 'Medicine, the Body and the Botanical Metaphor in Erotica', in Kurt Bayertz and Roy Porter, *From Physico-Theology to Bio-Technology. Essays in the Social and Cultural History of Biosciences* (Amsterdam and Atlanta, Ga., 1998), pp.197–223.

Peakman, Julie, 'Women, Whipping and Whims. Flagellation in Eighteenth-Century English Erotica' (MA Thesis, London, RHBNC, 1992).

Peakman, Julie, 'Initiation, Defloration and Flagellation: Sexual Propensities in *Memoirs of a Woman of Pleasure*', in Patsy Fowler and Alan Jackson (eds.), *This Launch into the Wide World: Essays on Fanny Hill*, (New York AMS Press, 2002)

Peakman, Julie, *Sexual Behaviour in Eighteenth-Century England* (London, Atlantic, forthcoming).

Peakman, Julie, 'Bodily Anxieties in Enlightenment Sex Literature', *Voltaire Studies* (forthcoming).

Pendred, John, *The Earliest Directory of the Book Trade, 1795* (London, Bibliographical Society, 1955).

Perry, Ruth, 'Colonising the Breasts: Sexuality and Maternity in Eighteenth-Century England', *Journal of History of Sexuality*, Vol. 2, No. 2 (1991), pp. 204–34.

Phillips, Kim M. and Barry Reay (eds.), *Sexualities in History* (London, Routledge, 2002).

Pinchbeck, Ivy, *Women Workers and the Industrial Revolution, 1750–1850* (1930, reprint, London, Virago, 1981).

Plomer, H. R., *Dictionary of the Printers and Booksellers who were at work in England, Scotland and Ireland from 1726–1775* (Oxford, Oxford University Press, 1932).

Poovey, Mary, 'Feminism and Deconstruction', *Feminist Studies*, Vol. 14, No. 1 (1988), pp. 51–63.

Porter, Roy, *English Society in the Eighteenth Century* (London, Penguin, 1982).

Porter, Roy (ed.), *Patients and Practitioners: Lay Perceptions of Medicine in Pre-Industrial Society* (Cambridge, Cambridge University Press, 1985).

Porter, Roy (ed.), *Lay Patients and Practitioners. Lay Perceptions of Medicine in Pre-Industrial Society* (Cambridge, Cambridge University Press, 1985).

Porter, Roy, 'Erasmus Darwin: Doctor of Evolution?', in James R. Moore (ed.), *History, Humanity and Evolution: Essays for John Greene* (Cambridge, Cambridge University Press, 1989).

Porter, Roy (ed.), *The Popularisation of Medicine*, (London, Routledge, 1992).

Porter, Roy (ed.), *Cambridge Illustrated History of Medicine* (Cambridge, Cambridge University Press, 1996).

Porter, Roy, *The Greatest Benefit to Mankind. A Medical History of Humanity from Antiquity to the Present* (London, HarperCollins, 1997).

Porter, Roy and Lesley Hall, *Facts of Life: The Creation of Sexual Knowledge in Britain, 1650–1950* (New Haven, Conn., Yale University Press, 1995).

Porter, Roy and Marie Mulvey Roberts (eds.), *Literature and Medicine During the Eighteenth Century* (London, Routledge, 1993).

Porter, Roy and Dorothy Porter, *In Sickness and in Health: The British Experience, 1650–1850* (London, Fourth Estate, 1988).

Porter, Roy and Mikuláš, Teich, *Sexual Knowledge and Sexual Science. The History of Attitudes to Sexuality* (Cambridge, Cambridge University Press, 1994).

Power, Eileen, *Medieval English Nunneries c. 1275 to 1535* (New York, Biblo and Tansen, 1964).

Power, Eileen, *Medieval Women* (Cambridge, Cambridge University Press, 1975).

Prior, Mary (ed.), *Women in the English Society, 1500–1800* (London, Methuen & Co., 1985).

Ramsden, Charles, *London Bookbinders, 1780–1840* (London, B.T. Batsford, 1956).

Reay, B., *The Quakers and the English Revolution* (Hounslow, Temple Smith, 1985).

Richardson, Major General Frank M., *Mars without Venus: a Study of Some Homosexual Generals* (London, Blackwoods, 1981).

Riley, Denise, *Am I that Name? Feminism and the Category of 'Women' in History* (New York, Macmillan, 1988).

Rivers, Christopher, 'Safe Sex: The Prophylactic Walls of the Cloister in the French Libertine Convent Novel of the Eighteenth Century', *Journal of the History of Sexuality*, Vol. 5, No. 3 (1995), pp. 381–402.

Roberts, M. J. D., 'The Society for the Suppression of Vice and its Early Critics, 1802–1812', *The Historical Journal*, Vol. 26, No. 1 (1983), pp. 159–76.

Robinson, Eric, 'Erasmus Darwin's Botanical Garden and Contemporary Opinion', *Annals of Science* (1954), pp. 314–20.

Rogers, Katherine, *Feminism in the Eighteenth Century* (Hemel Hempstead, Harvester Press, 1982).

Rogers, Katherine, 'Fantasy and Reality in Fictional Convents of the Eighteenth Century', *Comparative Literature Studies*, Vol. 22, No. 3 (1985), pp. 227–315.

Rogers, Pat, 'Publishers and Booksellers', in Newman (ed.) *Britain in the Hanoverian Age, 1714–1837*, pp. 573–75.

Rogers, Pat, *Grub Street: Studies in a Subculture* ((London, Methuen, 1972).

Rogers, Pat, *Hacks & Dunces, Pope, Swift and Grub Street* (London, Methuen, 1980).

Rogers, Pat, 'Publishers and Booksellers', in Newman (ed.) *Britain in the Hanoverian Age*.

Rolph, C. H., *Books in the Dock* (London, André Deutsch, 1969).

Roper, Lyndal, *Oedipus and the Devil. Withcraft, Sexuality and Religion in Early Modern Europe* (London, Routledge, 1994).

Rosario, Vernon A., The *Erotic Imagination. French Histories of Perversity* (Oxford, Oxford University Press, 1997).

Rose, Lionel, *Massacre of the Innocents. Infanticide in Great Britain 1800–1939* (London, Routledge & Kegan Paul, 1986).

Rousseau, G. S. (ed.), *The Letters and Papers of Sir John Hill 1714–75* (New York, AMS Press Inc., 1982).

Rousseau, G. S. and David Haycock, 'Voices Calling for Reform: The Royal Society in the Mid-Eighteenth Century', in Martin Folkes, John Hill and William Stukeley, *History of Science*, Vol. 37, No. 118 (1999), pp. 377–406.

Rousseau, G. S., 'The Much Maligned Doctor', *Journal of American Medical Association*, No. 8 (1960).

Rousseau, G. S., *Enlightenment Borders* (Manchester, Manchester University Press, 1991).

Rousseau, G. S. and Roy Porter (eds.), *Sexual Underworlds of the Enlightenment* (Manchester, Manchester University Press, 1987).

Rousseau, Jean-Jacques, *Confessions* (reprint; London, Everyman, 1931).

Rowlands, Marie B., 'Recusant Women 1560–1640', in Mary Prior (ed.), *Women in English Society 1500–1800* (London, Routledge, 1985), pp. 150–80.

Rudé, G., 'The Gordon Riots: A Study of the Rioters and their Victims', *TRHS*, 5th Series, Vol. VI (Cambridge, Cambridge University Press, 1956), pp. 93–114.

Sawday, Jonathan, *The Body Emblazoned. Dissection and the Human Body in the Renaissance* (London, Routledge, 1995).

Schiebinger, Londa, *Nature's Body. Sexual Politics and the Making of Modern Science* (London, Pandora, 1993).

Schiebinger, Londa, 'Gender and Natural History', in N. Jardine, J.A. Secord and E. Spary, *Culture of Natural History* (Cambridge, Cambridge University Press, 1996), pp. 163–77.

Schofield, R. S., 'The Measurement of Literacy in Pre-Industrial England', in J. R. Goody (ed.), *Literacy in Traditional Societies* (Cambridge, Cambridge University Press, 1968), pp. 311–25.

Scott, G. Riley, *Flagellation. The History of Corporal Punishment* (London, Tallis Press, 1968).

Scott, Joan W., 'A Useful Category of Historical Analysis', *American Historical Review*, Vol. 91, No. 5 (1986), pp. 1053–75.

Scott, Joan W., 'Deconstructing Equality-versus-Difference: Or, the Uses of Poststructuralist Theory for Feminism', *Feminist Studies*, Vol. 14, No. 1 (1988), pp. 33–49

Sharpe, J. A., *Judicial Punishment in England* (London, Faber & Faber, 1990).

Shell, Alison, 'Catholic Texts and Anti-Catholic Prejudice in the Seventeenth Century Book Trade', in Robin Myers and Michael Harris (eds.), *Censorship and the Control of Print in England and France 1600–1910* (Winchester, St. Paul's Bibliographies, 1992), pp. 33–57.

Shinn, T. and R. Whitley (eds.), *Expository Science: Forms and Functions of Popularisation* (Dordrecht, Reidel, 1985).

Shoemaker, Robert, *Gender in English Society, 1650–1850. The Emergence of Separate Spheres?* (London, Longman, 1998).

Shorter, Edward, *A History of Women's Bodies* (New York, Basic Books, 1982).

Sommerville, Margaret, *Sex and Subjugation. Attitudes in Early-Modern Society* (London, Arnold, 1995).

Spufford, Margaret, *Small Books and Pleasant Histories. Popular Fiction and its Readership in Seventeenth-Century England* (Cambridge, Cambridge University Press, 1981).

Stallybrass, Peter, 'Patriarchal Territories', in Margaret Ferguson, Maureen Quilligan and Nancy Vickers (eds.), *Rewriting the Renaissance* (Chicago, Chicago University Press, 1986), pp. 123–42.

Stolberg, Michael, 'Self-Pollution, Moral Reform, and the Venereal Trade: Notes on the Sources and Historical Content of *Onania* (1716)', *Journal of the History of Sexuality* Vol. 9, Nos. 1–2 (January/April 2000), pp. 37–61.

Stone, Lawrence, 'Libertine Sexuality in Post-Restoration England: Group Sex and Flagellation among the Middling Sort in Norwich in 1706-7', *Journal of the History of Sexuality*, Vol. 2, No. 4 (1992), pp. 525- 51.

Stone, Lawrence, *Broken Lives, Separation and Divorce in England 1660–1857* (Oxford, Oxford University Press, 1993).

Stone, Lawrence, *Roads to Divorce: England, 1530–1987* (Oxford, Oxford University Press, 1990)

Stone, Lawrence, *The Family, Sex and Marriage in England 1500–1800* (London, Weidenfeld and Nicolson, 1977).

Stone, Lawrence, *Uncertain Unions, Marriage in England, 1660–1753* (Oxford, Oxford University Press, 1992).

Straus, Ralph, *The Unspeakable Curll* (London, Chapman & Hall, 1927).

Suzuki, Akihito, 'Reading Signs of Pregnancy in the Eighteenth and Nineteenth Centuries', in Yasuo Otsuka, Shizu Sakai and Shigehisa Kuriyama (eds.), *Medicine and History of the Body* (Tokyo, Isiyaku EuroAmerica, 1999), pp. 313–26.

Talvachhia, Bette, *Taking Positions. On the Erotic in Renaissance Culture* (Princeton, NJ, Princeton University Press, 1999).

Taylor, Charles, *Sources of the Self. The Making of the Modern Identity* (Cambridge, Cambridge University Press, 1989).

Teich, Mikuláš, Roy Porter and Bo Gustafsson (eds.), *Nature and Society in Historical Context* (Cambridge, Cambridge University Press, 1993).

Thacker, C., *The Wilderness Pleases: the Origins of Romanticism* (London, Croom Helm, 1983).

Thomas, Donald, *A Long Time Burning. A History of Literary Censorship in England* (London, Routledge and Kegan Paul, 1969).

Thomas, Keith, 'The Double Standard', *Journal of History of Ideas*, Vol. 20 (1959) pp. 195–216.

Thomas, Keith, *Religion and the Decline of Magic*, (London, Penguin, 1971).

Thomas, Peter D. G., *John Wilkes, A Friend to Liberty* (Oxford, Clarendon, 1996).

Thompson, E. P., *The Making of the English Working Class* (Harmondsworth, Penguin, 1968).

Thompson, Roger, *Unfit for Modest Ears, A Study of Pornographic, Obscene and Bawdy Works Written or Published in England in the Second Half of the Seventeenth Century* (London and Basingstoke, Macmillan Press, 1979).

Tilly, Louise and Joan Scott, *Women, Work, and Family* (New York, Holt, Rinehart and Winston, 1978).

Tillyard, Stella, *Aristocrats. Caroline, Emily, Louisa and Sarah Lennox 1740–1832* (London, Vintage, 1995).

Todd, Sarah Annice, 'The Representation of Aggression in the Seventeenth-Century English Broadside Ballad' (PhD Thesis, University of Wales, Aberystwyth, 1998).

Tolias, G., *British Travellers in Greece, 1759–1820* (London, Foundation of Hellenic Culture, 1995).

Trapnell, William H., *Thomas Woolston. Madman or Deist* (Bristol, Thoemmes Press, 1994).

Trench, Charles Chenevix, *Portrait of a Patriot. A Biography of John Wilkes* (London, Blackwood, 1962).

Trevor-Roper, H. R., *Religion, the Reformation, and Social Change*, (London, Macmillan, 1967).

Trumbach, Randolph, *Sex and the Gender Revolution. Heterosexuality and the Third Gender in Enlightenment London* (Chicago and London, University of Chicago Press, 1998).

Tuana, Nancy, *The Less Noble Sex. Scientific, Religious and Philosophical Conceptions of Woman's Nature* (Indianapolis, Indiana University Press, 1983).

Turner, Cheryl, *Living By The Pen. Woman Writers in the Eighteenth Century* (London, Routledge, 1992).

Turner, Roger, *Capability Brown and the Eighteenth-Century Landscape* (London, Weidenfeld and Nicolson, 1985).

Van de Walle, Etienne, 'Flowers and Fruits: Two Thousand Years of Menstrual Regulation', *Journal of Interdisciplinary History*, Vol. 18 No. 2 (1997), pp. 183–203.

Van de Walle, Etienne, 'Flowers and Fruits: Two Thousand Years of Menstrual Regulation', *Journal of Interdisciplinary History*, Vol. 18, No. 2 (1997), pp. 183–203.

Vicinus, Martha, 'Who is Sylvia? On the Loss of Sexual Paradigms', in Vicinus, 'Sexuality and Power. A Review of Current Work in the History of Sexuality, *Feminist Studies*, Vol. 8, No. 1 (1982), pp. 133–56.

Vickery, Amanda, *The Gentleman's Daughter. Women's Lives in Georgian England* (New Haven, Conn., Yale University Press, 1998).

Vickery, Amanda, 'Golden Age to Separate Spheres? A Review of the Categories and Chronology of English Women's History', *Historical Journal*, Vol. 32 No. 2 (1993), pp. 383–414.

Wagner, Peter (ed.), *Erotica and the Enlightenment* (Frankfurt, Peter Lang, 1991).

Wagner, Peter, 'Introduction', John Cleland's *Fanny Hill or Memoirs of a Woman of Pleasure* (London, Penguin, 1985), pp. 7–30.

Wagner, Peter, *Eros Revived. Erotica of the Enlightenment in England and America* (London, Secker & Warburg, 1988).

Walkowitz, Judith R, *City of Dreadful Delight* (London, Virago Press, 1992).

Walsh, J. D., 'Methodism and the Mob in the Eighteenth Century', in G. J. Cuming and D. Baker (eds.), *Popular Belief and Practice*, Studies on Church History, Vol. VIII (Cambridge, Cambridge University Press, 1972).

Ward, Geoff (ed.), *Romantic Literature. From 1790–1830* (London, Bloomsbury, 1993).

Warner, Marina, *Monuments and Maidens the Allegory of the Female Form* (London, Vintage, 1996).

Wemple, Suzanne (eds.), *Women of the Medieval World* (London, Blackwell, 1885).

Wiles, R. M., *Serial Publication in England before 1750* (Cambridge, Cambridge University Press, 1957).

Williams, Tassie, 'Female Fraud: Counterfeit Maidenheads in the Eighteenth Century', *Journal of the History of Sexuality*, Vol. 6, No. 41 (1996), pp. 518–48.

Williams, Tom, *Polite Landscapes. Gardens and Society in Eighteenth-Century England* (Stroud, Alan Sutton, 1995).

Wilson, Adrian, 'The Perils of Early Modern Procreation', *British Journal for Eighteenth-Century Studies*, Vol. 16, No. 1 (1993).

Yeazell, Ruth Bernard, *Fictions of Modesty: Women and Courtship in the English Novel* (Chicago, Chicago University Press, 1990).

Yoseloff, Thomas, *Laurence Sterne, A Fellow of Infinite Jest* (London, Francis Aldor, 1948).

Reference books

Bibliographies

Fraxi, Pisanus [Henry Spencer Ashbee], *Index Librorum Prohibitorum, Centuria Librorum Absconditorum* and *Catena Librorum Tacendorum* (London, privately printed, 1877), reprinted as *Bibliography of Forbidden Books* (New York, Jack Brussel, 1962).

Kearney, Patrick, *The Private Case. An Annotated Bibliography of the Private Case Erotic Collection in the British (Museum) Library* (London, Jay Landesman, 1981).

Mendes, Peter, *Clandestine Erotic Fiction in English 1800–1930. A Bibliographical Study* (Aldershot, Scholar Press, 1998).

Rose, Alfred, *Registrum Librorum Eroticorum* (reprint; New York, Jack Brussel, 1965).

Dictionaries

Brewer's *Dictionary of Phase and Fable* (London, Cassell, 1981).

Dictionary of National Biography

Grose, Captain Francis, *A Dictionary of Buckish Slang, University Wit, and Pickpocket Eloquence* (London, C. Chappel, 1811; reprinted London, Senate, 1994).

Hoefer's *Nouvelle Bibliographie Universelle* (Paris, 1857–66).

Lass, Kiremidjian and Goldstein (eds.), *The Wordsworth Dictionary of Classical and Literary Allusion* (Ware, Wordsworth Editions, 1987).

New Larousse Encyclopaedia of Mythology (Twickenham, Hamlyn Publishing Group, 1985).

Oxford English Dictionary

Partridge, Eric, *A Dictionary of the Underworld* (London, Routledge & Kegan Paul, 1950).

Quérard , *La France Littéraire* (Paris, 1823).
The 1811 Dictionary of Vulgar Tongue.
Simpson, A. *Biographical Dictionary of Common Law* (London, Butterworth, 1984).

Papers and magazines

Bon Ton, November 1791.
Bon Ton, March 1792.
Bon Ton, June 1792.
Bon Ton, July 1792.
Bon Ton, December 1792.
Bon Ton, March 1793.
Bon Ton, March 1794.
Bon Ton, November 1795.
Bon Ton, December 1795.
Bon Ton, February 1796.
Bon Ton, January 1796.
British Magazine, June 1749.
British Magazine, February 1750.
British Magazine, March 1750.
British Magazine, May 1750.
Critical Review 1760, Vol. 18.
Gentleman's Magazine, January 1735.
Gentleman's Magazine, 1746.
Gentleman's Magazine, 1763.
London Journal, 14 May 1726.
Morning Herald, December 1781.
Philosophical Transactions, Abr. ix 200. (London, n. p., 1735).
The Public Advertiser, 2 June 1763.
Rambler's Magazine, January 1783, Vol. 1.
Defoe, *Review*, 1704.
The Times [then known as *The Daily Universal Register*], 1 January 1785.
The Times, 1 January 1785.
The Times, 2, 3, 4 July 1788.
The Times, 20 August 1788.
The Times, 18 September 1788.

Manuscripts

Dashwood, Sir Francis, Private Papers, West Wycombe.
Reddie, J C, [*see 'James Campbell'], Collection of bibliographical notes BM Add MS 38828–30
Owen, Richard, *Ranelagh Gardens* – MS notes, music, newspaper cuttings, etc.; CUP 401k8
Hogarth 'Transubstantiation Satirised' 1735, BM, DPD 3446 (plate 8)

Public Records Office

PRO, KB, 28/428/22.
PRO, KB, 28/176/19.
PRO, KB, 28/176/20.
PRO, KB, 28/176/21.
PRO, KB, 28/176/21.
PRO, KB, 28/347/4.
PRO, KB, 28/347/5.
PRO, KB, 28/353/6.
PRO, KB, 28/368/18.
PRO, KB, 28/387/2.

PRO, KB, 28/387/2.
PRO, KB, 28/391/12.
PRO, KB, 28/391/13.
PRO, KB, 28/428/22.
PRO, SP, 35/11/14, f. 33, 25.
PRO, SP, 35/55/102.
PRO, SP, 35/55/102.
PRO, SP, 44/83/462.
PRO, SP, 44/183/463.
PRO, SP, 44/83/456, 458,460.
Old Bailey February Session, 1792.
State Trials, XVII, p. 157.

Index